Rethinking Social Transformation

Criticism and Creativity at the Turn of the Millennium

Edited by
Ananta Kumar Giri

RAWAT PUBLICATIONS
Jaipur and New Delhi

ISBN 81-7033-698-8

Published by
Prem Rawat for ***Rawat Publications***
Satyam Apartments, Sector 3, Jawahar Nagar, Jaipur - 302 004 (India)
Phone: 0141-651748 / 657006 Fax: 0141-651748
e-mail : rawatbooks@pinkline.net

Delhi Office
G-4, 4832/24, Ansari Road, Daryaganj, New Delhi 110 002
Phone: 011-3263290

Typeset by Rawat Computers, Jaipur
Printed at Nice Printing Press, New Delhi

For

Sunderlal Bahuguna, Daya Krishna,
Manoranjan Mohanty & Ashis Nandy
inspiring embodiments of critical interrogations and creative interventions for a just and beautiful society

Contents

Contributors

Anindita N. Balslev is Associate Research Professor at the Department of Philosophy, University of Copenhagen. She has published numerous papers in professional journals in the area of cross-cultural studies, Indian as well as comparative philosophy. She is the author of *A Study of Time in Indian Philosophy* (1999) and *Cultural Otherness: Correspondence with Richard Rorty* (1999).

Amita Baviskar teaches sociology at Delhi School of Economics, University of Delhi and is the author of *In the Belly of River: Tribal Conflicts Over Development in the Narmada Valley* (1995).

Achyut Das is the most noted NGO activist in India today. Twenty years ago, he went to the backward tribal block of Kashipur, Orissa and began his work in political education with the tribals. He later co-founded the voluntary organization---Agragamee---which fights for rights of the tribals. He is based in Kashipur in the district of Rayagara, Orissa.

Chitta Ranjan Das is a Socratic teacher and creative experimenter in many fields of life----education, literature, religion, spirituality, and scholarly works in history and literary criticism. In his youth he had taken part in India's freedom struggle and also went to jail. Later, he continued his studies at Shantiniketan where at a relatively young age he produced important works on history and literature of Orissa such as *Mahima Dharma* and *Achyutananda* or *Panchasakha Dharma* which have become classics. Das combines in his work the best of East and West---Gandhi, Tagore, Sri Aurobindo, Karl Marx, Meister Eckhart, Baruch Spinoza, Erasmus and Victor Frankel. He has authored more than hundred books.

Vidya Das trained as an anthropologist and in her current work with Agragamee, of which she is a co-founder, she combines scholarly reflection and activist engagement in an inspiring way.

Fred Dallmayr is Packey J. Dee Professor in the departments of government and philosophy at the University of Notre Dame (USA). He holds a Doctor of Law degree from the University of Munich and a Ph.D. from Duke University. He has been a visiting professor at Hamburg University in Germany and at the New School for Social Research in Germany, and a Fellow at Nuffield College in Oxford. During 1991-92 he was in India on a Fulbright research grant. Among his publications are: *Twilight of Subjectivity: Towards a Postindividualist Theory of Politics* (1981); *Language and Politics* (1984); *Critical Encounters* (1987); *Margins of Political Discourse* (1989); *Life-World, Modernity and Critique* (1991); *G.W.F. Hegel: Modernity and Politics* (1993); *The Other Heidegger* (1993); *Beyond Orientalism: Essays on Cross-Cultural Encounter* (1996); *Alternative Vision: Paths in the Global Village* (1998); *Border Crossing* (1999); and *Achieving Our World* (forthcoming 2001).

Ananta Kumar Giri is currently on the faculty of the Madras Institute of Development Studies, Chennai and has an abiding interest in contemporary processes of social and spiritual transformations. He has also been a visiting fellow at International Social Science Institute, The University of Edinburgh; MSH, Paris; and International Institute of Asian Studies, Amsterdam. He has lectured in many universities in India and Europe and has published widely in national and international journals. He is the author of *Global Transformations: Postmodernity and Beyond*; *Values, Ethics and Business: Challenges for Education and Management*; *Conversations and Transformations: Towards a New Ethics of Self and Society; Building in the Margins of Shacks: The Vision and Projects of Habitat for Humanity.*

Nancy Weiss Hanrahan is Associate Professor of Sociology at George Mason University, where she teaches Social Theory, Feminist Theory and the Sociology of Culture. Before entering academia, she worked in the music business as a radio announcer for WBUR in Boston, and as programme director of New Jazz at the Public, a concert series of jazz and experimental music in New York City. Her publications include *Difference in Time: A Critical Theory of Culture* (2000) and *The Blackwell Companion to the Sociology of Culture* (forthcoming, 2002).

Amena Mohsin (MA, Hawaii, PhD, Cambridge) is Professor of International Relations, University of Dhaka, Bangladesh. She is one of the founding editors of the reputed social science journal of Bangladesh *Theoretical Perspectives* and is part of South Asian networks of scholarly and activist cooperation. Her areas of interest are minority, gender and human rights issues. She is the author of a widely acclaimed book, *The Politics of Nationalism: The Case of Chittagong Hill Tracts, Bangladesh* (1997) and is a member of the advisory board of the Global Encounter Series of Rowman and Littlefield, USA.

Daniel Moshenberg is Associate Professor of English and Women's Studies at George Washington University, Washington, DC, and a founding member of the Tenants' and Workers' Support Committee of Northern Virginia. He is the Guest Editor of the Prisons/Literacies/Cultures [P/L/C] Special Series of PRE/TEXT: A Journal of Rhetorical Theory. His book, *Policing Coherence: The Tenderness of Red Letters* is forthcoming and is currently working on a book on literary and cultural materialist geography.

Ramashray Roy is a distinguished social scientist who combines in his work philosophical reflection and social science explorations. He is one of the most creative interpreters of Gandhi and is known for his pathbreaking works such as *Self and Society: Studies in Gandhian Thought and Dialogues on Development*. He has written nearly a dozen books both in English and Hindi and his most recent work, *Beyond Ego's Domain: Being and Order in the Vedas* (1999), is an important contribution to social theory and critical philosophy. He worked at Centre for the Study of Developing Societies of which he was also Director and has been a National Fellow of Indian Council of Social Science Research, fellow of Indian Institute of Advanced Studies, Shimla, and recipient of Jawaharlal Nehru Award for Excellence in Social Sciences.

K. Raghavendra Rao is a distinguished political theorist and outstanding teacher. He is the author of many books. After his retirement from Department of Political Science, Mangalore University he is currently based in Dharwad, Karnataka. He has also been the President of Indian Academy of Social Sciences.

Prakash Chandra Sarangi is Professor of Political Science at the University of Hyderabad. Earlier he taught at Utkal and Rochester and was also a Fulbright fellow at the University of Wisconsin-Madison. He is the author of *Liberal Theories of State: Contemporary Perspectives* and of several research papers.

Chitra Sivakumar is Director, Centre of South and Southeast Asian Studies, University of Madras. She is the author of *Education, Social Inequality and Social Change* (1982) and has co-authored *Peasants and Nabobs: Agrarian Radicalism in Late Eighteenth Century* (1995).

Badri Narayan Tewari is a social historian and cultural anthropologist and is currently on the faculty of G.B. Pant Social Science Institute, Allahabad. He has also been a fellow at Indian Institute of Advanced Study, Shimla and visiting fellow with MSH, Paris. He has been a contributing member of Project of History of Science, Philosophy and Culture of the Center of Civilizational Studies, New Delhi and the project on *Purusartha* of Ecole Des Hautes Etudes En Sciences Soicale, Paris. He is the author of *Loka Sankruite Me Rastravad* (Nationalism in Folk Culture), *Sanskritika Gadhya* (The Prose of Culture), and *Documenting Dissent: Contesting Fables, Contested Memories and Dalit Political Discourse*.

Baas Weilinga has been teaching Social Analysis and Biblical Theology at Tamilnadu Theological Seminary in Madurai since 1975. He has published in the fields of Christian-Marxist dialogue, politics, economy/ecology and theology. He has earlier taught at Free University, Amsterdam and has an active association with many voluntary organizations and social movements. His publications include *Lenins Weg zur Revolution* (1971), *Marxist Views on India in Historical Perspective* (1976), *It's a Long Road to Freedom* (1981), and *Introduction to Marxism* (1984). He has recently published *Liberation Theology in Asia* in the Cambridge Companion to Liberation Theology, edited by Christopher Rowland (1999).

Preface

The present anthology is the outcome of a workshop on "Social Criticism, Cultural Creativity and the Contemporary Dialectics of Transformations", held at the Madras Institute of Development Studies in 1996, as a part of its silver jubilee celebrations. A suggestion from my colleague Professor S. Subramaniam helped me conceive the idea and encouragement from Professor S. Neelakantan, the then Director of the Institute, helped turn this idea into a reality. My thanks to both of them as well as to other colleagues and members of the staff of the Institute. I am also grateful to all the participants of the workshop for their contribution to this dialogue. I am sorry I have not been able to include many interested contributors in this volume out of the total 35 papers presented. I would here like to specifically record my thanks to Dr. P.M. Bhargava, Ms. Chandna Chakravarti, and Professors Makarand Paranjape, Rashida Chowdhury, Rajeswari Sunder Rajan, S.S. Sivakumar, Drs. Mujibar Rehman, Uday Kumar, S. Chandran, M. Bharathi, Nidhi Srivastava, T.T. Sreekumar and K. Sivasubramanian.

The volume is dedicated jointly to Shri Sunderlal Bahuguna, Prof. Daya Krishna, Prof. Manoranjan Mohanty and Prof. Ashis Nandy. They have, in their own unique ways, combined activist engagements with deep reflections and have helped us rethink social transformation and initiate new pathways of criticism and creativity. As a leading participant in the famous Chipko movement in the Himalayas, Sunderlaljee has stirred the conscience of the world about issues of ecological responsibilities. His critical engagements continue unabated even in his ripe age and in these new times of quick conformity to the idols of the market place. I recall vividly my meeting with him in July 1987 when we spent two days together in his ashram at Silvara near Tehri. During our discussion Sunderlaljee had pointed out to me the great danger that lies in leaving the task of social reconstruction in the hands of paid workers and professionals. In these days of corporatization of the much voluntary sector, even in a country like India, we shall do well to listen to the lone and courageous voice of crusaders like Sunderlaljee.

If Sunderlaljee has been a relentless crusader in the field of critical social action, Professor Daya Krishna has been a tireless crusader in the fields of foundational interrogations and philosophical reflections. What is important is that both Sunderlaljee and Dayajee pooh-pooh any comfortable boundary between social action and philosophical reflection, and in their own lives and works embody new modes of creative interpenetration between the two. Dayajee has raised many foundational questions to Indian philosophy and what he writes in his provocative, *The Problematic and Conceptual Structure of Classical Indian Thought About Man, Society and Polity* helps us come to terms with the crucial issue of self-other relations at the contemporary juncture: "Once we begin to see the 'other' as a subject in his or her own right and capable of being affected by one's actions one will begin to see the self as 'responsible' to the other and not just be concerned with the state of one's own being. Yajnavalkya's atman-centric analysis of the human situation and his contention that everything is dear for the sake of the self, then, seem to result from a one-sided analysis." Personally for me it has been an enriching experience to have had the opportunity to be in touch with Dayajee for the last ten years. Even at this ripe age and with partially poor eyesight, Dayajee embodies the critical explorations and restless dynamism of a young man and all of us concerned in the field of social transformation have a lot to learn from both Sunderlaljee and Dayajee.

Professors Manoranjan Mohanty and Ashis Nandy have come to us a generation after Sunderaljee and Dayajee and continue to work as inspiring social critics and outstanding 'public intellectuals' in their own inimitable ways. Both of them have not stopped dreaming even in these days of quick conformities and urge us to renew our commitment to the traditions of Indian freedom struggle, especially the aspirations of 'Swaraj'. In Professor Nandy's work, there is a critical interrogation of many of the taken-for-granted assumptions of modernity from the vantage point of tradition, and a continuous questioning of the self-closure of academic practice. A similar unorthodox and often militant border crossing is witnessed in the life and work of Professor Mohanty. He has been a participant in many struggles for freedom and a greater democratic experimentation and has made significant contributions to the theory and practice of a creative society. Dedicating this book to Professors Mohanty and Nandy, as well as to Sunderlaljee and Dayajee, we pay our tribute to this multi-faceted tradition of social criticism and and also pledge ourselves to the task of creative social criticism that awaits us at the contemporary juncture.

It is soon going to be five years when we spent four engrossing days during the workshop from which this volume arises. It has taken a long time to see the light of the day and it would have taken still longer time without the enthusiastic support from Mr. Pranit Rawat of Rawat Publications. My thanks to him for this. Finally, I hope, this collection of essays will contribute to our contemporary struggles---political, spiritual and moral---to make this world a more dignified place to live and to strive for yet unrealized dimensions of the spiritual and political evolution of humanity.

Ananta Kumar Giri

Chapter One

INTRODUCTION
The Calling of Creative Transformations

Ananta Kumar Giri

> ...all change or at least all radical change, that is, all creative change, begins with self-change, that is, with a prior (analytically and/or chronologically) transformation in one's transformative praxis. Moreover, all change also in a certain sense consists of (or involves) self-expansion...
>
> ...man is essentially God (and therefore also essentially one, but also essentially unique); and that, as such, he is essentially free and already enlightened, a freedom and enlightenment which is overlain by extraneous, heteronomous determinations which both (a) occlude, and (b) qualify this essential fact... Since God is also...*inter alia* unconditional love (unbounded peace and infinite joy or happiness) and we are essentially God-like, the most appropriate... ethical and political stance is one of unconditional love for our essential selves, and that of each and every being and the environment we inhabit.
>
> --- Roy Bhaskar (2000:68)

> It is society which is called upon to become a means for the free development of the individual, or, more precisely, the space in which each contributes to creating for all, and all for each, the conditions for a free development of their individuality.
>
> ---Andre Gorz (1999:66)

> Creative society embodies a methodology of viewing society in terms of liberation from multiple dominations—class, caste, race, ethnicity, gender and many more yet to be discovered sources of domination—and it points at processes already active or yet to be articulated, seeking to reconstitute society... The concept of creative society opposes any formation which suggests a terminal view of the history of society... the advanced industrial society may not be quite the example of a creative society that is fulfilling the people's democratic urges. It may actually be the picture of a system that manages instrumental creativity in a narrow framework... capitalism in modern history represents the taming of creativity and taming of reason. The creative society, therefore, is bound to break out of the capitalist process in pursuit of creativity and liberation.
>
> —Manoranjan Mohanty (1998:67-68)

> A spiritualized society would treat in its sociology the individual, from the saint to the criminal, not as units of social problem to be passed through some skilfully devised machinery and either flattened into the social mould or crushed out of it, but as souls suffering and entangled in a net and to be rescued, souls growing and to be encouraged to grow...The aim of its economics would be not to create a huge engine of production, whether of the competitive or the co-operative kind, but to give to men—not only to some but to all men each in his highest possible measure—the joy of work according to their own nature and free leisure to grow inwardly, as well as a simply rich and beautiful life for all... And that work would be to find the Divine Self in the individual and the collectivity and to realize spiritually, mentally, vitally, materially its greatest, largest, richest and deepest possibilities in the inner life of all and their outer action and nature.
>
> —Sri Aurobindo (1962:241-42)

I

We have stepped into a new century and a new millennium and "the expectations of the millennium are of moving towards a better society" (Thapar 2000:xviii). But this movement towards a better society which is decent (cf. Margalit 1996), creative and characterized by elimination of humiliation and institution of dignity in the lives of individuals and society, calls for new initiatives in criticism, creativity and transformation. The last century has witnessed the demise of many assured methods of moving towards a better society. Over the last few decades, all societies have been subjected to fundamental processes of transformation which have challenged the prevalent social and ideological systems. These processes have also challenged the familiar models of social criticism and methods of social transformation. The ideological systems of Marxism and liberal democracy had emphasized the proletarian class and political citizen as the main agents of social criticism. But contemporary changes have pointed to the limits of these categories as bearers of criticism, creativity and transformation. The collapse of state socialism and disenchantment with political parties in advanced industrial democracies suggest that now the agenda of criticism and transformation must be broadened.

At the turn of the new century as well as the new millennium, we thus face the challenge to rethink criticism, creativity and transformation in the context of changes taking place in self, culture and society. In familiar models of emancipation, political movements and political parties were to be the main agents of social criticism. As a consequence of the postmodern turn in culture and society, now, we are recognizing the significance of new socio-cultural and socio-spiritual movements as agents of social and cultural criticism. But this focus on new social movements now needs to be broadened by acknowledging transformative selves of individuals as agents of criticism and creativity. We get an intimation of such an agenda of criticism and creativity in the vision and experiments of many creative interlocutors of our times such as Roy Bhaskar, Alaine Touraine, Alberto Melucci, Roberto Unger, Sri Aurobindo, Fred Dallmayr, and Chitta Ranjan Das as well as in the work of movements such as Swadhyaya and integral education. To understand self-transformation as an important goal of criticism and creativity and transformative self as the agent of social criticism, we can begin with the recent intimate proposal of Roy Bhaskar. For Bhaskar, all creative change begins with self-change or "transformation of one's transformative praxis" (2000:68). The dialectic of self-transformation and social transformation are linked with each other and the task here is to overcome alienation and to practice the art of what Bhaskar calls 'de-alienation' or *yoga*. The dialectic of God-realization or self-realization are a mechanics of a 're-enchanted reality'. Love plays an important role in this path of criticism, creativity and transformation. As Bhaskar tells us: "The dialectics of de-alienation (of retotalization) are all essentially dialectics of love of, love of self (Self), of each and all (Totality) and in both inner and outer movements, both as essentially love of God. The essence of liberated man is therefore love of God and God, we could say, is not only essentially love but essentially to be loved" (ibid:44).

But to love God is also to love men, women and children and this world and to fight for justice when God is denied in our lives and social systems. In fact, there is a transformation in religion and spirituality now where people are relating to God in a spirit of practical service in the world. As Robert Wuthnow tells us about the emergent contours of practice-oriented spirituality in the contemporary US: "Although it is possible for people's spiritual practices to focus so much attention on themselves or on God that little energy is left for anything else, this possibility does not appear to be the typical result" (1998:192). For Wuthnow "spending time cultivating their relationship with God" frees people from "material concerns and other self-interested process so that they would focus on the needs of the other" (ibid). Wuthnow tells us that in a society like contemporary American society there is a transformation from a spirituality of dwelling to a spirituality of seeking and from a spirituality of seeking to spirituality of practice. "A spirituality of dwelling emphasizes *habitation*: God occupies a definite place in the universe" (ibid:10). But a "spirituality of seeking emphasizes *negotiation*: individuals search for sacred moments that reinforce their conviction that the divine exists..." (ibid:4). In practice-oriented spirituality such a seeking takes place in varieties of transformative practices which can hold Roy Bhaskar's proposal of universal self-realization as a dialectic of love. Practical spirituality touches all aspects of our life: "...the point of spiritual practice is not to elevate an isolated set of activities over the rest of life but to electrify the spiritual impulse that animates all of life" (ibid:198).

Practice-oriented spirituality provides us a new relationship with the sacred. The sacred here is not an instrument in fundamentalist mobilization of religion, which is active in all societies now, added as they are by the forces of globalization, but points to the realization of limits of instrumental rationality as the foundation of our lives. As Charles Taylor argues: "Acknowledging the transcendent means being called to a change of identity [that is, responding to the call for a], a radical decentering of the self [in relation with the divine]" (Taylor quoted in Dallmayr 2001:20). Transcendental sacred also works as a force of critical interrogation in contemporary societies when the power holders of society present the existing systems as Gods (Unger 1987). As Alberto Melucci argues: "Instrumental rationality has restored the world to mankind's scope of operation, but it also denies humanity all chances to transcend reality, it devalues everything that resists subsumption under the instrumental action. Society thus becomes a system of apparatuses identical with its own actions and intolerant of any diversity. The sacred thus re-emerges as an appeal to a possible other, as the voice of what it is not but could be. Divested of the ritual trappings of the churches, the sacred thus becomes a purely cultural form of resistance which counters the presumptions of power by affirming the right to desire... to hope that the world is more than what actually is" (Melucci 1996a:171). And here as Dallmayr would urge us to realize: "There are plenty of signs in our time that a narrowly confined immanence cannot satisfy human longings and aspirations. What needs to be recognised that longings for transcendence, even a transcendental holism, are vibrantly alive today in many societies on the level of the ordinary life-world—far removed from traditional power structures" (Dallmayr 2001:17).

An openness to beyond in our lives calls for our being attentive to our own 'inner planets' (Melucci 1996a:60). For Melucci, "concerning ourselves with the inner planet of an ecological mentality means that we are called to go beyond an ecology of the system to assume responsibility for our being in the world". In this context, "what we need is *a passionate capacity to change form*, to redefine ourselves" (ibid:50; emphases added). It also calls for an eulogy to wonder in our lives. This work of metamorphosis is facilitated by the work of creative and critical socio-spiritual movements which provide a laboratory for creative experimentation with self, culture and society. As Melucci tells us in his *Challenging Codes*: "Contemporary movements are prophets of the present. What they possess is not the force of apparatus but the power of the word. They speak a language that seems to be entirely their own, but they say something that transcends their particularity and speaks to us all" (Melucci 1996b:1). In fact, the ground for moral protest that many contemporary socio-cultural movements provide enable the actors to go beyond their instrumental concerns and engage themselves with something beyond. As James Jasper tells us: "Protest is like religious ritual: it embodies our moral judgements, so that we can express allegiance to moral visions through our actions. For those who no longer hold to traditional religious practices, protest is one of the few ways to express allegiance to moral visions through our actions" (1997:14). What is to be noted is that movements of protest which take us beyond the realm of instrumental and utilitarian self are not integration-seeking movements, seeking to be included within the existing frames of state and society but seek to transform the existing basis of organization and question what Homi K. Bhabha calls the existent 'ethics of social affiliation' (2000:108). Jasper calls some of these movements 'post-citizenship movements'. In Jasper's words: "In the nineteenth century post-citizenship movements often took the form of poor relief and anti-vice crusades; in the last thirty years they have pursued 'post-industrial' or 'post-material' aims like protection of the environment, peace and disarmament, alternative healing, lifestyle protections, and rights—goals which do not especially interest those seeking jobs, equal pay or the right to vote" (ibid:11).

Melucci presents metamorphosis as a path of criticism and transformation and this has close kinship with an appropriate politics and ethics of the subject, to what Touraine (2000) calls developing an appropriate 'subjectivation'. Touraine tells us in his *What is Democracy?* : "For a long time, modern philosophy regarded the interests of society as the principle of the Good: What was useful to society was good and what was harmful to society was bad. This rationalist, programmist faith in the correspondence between personal interests and collective interests is no longer tenable" (1997:19). For Touraine, "democracy serves neither society nor individuals. Democracy serves human beings insofar as they are subjects, or in other words their own creators and the creators of their individual and social lives" (ibid:19). For Touraine, "the subject is not merely a form of reason... it is also freedom, liberation and rejection" (2000:58); in fact, the "subject is at once reason, liberty and memory" (1997:127). To be a subject now is to recompose the world, especially as it is being torn asunder by the spread of global marketization and communitarian identity mobilization. Market forces recognize no subject nor do collectivist and communal identities. In our contemporary world, both market and collectivist mobilizations of identity are the triumphant forces which threaten our capacity for realization as subjects. For Touraine, "our real point of reference is not hope, but the pain of being torn apart. Because the world of objectification and its technologies has been so debased as to be no more than a market, whilst the world of cultural identities is locked into communitarian obsession, the individual who exists inside us all is suffering the agony of being torn apart, of feeling that his or her life-world is as decayed as the institutional realm or even the representation of the world itself... We are now experiencing a very different pathology: the pathology of formulating an 'I', because it is either drowning in a mass culture or confined within authoritarian communities" (2000:55). Touraine urges us to realize that "the reconstruction of the individual can come about only if that individual can recognize and assert himself as a subject, as a creator of meaning and change, as well as of social relations and political institutions" (2000:60).

Touraine's suggestions for developing an appropriate politics and ethics of the subject makes us realize that "the complete fulfilment of each individual now becomes the goal which society must make possible" (Gorz 1999:61). In this pathway, there is a need to produce alternative socialities which goes hand in hand with the creation of alternative subjectivities. But, in contemporary capitalism, production and employment are the dominant modes in which people relate to each other; society today is produced through the media of capitalist work and time. But now we have to think of new modes of creation of self and society other than the media of money and market. This calls for going beyond 'work', 'employment' and 'production' as the only foundation of self and society and to have a 'multi-active life' (ibid:73). As Andre Gorz tells us: "To change society, we have to change 'work' and vice versa. To change it by divesting it of all its reifying constraints ...which reflect its subordination to capital. To change it by reconciling it with a culture of daily life, an art of living, which would both extend and nourish instead of being cut off from them" (ibid:98-99). "We have to 'widen' as far as possible the gap between society and capitalism, that is to say, to increase as far as possible the space and resources which enable alternative socialities to be produced" (ibid:79).

Civil labour, as different from capitalist employment, can provide such a space for the production of alternative solidarity. In civil labour, people work for each other and for the common good and it is part of a "state-approved exit from the market" (Beck 2000:126). Today, civil society is on everybody's mouth but what needs to be stressed is that through concrete practices of civil labour where we share time and labour with each other, we can create and recreate civil society in an embodied and meaningful way. For Ulrich Beck who presents us this proposal of civil labour as a way of revitalizing state and society in his *The Brave New World of Work:* "There is no better way of breathing life into civil rights than to convert them, through civil labour, into the self-organized action of the sovereign many" (Beck 2000:134). There is a need now to rethink civil society not only as a space of political empowerment and political argumentation, but also as a space of self-realization and creative inter-subjectivity. Here, practices of concrete labour can give an embodied transformative content to the Habermasian disembodied space of moral argumentation (cf. Giri 2000). Beck makes it clear that civil labour provides opportunity for self-fulfilment also. It is not only a labour for helping the other; it is a labour which helps one to develop oneself. It is a labour which is neither altruistic nor egotistic; in fact it transcends the conventional boundaries of altruism and egotism. Thus participation in civil labour can create a condition for both the ethical and aesthetic development of self, where ethical development means development of an attitude of responsibility to the other, and aesthetic development means an appropriate care and cultivation of the self (cf. Giri 1999; Giri and Quarles van Ufford 2000). As Beck urges us to realize the connection between care of the self and attentiveness to the other: "For more and more people, 'social progress' is measured by the extent to which opportunities are created for self-fulfilment in the value dimension of one's own life" (2000:152). It is this "often-demonized individualism—and not the traditional duty orientation —which embodies a hitherto untapped source of engagement, a mighty 'social capital' lying dormant" (ibid).

Beck's discussion of self-fulfilment and civil labour as integrally connected, urges us to realize the transformative linkages between self-fulfilment and creation of social capital. As is well known, like civil society, social capital is an all-pervasive discourse of social and economic reconstruction at present (cf. Putnam 1993; Dasgupta and Serageldin 1999). Trust is at the root of the discourse of social capital but the theorists of social capital neither address the issue of how to generate trust nor do they explore ways of developing, what Fred Dallmayr has spoken of in another context, the "inner resources that are required to animate public commitment" (1999:19). This calls for a deeper foundation for civil labour, for a spiritual regeneration of social capital, a calling which we find animated in the vision and experiment of the socio-spiritual movement of Swadhyaya. As the essay of Ramashray Roy in this volume tells us, Swadhyaya has many *prayogas* or experiments where individuals work together for the generation of impersonal wealth and the creation of common goods. Swadhyayees consider their work in such projects as an instance of *shramabhakti*, devotion of labour. Devotional sharing of time and labour creates trust and social network among the participants and contributes towards a spiritual regeneration of social capital.

The vision and experiments of Swadhyaya not only transform the current discourse of social capital in the direction of a deeper spiritual renewal but also urge us to find much more fruitful pathways of connection between self-realization and the building of a just society. Here we can relate transformations taking place in spiritual horizons to new developments in social theory. The initial proposal of Roy Bhaskar regarding intimate links between self-development and social transformation gets an enriching corroboration in the work of radical sociologist, Goran Therborn. For Therborn, it is self-realization rather than emancipation which has to be the goal of a movement for a decent society and dignified life. For Therborn, a socialist or radical project can no more be summed up "in terms of emancipation" (1991:300). It is true and cannot be denied that "emancipation remains on the agenda in most parts of the world" and it has a salience in "the form of women's emancipation, but also of ethnicity/nationality and class" (ibid). "However, the concept of emancipation presupposes that of oppression/exploitation as a clear base line from which to move. In advanced capitalist democracies it is difficult, and unconvincing, to conceive of women or workers as generally and unqualifiedly oppressed and exploited" (ibid). In this context, human life-realization as the goal for struggles for liberation and freedom "has the advantage of not being tied to one linear movement, from oppression to freedom, but of connoting, at the same time, an infinite plurality of life-projects and a universal yardstick, the human life-span universally possible at a given level of world resources and medical knowledge" (ibid). But for this human life-realization to be a reality what is needed is a radical distribution of resources. Realization of universal self-realization calls for a just, humane, decent material and political foundation and in the context of present day systemic inequality it calls for both socio-spiritual and socio-political struggles. While the regnant ideology of neo-liberalism would make us believe that the contemporary moment heralds an end of history as an end of historical struggles for justice, in the contemporary world we continue to witness emergence of radical and anti-systemic people's movements and social struggles (Falk 1999; Wilfred 2000).

Enabling individuals to grow is a goal in both liberalism and democracy. While liberalism has failed in enabling universal self-realization as it is tied to capitalist rationality, the challenge here is to build on the inner resources of democracy and on the way transforming it as well. The task here is to use the emancipatory possibilities of democratic modernity in the fight against capitalist modernity and on the way to spiritualize both democracy and modernity as a project of universal self-realization.[1] As Chantal Mouffe argues: "... Once we acknowledge that what constitutes modern democracy is the assertion that all human beings are free and equal, it becomes clear that it is not possible to find a more radical principle for organizing society" (1992:1). Immanuel Wallerstein, the other radical thinker of our times who has not stopped dreaming even after the collapse of official socialism, makes a similar argument: "To most people democratization translates primarily as the demand for three things as equal rights: a reasonable income (a job and later a pension), access to education for one's children, and adequate medical facilities. To the extent there is democratization, people insist not merely on having these three, but on regularly raising the minimum acceptable threshold for each. But having these at the level that people are demanding each day, is incredibly expensive, even for the wealthy countries, not to speak for Russia, China, India. The only way every one can really have more of these is to have a radically different system of distribution of the world's resources than we have today" (1999:18). Thus, along with the contemporary politics of recognition, what needs to be stressed is an ethics and politics of redistribution, but the "the left is afraid to speak of distribution, when redistribution is becoming a question of life and death for society. Everything has to be redistributed from the top down---technology, resources, money, knowledge" (Kagarilsky 2000:9).

In Therborn, Mouffe, Laclau and Wallerstein, striving for universal self-realization is an integral part of realization of radical democracy and in the Indian context this linkage comes most forcefully in the works of Manoranjan Mohanty. Mohanty urges us to pay attention to multiple movements for a creative society in the contemporary world. For Mohanty, a creative society is a society where individuals become aware of the multiple sources of oppression and domination and continually seek to overcome these in quest for freedom and solidarity. Mohanty laments that now in the post-colonial societies, "memories of freedom struggle are transcended by new preoccupations" of market-led growth, global accumulation, etc. (1994:105). The task before post-colonial criticism here is to resist this evaporation of memory of struggle and to continue to fight for greater democratic realization. But such a charting of the path of post-colonial criticism, is different from what is globally applauded as post-colonial criticism. Post-colonial criticism has been part of the global cross-current of postmodern and post-structuralist cultural criticism but now it has become domesticated by global capitalism as most of the advocates of post-colonial criticism either work or have migrated to the US academia. Post-colonial criticism now seems to forget the memory and aspirations of freedom struggles. As Arif Dirlik writes: "Post-colonial ... is applicable not to all of the post-colonial period but only to that period after colonialism when, among other things, a forgetting of its essence tends to set in" (2000:216). For Dirlik, "post-colonial critics have engaged in valid criticism of past forms of ideological hegemony but have had little to say about its contemporary figurations" (ibid:231).[2]

Critique of essentialism has been an important part of post-colonial criticism, a goal which it shares with the global cultural and theoretical criticism of postmodernism and post-structuralism. This critique of essentialism has a liberatory potential as struggle for liberation calls for "the negation of divinification of every totality as negation of the negation of human person" (Dussel 1998:17).[3] But, the problem with post-colonial criticism, as with the broader genre of post-structuralism, is that it makes a fetish of anti-essentialism itself. As David Scott tells us about post-colonial criticism in his *Refashioning Futures: Criticism After Post-coloniality*: "For the anti-essentialists criticism is a practice of demonstrating the epistemological naivete of their adversaries" (1998:9). "The anti-essentialists are not interested in what constellation of historically constructed demands may have produced the supposedly essentialist formulations" (ibid:9). Marxism is often the object of the anti-essentialist wrath of post-colonial critics but here post-colonial critics neither translate Marxism "into a national (which is rejected) or local (which is affirmed) vernacular" nor replace it with local stories of criticism and creativity but put forward the universalist language of post-structuralism. The entry of an imperialist universalism that enters here through the back door should not escape our attention: a "critique that starts off with a repudiation of the universalist pretensions of Marxist language ends up not with its dispersion into local vernaculars but with a return to another First World language with universalistic epistemological pretension" (Dirlik 2000:218).

Decolonization and establishment of a life of what Gandhi calls *swaraj* or self-government is the enduring message of anti-colonial struggles for freedom and this has a continued significance in our contemporary world (cf. Terchek 1996). Now, the colonial masters may not be there in their classical forms but still we are subjected to ever newer forms of colonialism. As Jurgen Habermas tells us, our life-worlds are now increasingly subjected to a colonialism of the system world. The message of anti-colonial struggle needs to be retrieved here in terms of decolonizing our life-world from the colonialism of the system and making it a space of *swaraj* or self-government. The same challenge of criticism and creativity lies in decolonizing our mind, knowledge and future (cf. Pieterse and Parekh 1995). As Jan N. Pieterse argues: "The colonialism of the life world'---commodification, bureaucratization is a familiar metaphor. This includes a routinized process of colonization of futures, because of the concentration of forecasting and planning capabilities in government and computer hands. What is needed is a decolonization of futures or, to use more general language, a democratization of futures" (2000:3).

To decolonize future is to make "futures a matter of public concern" and it calls for decolonization of the public sphere. But, the public sphere is now being colonized by the forces of capitalist marketization and it is the advertisement for money and power which is written in bold letters there. In this context, the task of decolonization of public sphere entails the task of recreating it as a space of intersubjectivity and freedom, where freedom means not only consumer choice but what Zygmunt Bauman calls 'communal self-management' (1988:98). The task of criticism and creativity is to resist the privatization and reprivatization of the public sphere and to rescue it from the clutches of the new colonial masters of both state and market. But, as Bauman again tells us, now there is not only a privatization of public sphere, there is also a privatization of critique. While earlier social criticism was an activity in a 'shared household' now it has shrunk into an activity in the camping site (Bauman 2001). In the words of Bauman:

> One can think of the kind of "hospitality to critique" characteristic of present-day modern society as having the pattern of a camping site. The place is open to everyone who has their own caravan and money to pay the rent. Guests come and go, none taking much interest in how the site is run, provided that they have been allocated a plot big enough to park the caravan, that the electric sockets and water taps are in good order and the passengers in nearby caravans do not make too much noise and turn down their portable hi-fi and TV speakers after 10 p.m. ... If they feel they are being short-changed or find that the manager's promises are not kept, campers may complain and demand their due, but it won't occur to them to challenge and renegotiate the managerial philosophy of the site. They may, at the utmost, make a mental note never to use the facilities again and not to recommend using them to their friends (ibid:100).

For Bauman, such a privatization of critique instead of leading to critique of foundation of social arrangements leads to a 'compulsive *self-critique*' where one blames one for one's own misery, "seeking causes of one's own defeats nowhere except in one's own indolence and sloth" (ibid:106). Such a privatization of critique at the contemporary juncture makes urgent the need to retrieve the moral function of criticism as a connected activity in society (Walzer 1988).

Criticism as a connected activity is enriched by heeding to the challenge of 'triple transformation' at the contemporary juncture outlined recently by the sympathetic Portuguese critic Boaventura de Santos, where "power becomes shared authority, despotic law becomes democratic law; knowledge-as-regulation becomes knowledge as emancipation" (1995:482). But realization of this triple transformation calls for creation of new subjectivity and a new mode of knowing. The new subjectivity here is "constituted by the topos of prudential knowledge" (ibid:489) and the new mode of knowing overcomes the dichotomy between epistemology and ontology by calling for a new self-understanding of science. This, in turn, calls for a transformation in modernist positivist science as a secured foundation of knowledge of self and society. The task here is to transform science into a science of hope where it is a "search for new possibilities" (Sunder Rajan 1998:22). As Sunder Rajan further tells us, science as hope "is a post-critical hope in the transformative resources of the sciences" which strives for "certain intrinsic possibilities of a new self-understanding" (ibid). This calls for a mutual interpenetration between action, love and knowledge and a new epistemology of participation. In this transformational pathway, there can no longer be a divorce between epistemology and ontology and "knowledge of" is carried out in a caring condition of "knowing with". As Sunder Rajan tells us: "Caring gives us a unique mode of access, a kind of knowing which may be called knowing-with" (ibid:78).[4]

The preceding pages have presented us multiple visions of a desirable society towards which we need to strive. But this expected movement to a better society and a transformative self is not going to be painless or smooth; it would involve social struggles and we would have to be ready for this. At the same time we have to be ready for creativity as a foundation and art of life. Creativity is now no longer a choice, it is an obligation: "We feel obliged to create ourselves and choose our values" (Weiner 2000:268). As Robert Weiner tells us: "Short of divine intervention, it appears that none of our problems can be dealt with unless we think and work creatively" (ibid). But this task of creativity is not fulfilled by having or promoting extraordinary role models of creativity, rather it is to help all of us and each of us to be creative. As Weiner urges us to realize: "It will never suffice to have extraordinary role models of creativity. Our dream is to help everyone gain the insights of being on the margins without anyone being marginalized, to help the average person express him or herself in exceptional ways, and to help all of us progress together" (ibid:270).

Hope is an integral aspect of criticism, creativity and transformation. Critical initiatives in criticism, creativity and transformation are founded on hope and it cannot be carried on "without some sense of historical possibility" (Walzer 1988:17). But, the regnant ideology of neoliberalism would try to destroy hope for a life beyond the dominance of market. In this context, the fundamental task before us is to preserve, nurture and continually seek to transform what David Harvey (2000) calls 'spaces of hope'. Here it is a positive sign that despite the picture of no alternative created by state and market, people everywhere are struggling for new hopes and new freedoms. As Felix Wilfred writes in his heart-touching recent meditation, *Asian Dreams and Christian Hopes*: "Fired with hope, ordinary people resist abuses of power, take on the globalizing forces by small initiatives at the local level, affirm their identities against cultural domination and homogenization, claim their right for land and other natural resources against exploitative forces. Are these not truly the sling of David in the face of the mighty Goliaths? There is only hope and no room for despair" (2000:xvi). What Wilfred writes provides us further challenges in rethinking criticism, creativity and transformation at the contemporary juncture:

> Hopeless is the situation when one segment of humanity, one culture or civilization pretends to be all. It is a process that weakens humanity. That is why we look forward to a century of greater

> human solidarity and togetherness, and not clash of civilization. We cannot forget for a moment that a nuclear conflagration of the world is a real possibility that hangs over the head of humanity like Democles' sword. It provides an added reason to invest our energies in bringing peoples and nations together in mutual understanding and cooperation. The meeting of peoples and races, cultures and regions will be the most hopeful thing that could happen to humanity and signify a fresh epoch of richness. It is the direction in which we need to move and look for ways and means to realize the future of humankind as one family (ibid:xiv).

II

The above account presents a glimpse of new challenges and possibilities in rethinking criticism, creativity and social transformation at the contemporary juncture. The contributors to this volume in various ways take part in these conversations and contribute to the broadening of agenda of criticism, creativity and transformation at the present time. In his opening essay, discussing the challenge of going beyond the modernist preoccupation with power and rationality in the discourse and practice of social criticism, the editor of this volume, Ananta Kumar Giri, argues that both work on transformation of undemocratic structures of power and self-transformation which enables the actors to use power with a will to serve—rather than with a will to dominate—-ought to go together. He urges us to have a notion of transformative self as a bearer of social criticism and cultural creativity. For Giri, culture, while implicated in a field of power, nevertheless contains "within it a dimension of ideal seeking vis-a-vis self-realization, modes of intersubjectivity and the constitution of a good society which puts it in a relationship of conflict and transcendence with the structures of power".

In his paper, "Culture and Development: Lessons from Swadhyaya", Ramashray Roy helps us further in having a creative, critical and transcendental view of culture. In place of the contemporary regnant view which puts culture at the service of development, where development primarily means socio-economic development, Roy pleads for putting development at the service of culture. But this requires going beyond the contemporary mode of culture as consumption and entertainment, and rethinking both the concept of man and development. For Roy, "the point of departure for a fresh thinking on development is man himself". While offering a critical genealogy of modern individualism and its preoccupation with felicity, Roy urges us to jettison the Cartesian concept of man as "a body-mind complex" and go back to "the traditional notion which treats man as incomplete without the soul as the sensorium of the divine". For Roy, "when attuned to the divine ground of being, the social develops the capacity to resist attempts by passions to rule over it...". Roy presents the vision and practice of Swadhyaya Parivara----an exciting socio-spiritual initiative in multi-dimensional transformation----as an instance of such an alternative conception of man and cultural creativity. According to Roy, in Swadhyaya, to know "is not only to reflect and comprehend, but also to shape and create. For, to know oneself is simultaneously to perfect oneself and help others to perfect themselves". He further tells us that "action, in Swadhyaya perspective, is an offering to God, an offering for covering this world with God's love". In Swadhyaya, we see glimpses of the liberation of religion from lifeless rituals where the movement becomes a catalyst of self-development and social transformation.

If Roy presents the new voices of liberation from Hinduism, in his contribution Fred R. Dallmayr presents new voices of liberation from Buddhism and Islam. Dallmayr puts forward two radical voices each from Buddhism and Islam. In contemporary Buddhism, he first draws our attention to the Japanese Zen Buddhist philosopher, Maso Abe. Inspired by his teacher, Hiscamatsu Sinchi, Abe has been actively involved in a "loosely structured lay movement," which aims at "transgressing the traditional Zen focus on monastic practices and private-individual illumination in the direction of a concern for social transformation". For Abe, "in order to promote this transformation, more concretely, liberation of people from oppression and injustice, lay Buddhists had to be ready to serve as emancipatory agents—without, however, embracing the modernist premises of anthropocentrism or sovereign self-constitution". Abe bases himself on a critical view of *sunyata* which encourages a "continual transgression of self-being toward otherness" and "harbors within itself a deep compassion in the light of which existing forms of oppression or domination can be 'freely turned over' or at least alleviated". The second voice from Buddhism that Dallmayr presents is that of Buddhadasa Bhikhu of Thailand whose agenda of Dhammic Socialism proposes a form of democracy which is "respectful of the spiritual authority of *dhamma* (or *dharma*) and mindful of the continuous need of human self-transformation".

The two voices of liberation from contemporary Islam that Dallmayr delineates also contribute to the broadening of agenda of criticism and transformation. In his *Rethinking Islam*, Arkoun argues that, "as opposed to ideological-fundamentalist mobilization, liberation must tap deeper religious resources located beyond, and even repressed by, sheer power politics". The second voice, that of Ali Shariati of Iran, offers a profound critique of the "western propensity toward materialism, consumerism and secular anthropocentrism" as well as the suppression of freedom under the regime of clerical traditionalism. What is quite insightful is that Dallmayr links these voices of liberation to contemporary reconstructions of the agenda of freedom and emancipation as in certain postmodern moves which decenter "sovereign autonomy and self-constituting agency".

Dallymayr's attempt to outline pathways of liberation beyond liberalism is taken up to new heights and depth in Chitta Ranjan Das' discourse on integral evolution and education. Das writes: "One liberates oneself by collaborating with a liberating process and that is perhaps how we all collaborate in the march of this world of ours". Evolution, for Das, who builds on Sri Aurobindo's agenda of integral evolution, is collaborating with oneself and the world to make this world a more dignified place to live. For Das, "once you decide to believe in evolution, you begin to feel that you have an errand to deliver through living your life and decide no more to lecherously prey and pine for your own salvation". Indian society has, more often than not, forgotten this ethics of identification and responsibility. Das finds it deeply problematic that in India, as a result of traditional preoccupation with individual salvation and world renunciation, "the best people have chosen to run away in a sort of religious disgust from everything that stands for this world. World-hate has got the better of being drawn toward the world with a love and determination to change it."

Das also describes the vision and an experiment of integral education. While inviting to appreciate the life of austerity that the teachers of such alternative educational schools lead, Das is, at the same time, critical of the organizers of these schools who cling to money and power. In fact, what Das writes is a remarkable model of critical engagement: "The organizers belong to the old society, they are somewhat successful in the old society and are people who matter in the old order of things. But there has been no personal revolution in their lives."

Das' self-critical approach to the transformative movement that he himself belongs to, finds a creative correspondence in Nancy Weiss Hanrahan's approach to cultural practice and social change. Of the women's movement in the US, Hanrahan asks: "Does cultural creativity generate more possibilities for women, or does it reproduce new images of femininity and constrain women's options?" Furthermore, "the same categories of analysis may also be applied to the women's movement itself. Is it hierarchical or egalitarian? Does power flow from the top down or bottom up?" For Hanrahan, "...there is no liberation without the internal grounds for a critique of the normative claims to that liberation". She also offers a critique of power as the telos of human emancipation: "One of the dangers of culturally structured social movements is the tendency to equate empowerment with power---which in the worst cases, substitutes private liberation for social freedom... Nazism could be seen as liberating in that it personally and collectively empowered the German people. But as we know, it was politically repressive, not only with respect to the Jews, but also within its own ranks" (p.2). The key question in thinking about criticism and creativity now is: "How do we construct critique in the absence of categorical or fixed guideposts?" Furthermore, "the analytical distinctions between hierarchy and egalitarianism, between cultural objects and cultural practice, do not serve the analysis of either the movement or its cultural representations particularly well. It is not that there is not a liberatory ideology at work, or that it is not actually negotiating the problems and ideals of a democratic society. It is that these categories, even if constructed as dialectically related pairs, do not grasp the complexity, or the contingency, of the processes of cultural creativity and social transformation."

Hanrahan's arguments that "movements of social change also internally reproduce power and have repressive tendencies" and that "these issues are not solved by virtue of whether a movement is grass roots or organized through centralized institutions of power", find an ethnographic correspondence in Chitra Sivakumar's evocative, moving and sympathetic study of the Tamil militants of Sri Lanka. While the militant violence against the genocidal violence of the Sri Lankan State has been looked at as the panacea by the Tamil minorities, Sivakumar also evaluates this violence as presented by the actors themselves. But, at the same time, she urges to realize that, in the first place, this violence was a response to the sufferings and pangs of the Sri Lankan Tamils. For Sivakumar, "...the Sri Lankan Tamil collective consciousness responded to the 1983 'magma' of experience by opting for violence for its recovery". In this process, there emerged a transformed hermeneutics of death: "Death, for the Sri Lankan Tamils, not only became a polysemic emblem, signifying not merely the recovery of dignity, honour, self-respect, nationhood and freedom, but also an instrument for the recovery of the Tamil ontic self in its hiddenness."

The Tamil militants are struggling for a space for autonomy and freedom in a nation-state which does not recognize its difference and wants to destroy its being. This draws our attention to the problem of thinking about nationalism as an emancipatory ideology. The challenge is that emancipatory movements, fighting against the nation-state, should not fall into its ideological trap and reproduce the same logic of annihilation and domination. This point has been made forcefully in this volume by Amena Mohsin in her study of what she calls 'traps of nationalism' in the Chittagong Hill Tracts (CHT). While pleading for making Bangladesh a multi-national state, she argues that though nationalism is "looked on as counter-hegemonic", in reality it "entraps human beings within the same divisive and hegemonic grove, due to the discourse's inherent bias towards the majority dominant community". In this context, she questions how the demand on the part of Jumma nationalism in CHT to "merge three districts into one political unit works against the very principle and logic of decentralization".

In rethinking emancipation, if Mohsin points to the traps of nationalism, Amita Baviskar, herself a sympathetic scholar of ecology movements, presents many pitfalls of environmentalism. In her article, "The Dialectic of Environmentalism", she draws our attention to the loss of traditional rights of the local people over the use of forest resources by the establishment of a wildlife conservation park in Himachal Pradesh. Baviskar shows how "ecodevelopment begins with the assumption that wildlife conservation is a priority that overrides people's rights to resources within the protected area". Furthermore, "its underlying philosophy is statist in that it ignores the crucial issue of redressing a fundamental inequality, viz., the denial of rights to local people, a systemic bias begun by the colonial state and continued in independent India." This issue of the suppression of the rights of the local people is also discussed evocatively by Vidhya and Achyut Das in their contribution, "State, Market and the Voluntary Sector: Agragamee, Social Criticism and the Contemporary Dialectics of Transformations".

Thus, Mohsin, Baviskar, and Achyut and Vidhya Das help us to be aware of the dangers to human emancipation when frames of emancipation turn into hegemonic orthodoxies. In a very novel way, Baas Weilinga contributes to this critical awakening by drawing our attention to the trap of productivism in modernity—a trap from which revolutionary alternatives to capitalism have not been able to fully come out. In his paper, "Rethinking Social Transformation: An Eco-Socialist Perspective", Weilinga argues how Marx and the subsequent Marxist attempts in social transformation, such as those of Lenin and Stalin, did not offer any fundamental critique of industrial production itself. Speaking of the Bolshevik Revolution in Russia, Weilinga tells us how "all Bolshevik leaders have been looking forward towards the USA when trying to imagine the future of a prospering socialism". Furthermore, Weilinga asserts that though eco-socialists find traces of awareness in Marx about the entropic limits of industrial production, Marx and Engels did not have a proper response to the entropic critique of industrial production. Such a bondage to the traps of productivism did not help in discovering any alternative to "the formidable capacity" of capitalism to "orient human longings and ambitions towards profit producing objects and objectives". The dictatorial definition of needs in socialist countries was no real alternative since in these countries "the need of participation in discussing and deciding which needs are basic and which desires are socially acceptable was suppressed". For Weilinga, it was forgotten in these efforts in defining human well-being that "the satisfaction of basic needs is not just a quantitative task, but a cultural task as well". For Weilinga, there is an epochal need to "transform the politics of transformation" and a fundamental challenge here is to re-orient human desire, a reorientation which calls for "major efforts in aesthetic education and cultural action as the only way to counter the onslaught of the media". The work on aesthetic education, at the same time, must be accompanied by a project of what Weilinga calls 'radical democratization' simultaneously in civil society and political arena.

Roberto M. Unger, a Brazilian thinker teaching at Harvard, is one of our most engaging contemporary interlocutors who has presented us an invitational outline of the programme of a radical democracy which involves both personal revolution and structural transformation. In his contribution, Prakash C. Sarangi attempts to give an intimation of the calling of transformative politics that awaits us through a discussion of the work of Unger. Sarangi shows how in Unger's programme of empowered democracy, transformative movements and voluntary associations play an important role by keeping "the state humble" and facilitating "the self-organisation of society outside government". But, the language of the transformative movements is not just the language of the present; it must embody a prophetic vision of the future. Furthermore, Unger wants the transformative movements "to be an experimental model in anticipation of the empowered democracy".

But the further challenge that transformative initiatives face and the constraints that bind are still formidable, and we can estimate the significance of contributions of Anindita N. Balslev, Daniel Moshenberg and Badri Narayan Tewari in terms of such further challenges and constraints. In her contribution Balslev shows how cross-cultural conversation is an important task before any transformative initiative now. Cross-cultural conversation performs a bridge-building task and must seek to build a global community in the contemporary epoch of globalization. Such conversations, for Balslev, must help us explore "new ways of thinking about the 'otherness' of others".

But, in reality, even in our contemporary postmodern world, the 'otherness' of the other is being suppressed by simply not recognizing the face and existence of the other. In his contribution, Daniel Moshenberg calls this the problem of 'inattention'. He shows how the school board of Washington DC, USA does not recognize and attend to the desire of the illiterate women of colour and the migrant women from Latin America to study further and improve their life-standard. In the educational discourse of the state, only children are valorized where the faces of the poor migrant women are forgotten: "the crisis touches only children, because only children can be at risk". In this context, critical literacy calls for "being with and being for those articulated as forgotten and forgettable, as ignored and ignorable and entails attempting to destroy and transform the appareti and agencies of articulation". But here, the state alone is not guilty of inattention; similar is the case with the so-called transformative movements within the civil society as well. Moshenberg here points to "the failure of western models of women's liberation to see women's domestic labor as an everyday practice".

One important part of the strategy of 'inattention' is the erasure of the struggling people's memory of resistance and struggle. This constitutes the crux of Badri Narayan Tewari's contribution to this volume. Tewari presents his study of the folk memory of Chuharmal who is a 'hero' of the lower castes in central Bihar, India. In the narrative, Chuharmal, a member of the low caste of Dusadh, elopes with a girl from the upper Bhumihar caste. But when this folk narrative is played out even today, the higher castes attempt to stop its staging, and sometimes even kill the person who plays the part of low-caste hero, Chuharmal. In fact, because of the popular myth of Chuharmal, four caste riots have taken place in the Bhojpur region of Bihar between 1970 and 1990. Through his study, Tewari seeks to show how memory has been used as a method of dominance as well as a method of protest. In this context, an important task before transformative movements is to preserve and nurture alternative memories of struggle and imagination.

But, this is a task not for the leaders and the literate alone. Here, it is helpful to go back to Moshenberg. He argues that the notion of the transformative agent, in many theories of transformation such as the Marxian, is a biased one. It privileges vanguard leaders who are almost always literate at the expense of the masses. In such a view, the folk hero, Chuharmal, would not probably have much significance. But Moshenberg's meditations go further and he urges us to explore alternative to dialectics. Writes Moshenberg: "I suggest that the very notion of dialectics within the Marxist and neo-Marxist traditions presumes a certain kind of and level of literacy always inscribed within the mass, or at least among the vanguard leadership of that mass. Thus, the educational work, as dialectical, is always directed towards that leadership." In this context, Moshenberg proposes, as alternative to dialectics, antagonistics, as suggested by Antonio Negri and the Italian autonomy movement. But it is not clear from Moshenberg's account how Negri's antagonistics is free from the presuppostions of dialectics.

Nevertheless, the challenge for rethinking dialectics at the contemporary juncture for radical transformative imagination requires urgent attention now. Dialectical thinking, whether of the Hegelian or Marxian kind, has deeply influenced collective action and critical reflection in the last one hundred and fifty years. But, how do we look at the theory and practice of dialectics in the light of contemporary changes, namely, the collapse of social systems governed by the philosophy of historical materialism? Does dialectic involve only the conflict between thesis and anti-thesis leading to an inevitable synthesis or is there also a process of cooperation at work? What is the significance of reflection, more importantly, self-reflection, in the dialectical process? Giri addresses some of these questions. Giri presents Roy Bhaskar's rethinking of dialectics for whom "dialectical processes are not necessarily characterized by opposition or antagonism". Furthermore, an important part of dialectical engagement for Bhaskar is the discovery of what Bhaskar calls 'open totality'.

Bhaskar helps us to relate dialectic to what he calls "the pulse of freedom". Giri concludes by relating it to the pulse of dialogue. Dialogue is different from oppositional confrontation and is always characterized by a reflexivity about one's own position and transformation of the initial starting point. K. Raghavendra Rao's concluding contribution to this volume also helps us realize this. Taking inspiration from Gandhi, Rao provides us further challenges for listening and dialogue and in the process strive to continuously overcome the separating lines of friends and foes. The challenge of creative transformation now calls for an evolutionary synthesis of dialectics and dialogue, a struggle for realizing self-transformation of individuals, and the structural transformation of the bases of unjust power and exploitative capital.

Notes

1. Partha Chatterjee (1997) draws our attention to the hiatus between capitalist modernity and democratic modernity. But he does not wish to push democratic modernity in a direction of spiritualization, an agenda which I would like to stress here.
2. For Dirlik, "in their simultaneous repudiation of structure and affirmation of the local in problems of oppression and liberation" post-colonial critics "have mystified the ways in which totalizing structures persist in the midst of apparent disintegration and fluidity" (Dirlik 2000:231).
3. What Dussel writes here as the objective of liberation philosophy deserves our careful attention: "It is necessary to negate the moments that negate the person, and to develop the moments that justify liberation. If there is an absolute, it cannot but affirm and develop the person in justice, autonomy, and freedom" (Dussel 1998:11).
4. Sundar Rajan's call for a new epistemology of participation is partly realized in new computer-mediated communication technologies. Jim Walch (1999) provides us several glimpse of this (also, Castells 1997).

References

Bhabha, Homi K. 2000. "Postcolonial Criticism." In Diana Brydon (ed.), *Postcolonialism: Critical Concepts in Literary and Cultural Studies*. London & New York: Routledge. Vol. 1, 105-133.

Bauman, Zygmunt. 1988. *Freedom*. London: Open University Press.

—, 2001. *The Individualized Society*. Cambridge: Polity Press.

Bhaskar, Roy. 2000. *From East to West: Odyssey of a Soul*. London: Routledge.

Beck, Ulrich. 2000. *The Brave New World of Work*. Cambridge: Polity Press.

Butler, Judith, Ernesto Laclau and Slavoj Zizek. 2000. *Contingency, Hegemony, Universality: Contemporary Dialogues on the Left*. London: Verso.

Castells, Manuel. 1997. *The Power of Identity*. Basil Blackwell.

Chatterjee, Partha. 1997. "Beyond the Nation or Within." *Economic and Political Weekly*, January 4-11.

Dasgupta, Partha and Ismail Serageldin (eds.), 1999. *Social Capital: A Multifaceted Perspective*. Washington, DC: World Bank.

Dirlik, Arif. 2000. "The Post-Colonial Aura: Third World Criticism in the Age of Global Capitalism." In Diana Brydon (ed.), *Postcolonialism: Critical Concepts in Literary and Cultural Studies*. Vol. 1. London & New York: Routledge.

Dallmayr, Fred. 1999. "Achieving Multiple Countries: Millennial Reflections." *Journal of Contemporary Thought 10 (Winter)*: 5-26.

—, 2001 "Global Modernization: Toward Different Modernities." University of Notre Dame: Manuscript.

Dussel, Enrique. 1998. *The Underside of Modernity: Apel, Ricouer, Rorty, Taylor and the Philosophy of Liberation*. New York: Humanity Books.

Falk, Richard. 1999. *Predatory Globalization: A Critique*. Cambridge: Polity Press.

Gorz, Andre. 1999. *Reclaiming Work: Beyond the Wage-Based Society*. Cambridge: Polity Press.

Giri, Ananta K. 1999. "Self-Development and Voluntary Action." *Gandhi Marg* 21 (2): 195-207, July-September, 1999.

—, 2000 "Rethinking Civil Society." *Review of Development and Change* V (1): 99-127.

Giri, Ananta K. and Quarles van Ufford. 2000. "Reconstituting Development as a Shared Responsibility: Ethics, Aesthetics and a Creative Shaping of Human Possibilities". Madras Institute of Development Studies: Working Paper.

Harvey, David. *Spaces of Hope*. Edinburgh University Press.

Jasper, James. 2000. *The Art of Moral Protest*. Chicago: University of Chicago Press.

Kagarlitsky, Boris. 2000. *The Return of Radicalism: Reshaping the Left Institutions*. London: Pluto Press.

Margalit, Avishai. 1996. *The Decent Society*. Cambridge, MA: Harvard University Press.

Melucci, Alberto. 1996a. *The Playing Self: Person and Meaning in the Planetary Society*. Cambridge: Cambridge University Press.

---, 1996b. *Challenging Codes: Collective Action in the Information Age*. Cambridge: Cambridge University Press.

Mohanty, Manoranjan. 1994. "Swaraj and Jiefang: Freedom Discourse in India and China." In *Understanding the Post-Colonial World: Theory and Method*, ed., Neera Chandhoke. Delhi: Sterling.

---, 1998. "Towards a Creative Theory of Social Transformation." In *People's Rights: Social Movements and the State in the Third World*, eds., Manoranjan Mohanty and Partha N. Mukherjee. New Delhi: Sage Publications, pp. 9-26.

Mouffe, Chantal. 1992. *Dimensions of Radical Democracy: Pluralism, Citizenship, Community*. London: Verso.

Pieterse, Jan N. and Bhikhu Parekh (eds.) *The Decolonization of Imagination*. London: Zed Books.

Pieterse, Jan N. (ed.) 2000. *Global Futures: Shaping Globalization*. London: Zed Books.

Putnam, Robert D. 1993. *Making Democracy Work: Civic Traditions in Modern Italy*. Princeton: Princeton University Press.

Scott, David. 1998. *Refashioning Futures: Criticism After Postcolonialty*. Princeton: Princeton University Press.

Santos, Boaventura de Sousa. 1995. *Toward a New Common Sense: Law, Science and Politics in the Paradigmatic Transition*. London: Routledge.

Sri Aurobindo. 1962. *The Human Cycles: The Ideal of Human Unity, War and Self-Determination*. Pondicherry: Sri Aurobindo Ashram.

Sunder Rajan, R. 1998. *Beyond the Crisis of European Sciences*. Shimla: Indian Institute of Advanced Studies.

Terchek, Ronald J. 1996. *Gandhi: Struggling for Autonomy*. New Delhi: Vistaar Publications.

Thapar, Romila. 2000. *India: Another Millennium*? Delhi: Viking.

Therborn, Goran. 1991. "Virsprung durch Rethink." In Robin Blackburn (ed.), *The Future of Communism and the Future of Socialism*. London: Verso, pp. 298-309.

Touraine, Alain. 1997. *What is Democracy*? Boulder, CO: Westview Press.

----, 2000. *Can We Live Together? Equality and Difference*. Cambridge: Polity Press.

Walch, Jim. 1999. *In the Net: An Internet Guide for the Activists*. London: Zed Publishers.

Wallerstein, Immanuel. 1999. *The End of the World as We Know It*. Minneapolis: University of Minnesota Press.

Walzer, Michael. 1988. *The Company of Critics: Social Criticism and Political Commitment in the Twentieth Century*. New York: Basic Books.

Weiner, Robert P. 2000. *Creativity and Beyond*. Albany: SUNY Press.

Wilfred, Felix. 2000. *Asian Dreams and Christian Hopes*. Delhi: ISPCK.

Wuthnow, Robert. 1998. *After Heaven: Sprituality in America since the 1950s*. Berkeley: University of California Press.

Unger, Roberto M. 1987. *False Necessity: Anti-Necessitarian Social Theory in the Service of Radical Democracy*. Cambridge: Cambridge University Press.

Chapter Two

Social Criticism, Cultural Creativity and the Contemporary Dialectics of Transformations

Ananta Kumar Giri

I can't help but dream about a kind of criticism that would not try to judge, but bring an *oeuvre*, a book, a sentence, an idea to life; it would light fires, watch the grass grow, listen to the wind, and catch the sea-foam in the breeze and scatter it. It would multiply, not judgments, but signs of existence; it would summon them, drag them from their sleep.

— Michel Foucault (1988:326)

[A contemporary critique of capitalism] is perhaps more needed than ever, as the demise of state socialism has increased capitalism's self-assertion. Today, there is scarcely anyone who wants to criticize capitalism. And yet, in the European Union alone we have seventeen million unemployed. ... We have to imagine something new in order to criticize this system. But, the standard of criticism can only be the realization of a radical democracy, which naturally involves taming capitalism by means of a social state to a degree yet unknown

—Jurgen Habermas (n.d.:11)

To go inside, in the life of the spirit, is also to expand oneself in terms of consciousness, to break down the separating wall between

> oneself and the all. Self-realization with the medieval saints of India was not a running away from the world to what is called to save one's soul; it is being reborn egoless, so that you are able to look at the whole world in a different eye. You become a rebel because you want the relationships and arrangements of society to be determined anew.
>
> —Chitta Ranjan Das (1982:80)

I

Social criticism is part of a wider criticism of life and is animated by a passion of both critique and construction. It begins with an enquiry into the foundations of our life and an awareness about its multi-dimensional origin and dynamics----the material and the spiritual, the collective and the individual; it evaluates the nature of our contemporary social institutions from the point of view of justice and human dignity. Life means multiple webs of relationships and criticism is an inquiry into the quality of these relationships. Criticism also seeks to understand whether the modes of togetherness suggested in life's architecture of relationships genuinely holds together or not. Criticism begins with a description of the dynamics of relationships in life; observes and describes both coherence and incoherence, harmonies and contradictions at work in life; and seeks to move from incoherence to coherence, darkness to light, and from light to more light. An eternal desire to move from one summit of perfection to another is the objective of criticism which is not a specialized attribute of life; it is life itself.

Sociologically, self, society and culture are three dimensions, domains or levels of reality where the webs of relationship called life are at work. Though social criticism has definitely more to do with the field called the social, it is not separated from the dynamics of criticism and creativity in the field of self and culture. Society consists of the dialectic of value and power and social criticism is an enquiry into the mode of this dialectic without presupposing that this dialectic is a process of determination where power determines the terms of discourse and holds the keys to human emancipation (cf. Beteille 1980; Giri 1996). Social criticism is an inquiry into the nature of legitimacy of a society's structure of power and the dignity of its institutional order. But, the process of social criticism goes hand in hand with the process of self-criticism (i.e., self-criticism in the life of the subjects as well as an object of concern in the life of fellow beings) and cultural criticism. In fact, self-criticism is the base of social criticism while cultural criticism constitutes its sky.

The task of social criticism is one of interrogating the foundations of one's society (also of another's; consider the exemplary social criticism of American democracy presented to us by the French Alexis de Tocqueville) and reinterpreting it. What is the dynamics of such criticism and who are its actors? The actor can be an individual, a group of like-minded individuals whom we can call a community of critics, a group or a movement. The actors of social criticism can either conceive their role as one of just standing by the side of the river and never jumping into it or immersing themselves totally in it and presenting a critique from the inside out. In the case of the former, the critics perceive their role as one of pointing out the faults and contradictions of the society concerned but they do not take responsibility for their critical positions. Here, social critics behave as marginal men and women; like Simmel's strangers, "they are in but not wholly of their society" (Walzer 1988:32). In contrast to this, we can find critics who are related to the society they criticize both politically and morally. "It is opposition, far more than detachment, that determines" the shape of such social criticism. Here, the critic takes sides and "sets himself against the political forces" (ibid:48).

But, while a critic or a community of critics or a movement takes a political side; he or she may not feel the necessity of taking the beliefs and values of the people whose life is the object of her/his criticism seriously. The critic may proceed with an assumption or arrogance that she is endowed with a uniquely revealed truth and it is his destiny to preach it to the many unfortunate whose life is in urgent need of redemption. Therefore, the politically responsible criticism that Walzer associates with connected social criticism, can go without taking seriously or having a dialogue with the internal tradition of a society. This seems to have been the case with many of the major movements of criticism in the modern world, for instance, Marxism, psychoanalysis, and feminism. True, many creative critics within these movements of criticism have tried to make a dialogue between their modernist agenda of criticism and their lived traditions giving rise to a Buddhist Marxism or a Vedantic psychoanalysis or a truly indigenous feminism, but such moves have, by and large, been on the fringe and have been looked with suspicion by the ideological proponents of such systems of social criticism.[1]

But, in order to make social criticism a worthwhile engagement, there is a need to take the tradition of a society seriously. This seems to constitute the difference between a Platonic approach to social criticism and an Aristotelian mode which takes people's practices as the starting point of an inquiry. While "for Plato, the opinions of finite and imperfect people, as embodied in their traditions, are hardly a sufficient basis for an account of what is really good, even good for these very same people," Aristotle urges the critics to "seek conviction through arguments using the traditional beliefs as our witnesses and standards" (Nussbaum and Sen 1987:23). But, at the same time, the evaluation of tradition in the Artistotelian agenda also involves a movement "beyond the superficial desires of participants to a deeper and more objective level" (ibid). Criticism here is a deliberative process which "confronts the reflecting participant with all of the alternative views on a topic, leads him or her through a thorough imaginative exploration of each," leading to modification of their many unconsidered positions. Yet, "this modification, if it takes place, will take place not as an imposition from without, but as a discovery about which, among that person's own values, are the deepest and the most central. This is self-discovery and discovery of one's own traditions" (ibid:24).

While taking seriously the internal tradition of a society in one's act of criticism, two points have to be born in mind. *First*, sources of social criticism are not solely internal to a society concerned; they are invariably born out of a global interpenetration of traditions, societal consciousness and civilizational perspectives. For example, in understanding the sources of criticism in a seeker such as Gandhi, we find that these are not solely internal to Indian tradition; rather it is born out of the dialectic between the emancipatory traditions in the West represented by Thoreau, Ruskin and Tolstoy and Indian traditions of spiritual criticism. The same is the case with Sri Aurobindo and Swami Vivekananda whose critical agenda is difficult to understand without understanding their dialogue with the emancipatory agenda of modernity. Such a view of the multiple sources of social criticism is particularly important in the present day world where societies and cultures are increasingly part of a process of mutual interpenetration, where the vision and the experiment of good life in one, holds a critical mirror for the unjust social arrangement that is perpetuated in the other. *Second*, the dialogue between tradition and critique may not be a smooth one and social criticism must have the courage to break away from tradition and create new ones for the sake of justice and human dignity.

In fact, social criticism involves taking a hypothetical attitude to one's culture, society and one's taken-for-granted conceptions of self. Taking such a hypothetical attitude is a difficult task, but an inevitable challenge to be overcome, because "individuals who have been socialized cannot take a hypothetical attitude to the form of life and the personal life-history that have shaped their own identity" (Habermas 1990:104). For many interlocutors within the western critical tradition—from Aristotle to Habermas—this overcoming of the natural blindness is possible by participating in a rational deliberation on the form of life to which one belongs. Habermas calls such modes of engagement discourse ethics and argues that "for the hypothesis-testing participant in a discourse, the relevance of the experiential context of his life world tends to pale. To him, the normativity of existing institutions seems just as open to question as the objectivity of things and events" (ibid:109). Habermas (ibid:108) further tells us in his memorable phrase: "Under the unrelenting moralizing gaze of participants in discourse ... familiar institutions can be transformed into so many instances of problematic justice."

But, after taking a hypothetical attitude to one's society, a critic has to come back to the society in order to transform it. To put it in the words of historian Arnold Joseph Toynbee: "the process of withdrawal has to be accompanied by a process of return and an attempt at a new life based on self-realized, transformed values". Habermas also helps us understand this: "Concern for the fate of one's neighbour is a necessary emotional prerequisite for the cognitive operations expected of participants in discourses". But how do we achieve "integration of cognitive operations and emotional dispositions" in our critical engagements? Here is the rationalist binding in the Habermasian discourse ethics adequate and enough? Realizing this integration also involves going beyond one's rational mind and discover the spiritual dimension in one's self and the other. But even while looking for hermeneutic supplements after realizing that "the discursive justification of norms is no guarantor of moral insights," the farthest Habermas can go is towards neighborhood solidarity and "internalization of authority" (ibid:170).

But, the problem with such a supplementary exercise is that it fails to realize that "reflective dialectical examination" also requires "reflective self" whose sources are not only material and rational but also spiritual. Critical theory from Aristotle to Habermas has shared an uncritical faith in the ability of rationality to arrive at integration of our life and in thinking about the task of social criticism. Today there is probably a crucial need to think about the limit and possibility of such a preoccupation. There is a commitment here to a "rational criticism of culture" which leaves untouched the question of the infrarational and the superrational or the supramental challenges of the human condition, not to mention that it is not reflective enough about such a basic problem as the cultural construction of rationality itself. But, as Sri Aurobindo (1962:206) has argued, in realizing an integration between cognitive distantiation and emotional care, "a rational satisfaction cannot give (a person) safety from the pull from below nor deliver him from the attraction from above." "It is spiritual, a greater than rational enlightenment that can alone illumine the vital nature of man and impose harmony on its self-seekings, antagonisms and discords" (ibid).

I wish to submit for your consideration that social criticism now needs to have an agenda of spiritual criticism which encompasses rational criticism. More specifically, the Habermasian agenda of practical discourse needs to be a part of an agenda of what can be called practical spirituality. Practical spirituality, as Swami Vivekananda argues, urges us to realize that "the highest idea of morality and unselfishness goes hand in hand with the highest idea of metaphysical conception" (1991:354). This highest conception pertains to the realization that man himself is God: "You are that Impersonal Being: that God for whom you have been searching all over the time is yourself----yourself not in the personal sense but in the impersonal" (ibid:332). The task of practical spirituality begins with this self-realization but does not end there: its objective is to transform the world. Vivekananda thus challenges us: "The watchword of all well-being, of all moral good is not 'I' but 'thou'. Who cares whether there is a heaven or a hell, who cares if there is an unchangeable or not? Here is the world and it is full of misery. Go out into it as Buddha did, and struggle to lessen it or die in the attempt" (ibid:353).

The objective of practical spirituality is to solve the concrete problems of men and women and enable them to move from food to freedom. Spiritual criticism is animated by such a passion of integration and transformation. Let us try to understand the varieties of spiritual criticism at work in society and history. Prophetic criticism about which Michael Walzer (1988) has told us so insightfully is an instance of spiritual criticism of society where prophets use the name of God to build their movements against the forces of oppression. Not only in traditional societies but also in a variety of contemporary societies one is back to the beginning where social critic is a prophet. The prophets are not only opposed to priesthood but also to the state. As Walzer speaks of the Prophet Amos: "In the dispute between Amos and the priest Amaziah, it is the prophet who appeals to religious tradition, the priest only to the reason of the state." For Walzer, "prophecy aims to arouse remembrance, recognition, indignation and repentance" (ibid:63).

Prophecy also aims to arouse realization in each one of us that we contain the reality and possibility of being a prophet ourselves. As we think about prophetic criticism, it is essential to realize that "the typological differentiation between man and overman no longer makes much sense, if it ever did" (Connolly 1991:182). As Connolly tells us: "The 'overman' now falls apart as a set of distinct dispositions concentrated in a particular caste or type and its spiritual qualities migrate to a set of dispositions that may compete for presence in any self" (ibid). In an exciting way, developments in quantum physics buttress such a view of criticism and creativity. For Donnah Zohar and Ian Marshall: "If we are looking for 'God' within physics, the vacuum would be the most appropriate place to look, ... the vacuum has all the characteristics of the immanent God, or the Godhead, spoken of by the mystics, the God within, the God who creates and discovers Himself through the unfolding existence of His creation" (1993:197-98). But, "there is nobody here to act but us... Perhaps, the 'Second Coming' for which so many people have waited is nothing else but the realization that we are that 'coming'. The job of transforming ourselves and saving the world is down to us" (ibid).

Closely related to prophetic criticism is the agenda of martyrdom. J.P.S. Uberoi tells us in his recent provocative study of Sikhism and Gandhism that in their struggle against the power of the state the martyrs show that "no power on earth can make the self do anything against its nature, except indirectly confer martyrdom on it" (1996:88). For Uberoi, the elementary structure of martyrdom is "manifestly the non-dualism of loving self-sacrifice...but equally it is the responsibility of "arising to bear witness" on the duality of the true and false, religion and irreligion, liberation and bondage" (ibid:130). Furthermore, "the martyr is one who must love his enemy in some sense since he or she is the perfect witness (saheed-ul-kamil) that God, who at this time takes an interest in history and politics, does not want his servant to suppose, as the dualist would, that Satanism has any true independent existence, and so *dharmayudhha*, the righteous war, can be transformed into *satyagraha*" (ibid:124). Giving the examples of Antigone, Socrates, Jesus Gandhi and the Sikh Gurus, Uberoi urges us to realize that martyrs as social critics criticize the existing structure of power for the sake of "self-rule, self-reforms" and the "self-management of society".

Bhakti movements in Indian traditions have been yet another example of spiritual criticism where we meet social critics as saints who dissolve the category between the priest and the laity and fight for a relationship of dignity. Some proponents of the Bhakti movement in medieval India such as the poet Achyutananda Das of Orissa have made a distinction between different kinds of *bhakti*---Brahmana Bhakti, Vaishya Bhakti,

Khastriya Bhakti and Shudra Bhakti—and have put Shudra Bhakti at the top.[2] Shudra Bhakti is characterized by a passion to serve God, society and the other without any precondition. The objective of criticism and creativity then is to enable human beings to be Shudras—servants of God, servants of an ideal relationship and good society which grants human dignity to all. Shudras represent labour in Indian tradition and in Bhakti movements labour and devotion, that is, *shrama* and *bhakti* come together for the sake of transformation.

Prophetic criticism, martyrdom and Bhakti movements are examples of spiritual criticism in society and history. They are not innocent of the dynamics of power, both in their method and object of social criticism but, they are not confined to it. They propose a different relationship between knowledge and power where knowledge does not end in the acquisition of power but in the cultivation of an understanding and *sraddha*. These initiatives in criticism help us to realize that the social critic is a *tapashyi* and the *tapashya* of criticism is a *tapashya* of *sraddha*. As Chitta Ranjan Das argues: "Like the demon [the critic] is not engaged in this *tapashya* for the acquisition of more power but for more *sraddha* (reverence for life). It is *sraddha* which makes knowledge radiant, expands it to right fields of activities and makes one capable of more giving and true *sraddha* acts as the mother of courage" (1991:35).

Das also argues that the bearer of social criticism is a "creative man" who looks at the world through the eyes of a friend---*mitrashya chakhusya*, as he calls it. Social criticism in the modern world has been governed very much by the ideals of liberty and equality but criticism as friendship reiterates the transformational significance of fraternity and sisterhood in our critical engagement. A social critic is primarily a friend of the man/woman on the street and a friend of the world. This view of criticism is illumined by Dallmayr's (1993) recent discussion of Heidegger as a "friend of the world". Neither Dallmayr nor I condone Heidegger's initial support for fascism and his total silence on the holocaust but that should not disable us to draw lessons from his critical and creative *oeuvre*; from an "other Heidegger", as Dallmayr presents it. From Heidegger we can have a vision of the social critic as a "house friend" who comes and sits in our backyards but encourages us to discover the depth dimension of our lives as well as other horizons. Social criticism is a genuine dialogue between fellow beings whom Heidegger calls "co-beings".[3] What Heidegger writes of genuine dialogue is true of criticism: both of these are located at the "midpoint of friendship of friends". For Heidegger, "the partners of such dialogue recognize each other in their difference or distinctiveness, a distinctiveness that involves not separation but a mode of 'letting be' and 'setting free' which allows human 'truth' to emerge; the emblem of such truth again, is friendship" (ibid).

As we are invited by the calling of social criticism as friendship, it has to be noted that social criticism also involves serious social antagonism and many critics in society and history have used explicit political insurrection as a method as well. These moves have also helped to make the world a better place to live in as much they have contributed to the creation of a more democratic arrangement of power.

II

If rationality has been a deep structure of social criticism in the western critical tradition, so has it been a preoccupation with politics and power. It is quite striking that power as a tool of criticism and emancipation is such an uncritically taken for-granted assumption under the regime of modernity that critics cannot but think of discourse without politics and can not utter a sentence without the adjective and the noun---political and politics. Thus, Seyla Benhabib cannot proceed further in her meditation on norm and utopia without talking about the "politics of fulfilment" and "politics of self-transfiguration" and Anthony Giddens cannot talk about self-identities without talking of "life politics". I do not want to belittle the significance of politics in the agenda of social criticism and I agree with Derrida (1994) that deconstruction could not have been possible in a "pre-Marxist space". As it is difficult for a hungry person to realize God, it is equally for a society governed by unjust power to realize its spiritual worth. At one point, the relationship between power and spirituality has a relationship of succession, very much like the primary need and secondary needs in Maslow's hierarchy of needs.[4] But, my submission is that both work on transformation of undemocratic structures of power and self-transformation which enables the actors to use power with a spirit of *bhakti*---not with a will to dominate----ought to go together and, in fact, can go together. Without essentializing, we can understand the significance of Gandhi in terms of both these simultaneous---not merely successive---seekings.

One contemporary interlocutor whose work has been very influential in terms of a power perspective is Foucault. For Foucault, social criticism is a criticism of not only macro power but also micro power: "critique must begin from an analytic of relations of power" (quoted in Caputo and Yount 1993:7). But as J.N. Mohanty (1993:33) argues, like the Heideggerian "cunning of reason". Foucault's "power" also succeeds by "hiding its own mechanism", and I should say, by hiding its own limitations. But in Foucault, we also find a realization of the limitation of power as a tool and object of criticism in ensuring human emancipation. There is also another stream in Foucault which questions the primacy of the political in the craft of social criticism. As Foucault writes: "In fact, I have especially wanted to question politics, and to bring to light in the political field, as in the field of historical and philosophical interrogation, some problems that had not been recognized there before. I mean, that the questions I am trying ask are not determined by a preestablished political outlook and do not tend to the realization of some definite political project" (1984:376).

In reflecting on the task of social criticism, we have had a dialogue with Habermas and Foucault. How do we relate to another major interlocutor of criticism and creativity of our times, namely, Jacques Derrida? Derrida's project of "difference" is a radical project in as much as it is integrally linked to the critique of the system and the dynamics of movements (Barnett 1989). But as we make a dialogue with Derrida, we realize that "deconstruction alone is not enough, it must be accompanied by an at least tentative reconstruction grounded in the political and theoretical demands of the contemporary world" (Soja 1989:74). Seeing the work of deconstructionists in the contemporary world we are also bound to ask, "Is there nothing for the philosopher to do, after the demise of the metaphysical seriousness, but to be an intellectual 'Kibitzer', a concern-free creator of abnormal discourse; an insouciant player of deconstructive and fanciful word games, an agile figure shaken on the thin ice of a bottomless chessboard?" (Madison 1989:107).

Derrida has a horizontal notion of difference and cannot think of difference in terms of what Taylor (1989) calls "qualitative distinction" and what Heller (1987) calls "beyond". It is to be noted that "beyond" here does not refer only to being different but to something "higher". True, Derrida speaks of God but for him God is "wholly other" but such a perspective heightens the difference between God and self, self and other rather than help us realize that God is also part of the self. Furthermore, Derrida urges us to understand the work of "deferral" of differences but does not either urge or help us to understand the frame of coordination between differences. But to strive to arrive at a framework of coordination is not to clear the grounds for totalitarianism or totalization. The task for deconstructive politics is now to realize, as Laclau has so forcefully argued, that a "politics of pure difference" is not enough (Giri 1995; Laclau 1994). Both the Foucauldian agenda and Derrida's share a suspicion of the universal and urge us for a "critique of universality".[5] While being enriched by this critical suspicion about the violence of universal categories and processes, the task of social criticism is also to describe and understand the manifold relationship between the universal and the particular that exists today with a view to working out an emancipatory space which inhabits both universal and the particular and transforms their respective arrogance and narrowness to one of creative reconciliation.

In fact, description of existing processes, forms of life and movements is/has to be an integral part of a project of critical engagement. Such a project gets inspiration from the project of a critical anthropology/ethnography which submits that it is possible to make a move from description to critical dialogue. Criticism begins with a description of the society it seeks to understand, a description which is not bound by any particular theory of social criticism and model of social transformation. In fact, the problem with contemporary criticism is that it is too much theory-driven and has very little passion to understand the critical movements that are at work in a form of life without fitting them to apriori theoretical models or using one's critical engagements to prove or disprove a theory.

If social criticism has to maintain a mutually enriching dialogue with theories, it has to maintain a cautious distance from the use of adjectives. Characterizing either the mode of social criticism or the form of life by certain adjectives—for example, a Marxian criticism or a Gandhian society—does not lead us anywhere and the challenge that confronts us now is to be liberated from such an adjectival regime.

It was Richard Rorty (1989) who had challenged us some time ago with his argument that human solidarity is achieved not by theory but by description---description of the unfamiliar and redescription of the familiar. If the task of social criticism is to create solidarity between human beings through the help of description, then how do we make sense of the critical engagements/works of our times? Here, we can take the work of Veena Das (1995), a thought-provoking intellectual of India, as a case in point. In her *Critical Events*, Das urges social theory and analysis to be sensitive to social suffering and understand the need for creating an embodied solidarity which dissolves the distinction between the self and the other. She speaks about the suffering of the abducted women during the partition of India and the victims of Bhopal gas disaster, among others. But she does not provide a single life-story of the victims nor of those who have come forward to establish embodied solidarity with them. In fact, in case of a tragedy like the Bhopal, an ethnographic (i.e., critically-descriptive) portrayal of lives and communities could have inspired efforts for creating solidarity and could have given rise to an engaged public debate on this issue. But Das does not do this. One of the few voices we hear in this text is the one by an illiterate woman who address her speech towards the judges of the Supreme Court of India: "We only ask the judges for one thing. Please come here and count us" (ibid:164). But Das' anthropological discourse on suffering is not very different from the judicial discourse in as much as she does not establish our friendship with a few real life victims and noble souls. In Das' text, suffering of real human beings thus gets displaced by the passion for theory and interpretation. This suggests that the mode of writing crucially determines the impact of our critical engagement. If social criticism is written descriptively and ethnographically it has the potential to create multi-dimensional and multi-pronged solidarity between the victims and the concerned citizens of society than if it is written in an abstract, theoretical mode.

Another critical work in the recent times which succeeds in performing such a task is *Creating a Nationality: Ramajanmabhoomi Movement and the Fear of the Self* by Ashis Nandy (1996) and his colleagues. A sympathetic and critical discussion of the victims of communalism in this has the potential to create a solidarity for collective action against this all-pervasive virus. The first chapter of this book, "Hindutva as Savarna Purana", is remarkable from this point of view. But, the authors seem to lack a deep engagement in few other instances of their narrations. They find the house of a victim in Ayodhya and even though they find his story heart-rendering, they are in a hurry to leave the village before the fall of night. They cannot wait. But it is needless to reiterate that social criticism requires a deep immersion in the life of fellow beings---an immersion which one misses in Nandy and his colleagues' critical text.

In thinking about the efficacy of social criticism its language is a very decisive factor. Many of our social critics today do not write in the language of the people. Even in a society such as India, our critics hoping to create revolution in people's consciousness through their critical exegesis, write only in English. Common men and women do not become part of such a conversation. But such a mode creates a division between people and writers in the present day world similar to that between people and the court pundits in the days of the Maharajas (Devy 1992).

But the problem here is not simply one of writing in English rather than in the vernacular. The key question is one of comprehension, commitment and desire for dialogue. What is written in the name of social criticism in a language---English or Oriya---may not be understood by people who speak the same language. As Jacoby (1987:236) tells us about the intellectuals in the contemporary US, it is difficult for common people to understand their "professional and arcane languages" which symbolize their "refuse as well as flight". Social critics today have become professionals and they are no more a Socrates on the street but members of the system world of the university or the kindred institutions. This spells of "privatization", "withdrawal from a larger public discourse" and lack of concern for the ongoing dynamics and struggle in the outside world. In this context, it is no wonder then that the radicals among the critics and intellectuals today in a society such as the contemporary United States suddenly turn to new fields like semiotics "as if the really interesting thing about the homeless were the variety of coded messages of protest that cardboard boxes could convey" (Harvey 1991:69).

We began this journey with the view that self-criticism is the foundation of social criticism and now we should try to understand some of its implications. The first step here is that social critic has to make his or her own life subject of criticism. He or she has to reflect whether the transformation that is desired in institutions and society in her critical agenda is also at work in her own life. Self-criticism as a mode of criticism is also meant to enable others to be critical of themselves. As a mode of critical engagement, it is meant to help us realize the distinction between ego and self. Self-criticism also seeks to interrogate the life that one is leading keeping in mind the condition of the majority and the agenda of transformation. If the two-third of the world are not able to have two square meal a day then the object of self-criticism is to make us think about our life governed by conspicuous consumption. Self-criticism also goes beyond a formal legalistic view of one's goodness and responsibility. For instance, one may not be violating any law but if the society is itself unjust then the task of self-criticism is to make one realize the responsibility one has to change the current social arrangement and create a new one.

III

Having discussed at great length some of the questions that confront us in the craft of social criticism, now I wish to discuss some of the issues that call for our reflection in the field of cultural creativity. The first issue here is the issue of culture as a source of criticism and creativity in the field of society. Culture is not a mirror image of the political and economic structures of a society. Culture contains a critical possibility to interrogate the foundations of society and its structure of power. Even Edward Said, who is known for his outstanding work on the relationship between culture and power, tells us: "Culture palliates, if it does not altogether neutralize, the ravages of a modern, aggressive, mercantile, and brutalizing urban existence. You read Dante or Shakespeare in order to keep up with the best that was thought and known, and also to see yourself, your people, society and tradition in these best lights" (1993:xii). As culture is a pattern implicated in a field of power, culture also contains within it a dimension of ideal seeking vis-a-vis self-realization, modes of intersubjectivity, and the constitution of a good society which puts it in a relationship of conflict and transcendence with the structure of power.

Indian philosopher G.C. Pande helps us in understanding this ideal dimension in culture. For Pande, "it is only with reflective consciousness that the subjective-objective world of culture can be apprehended" (1982:23). For Pande, culture is a dialectical process of value-seeking: "To seek a value is to seek progress in infinite direction, for it is in the nature of value to be a standard of perfection which judges all alternatives to fall short of ideal. From the lower realization of the self in terms of finite accidents (*upadhis*) to their complete transcendence in pure self-experience, the human seeking follows a process of dialectical evolution." Pande urges us to realize that the "the dialectic of value-seeking is the dialectic of self-transformation through the interaction of vision and praxis. *It implies not merely progress within a plane of consciousness but a change in the plane of consciousness*" (Pande 1982:26-27; emphasis added).

Culture has a dimension of "beyond" within it which resists its absolutization and political fixation. Every culture has and ought to cultivate a "metaculture" which can radicalize both culture and self (Bidney 1967).[6] As Homi Bhabha (1994:7) argues: "...to dwell in the beyond is also...to be part of a revisionary time, a return to the present to redescribe our cultural contemporaneity; to redescribe our human, historic commonalty, to touch the future on its hitherside. In that sense, the intervening space of beyond becomes a space of intervention in here and now." But this "beyond" dimension of culture is not fully appreciated in contemporary reflections on it. For instance, in her provocative essay, "The nice thing about culture is that everyone has it," anthropologist Marilyn Strathern (1995) points to the need for sources of creativity in culture in an "elsewhere". But she just leaves her critical exploration at that and fails to realize that it is the ideal and "beyond" dimension in culture which constitutes that "elsewhere".

Confronting the challenge of cultural difference as such difference is becoming a ground for new exclusionary practices such as racism and violence against the cultural alien in one's land is an important task now, a task which requires for its fulfillment "certain readjustment in both our rhetorical habits and sense of mission" (Geertz 1986:119). The creation of exclusion in the name of culture is most evident in the anti-immigration rhetoric and law in Europe, North America and now in many parts of the world. As a commentator helps us understand this: "Immigrants threaten to swamp us with their alien culture and if they are allowed in large numbers, they will destroy the 'homogeneity of the nation'. At the heart of this new racism is the notion of culture and tradition" (Barker quoted in Stolcke 1995:3). While earlier racism inferiorized the other, the new racism, in the name of culture, as anthropologist Verena Stolcke argues, can even assert the "absolute, irreducible *difference* of the 'self' and the incommensurability of different cultural identities" (1995:4).

Stolcke argues that contemporary cultural fundamentalism's rhetoric of exclusion and its reification of cultural difference draws, for its argumentative force, "on the contradictory 19th century conception of the modern nation-state which assumed that the territorial state and its people are founded on a cultural heritage that is bounded, compact, and distinct..." (ibid:12). A way out of the erasure of the other in the name of culture requires going beyond such politicization of culture and the accompanying conflation between society and culture and state and culture. According to Stolcke, "genuine tolerance for cultural diversity can flourish without entailing disadvantages only when society and polity are democratic and egalitarian enough to enable people to resist discrimination (whether as immigrants, foreigners, women, blacks) and develop differences without jeopardizing themselves and solidarity among them" (ibid:13). But it is instructive that Stolcke herself writes in the very next line of her essay: "I wonder whether this is possible within the confines of the modern nation-state or, for that matter of any state"(ibid). Thus, Stolcke is sensitizing us to the limits of the state-centric approach in dealing with the problem of the other and the fundamentalism of culture though others characterize her diagnosis as utopian.[7]

It is precisely the utopian dimension in self and culture that needs to be retrieved, articulated, and lived by at the contemporary juncture. The tendency to erase an "other" because of difference of culture cannot be fought only at the level of State and now creative responses to it has to be explored in the domains of self and culture. But such a sensitivity to the limits of politics in addressing the challenge of cultural difference and the fundamentalism of culture seems to be lacking in the contemporary debate on multi-culturalism. Starting in North America, like all fashions, the discourse of multi-culturalism is now catching up with the rest of the world as if it contains a new revelation about toleration. But the proponents of this debate can only talk of "politics of recognition". The most obvious example here is Charles Taylor's (1994) agenda of multi-culturalism. It is striking that Taylor does not bring the project of a "reflective self" (cf. Taylor 1989) to his project on multi-culturalism as a bearer and agent which would have helped to create a deeper ontological ground for the acceptance of cultural difference and helped to transform it from the present state of juxtaposition and hyphenation to one of interpenetration and dialogue.

The project of multi-culturalism also can valorize one's cultural identity and demand for cultural rights. But this can lead to the suppression of the right of individuals and their capacity for creative ways. Both K. Anthony Appiah and Veena Das quite insightfully draw our attention to this problem. The identities whose recognition are pleaded for in the politics of multi-culturalism are the collective identities but valorizing these can lead to the suppression of creative variations within a collective. Appiah urges us to be attentive to the two levels of authenticity---the collective and the individual---and cautions us: "...a politics of identity can be counted on to transform the identities on whose behalf it ostensibly labours. Between the politics of recognition and the politics of compulsion, there is no bright line" (1994:163). In a similar way, Veena Das also helps in widening our universe of discourse when she writes: "An individual's capacity to make sense of the world presupposes the existence of collective traditions; but individuals must be able to experiment with these collective traditions by being allowed to live at their limits. A simultaneous development of the rights of groups and individuals will depend on the extent to which these paradoxes can be given voice, both in the realm of the state and in the realm of the public culture of civil society" (1995:116).

Now, let us direct our attention to two exciting emergent processes where cultural creativity is embodied at the contemporary juncture. One is the rise of what is called the new social movements both in the advanced societies and the developing world which "fight for symbolic and cultural states, for the achievement of new meaning in social action" (Walker 1988:96). These movements are considered socio-cultural rather than socio-political insofar as their objective is to realize a new grammar of creativity in social life rather than capture power. These movements have been bearers of cultural creativity and have offered alternative imagination of self and society often denied by the media-steered systems of our society. They provide an alternative language of self-actualization and social governance---reciprocity, sharing, cooperation and renunciation.

Whether we talk of liberation theology in Latin America, Habitat for Humanity in the USA, Swadhyaya in Western India, new social movements in Western Europe, the Chipko in the Himalayas we find a new mode of social criticism whose objective is not the capture of power but realization of what one such movement, Swadhyaya, calls *sanskrutika kranti*, a cultural revolution.

Another aspect of the culture shift in contemporary advanced societies is the rise of what Roland Inglehart calls a 'post-materialist culture'. In the words of Inglehart (1990:278), "the major existing political parties were established in an era when economic issues were dominant and the working class was the main base of support for socio-political change. Today, the most heated issues tend to be non-economic, and support for change on these issues comes from postmaterialists, largely of middle-class origin." But Inglehart leaves unexplored the way the emergent post-materialist culture relates to the material deprivation in the advanced industrial societies and the world at large. For instance, what happens to the issue of poverty and unemployment in the discourse of post-materialism? As one of Alain Touraine's informants puts it: "The ecology movement has been totally incapable of explaining to workers and discussing with them the importance of those themes for their day-to-day problems" (1983:71).

This points to the need for developing a cultural critique of the economic system which binds us to many chains of unfreedom. Culture plays an important role in the dynamics of the economy at present. As Scott Lash and John Urry (1987) argue, culture is not simply an object of production now, production itself is becoming increasingly cultural. Thus, it is no wonder then that the production of aesthetically beautiful and lofty apartments is a vital part of the speculative regime of late capitalism today. But Lash and Urry do not analyze the human cost of such an economy and the enormous problem of homelessness that the shift of capital from production to speculation in lofty real estate creates. Their account of the shifting trajectory of capitalism and its increasing cultural turn is devoid of a normative criticism. We here need a cultural criticism of contemporary capitalism as an institutional regime. As Alf Hornborg argues: "The counterdrive to total commoditization is the cognitive discrimination we know as culture" (1993:317).

To speak of culture and the contemporary condition without speaking of the communications revolution underway in the present-day world would be an incomplete exercise. Now television is a household reality for many of us in all corners of the world. Television has helped to dissolve the distinction between the "high culture" and "low culture" and we must not fail to acknowledge the democratizing potential in this dissolution. But, at the same time, we have to realize that television has made us consumers of culture, making us believe that the vicarious consumption of culture is the same thing as its creation (see, Das, 1994). But if many of us become consumers of culture when culture means soap operas, media-steered system images and advertisements for the system of money and power then what is the fate of culture as a source and process of transformation?

A contemporary meditation on self, other and culture cannot absolve itself of the obligation of criticism and creativity. The challenge for us is to continue to create culture in an age where culture itself has been made an object of consumption and commodification. When consumption of what on an average is understood as culture seems to be our new weltanschauung---our new *yugadharma*—the task for us is to recover the ground where cultural creativity as a *sadhana* of self and institutional transformation becomes a powerful ideal in our individual lives and in our public sphere. It is needless to mention that the realization of such a task requires multi-dimensional effort at both individual and collective levels.

Creation of culture is a work of *sadhana*. It is a work of silence. But the culture of TV is the culture of the bombardment of words (Miller 1988). So the first step is to learn to be silent in our age of communications revolution. Silence would help us realize that if we watch television four hours a day or even two hours a day then even God cannot help us from being slipped into what Baudrillard calls the "silent majority" and Toynbee called the "uncreative majority". But this desired silence may not come so spontaneously. The struggle for the meaning of culture in the next century may begin with the breaking of television sets which would complete the unfinished agenda of transformation inaugurated by the Luddite breaking of the machines of industrial production in the last century.

IV

Certain features of the contemporary processes of change immediately arrest our attention. One is having to do with the increasing significance of science and technology in creating ever more powerful systems where the professionals who manage these are our new "colonial masters", to put it in the memorable phrase of Habermas. Along with this new colonialism of the elites and the holders of power what American social critic Christopher Lasch characterizes as the revolt of the elites, we also witness movements for freedom everywhere which is passionately put in the following lines of Ken Saro-Wiwa (1995:15), the great soul of the Ogoni tribe whose life was terminated by the dictator of Nigeria: "We are witnessing the birth of a new phenomenon, the decision of a small group of people that they will not tolerate their dehumanization...and all the guns of the world, the casuistry of dictatorship and the threat of death and imprisonment cannot deter a people to secure their God-given rights..."

Saro-Wiwa's struggle and martyrdom emphasize the crucial significance of the issue of autonomy and "self-organization", what Gandhi had identified long time ago as the issue of *swaraj*. Speaking of his own predicament and at the same time identifying himself with the sorrow of annihilation of groups and individuals everywhere in the world, Saro-Wiwa tells us: "In virtually every nation-state are several 'Ogonies'---despairing and disappearing peoples suffering the yoke of political marginalization, economic strangulation and environmental degradation...What is their future?". The future, as Saro-Wiwa himself (1995:76) tells us lies in creating what he calls "undiluted federalism". Autonomy movements all over the world are fighting for "self-organization" and the answer to their struggle lies in creating genuine federal frames of coordination. But, the question of "self-organization" of groups is related to the "democratic self-legislation" of individuals (cf. Habermas 1995). Many of the leaders of the autonomy movements use authoritarian means to achieve their goal and one does not know whether their realized *swaraj* would replace one tyranny with another.

Realization of radical democracy is an important challenge at the contemporary juncture and this can provide us an yardstick to evaluate our struggles for autonomy as well as our current economic systems which is based on the split between what Amartya Sen calls "food and freedom". It is not possible here to go into in all its details the exciting question of radical democracy except to point out four most crucial issues in this regard. The first is the issue of economic democracy. The second relates to the need for creating a "reflective self" as the actor and bearer of democracy who is able to overcome the dualism between negative freedom and positive freedom. The third relates to the issue of civil society. Civil society, like the discourse of democracy, has become a globally influential ideal today. But the idea of civil society is very much state-centric and its essential political and modernist bias needs a spiritual and universal opening today (cf. Giddens 1994; Uberoi 1996). Furthermore, the way globalization both threatens and opens up new possibilities for civil society has to be understood. Dahrendorf's argument that "the condition of global competition coupled with social disintegration is not favorable to the constitution of liberty" helps us to understand the threat to civil society because of its consequent twin processes of "individualization" and "centralization" (Dahrendorf 1995:17). At the same time, the transnational initiatives that proliferate today in the form of transnational people's movements and international NGO activities open up a creative space for establishing people-to-people solidarity without the mediation of the nation-state.

The fourth issue in striving for the realization of radical democracy relates to the creation of transformative institutions and transforming existing institutions. It is because the foundation of many of the existing institutions---from the family to the university---do not fit in well with the agenda of a radical democracy. We now need to move from our preoccupation with electoral democracy to what can be called "dialogic democracy" (cf. Giddens 1995; Giri 1996) both in the sphere of intimate relations and in our pubic sphere. But the realization of "dialogic democracy" is not possible today without a "radical form of self-government" (cf. Beck and Beck-Gernsheim 1995:194). The transformative institutions have to create a ground for such a flowering of criticism and creativity in the life of the individuals. As Claus Offe urges us to realize, "institutional conditions of collective action within civil society" today are "significant factors in the development of moral competence" (1992:80). Offe and his colleague Heinze further argue that institutions today have a moral responsibility to educate our desire when we are enmeshed in an "inner conflict between" our "more desirable" and "less desirable desires" (1991: 167).

But how do we create transformative insitutions at the contemporary juncture? Can they be created by socio-political struggles alone? Institutions are not manufactured but they are nurtured like flowers and this requires both transformative practice in the life of individuals and an alternative relation of inter-subjectivity dynamically at work in the field of culture and society. Alternative relationships founded on intimacy, sincerity and egolessness can be the genealogical grounds of new institutions. Transforming existing institutions requires the work of what Pantham (1995), following Gandhi calls "experimental subjectivity". Such a work brings self-transformation and transformation of society together. As Roberto M. Unger (1987:400) argues:

> The ability to see institutional transformation as part of an attempt to change the character of our most elementary personal interactions pushes the conflict over the form of society beyond the instrumental struggle over material advantage. It extends strategic prudence into visionary ardor, thereby offering the incitement to sacrifice and self-restraint that cold calculation is rarely enough to ensure.

The agenda of transformation also involves the task of reinterpreting emancipatory ideals and concepts currently in vogue. In a recent insightful paper Immanuel Wallerstein (1995) argues that the first task here is "undoing of the Eurocentric assumptions that have dominated for the last two centuries", an undoing which involves "acute and constant political and cultural struggle". As Wallerstein cautions us about the aristocratic bias and the anti-democratic thrust of liberalism and argues: "We can contribute nothing to a desirable resolution of the terminal crisis of our world system unless we make it very clear that only a relatively egalitarian, fully democratic historical system is desirable" (ibid 1995:16).

But Wallerstein seems to have taken for granted the meaning of egalitarianism and democracy. Similar is also the problem with the work of an engaging critic such as Manoranjan Mohanty who concludes his fascinating critique of the contemporary discourse of empowerment with the argument that the concept of empowerment now has to contend with other "concepts like liberation, freedom, and equality" (1995). But Mohanty does not discuss the need for critically examining the genealogies and relevance of these concepts as they proliferate today. An engagement with transformative practice can suggest that all these three concepts are in need of reinterpretation today---a reinterpretation not simply for the sake of pleasure of semantic jugglery but as a guide to transformative action. Consider, for instance, a concept like equality and the conjoint ideal of egalitarianism. How do we realize an egalitarian society in the light of failure of both socialism and welfare state to achieve distributive equality? Just reiterating the slogan of equality now won't do. In this context, Anthony Giddens' (1994) distinction between distributive equality and "generative equality" has the potential for a new departure. A generative model of equality emphasizes upon the mutual collaboration between the affluent and the poor in building the collective foundations of a good life and in overcoming "collective bads" (ibid:191). Equalization here is primarily understood in terms of equalization of a quest for a meaningful life and relationship. In a generative striving for equality, inequality in life chances is tackled through changes in lifestyle (ibid 1994:194).

Similar is also the challenge of reinterpretation with an ideal like justice. In thinking about the calling of justice in the human condition the most important challenge is creating what John Rawls (1972) himself calls a "capacity for justice" within the individual. But the Rawlsian project is silent about the ontological preparation for this capacity which requires for its fulfilment the realization that "I am more than just my brother's keeper, I am my brother" (Zohar and Marshall 1993:174). And now finally coming to the question of rethinking dialectics at the contemporary juncture. Dialectical thinking whether of the Hegelian or Marxian kind has deeply influenced collective action and critical reflection in the last one hundred and fifty years. But, how do we look at the theory and practice of dialectics in the light of contemporary changes? As a prelude to this rethinking we can consider the following points: First, dialectics does not always involve the conflict between thesis and anti-thesis and there is also a process of cooperation at work.

Second, the dialectical process is a reflective process where self-reflection is an important agent, leading to a fundamental transformation of the phenomena and persons engaged in the process of dialectical interpenetration.

In a recent important work Roy Bhaskar (1993) helps us in this journey of rethinking. He (ibid:3) argues that "dialectical processes and configurations are not always sublatory (i.e., suppressive), let alone preservative. Nor are they necessarily characterized by opposition or antagonism..." Reminding us of the ideal of 'permanent criticism' discussed in the beginning of this paper, Bhaskar (ibid:20) tells us: "Dialectic is a method...which enables the dialectical commentator to observe the process by which the various categories, notion or forms of consciousness arise out of each other to form ever more inclusive totalities until the system of categories, notions or forms as a whole is completed." But Bhaskar quickly urges us to realize the distinction between "bad totalities" and "good totalities". While "good totalities" are open; bad totalities are, "whether constentionally or otherwise, closed" (ibid 1993:24). While for Hegel, totality is "constentionally closed" and the idea of "an open totality would conjure up the specter of an infinite regress" (ibid 1993:25), the objective of a transformed dialectical engagement is to realize open totality.[8]

Bhaskar helps us to relate dialectic to what he calls "the pulse of freedom". I wish to conclude by relating it to the pulse of dialogue. Dialogue is different from oppositional confrontation and is always characterized by a reflexivity about one's own position and transformation of the initial starting point. It is also characterized by a process of resynthesis where people discover that "they have to listen to each other in a new way" (Zohar and Marshall 1993:236). Like the dialectical objective of realization of an open totality, the objective of dialogue, after the transformation of one's own initial point of view and mutual deconstruction of one's own positions, is to move in a new order. As Zohar and Marshall (ibid) help us understand this: "This new order is a whole new, emergent level of consciousness in which the participants get beyond the fragmented state of individual consciousness to a shared pool of meaning and value..." Zohar and Marshall (ibid:248) further tell us: "Every time that we try to understand another person's point of view it is a small religious act. It is also a small political act." As we address the challenge of social criticism, cultural creativity and the contemporary dialectics of transformations there is probably an epochal need to understand the spiritual and political significance of dialogue and to transform the world in accordance with such an understanding.

Notes

1. As Ashis Nandy (1995:112) helps us understand this: "Thus, psychoanalysts such as Carl Jung, who were especially open to the Indian world view, found few adherents in India; Marxist scholars such as Ernst Bloch, who sought to establish a continuity between the Marxist vision and the older religious worldviews, never enjoyed a vogue in non-European societies organized around religion."
2. Achyutananda Das says that in the spiritual life of a person, the first *bhava* or feeling is the *bhava* of Kshatriya. First he has to fight, fight with one's ripus (enemies) and annihilate them. Then comes the feeling of Vaishya. At that time, a *bhakta* wants to do commerce with one's god, he wants to enhance his wealth. The third step in this ascending order is the step of Brahmana *bhava*. At that time one spends time with rituals; the worship continues with *mantra* and *murti*. And the fourth stage is the stage of Shudra *bhava* during which one wants to serve God and the other without any precondition. For Achyutananda Das, the highest stage of self is the stage where one acquires Shudra *bhava* (cf. Das 1992).
3. For Heidegger, "co-being means not a social juxtaposition but rather a constitutive juncture or correlation" (Dallmayr 1993:182).

4. What Nandy writes about bread and freedom applies to the logic of a hierarchical and successive formulation (in terms of freedom coming after paper) between power and freedom: "...there is not only Maslow's theory of hierarchy of needs but also a half-articulated anti-Maslowian logic which says that if freedom can be an ego defense and not a real substitute for bread, bread too can be an ego defense and not a real substitute for freedom" (Nandy 1986:250).
5. For Foucault, a critic is a "specific intellectual" as different from a "universal intellectual" and "one dimension of criticism for the specific intellectual is the critique of universality per se..." (Caputo and Yount 1993:8).
6. In order to understand the work and the critical significance of "metaculture" let us consider the way three different thinkers use it in three different contexts. Speaking of the predicament of globalization, anthropologist Ulf Hannerz uses it in the following manner: "A more genuine cosmopolitanism entails a certain metacultural position. There is first of all a willingness to engage with the other.." On the other hand sociologist Roland Robertson uses it in the following manner: "There is a need for more discussion of what I call metaculture as a way of addressing the varying links between culture and social structure and individual and collective action" (Robertson 1992:34). Theologian Rienhold Niebuhr sums up its significance in the following lines:

   > We cannot expect even the wisest of nations to escape every peril of moral and spiritual complacency; for nations have always been constitutionally self-righteous. But it will make a difference whether the culture in which politics of nations are formed is only as deep and high as nation's ideals; or whether there is a dimension in the culture from the standpoint of which the element of vanity in all human ambitions and achievements is discerned.

7. For instance, Jonathan Benthall, in his comments on Stolcke's essay writes: "The last seven words of Stolcke's lecture suggest that she wants all state power to be weakened which sounds utopian" (Benthall 1995:13)
8. In this context, what Bhaskar (1993:26) writes is noteworthy: "Even if it is admitted that there is some kind of inadequacy or lack in an open totality..., there is no inadequacy in the *thought* of an open totality, which is what is at stake here."

References

Appiah, K. Anthony, 1994, "Identity, Authenticity, Survival: Multicultural Societies and Social Reproduction." In Amy Gutman (ed.), *Multiculturalism: Examining the Politics of Recognition*. Princeton: University Press.

Barnett, Eve T., 1989, *Structuralism and the Logic of Dissent*. London: Macmillan.

Beck, Ulrich and Elizabeth Beck-Gernsheim, 1995, *The Normal Chaos of Love*. Cambridge: Polity Press.

Benhabib, Seyla, 1987, *Critique, Norm and Utopia*. NY: Columbia University Press.

Benthall, Jonathan, 1995, *Comments on Verena Stolcke's Essay*. In Stolcke, 1995.

Beteille, Andre, 1980, *Ideology and Intellectuals*. Delhi: Oxford University Press.

Bhaskar, Roy, 1993, *Dialectics: The Pulse of Freedom*. London: Verson.

Bhabha, Homi, 1994, *The Location of Culture*. London: Routledge.

Caputo, John and Mark Yount, 1993, *Foucault and the Critique of Institutions*. University Park: Pennsylvania State University Press.

Connolly, William E., 1991, *Identity/Difference: Democratic Negotiations of Political Paradox*. Ithaca: Cornell University Press.

Dahrendorf, Ralph, 1995, *Economic Opportunity, Civil Society and Political Liberty*. UNRISD Discussion Papers.

Dallmayr, Fred R., 1993, *The Other Heidegger*. Ithaca: Cornell University Press.

Das, Chitta Ranjan, 1982, *A Glimpse into Oriya Literature*. Bhubaneswar: Orissa Sahitya Akademi.

---, 1991, *Sikhya O. Chetana* [Education and Consciousness]. Berhampur: Suhrut Gosthi.

---. 1992, *Odia Sahityara Itihasa: Samajika-Sanskutika Bhittibhumi* [Thc History of Oriya Literature: Social and Cultural Foundations]. Cuttack: Sabdaloka.

---, 1994, *Sukara O. Socrates* [The Pig and the Socrates]. Berhampur: Pustaka Bhandara.

Das, Veena, 1995, *Critical Events: Anthropological Perspectives on Contemporary India*. Delhi: Oxford University Press.

Derrida, Jacques, 1994, "Specters of Marx." *New Left Review* 205: May-June.

Devy, G.N., 1992, *After Amnesia: Tradition and Change in Indian Literary Criticism*. Delhi: Orient Longman.

Foucault, Michel, 1984, "Politics and Ethics: An Interview." In Paul Rabinow (ed.), *The Foucault Reader*. New York: Pantheon Books.

----, 1988, "Practicing Criticism." In Lawrence D. Kritzman (ed.), *Michel Foucault: Politics, Philosophy, Culture*. New York: Routledge.

Geertz, Clifford, 1986, "The Uses of Diversity." *Michigan Quarterly Review*, Winter: 105-123.

Giddens, Anthony, 1991, *Modernity and Self-Identity: Self and Society in the Late Modern Age*. Cambridge: Polity Press.

----, 1994, *Beyond Left and Right: The Future of Radical Politics*. Cambridge: Polity Press

Giri, Ananta, 1995, "Gender and the Overcoming of Ego." Paper presented at the Indian Political Economy Association's Conference on "Gender".

----, 1996, "Democratic Transition and the Challenge of Transformation." *Economic and Political Weekly*, August 10.

Habermas, Jurgen, 1990, *Moral Consciousness and Communicative Action*. Cambridge: Polity Press.

----, 1995, "Reconciliation Through the Public Use of Reason: Remarks on John Rawls' Political Liberalism." *The Journal of Philosophy* XC11 (3): 109-31.

----, n.d., *Overcoming the Past*.

Hannerz, Ulf, 1990, "Cosmopolitans and Locals in World Culture." In *Global Culture: Nationalism, Globalization and Modernity*. London: Sage.

Harvey, David, 1991, "Flexibility: Threat or Opportunity?" *Socialist Review* 21 (1): 69-77.

Heller, Agnes, 1987, *Beyond Justice*. Oxford: Basil Blackwell.

Hornborg, Alf, 1993, "Money and Meaning: Towards a Multi-Centric Economy." In *Entropy and Bioeconomics*. Milano, Italy: European Association for Bioeconomic Studies.

Inglehart, Ronald, 1990, *The Culture Shift in Advanced Societies*. Princeton: University Press.

Jacoby, Russell, 1987, *The Last Intellectuals: American Culture in the Age of Academe*. New York: Basic Books.

Laclau, Ernesto, 1994, "Subject of Politics, Politics of Subject." Center for Theoretical Studies, University of Essex.

Lash, Scott and John Urry, 1987, *The End of Organized Capitalism*. Madison: University of Wisconsin Press.

Madison, G.B., 1988, *The Hermeneutics of Postmodernity*. Bloomington: Indiana University Press.

Miller, Mark, 1988, *Boxed In: The Culture of TV*. Evanston, II: Northwestern University Press.

Mohanty, J.N., 1993, "Foucault as a Philosopher." In John Caputo and Mark Yount (eds.), *Foucault and the Critique of Institutions*. Pennsylvania State University Press.

Mohanty, Manoranjan, 1995, "On the Concept of Empowerment." *Economic and Political Weekly* 24.

Nandy, Ashis, 1986, "The Idea of Development: The Experience of Modern Psychology as Cautionary Tale and as an Allegory." In Carlos A. Mallman and Oscar Nudler (eds.), *Human Development in its Social Context: A Collective Exploration*. London et al.: Hodder & Stoughton.

----, 1995, *The Savage Freud and Other Essays on Possible and Retrievable Selves*. Delhi: Oxford University Press.

Nandy, Ashis et al., 1996, *Creating a Nationality: The Ramajanmabhoomi Movement and the Fear of the Self*. Delhi: Oxford University Press.

Niebuhr, Rienold, 1952, *The Ironies of American History*.

Offe, Claus, 1992, "Bindings, Shackles, Brakes: On Self-Limitation Strategies." In Alex Honneth et al. (eds.), *Cultural-Political Interventions in the Unfinished Project of Enlightenment*. Cambridge, MA: The MIT Press.

Offe, Claus and Rolph G. Heinze, 1991, "Democratic Institutions and Moral Resources." In David Held (ed.), *Political Theory Today*. Cambridge: Polity Press.

Pande, G.C., 1982, "The Nature of Social Categories." In Ravinder Kumar (ed.), *Philosophical Categories and Social Reality*.

Rawls, John, 1972, *A Theory of Justice*. London: Oxford University Press.

Said, Edward, 1993, *Culture and Imperialism*. London: Chatto & Windus.

Saro-Wiwa, Ken, 1995, *A Month and a Day: A Detention Diary*. London: Penguin Books.

Soja, Edward, 1989, *Postmodern Geographies: The Reassertion of Space in Critical Social Theory*. London: Verso.

Sri Aurobindo, 1962, *The Human Cycles: The Ideal of Human Unity, War and Self-Determination*. Pondicherry: Sri Aurobindo Ashram.

Stolcke, Verena, 1995, "Talking Culture: New Boundaries, New Rhetorics of Exclusion in Europe." *Current Anthropology* 36 (1): 1-24.

Taylor, Charles, 1989, *Sources of the Self*. Cambridge, MA: Harvard University Press.

—, 1994, *Multiculturalism and the Politics of Recognition*.

Touraine, Alain, 1983, *Anti-Nuclear Protest*. Cambridge: University Press.

Uberoi, J.P.S., 1996, Religion, *Civil Society and State: A Study of Sikhism*. Delhi: Oxford U. Press.

Vivekananda, Swami, 1991, *The Collected Works of Swami Vivekananda*.

Walker, R.B.J., 1988, *One World, Many Worlds: Struggles for a Just World Peace*. London: Zed Books.

Walzer, Michel, 1988, "Interpretation and Social Criticism." In S.M. McCurrin, (ed.), *The Tanner Lectures on Human Values*. Universities of Utah and Cambridge Press.

Wallerstein, Immanuel, 1995, "The Agonies of Liberalism." *New Left Review*.

Zohar, Donnah and Ian Marshall, 1993, *The Quantum Society: Mind, Physics and a New Social Vision*. London: Flamingo.

Chapter Three

Cultural Practice/Social Change: Nurturing a Self-Critical Ground

Nancy Weiss Hanrahan

Weber's classic critique of Marx—that social change must be explained on the basis of the meaningful social action of individuals, rather than through the blind processes of dialectical materialism—has become the basic assumption guiding contemporary analyses of culture and social change.[1] Weber understood that culture is inseparable from the particulars of social development, insofar as it as part of the structure of meaning through which strategies of social action are constructed. If we accept the proposition of the centrality of culture in social transformation, the question of how the dynamics of culture are theorized with respect to both social movements and structures of power is a central concern.

This paper is both a critical reflection on the existing categories of analysis used to describe cultural creativity and social transformation, and a series of suggestions for revising them, given a more complex understanding of temporality and culture. Those suggestions are premised on the notion that social transformation and cultural creativity are processes, not objects. From a pragmatic point of view, this is, of course, entirely self-evident. But, how that understanding is translated into theoretical concepts or constructs is far less obvious. To date, the dynamic aspects of social reality have received significantly less theoretical attention than the structural ones, and the vocabulary of social theory remains primitive in its conception of process. The teleology of change as progressive and transformation as transcendent persist, despite our understanding that processes of social change are non-linear, contingent, and both the result and the origin of unintended consequences. In the face of this complexity, social theory presents the Enlightenment model of historical change as progress, or as increasing rationalization (however paradoxical), or as dialectics. None of these are adequate; history teaches us that change is always contradictory, and that cultural change is temporally complex.

Cultural creativity is always contingent and paradoxical because it operates within a field of temporal and spatial complexity. Further, it is the reflexive awareness of complexity that provides the basis for meaningful critique of this process. In presenting these arguments, I take it as given that time and space are mutually constitutive variables of both our environment and our social reality. Yet, rather than a model like Anthony Giddens' structuration theory, which suggests that processes take place within structures and therefore prioritizes the latter as the context for the former, I take a more Simmelian turn and suggest that structures are the patterned actualizations of processes. Structures of meaning and power are constituted by processes which have social, temporal, and material dimensions. In other words, some consensus has to be achieved, they have to have duration, and they have to acquire some objectivity or materiality.[2] Regardless of how observation frames social reality as stasis, it is fundamentally eventful. Long-term processes of social transformation have a far more complex temporal structure than simple events, and the dynamics of culture have historically been at a variance with other aspects of social change. This complex temporality must be taken into account in the analysis of cultural creativity and social transformation.

The Categories of Cultural Analysis: Modern/Postmodern

Culture is itself a category in flux, as has been its incorporation into social theory. Historically, the link between culture and claims to social justice in the modern period, or in the modernist politics of liberation, de-emphasized ethnicity or culture as lived experience. The overarching human, liberal values of freedom and justice are, or were, supposed to be culture blind. The tendency in the Marxist tradition, particularly in later European Marxism of Frankfurt School, was to cast the liberatory dimension of culture in terms of the most advanced art forms. Great art, specifically, the formal works of high modernism, resisted both the commodity logic of capitalism and the folk mythology of fascism. As such, this work was in itself a critique of the domination of authoritarianism and the totally administered forms of capitalist production. Over time, this resulted in the relentless pursuit of esoteric aesthetic forms, the logic of which was unavailable to all but a small elite. The fact that these highly formal works had no real social base undermined the claims to cultural resistance and, contrary to the intentions of its authors, was reduced to a celebration of high art. Nevertheless, the enduring legacy of critical theory is a significant body of work that clearly implicates culture in the reproduction of power. The reproduction of ideology through the manipulation of cultural symbols was analyzed as an aspect of both the fascist mobilizations, and of the culture industry as an agent of capitalist social control. The overriding tendency in this period was to read culture from the top down, analyzing its implication in social domination rather than as an aspect of lived experience that could be utilized for non-totalitarian ends.

Now, in the postmodern moment, culture is theorized as the water we're all swimming in. In a reaction to the modernist reading of culture, a more anthropological understanding is current. Rather than viewing culture as the preserve of either a power or a cultural elite, culture is something that ordinary people make, live in, interact with, and reinvent in their daily lives. Culture is cultural practice, or a multiplicity of practices. The view of culture as lived experience carries the presumption that culture is egalitarian. The notion of cultural creativity is linked to this, more postmodern, reading.

The modern/postmodern debate over the orientation of cultural analysis can be mapped through a few simple dichotomies:

modern	postmodern
art	culture
objects	practices
hierarchical	egalitarian

In the context of a liberatory politics, both sets of categories are used in the service of articulating a final judgment on culture, which acts as the subtext of analysis. Where the modernist analysis turned on the dialectic of liberation vs. domination; the postmodern offers a simpler, non-dialectical, notion of resistance.

However useful these categories may once have been as the analytical distinctions to ground cultural theory, they are no longer adequate to the task. First, it can be demonstrated fairly easily that in most analytical situations, these oppositional concepts actually coexist as two parts of a single analytic. Second, where the modernist reading tends to be hierarchical, or top down, the postmodern one is egalitarian, or bottom up; both of which make the negotiation of power appear far more straightforward than it actually is. Third, these dichotomies do not account for the contingency of processes, which make them particularly unsuitable as the basic analytic categories for cultural creativity and social change. In the following sketch of the women's movement, I will use the conceptual vocabularies of modern and postmodern cultural sociology both to underscore their inadequacies and to demonstrate that the contrast between them constitutes a false dualism.

Cultural Creativity

The women's movement was organized around the articulated goals of equality of economic opportunity and equal participation in public life. To the extent that exclusion and inequality are supported by assumptions about what women are like, how they are expected to behave, or social ideals of femininity, the struggle for equality takes place not only in the arena of public policy, but also in the battle over cultural representations of women. Social roles are the mediating point between individuals and social reality; they are the ways in which individuals enter into a truly social world and understand it as their own. In the construction of new social roles for women, collective forms of representation are iconic. The entrance of feminism into the cultural terrain of television and film has produced depictions not only of the working mother but also of the woman cop, the corporate executive whose husband stays home with the baby, the opinionated working class woman, the liberated call girl, as well as the feminist politician or organizer herself. What do the basic categories of cultural analysis demonstrate about the proliferation of cultural representations of new social roles for women? For instance, are these different depictions of roles coming from the bottom up or top down? Are they the product of the imaginations of Hollywood moguls, or of the lived experience of women in the US? Where is the line between cultural objects and cultural practices? Certainly, Hollywood is reacting to ongoing cultural creativity and social change, and is also participating in it. The more those roles are depicted, the more available they become for women, at least as the ground of contestation. But they wouldn't have much currency, or much profitability, if they weren't tapping into some pre-existing social drama. The flow is multi-directional. At the same time, there are important qualifications on the "real" content of these roles. First, it's fairly obvious that no human being's "real life" is depicted in a Hollywood movie, so even positive depictions of new social roles carry an element of distortion, selection, or glamorization. At the same time, some of the depictions of working women are very unflattering, and retain the subtext that equality of opportunity is unfeminine, or emasculating. The real situation for women is contradictory and conflict ridden; Hollywood is not, or at least pretends that it can't afford to be.

Given the multi-directional flow between objects and practices, from the top down and the bottom up, how do we make a judgment about the effects of these processes? Does cultural creativity generate more possibilities for women, or does it reproduce new images of femininity that constrain women's options? Are the representations striving to fit women, or are women now striving to fit the representations? Are existing structures and relations of women's oppression reproduced or transformed? It is in fact nearly impossible to frame such a judgment, because what we're looking at are ongoing processes, not results. We can observe moments in the process, but we cannot predict the outcome of contingency. To the extent that it is possible to observe results, they are only available in the specific case, or on a case by case basis. Perhaps, all that can be said with certainty is that cultural creativity keeps the process in motion, and, in this case, keeps it public.

The example of Hollywood and television is useful in part because these are the media viewed by the largest number of people in the US, and by certain measures have a bigger impact on the issue of collective representation. Clearly, these media are important structures of power in themselves, subject also to internal constraints of profitability, risk, etc., all of which deserve a fuller analysis than can be presented here. But, the example also serves a larger argument. The postmodern tendency is to think of culture in a pure or organic state because it is in some sense given with our humanity. But, the fact is that it, too, is reproduced within, and reproduces, structures of power, even in the sense of cultural practice or creativity. Culture is a problem of meaning, as well as of expectations of behavior, which includes anthropological categories such as practices and ethnicity, but is also negotiated in much less predictable ways through the objects and processes of material culture. These are not mutually exclusive. The symbolic aspects of material culture are appropriated and reproduced by existing structures of power such as the culture industry as well as by identity groups in creating solidarity, and are used as symbols of political representation or legitimation.

The same categories of analysis may also be applied to the women's movement itself. Is it hierarchical or egalitarian? Does power flow from the top down or from the bottom up? These are in fact very difficult questions to answer with regard to any culturally structured social movement, since so much of the "movement" takes place in private conversations, in classrooms, as a subtext for workplace relations; that is, ideationally, or outside of any real institutional structure. There have been power struggles within the more organized branches of the movement, as different individuals and groups compete to put their claims forward, and charges of elitism have been levelled at a predominantly white, middle class and educated stratum of both membership and leadership. While contestation over agenda and priorities is the heart of a democratic process, it is certainly true that as the movement expands, there is more and more division within the ranks, on the basis of class, race and ideology, particularly between working class women and intellectuals, between the rich and the under-represented poor. With respect to the public, as opposed to the internal, aspects of power, can we detect a clear trend toward liberation for women? In the sense of expanding opportunities, and more public visibility for women's issues and women's oppression, the answer is clearly yes. But again, there has to be a more nuanced reading. There has also been a lot of backlash against women, and questions remain as to how deep the change is. There are more women CEOs, but most working women still earn less than 80 cents to the dollar for equal work. And, while women have entered the official economy, men still don't do the laundry.

The analytical distinctions between hierarchy and egalitarianism, between cultural objects and cultural practices, do not serve the analysis of either the movement or its cultural representations particularly well. It is not that there is not a liberatory ideology at work, or that it is not actively negotiating the problems and ideals of a democratic society. It is that these categories, even if constructed as dialectically related pairs, do not grasp the complexity, or the contingency, of the processes of cultural creativity and social transformation. Social change is not linear, it embodies its own counter-tendencies, reproduces the very conflicts in society that it most seeks to avoid. We cannot assume that social solidarity and individual commitment are pure forms of agency not subject to other social processes. The very notions of solidarity and commitment are the constructs of a given society and its concrete history. Movements of social change also internally reproduce power and can have repressive tendencies, codes of inclusion and exclusion, charismatic leaders, or chosen texts. These issues are not solved by virtue of whether a movement is in its grass roots or organized through centralized institutions of power. The tendencies in one are reproduced in the other because they partake in a shared, lived culture.

The following theoretical points are offered in summary:

1. Cultural creativity and movements of social change cannot be analyzed in isolation. They occur as aspects of, and are framed by, a larger society and will therefore reproduce many of its tendencies.
2. In the dynamics of social processes, distinctions between objects and practices, egalitarian and hierarchical organization, and the flow of power from top down or bottom up become increasingly blurred. On the contrary, these seeming dichotomies most often appear as two, of the possibly several, sides of a single phenomenon.
3. Cultural creativity produces difference.[3] The category woman becomes gay or straight, working or domestic, black or Asian or white, working class or upper class, first

world/third world, pro-choice/pro-life, etc. In addition, some differences solidify, given the goals or direction of social action, the type of leadership structure, or other variables.

4. Cultural creativity produces complexity, but not necessarily liberation.

Temporal Complexity

The challenge is to think critically about culture and social transformation, rather than categorically. Given the common assumptions, and problems, of critique, one might be less than sanguine about the prospects. How do we construct critique in the absence of categorical or fixed guideposts? What should be the criteria? How do we judge a process which has not, and may never conclusively, yield results? And finally, how do we value, or evaluate, complexity? I'd like to suggest two conditions of critique in this context. The first is thinking in time; the second, making distinctions.

In his classic essay "Traditional and Critical Theory", Max Horkheimer suggests that critical theory situates the theorist both within the object domain of society, and in history. In contrast, the sociology of knowledge, the project of periodizing thought, is an example of the model of traditional theory, where the theorist is situated outside both the object and time. Horkheimer's claim that the thinker him/herself is in historical time has significant consequences for theory. It is a direct challenge to orthodox forms of Marxism, which rely on universal concepts of historical development, and seek to fit historical change into an unchanging theoretical paradigm. While retaining Marxism's "existential judgment"[4] on the nature of capitalism as a system of domination, critical theory, according to Horkheimer, must change its concepts to fit changing historical conditions. Critical theory is therefore constituted as continuing self-reflection on the changing historical conditions of its own project, that is, of critique.

It is in this spirit of critical self-reflection that I propose rethinking, not only of the historical conditions of critique, but also the category of "historical conditions" itself. This is not an idea without precedent. In *The Postmodern Condition*, Lyotard heralds the collapse of the grand narratives of modernism, including those of Marxist theory, and the modernist conception of time progressing infinitely into the future. In contrast, he offers the notion of petits, recits small narratives, which would open up narrativity to a plurality of possibilities. While much is left to the imagination, including how the temporal structure of postmodern narratives would differ from the modern, the work presages the disruption of overarching historical or temporal categories. In more recent literature on postmodernism, the shift from broad historical markers to a more complex notion of historical time is articulated in Andreas Huyssen's work on culture, memory, and the avant-garde. His thesis is that the relationship between progress and the destruction of cultural forms, between modernity and tradition, has changed. If there is anything really new about postmodernism, according to Huyssen, it is the tension between tradition and innovation, conservation and renewal, that cannot be judged as politically left or right, progressive or conservative. He writes:

> ... we are confronted with a multi-faceted and diverse search for the past (often for an alternative past) which, in many of its more radical manifestations, questions the fundamental orientation of western societies toward future growth and toward unlimited progress.[5]

In theory, as well as in social movements, historical time referents are complex and open to contestation.

Rather than situating the thinker in history, understood as a historical era, the theorist can be situated in time, understood as a present. In part, this is a criticism of the utility of historical categories, such as modern/postmodern; liberal capitalist/monopoly capitalist; bourgeois/socialist, which articulate every moment of the present as an unproblematic reproduction of a larger temporal structure. It is also a criticism of the tendency to situate ourselves in place-by virtue of geographical location, theoretical location, or identity, which has become the dominant contemporary form of "location". The idea of "point" of view is spatial; through it we establish an observation post. But observation is also eventful, and in the act of observing, we frame or constitute a specific present. This present is layered, in that it is constructed through the present of biography, the present of theory or conceptualization, and the present of the object that is being observed. Each of these is in itself complex. Theory is always negotiating the utility of old ideas in new situations, making predictions on the basis of present behavior and past patterns, layering new concepts within existing frameworks developed to analyze conditions that no longer obtain. Nor are social processes, the object of observation in this instance, simple, linear or teleological. Processes have junctures or moments, one could even say, different rhythms. Processes always negotiate time, and, like music, refer to other moments, work variations on existing themes, prefigure their resolution, and occasionally repeat themselves. They are open to surprise, just as they experience occasional periods of relative stasis. Social processes, regardless of how rationalized they are, are far too contingent ever to proceed as direct unbroken lines toward a goal or end result.

Situating theory in time also means that at the moment of observation, what is observable is only a moment, however complex. Observation frames that moment as a situation, but it is not static; any present is subject to change. Observation is a situated event, just as the moments we grasp are situated events. Thinking in time means taking this temporal complexity into account. The critical theory project of historicizing theory can be reconstructed as a critical project in temporalizing theory.

Temporality and Culture

Analytical distinctions used to articulate temporal complexity do more than present an elegant theoretical alternative to the analysis of social or cultural hierarchies, or the directionality of power. They speak to some of the most significant issues of social movements today; specifically, the direction and tempo of change, and how notions of progress or liberation are articulated. The first task of theory is to describe this complexity and analyze how claims to social justice are elaborated. The second, to use public and private frames of reference as the basis for their critique.

Cultural creativity is a form of lived temporal complexity. In constructing new social roles for women, old ones are redefined, the history of working women in the US is discovered or reinvented, changing notions of family are periodized rather than universalized, and the boundaries between men and women are redrawn at the same time that their elimination is actively sought. What is more, the contest over images of women, or of femininity, always engages a future toward which these images are projected as forms of liberation or fulfillment. In all of these processes-recuperative or innovative-time is subject to continual rearticulation. It is never the case that old temporal structures are simply replaced with new ones, just as traditional roles do not disappear with the creation of the new. These temporal structures coexist, in what Reinhart Koselleck calls the contemporaneity of the noncontemporaneous.[6] Similarly, many new social movements in India draw on spiritual traditions in order to promote social development and new notions of social progress. What is being negotiated here is not just the dichotomy between the spiritual and the secular, but that of ancient and modern, traditional and new---a conservation of tradition to serve a future of social justice. These time references (past, present, future) become so internally complex, it is reasonable to question whether or not they are still viable.

The temporality of cultural creativity is always complex because culture is itself both retentive and protentive. Culture is by definition historical, in the sense that it both has duration and develops over time. It also is future directed in that cultural practice establishes expectations of behaviour. Cultural practices outlast many other social arrangements, such as forms of production and political systems.[7] For instance, we can legislate equal opportunity for women in the workplace, and can even point to the growing numbers of women working in the official economy in the US, but the notion of the feminine as either the sex object or the mother persists, with real economic and political consequences in the struggle for equality. In the immortal words of Astor Piazzolla, in Argentina you can change the government, you can change the currency, but you cannot change the tango.

To the extent that notions of progress and liberation are temporal concepts, this negotiation of time is of particular importance for liberatory politics. Claims to social justice in the modern period were made on the basis of an unlimited progress into the future, and the utilization of the productive capacity of modern technology in the name of a better life. Utopian visions, socialist or otherwise, are always a projected future which re-enters the present as a critique of existing conditions. The temporality of liberation, even in the theological sense, has a future trajectory; that of domination, a static present; that of repression, a return to older forms of authority and the past. These concepts can be mapped on two axes, the vertical of power, the horizontal of time. On the vertical axis, liberation is mapped as power flowing from the bottom up; repression as power flowing from the top down. On the horizontal axis, liberation is time going forward into the future; repression is a return to the past. These latter categories are linked to the Enlightenment notion of history as the progress of reason and rational authority, on the one hand, or traditional forms of authority on the other.

This scheme cannot account for the contemporary situation. What is increasingly evident in many social movements is the reintroduction into the present, and therefore also the intended future, of elements of the past. The present as such is made problematic as history and preservation coexist with construction and innovation. New concepts of social justice are based on this complexity, rather than on a teleology of progress, or an understanding of liberation as an uninterrupted march into the future. Liberation is often the freedom to link present identity to a retained cultural heritage, or to construct a vision of progress that preserves a traditional culturally articulated notion of human dignity. Sometimes, as in the case of fundamentalist and back to nature movements, liberation is even understood as a return to a past, real or imagined. But even in these instances, it is never a simple return, but rather a past inscribed in the present or future. Cultural creativity also generates temporal difference within social movements-differences in negotiating time. Who wants to modernize, who to conserve? Which aspects of the past are newly understood to be progressive, which ones cannot make the leap into an already complex present? A critical project must articulate the temporal complexity of social movements if it is to account for new notions of liberation, and subject them to critique.

Spatial Complexity

The foregoing sketch of the temporal complexity of cultural creativity and social transformation is but one aspect of a theoretical project, or a social reality, in which time and space are mutually constitutive. Analysis cannot proceed without frames of reference which situate observation. Yet social processes cannot be situated in a static, unchanging notion of place. Just as temporality becomes complex as past and future reenter the present, situation must be articulated as an ongoing process of distinction that enters the space of observation and marks its terrain.[8] I suggest that that distinction be the one between public and private forms of reference.

The distinction between public and private, or between internal and external forms of reference, both establishes the identity of the social movement as a frame within society, and functions as an internal distinction within the movement itself. First, the women's movement is distinguished from other forms of social practice and advocacy in that meaningful communications within the movement are based on the difference between equality and inequality for women. The distinction does not establish a static, or fixed, terrain. The boundaries of the movement are not institutionally stable; they are continually being articulated, and shift with every moment of communication. Women's oppression becomes an element of the debate over the national welfare system, just as it reappears in an argument over the division of labor in a specific household. The women's movement, like any culturally structured social movement, is not a definite set of practices or institutional affiliations; it is simultaneously a matter of public policy and private experience. In either case, it is identified by communication organized around the issue of gender equality as articulated within the movement and made publicly available. Each such communication contributes to the ongoing reproduction of the movement itself, and reconfigures its terrain.

Unlike dualism, which inheres in the modern vs. postmodern categories of cultural analysis, the distinction between public and private frames of reference is not an either/or distinction. Rather than being mutually exclusive, these are mutually constitutive categories. The two sides of the distinction always occur together, and are always articulated with respect to one another. The distinction functions publicly in establishing a communicative terrain that is distinct from other aspects of social reality based on the internal, or private, premises of communication within the movement. But, the distinction between public and private reenters the terrain of the movement itself, as a frame of reference for its own internal communication. It functions privately, in this sense, in structuring the communication of feminists amongst themselves. It accomplishes this in two ways; first, in that the criteria of equality and inequality are applied reflexively to the structure of communication, and second, the grounds of debate over the determination and articulation of needs are established with reference to the publicly stated goals of the movement. Internal discussions are always conducted with an eye toward public dissemination, and they are subject to critique on the basis of the very norms of equality proposed by the movement. The public nature of the distinction as it functions privately in this sense is that the issue of equality vs. inequality becomes a matter not only of the social construction of gender relations, but also of the movement's construction of its own communicative relations.

Public and private frames of reference articulate space at the same time as they are constituted by lived practices. The public/private distinction is particularly meaningful with respect to the women's movement, which has argued for some time that the privatization of the domestic sphere has led to the invisibility of women's labor as a contribution to the official economy, and to keeping the social issue of domestic violence against women hidden behind the closed doors of the home. My argument is that within both public and private spheres, an ongoing set of practices occur which are both public and private, or have both public and private functions. Habermas speaks, in his discussion of the public sphere, of the public functions of many allegedly private corporations.[9] We also know that a great deal of public decision-making is conducted in private and serves private interests. Institutional definitions alone tend to obscure the public and private aspects of how institutions actually function. Public and private designations are even more complex in the case of social movements, in that they also function on the individual level. In an argument between a husband and wife over who does the dishes, the publicly articulated issue of equality between men and women enters into the private relationship between two human beings.

Critique

The utility of these frames of reference, understood as an ongoing distinction, is not only that they provide a better description of how cultural creativity actually functions within the larger social context, but also that they provide the basis for meaningful critique. Indeed, the criterion of utility rests precisely in the critical function of theory.

Traditional conceptions of public and private have been articulated along institutional lines, and take the form of categorical or fixed oppositions. More recently, given the emergence of identity politics and the social movements associated with it, the claim is frequently made that the public and the private, the personal and the political, so completely overlap that no meaningful distinctions can or need be made. Both of these positions are very problematic from the point of view of theory as well as that of social practice. First, static concepts may be able to describe what things are at a specific moment in time, but they can't articulate how they work. Second, the institutional frame tends to privilege the public over the private. Third, an institutional basis for these categories is reductive in that internal distinctions based on public and private functions are subsumed within the larger institutional category. Fourth, and the two frameworks converge at this point, without distinctions between the personal and the political, no internal critique is possible. One of the dangers of culturally structured social movements is the tendency to equate empowerment with power-which, in the worst cases, substitutes private liberation for social freedom or makes claims to social justice on the basis of internal forms of repression. Social movements that are culturally structured carry this potential contradiction between the public and the private, the personal and the political. As an extreme example, without the criteria of these distinctions, nazism could be seen as liberating in that it personally and collectively empowered the German people. But as we know, it was politically repressive, not only with respect to the Jews, but also within its own ranks. Without a functional distinction between public and private, the very notion of liberation cannot be subjected to critique. This constitutes the second, and most important, grounds for the utility of these categories.

If the words liberation, freedom, or social justice are to have any meaning at all, it cannot rest solely on private or public, personal or political notions. These are internally complex and mutually constitutive categories which occur and recur within an ever changing social landscape. Most importantly, there is no liberation without the internal grounds for a critique of the normative claims to that liberation. The temporal structure of claims for social justice can only be critiqued against their lived moments of public and private practices.

Conclusion

I have argued that temporal complexity is a constitutive aspect of processes of cultural creativity and social transformation, and therefore must be a premise of theory itself. Temporalizing theory in this way, and taking the real contingencies of social processes into account, is an implicit argument against the predictive disposition of the social sciences. Rather, the first task of theory is to describe the present complexity; to prioritize critical reflection over prediction.

I have also argued that the analytical distinctions between object and practices, elitisim and egalitarianism, no longer serve a critical project in social and cultural theory. Social movements negotiate time both in internal processes of meaning-construction and in articulating claims to social justice or liberation vis-a-vis existing structures of power. Those claims are either validated or subjected to critique in the space constituted by public and private practices. The distinctions of time and space better serve contemporary analysis.

Finally, it is my belief that description and observation are communicative forms of social practice. Criticism of processes of social change is not a counter-movement, but rather contributes to the ongoing reproduction of communication on the terrain of social movements, and offers the best possibility for their analysis. Embedded in this idea is a plea not to take for granted the claims to liberation of social movements, but rather to use frames of reference to assess how they structure actual practice. It is also a plea not to predict outcome on the basis of either past results or present ideology. These remarks are offered as analytical possibilities for that project.

Notes

1. For examples of how this understanding has informed contemporary literature, see: Pierre Bourdieu, *The Logic of Practice*, (Stanford: Stanford University Press) 1990; Orville Lee and Meredith Phillips, "Culture, Structure and Poverty: The Uses of Culture in the Study of Social Inequality", unpublished conference paper, ASA, 1996; William H. Sewell, Jr., "A Theory of Structure: Duality, Agency and Transformation," *American Journal of Sociology*, Vol.98, 1, (July 1992); and Ann Swidler, "Culture in Action: Symbols and Strategies", *American Sociological Review*, Vol.51, 2 (April 1986); among others.
2. These three dimensions are described by Niklas Luhmann, "Meaning as a Basic Concept" in *Essays on Self-Reference* (New York: Columbia University Press) 1990, p.36.
3. I owe this specific formulation to Craig Calhoun.
4. Max Horkheimer, "Traditional and Critical Theory" in *Critical Theory* (New York: Continuum), 1972, p. 227
5. Andreas Huyssen, "The Search for Tradition: Avantgarde and Postmodernism in the 1970's" in *After The Great Divide: Modernism, Mass Culture, Postmodernism* (Bloomington: Indiana University Press), 1986, p.171.
6. Reinhart Koselleck, *Futures Past, On the Semantics of Historical Time*. K. Tribe, trans. (Cambridge, MA: MIT Press, 1985).
7. This notion first appears in the sociological literature in Max Horkheimer's concept of "cultural lag" presented in the 1936 essay "Authority and the Family", in *Critical Theory* (New York: Continuum), 1972.

8. The notion of recurrent distinction is indebted to Niklas Luhmann's work in systems theory.
9. Jurgen Habermas, "The Public Sphere" in Steven Seidman, ed., *Jurgen Habermas on Society and Politics* (Boston: Beacon Press), 1989.

Chapter Four

Rethinking Social Transformation: An Eco-Socialist Perspective

Baas Weilinga

The Outcome of the Revolutions of the 20th Century

"The revolution is also no more what it used to be", remarked Henri Lefebvre, the French Marxist, already in 1977, even before the once more hope giving victory of the Sandinistas in Nicaragua. Hardly twenty years later, close to the end of the century which saw successful revolutions in Persia, Turkey, Russia, Mexico, China, Yugoslavia and other places, followed by a wave of anti-colonial liberation struggles, the very terminology of revolution is being avoided, at least among leftists. The advertisers have appropriated the word, in order to promote the sale of the latest fashionable luxury products. And then came Ronald Reagan, the former US president, who on the last day of his eight years in the White House said: "We were all revolutionaries and the revolution has been a success."

That was one year before 1989. In that watershed year we could learn once more—as already before in Iran, the Philippines and other places—that political revolutions are still possible. Unarmed mass mobilizations have brought down heavily armed dictatorial regimes. What seems to remain beyond reach, as the same year dramatically demonstrated, is the realization of a social revolution which would bring about and consolidate a socio-economic and socio-cultural base for a truly democratic society in which people's needs are being met in an equitable way because people are in control of resources and decision-making. The year 1989 saw not only the collapse of such hopes which had been associated with 1917, but also of the hopes of many of the actors in the democratic upheavals of that year itself, people who are deeply disappointed today about the outcome of their struggles, as they had set out in the expectation that 'perestroika' and democratization would eventually lead to a form of democratic socialism.

Similarly, we may ask what has remained of the hopes and dreams of social transformation which accompanied the struggle for independence in India and other colonized countries. How do we explain that the visions of Gandhi or Nehru, of Lohia or Ambedkar, or of various communist tendencies, seem to have lost their capacity to protect people against the spirit of surrender. How is it that liberalization is being accepted as substitute for liberation from the dominance of global capital? Why is the aim of economic self-reliance being given up, not to speak of people's control of resources?

Many reasons can be quoted to explain the—unexpected and unpredicted---triumph of capital at the end of this century. In this paper I want to focus on those reasons which are connected with its capacity to orient human desires towards commodity-centred ways if fulfilment which contribute to its ongoing, never-ending drive for accumulation. This is not to deny the importance of other factors such as economic and military superiority. But the most formidable strength of capitalism may be its power over human souls, its capacity to orient human longings and ambitions towards profit-producing objects and objectives. Both capitalism and state socialism as it was constructed after 1917, have been ruthless in their destruction of traditional forms of satisfaction of human desires. The difference is that capitalism was able to fill the vacuum which its destructiveness created with the longing for commodities that offered a type of satisfaction, however problematic, with which the boring daily life patterns and political rituals in austere Soviet society in the long run could not compete.

From among a variety of possible candidates, Ford may be selected as a leading and typical representative of this victorious capacity of 20th century capitalism. Ford who launched his mass production of automobiles in 1909 has been the winner of this century, absurd as it may be. When the Berlin wall was opened, people going to the West were most eager to buy a western car, never mind second or third hand. And one of the most conspicuous symbols of liberalization in India is the opening of the market for the production and sale of a wide variety of cars, with, as it happens, Mahendra Ford a front-runner.

The private car is much more than a comfortable means of transport. It is indeed a symbol of what 20th century capitalism stands for, both of its attractive and its destructive character. It stands for the private dreams and longings which it promises to satisfy, as an analysis of the advertisements, e.g., in *India Today*, can demonstrate. And it stands for the sacrifices of human lives and limbs on the altar of those dreams, for the promotion of an irrational transport policy, for the demolition of neighbourhood,[1] and landscapes, for an unsustainable burden on local environments and global climate, for the depletion of limited resources, and for the impossibility of providing all with that what the advertisements broadcast to all. In a more hidden but hardly disputed way it stands for the "way of life" in whose "defense" capitalist countries led by the USA, are ready to go to war, as the Gulf War of 1991 brutally demonstrated.

Revolutionary Captives to the Dream of "Catching Up"

Long before GDR citizens could flock to the showrooms of the West and Indian aspirants could rush to get a loan from the Bank of America to book a Ford Escort (*The Hindu*, 9 September 1996), there were staunch revolutionaries nurturing that very dream of speed, freedom and civilized progress which is supposed to be incarnated in the automobile. In 1929, the USSR signed an agreement with Ford (Detroit) for the construction of a plant with a planned output of 2,00,000 cars per year. Celebrating in the same year the anniversary of the October Revolution, Stalin wrote:

> We are going full steam along the road of industrialization to socialism, leaving behind our age-long 'Russian' backwardness. We are becoming a country of metal, a country of the automobile, a country of the tractor. And when we have seated the USSR in an automobile, and the peasant on a tractor, then let the honourable capitalists who plume themselves on their 'civilization' try to catch us up. We shall see which countries can be counted as backward and which as advanced.[2]

In this orientation Stalin was not an exception. Almost all Bolshevik leaders have been looking towards the USA when trying to imagine the future of a prospering socialism. On the one hand, there was the revolutionary rhetoric of radical confrontation with capitalism and the promise of an alternative socialist society. The world was confronted with the picture of a conflict between diametrically opposed systems. In certain aspects there were indeed basic differences, particularly in terms of property relations. That nurtured hope among exploited classes and nations around the world that the USSR offered a way of escape from capitalism and imperialism. There was a society in which under the most trying circumstances other priorities were set: right to work, provision for the basic needs of all, health care and education for all. It appeared to be a place which could be a homeland for hope as it seemed to be no longer under the sway of capital.

But what easily got overlooked was that the adversaries were moving into the same direction, as the idea of "catching up" indicates. It was left to the capitalist front-runners to choose the direction of technological development and set the aims and standards of production, while their rivals were concentrating on raising the resources to emulate them, becoming exploitative themselves in the process, and thus losing their legitimacy in the long run.

For a long time the socialist countries, in their efforts to build an industrial and military independent base concentrated on the technological race---for example, in space—while ignoring the emergence of new needs and desires among its citizens after the basic needs were more or less satisfied.[3] Capital accumulation for the technological race implied continuing austerity for the consumers. High levels of education increased the scope of aspirations. Promising attempts to satisfy these aspirations through the creation of democratic space for participation in politics, artistic freedom of expression, and socio-cultural pluralism were crushed by anxious bureaucratic-dictatorial regimes, as it happened in Czechoslovakia in 1968. To compensate its frustrated citizens for the curtailments of freedom they imposed, these regimes offered the increase of imitation-style western consumption such as cars, and other gadgets. They suppressed the democratic and creative desires which could have contributed to the development of an attractive socialist alternative and promoted the nurturing of those addictive, commodity-centred desires which ultimately western capitalist society can satisfy much better, be it not for all. In India and other post-colonial societies, we can observe a similar contradiction between confrontation with imperialism and emulation of its civilization and economic and technological achievements. When Jawaharlal Nehru was impressed with planned modernization policies in the USSR, he drew from it the hope that backward countries could escape from imperialist control and at the same time catch up with modern development through central planning. His vision of industrialization and modernization as the way to build a base for self-reliant development and gradual transition to socialism won the day over alternative proposals of Gandhians, M.N. Roy and a few others, and gained widespread support including from the communist left. Today, this project has collapsed, as the aim of self-reliance is given up and that of socialism has been discarded after liberalization policy with its consumerist lure has gained the support of the pampered prosperous sections of the population.

Once we accept that there is only one way of economic development and progress, only one criterion of what is forward and backward, we have to admit that the revolution in backward Russia and the struggle for independence elsewhere were futile as far as the ambitions to find an escape route to an alternative society are concerned. They could at best have meaning as phases in the harsh process of modernization, while the sacrifices were then legitimized in the name of nationalism and socialism or development.

This has been the approach of non-Marxist modernization theories as well as of those Marxist tendencies which explain the failure of the October Revolution as the unavoidable outcome of the fact that the revolution did not take place, as expected by Marx, in the "most developed" capitalist countries. This reasoning is based on an understanding of the dialectic of productive forces and production relations as the motor of all social revolution, within a linear evolutionary scheme of successive phases of historical progress.[4] This theoretical paradigm is primarily derived from the historical case of the transition from feudal to bourgeois property relations and society in Western Europe.[5] Within this framework Marx, Engels and Lenin at times have welcomed the destructive dynamism of capitalist development which sweeps away the relics of petty production and social structures of traditional pre-capitalist society.[6] Capitalist progress, with all its cruelty, was seen as promoting the socialization of labour, the development of the market, technical advance, destruction of patriarchal conditions in the countryside, and so on.[7] Such destruction was to be welcomed, as only in that way the "naked conflict between capital and labour" as "the one contradiction of world-historical significance" would become apparent.[8]

Unfortunately, this tendency in the works of Marx and Engels has become dominant in the theoretical and practical outlook of the Second International, whereas the relevance of rethinking and of new explorations in the later work of Marx and the warning of counter-voices as that of Walter Benjamin were ignored.

Revolution as Escape from Disastrous Progress

It is a speculative question whether communists in Russia and nationalists in India and elsewhere could have followed another path, an alternative way to break successfully free from capitalist domination. Some half-forgotten, dissenting voices have been arguing in favour of other approaches. They deserve to be given a fresh hearing as part of the renewed search today—under changed circumstances—for alternative development. The triumph of global capitalism has not solved any of the problems which it creates, on the contrary it has aggravated them. Its social, cultural and ecological destructive impact makes the search for an alternative more urgent than ever before.

Not all Marxists have subscribed to the theory that the "mission" of capitalism to make tabula rasa of traditional society had to be welcomed in the interest of a socialist future. Marx himself became much more critical of the hindrances which capitalist destructiveness eventually—instead of clearing the way—might throw up. In *Capital* itself he has shown how the productive forces can turn into destructive forces.[9]

The "late Marx" of the 1870s moves away from a revolutionary perspective which fully relies on capitalist technological progress. The Paris Commune brings the insight that the working class needs an alliance with the peasantry that is based on its "vital interests and real needs" (MEW 17,550). Intensive study of the Russian situation in interaction with populist revolutionaries there[10] leads to the hypothesis that traditional village commune and peasantry could play a crucial role in a revolutionary regeneration of Russia. Capitalist development as it was promoted by the Tsarist state and merchant and usury capital appears no longer as an unavoidable and necessary phase in the progress of history, but as a destructive intervention and parasitic threat to common property relations in the village commune and to the peasants as Russia's "greatest productive force". A successful revolution as envisaged by the Narodniki of Narodnaya Volya, could, if it would happen in time, interrupt the destructive development and make it possible to avoid capitalism. "To save the Russian Commune there must be a Russian Revolution."[11] Such a revolution would open a new chapter which would "not begin with its own suicide". Instead of a phase of destruction there would be a way of transformation which with the help of technological achievements of capitalism elsewhere could bring about a new society, which could be considered as a "revival in a superior form of an archaic social type".

Marx's rethinking on the peasant commune links up with his analysis of the Paris Commune, the "greatest revolution" of the 19th century which is understood as a "revolution against the state itself", namely, through a "reabsorption of state power" through the masses, a "resumption by the people for the people of its own social life". This differs from the tabula rasa approach before. Obviously not everything of traditional society deserves to be destroyed. Return of archaic elements on a higher level, reabsorption, regeneration point at a more dialectical approach.

The same is the case with reference to the role of colonialism. Marx speaks in the 1850s of the revolutionary mission of England in India in a double sense: "One destructive, the other regenerating---the annihilation of old Asiatic society and the laying of the material foundations of western society in Asia."[12] He appreciated England as the "unconscious tool of history" in bringing about the only "social revolution" in Asia as it destroyed the village communities. In the context of his discussion of the Russian situation he revises this approach and emphasizes the negative effects of the colonial intervention in India. In one of the drafts of his letter to Vera Zasulic he speaks of the "suppression of communal land ownership" as "nothing but an act of English vandalism which drove the indigenous population backward rather than forward."[13]

Space does not permit to show that Lenin, especially in his last writings about "cooperatives" comes closer to a more constructive appreciation of the role of the peasantry. Unfortunately, neither the "late" Marx nor the "late" Lenin were taken into consideration when their successors in their name opted for a devastating bureaucratic-technocratic "bulldozer" approach which in its course destroyed also valuable social and cultural elements. It has had far-reaching negative consequences that the followers of Marx and Lenin remained captive to the dominant paradigm of economic, social and cultural progress through industrialization---even at break-neck speed---and were unable to pursue the critical and self-critical questions they had thrown up. Today, with hind sight and in view of the looming eco-catastrophes, we may wonder why Marx and others as revolutionary critics did not pursue those questions more forcefully.

After all Marx and Engels were contemporaries to the discovery of the law of entropy in the 1850s. Joan Martinez-Alier, who untiringly draws attention to the ecological basis of all economics,[14] has documented that Marx and Engels have been confronted with the economic implications of entropy. The Ukrainian Narodnik Socialist Sergey Podolinski discussed some of those implications in an essay published in leading socialist magazines in France and Germany (*Die Neue Zeit*). Marx, who was asked by the author for his comments, consulted Engels, who did not deny the scientific argument but advised against mixing up economics and physics.[15] This mixing is what liberal economists would like to avoid even today. And it is on the basis of this refusal to take into consideration the physical base and limits of all economics that later Marxists joined them in believing in the inexhaustibility of natural resources and competed with them in unfettering the productive forces.

Eco-Marxists have shown that there are traces in Marx's writings of an awareness that capitalist technological development is heading for disaster. He ends his chapter on machinery and modern industry[16] with a critical perspective on the contradiction between the capitalist mode of production and the natural conditions of production. Marx writes:

> All progress in capitalist agriculture is a progress in the art, not only of robbing the labourer, but of robbing the soil; all progress in increasing the fertility of the soil for a given time, is a progress towards ruining the lasting sources of that fertility. The more a country starts its development on the foundation of modern industry, like the United States, for example, the more rapid is this process of destruction. Capitalist production, therefore, develops technology, and the combining of various processes into a social whole, only by sapping the original sources of all wealth - the soil and the labourer...[17]

James O'Connor and other authors around the journal *Capitalism, Nature, Socialism: A Journal of Socialist Ecology* speak of the second contradiction of capital, namely, the contradiction between capital and the conditions of production which include the natural environment, the life-world of people and the social infrastructure. In these areas capital is confronted with rising non-productive costs, because it cannot solve the problems its impact has created: eco-catastrophes, health problems, transport problems, socio-cultural protest, demands of women and the accumulation of side-effects of technocratic pseudo-solutions to these problems. All these costs are compensated through reduction of social welfare costs, which results in further conflicts.[18]

An adequate understanding of these accumulating, unsolvable problems leads to the insight that life-saving anti-capitalist revolutions and struggles for social transformation have to abandon firmly and clearly the idea of catching up with or surpassing capitalism. Social transformation with the aim of overcoming mass poverty and eco-destructive economics and consumerist civilization has to look for other, sustainable ways of ecological-economical and socio-cultural reproduction and regeneration. That may sound utopian, but is based on the down-to-earth, materialist insight that we have to start from the limited capacities of natural environment and humans to regenerate and sustain themselves, which radically differs from the unlimited capacity of capital to accumulate.

Confirming the insight that social being determines consciousness, we will find socially marginalized people, such as women, indigenous peoples and other subsistence producers, small peasants, workers in the informal sector, artisanal fishers, development-refugees, etc., being the first to articulate protest against the destructive effects of present-day capitalism. Yet, the same spreads also in core sectors. The survival struggles of the marginalized—who had been written off long ago by liberals as well as leftists—are gaining an unexpected new relevance for the more privileged sections which now feel the pressure of flexibilization policies. However great the differences, the insight emerges, that there are worldwide common interests to stop the locomotive of the capitalist revolution. Marx spoke of revolutions as the locomotives of history. Following his own hope for a Russian revolution as timely intervention this metaphor ought to be replaced by that of Walter Benjamin who spoke of revolution as pulling the emergency brake. That metaphor evokes not only the image of a general strike which brings all wheels to a standstill, it suggests that the blindly forward rushing locomotive of progress leads to disaster. All over the world we find attempts to slow down, to get out, to reorient. Protests against destructive mega projects, boycott actions, alternative projects, struggles for democratic space to protect certain viable traditions (Zapatistas), re-vitalization of local and regional economies, resistance against MNCs, and so on. These attempts can be seen as signs of a beginning, complex and difficult, but vital epochal reorientation, in search of new ways of life, of a new, sustainable type of civilization. This will be a long process, in which the reorientation of human desires through a cultural regeneration and reorientation will play a crucial role.

Regarding the Reorientation of Desires

Human needs, wants and desires are changing in the course of history. Even so called basic needs are changing, at least regarding the forms in which people seek their satisfaction.

Capitalism has demonstrated a tremendous capacity to restructure the human psyche, its desires and emotions to its advantage. In its early phase accumulation was based on the repression of even the most elementary needs of the workers, while it developed the logic of creating ever changing artificial wants among the rich and the desire for money as the alien power which gives access to satisfaction of all possible wants. As Marx puts it:

> The less you eat, drink and buy books, the less you go to the theatre, the dance hall, the public house, the less you think, love, theorise, sing, paint, dance, etc., the more you save—the greater becomes your treasure which neither moths nor rust will devour—your capital...[19]

In a later phase, represented by Ford's mass production, a larger section of people got hooked up to new consumption wants by means of immense advertisement campaigns and loan-schemes in order to sustain the growth of capitalism. In a fascinating study Trevor Blackwell and Jeremy Seabrook have shown how post-World War II welfare capitalism turned what seemed to be an advance if not victory of labour into a new enslavement, which then three decades later became the base for the gradual dismantling of the welfare deals.[20] In the benevolent guise of the welfare state capitalism was "able to extend its transforming power deeper and deeper into the lives of men and women", making at the same time "alternatives appear increasingly unimaginable".[21] The authors do not argue that the working class needed no relief from poverty, or that the workers were corrupted by affluence. Their point is that capitalism offered relief on a private basis with purchased commodities as consolations for the non-fulfilment of the social needs which the vision of solidarity in socialism had promised to satisfy.[22]

The east bloc of socialist countries used the "iron curtain" to keep the glittering attractions of western consumerism out of sight and to prevent an exodus towards the "fleshpots of Egypt". In pursuit of a rigorous program of industrialization the state with its central planning had established a "dictatorship over people's needs".[23] The need of participation in discussing and deciding which needs are basic and which desires are socially acceptable was suppressed. These dictatorial regimes themselves in a later stage prepared the way for an uncritical consumerism which left the citizens of these countries unprepared to face the onslaught of the superior consumerism of the West.

The outcome of these processes seems to be an irresistible sway of capital in defining, directing and attracting human desires. However, it is of crucial importance to discern the fundamental weaknesses of its regime, the vulnerability of this god on clay feet. Firstly, while it promises satisfaction, it unceasingly spreads dissatisfaction. This applies not only to those who hardly can satisfy their minimum basic needs, but also to those who do manage to buy the latest products, as they are rather sooner or later persuaded by the next advertisement campaign that they are no longer up-to-date or out of tune with the latest fashion). Both non-consumers and consumers are kept up their toes, are not allowed to slow down and rest, as capital has to accumulate, and as the economy has to grow. But, secondly, the economy cannot continue to grow in the same way as in the past. The ecological limits have become visible, however blindly economists and politicians still measure their performance in terms of growth. The dynamism and speed required by the logic of accumulation clashes violently with the processes of regeneration of nature which require a drastic slowing down, a ban on certain types of production and carefully prioritized selection of branches in which growth is needed. The laws of the market violate the laws of nature.

Whatever its promises, global capitalism cannot solve the problem of mass poverty, because it has to go on accumulating, it cannot satisfy the rich, because it has to go on innovating, and it cannot generalize globally the living standards of the "most developed" countries, because the planet earth would not be able to cope with it.

This leaves only two options: either the rich minorities barricade themselves in guarded enclaves surrounded by masses of envious and angry poor, in the style of Maxworth Nagar's with all facilities, like abundant supply of water---to wash their cars---in the midst of water-starved masses and fields or a process of radical social transformation towards an equitable and ecologically sustainable society.

The second option implies the frank recognition that there is a limit to the satisfaction of needs, if all are going to be satisfied, including generations after us. The "American way of life", the consumerism of the rich capitalist countries can no longer be accepted as a model to be emulated and is morally and politically unacceptable, as it is based on the exploitation of limited resources at the cost of others.

This means, the old anti-imperialist struggle, has to continue, this time in the form of denying access to MNCs. But this has to be led by a new vision of an alternate society which is no longer captive to the "American dream".

Is that possible? Is a reorientation of human desires possible? This is not the place to review the complex debate about theories of human needs, wants and desires.[24]

The following points seem to me to be particularly important for further reflection. Firstly, it must be possible to identify and to agree in the course of public, democratic discussion on basic human needs whose satisfaction for all has to be secured first. This is the priority of social justice to which the socialist movement has been committed.

Secondly, the insight that even basic needs are culturally mediated with regard to the forms in which they are satisfied has to be taken seriously. It means that the satisfaction of basic needs is not just a quantitative task, measured only in statistics of productivity, but a cultural task as well. It was one of the failures of state socialism and central planning that it did not give space for democratic participation, local initiatives and freedom in designing and choosing patterns of production and consumption---e.g., house construction---in which cultural, social and aesthetic desires could find satisfaction already in the process of satisfying basic needs.[25]

Thirdly, the concept of basic needs has to be distinguished from felt needs and desires which are ambiguous as they may include ecologically destructive and self-destructive desires. The addiction to tobacco and drugs or speed may shape the desires of many people, but these desires cannot be recognized on par with the desire for decent food, shelter, social interaction and so on. The question is how society can cope with such harmful desires. While measures of control---such as banning---may be necessary, it is clear from the experiences of campaigns against alcoholism that the re-animation of other desires which can replace them is crucial. The same applies to dealing with the problem of ecologically harmful desires.

Fourthly, all this calls for major efforts in aesthetic education and cultural action as the only way to counter the onslaught of the media. The task seems to be daunting in view of the fascination with the media. But, the in-built tendency to leave people dissatisfied offers openings. A good participatory sport, games or drama programme in any village or slum can draw children away from the screen. There are many desires of a social and cultural nature---as articulated, e.g., by Marx and Morris---which are left dormant or suppressed by capitalism, not to speak of the "radical needs" identified by Agnes Heller.

The Need to Transform the Politics of Transformation

The strategy of the traditional left has been based on the concept of a vanguard party leading the struggle for the conquest of political power and subordinating all other struggles to that overriding purpose. Whether women or dalits or peasants or indigenous peoples, all were supposed to identify primarily with the class struggle for political power. Social transformation would follow the successful political revolution.

Independent social movements have been challenging this approach, by launching struggles on particular issues while leaving the question of political power open or even unaddressed. Some scholars see this as a welcome development of civil society over against an earlier state-focussed approach. However, recent calls for a "new politics" are based on the insight that the questions of political power cannot be avoided. A radical democratization is needed which has to be fought for simultaneously in civil society and in the political arena.[26] In this process the traditional left based on the organized working class and the new social movements need each other and need to learn from each other while leaving space for different roles, forms of organization and ways of struggle, while aiming at an alliance of forces which will be able to focus as well on the first as on the second contradiction of capital. This will be difficult but it has the potential of opening up a renewed socialist perspective.

The red-green Chattisgarh Mukti Morcha has become an outstanding and inspiring example of innovative ways in which a working class movement can link typical working class demands with a much wider agenda which addresses problems of health care, education, rural economy and socio-cultural identity in a perspective of radical social transformation.

On the other hand, we find a growing trend towards unionization in the informal sector. Traditional artisanal fishers have organized themselves successfully as fishworkers and have shown their capacity to operate on regional, national and even global levels. Forest dwellers start organizing themselves as 2forest workers. Women movements have launched into cooperatives and union work.

These developments have the potential to link up questions of the exploitation of labour and of the control of resources. Fishworkers, forest-based *adivasis*, peasants and women are raising the question of access to resources as well as the question of sustaining the resource base. Peasant movements have started confronting multinationals like Cargill over the control of seeds and aquaculture companies over the issue of land and environment.

Politically, these movements and struggles are very heterogeneous, a nightmare for those who dream of strong, monolithic organizations, as the only means to move towards social transformation. But, in the process, we may discover that there may be also advantages in fighting the goliath of global capital with its concentrated power in a wide variety of ways. A reflection on the political implications of an ecological approach may help to discover its potentialities as well as its problems.

Ecologically, a decentralization of production is needed, which is counter both to the market-based centralization and accumulation of capital and to the plan-based centralization of state socialism which are both not sustainable. Such reorientation for ecological reasons converges with the strategy to fight poverty by starting from organizing local resources to meet local needs. Ecologically, survival depends on bio-diversity. Accordingly, viable socialism requires planning and decision-making from below, which is responsive to people's concrete needs and nature's concrete possibilities and limitations. Instead of homogenizing centralistic state planning from above or marketing strategies from abroad, this approach would have to be democratically based on people's control and management of resources.

Sustaining the environment requires skills and attitudes which have been sidelined or destroyed by modernization. An ecologically informed reorientation will revise the marginalization of artisan, peasant and tribal communities and appreciate the contribution which their traditional skills and attitudes oriented towards the production of life can make, in combination with non-destructive, democratically controllable, appropriate technologies and high-tech inventions. Eco-feminists have shown how women have a central role to play in such a reorientation which would imply overcoming the sexual division of labour by drawing men "into the field of production and sustenance of life".[27]

Ecologically, we need an economy without accumulation through interest on capital.[28] Non-Marxist critics of the capitalist finance system such as James Robertson are suggesting a break with the interest logic in order to get away from the exponential growth rates of capital. Does this not provide a base for a call "all debtors of the world unite"?

Ecologically, all life is interconnected. Ecological awareness forbids to separate micro and macro levels. Eco-concerns reach from the local through the regional and national to the international and global. This implies that a sound ecological orientation cannot go together with chauvinist, exclusivistic movements. Religious communalists and caste associations may appeal to the same concerns of daily survival, connected with the life-worlds of people, but they cannot adequately address the eco-problems as long as they make exclusive, chauvinistic claims. Ecosystems, local watersheds, river waters, groundwater tables, etc., are the common base for people of different social communities and eco-politics is possible only on the basis of cooperation across social and political boundaries.

This opens a perspective on a material-collective basis for the democratization of civil society in ever-widening circles, which correspond with the interconnectedness of ecosystems.

In terms of political systems this poses the need of combining forms of direct, participatory democracy---as in gram sabhas, cooperatives and water user associations---with forms of representative democracy on higher levels. Dalits and others who suffer from traditional forms of discrimination must have the possibility to appeal to higher instances which have the power to interfere to protect their rights. Conflicts over the sharing of common resources, e.g., river waters, have to be settled on higher levels. The present tendency of devolution of power to the states and abandoning ecological responsibility on the level of the central government may speed up short-term economic growth but invites eco-disasters in the long run.

In terms of political and social activity this calls for constructive, innovative work on local levels, aiming at people's control and management of resources, linked with political mobilization for influencing legislation and policies on regional, national and international levels. That is where alliances of people's movements and radical parties have to find new equations based on the emerging perspective of an alternative development. Without such an evolving ideological-political perspective it will be hardly possible to resist the large-scale attempts to co-opt the ambiguous NGO activities which tend to borrow ideas and credibility from social movements into the civil society project of the market-oriented forces.

On the other hand, those who insist rightly on the need for a radical political perspective, have to rethink on the potential contribution of local alternative experiments. The Marxist critique of utopian socialism has created a deep skepticism regarding such experiments. The critique is valid when the assumption would be that it is just a matter of multiplying alternative projects in order to achieve an overall transformation of society. Such an approach would ignore the necessity of struggle against the powers that are bound to resist the advance of successful alternatives, either by co-optation or repression. Such experiments cannot replace the political process and struggles but they are an important part of it. They are needed as eye-openers, as consciousness-reorienting practical arguments against the widespread, paralyzing, fatalistic skepticism that there are no alternatives. A growing number of people know that the present capitalist civilization is not viable in the long run. But they are unable to act according to this insight, as long as they believe that nothing can be done about it. This skepticism cannot be broken by the promise that everything will be possible "after the revolution".

An alternate development paradigm is evolving from local struggles and experiments and is bound to attract more people when pioneers succeed in showing that things can be done in a better and sustainable way. This itself can generate a pioneering enthusiasm which offers an alternate satisfaction to the basic human desire of creative participation in common ventures. The release of creative and constructive social energies will not make confrontational political struggles based on mass mobilization and organization superfluous, but it will give them hopefully another depth and human quality and provide a base for a vision which is organically connected with people's lives and desires and has the potential to become hegemonic.

Notes

1. Cf. Marshall Berman, *All that is solid melts into air: The experience of modernity* (London, Verso, 1983).
2. Kendall E. Barks, *Technology and Society under Lenin and Stalin* (Princeton, 1978), p.170f, quoting Stalin "The Year of the Great Breakthrough".
3. See C.T. Kurien, *The Economy: An Interpretative Introduction* (New Delhi, Sage, 1992), ch.6.
4. Usually with reference to Karl Marx, Preface to *A Contribution to the Critique of Political Economy* (1859), see Marx/Engels, *Selected Works*, Vol. I, pp.502ff.
5. Summed up in *Capital* I, ch. XXXII.
6. See the eloquent praise of the role of the enterprising bourgeoisie in: *Manifesto of the Communist Party*.
7. See Lenin about the "mission" of capitalism in: "Development of Capitalism in Russia", *Collected Works*, Vol.3.

8. F. Engels, "The Prussian Military Question and the German Workers' Party" (1865) in: Marx/Engels, *Collected Works*, Vol.20, p.70.
9. See T. Shanin (ed.), *Late Marx and the Russian Road* (New York, 1983).
10. See K.K. Dasgupta, *Marx, Chernyshevskii and the Theory of Non-capitalist Development* (New Delhi, 1991).
11. Shanin, op.cit., p.116.
12. "The Future Results of the British Rule in India." in: *On Colonialism* (Moscow), p.84.
13. Shanin, *op.cit.*, p.118.
14. See J. Martinez-Alier, *Ecological Economics: Energy, Environment and Society* (New York, 1987).
15. See Martinez Alier, "La Confluence dans l'eco-socialism" in: J. Bidet/J.Texier, *L'idee du socialisme a-t-elle un avenir?* (Paris, 1992) Cf. Letters of Engels to Marx on 19 and 22 December 1882 in Marx/Engels, *Sel. Correspondence.*
16. *Capital I.*, ch.15.
17. *Capital I* (Moscow), p.474f.
18. E. Altvater, *The Future of the Market* (London, 1993).
19. Economic and Philosophical Manuscripts, Marx/Engels, *Collected Works* 3, p.309.
20. Trevor Blackwell/Jeremy Seabrook, *A World Still to Win. The Reconstruction of the Post-War Working Class* (London, Faber, 1985).
21. Ibid., p.82.
22. Ibid., p.51.
23. See the critique of Ferenc Feher and Agnes Heller of the Budapest School, *Diktatur uber die Beduerfnisse* (Hamburg, 1979).
24. See the writings of Agnes Heller, Kater Soper, Len Doyal/Ian Gough. Kater Soper: *On Human Needs* (Brighton, 1981); Len Doyal/Ian Gough, *A Theory of Human Needs* (London, 1991) and the discussion between them in *New Left Review* 197 and 201. Important would be also the mimesis-discussion, responding to the theories of Rene Girard. See also William Leiss, *The Limits to Satisfaction: An Essay on the Problem of Needs and Commodities* (Toronto, 1976; Kingston, 1988).
25. This point is made by William Leiss, op.cit.

26. Neera Chandhoke, *State and Civil Society. Explorations in Political Theory* (New Delhi, 1995).
27. Gabriele Dietrich, *Women's Movement in India* (Bangalore, 1988), p.179.
28. E. Altvater, op.cit.

Chapter Five

Liberation Beyond Liberalism: New Voices from Buddhism and Islam

Fred R. Dallmayr

As inhabitants of the West, we live in what is called the "free world". Taken literally, this phrase suggests that other parts of the world are unfree and perhaps even unfamiliar with the concept of freedom. Seen in a historical perspective, the phrase also intimates that the West has undergone, and now is the product of, an intensive process of liberation---a process which again is absent in the non-western world. The main purpose of the following presentation is to challenge these assumptions or at least to show their skewed and lopsided character. What should emerge from these pages are at least two points: first, that the concepts of freedom and liberation are by no means as straightforward and univocal as is frequently claimed in western literature; and secondly that so-called non-western religions---that is, those outside the Judaeo-Christian orbit narrowly defined---are by no means strangers to liberation and are in fact deeply rooted in (soteriological) conceptions of freedom.

Regarding the first issue---the meaning of freedom and liberation---my comments here have to be brief and can only convey a sketchy glimpse of the problem. Proceeding in a summary fashion one might say that, in modern western thought, freedom has tended to be viewed as a property or attribute of human subjects and that liberation, accordingly, was seen as an intentional or deliberate movement carried forward by individual or collective agents. In this respect, recent western philosophy has problematized or called into question such modernist assumptions. One of the prominent features of recent Continental thought---sometimes styled "post-modern" or "post-structuralist"---has been the effort to dislodge or "decenter" the linchpin of modern post-Cartesian philosophy: human subjectivity (or the *cogito*) together with subject-centered or anthropocentric forms of agency. Needless to say, this decentering move also casts its shadow, or a new light, on the meaning of liberation or emancipation (and by implication on the concept of "liberation theology"). For clearly, on the premises of a decentered subjectivity, one is compelled to ask or renew such questions as: in an emancipatory, perhaps even revolutionary, process, who or what is liberating or being liberated, and from what? On the same premises, does freedom become unintelligible or is it perhaps necessary to rethink its meaning and role?

As it happens, there are some succinct statements or guideposts on these issues in recent social-theoretical literature---statements toward which I can only gesture here in all brevity. In a broad overview easy on the status of "liberty" and "emancipation" in our time, the Dutch theorist, Jan Pieterse has emphasized the need to distinguish---without radically segregating---"modern" from "post-modern" treatments of the topic. In his presentation, the concepts have been bequeathed to us by the Enlightenment and its liberal offshoots, a tradition which construed "emancipation" basically as a linear process or movement, that is, as a humanly engineered exit from oppression into the "reign of freedom". This approach, Pieterse notes, is contested or at least complicated by recent Continental literature. While the "grand theme" of modernity, he writes, revolved around "human beings taking responsibility for their own destiny" and thus around the "conscious programming and production of society," post-modernism offers a critical postscript to this trajectory (without denying freedom as such). In still more poignant fashion, the issue of liberation/emancipation has been explored by Ernesto Laclau, with an accent on the quandaries besetting the modernist paradigm. In Laclau's portrayal, that paradigm was wedded to a number of dubious premises, including a binary metaphysics and the utopia of ultimate self-transparency. The contemporary challenge, in his view, is not to discard freedom or liberation but to reconceive them along loosely "post-modern" lines: by decentering sovereign autonomy and self-constituting agency.[1]

As it seems to me and as I intend to show, such new initiatives or reconceptualizations bear an affinity (but, of course, do not coincide) with understandings of freedom and liberation found in some non-western cultures, including non-western religious traditions. In fact, as stated before, many non-western religions are firmly anchored in freedom---though a freedom not construed in subject-centered or anthropocentric language. Parallels with post-modern initiatives can be found especially in the confines of recent discussions in Buddhism and Islam---discussions which are often silhouetted against the stark backdrop of western colonial domination or post-colonial hegemony. Given the vast panorama of Buddhist and Islamic literature and ideas, my approach has to be again quite selective. Basically, my endeavor is to explore recent understandings of freedom and liberation by focusing on a limited number of "new voices" in Buddhism and Islam---voices which, because of their intellectual verve and integrity, have gained widespread respect both inside and outside their respective religious communities.

I

The linkage between Buddhism and freedom is evident at a first glance---though a closer look reveals many difficulties and quandaries. As is well known, the central point of the four "noble truths" is freedom or liberation from suffering (*dukkha*), a suffering induced primarily by self-centeredness or selfish desire (*tanha*) as well as blind ignorance and delusion (*avidya*). In the teachings of the Buddha Sakhyamuni, the overcoming of suffering was articulated in detail as an "eight-fold path" of enlightenment and emancipation, a path pointing ultimately to a realm of freedom beyond desire (*nirvana*, *nibbana*). Given this traditional emphasis on emancipation, Buddhism seems to be well-equipped to provide inspiration for a liberation perspective---perhaps even liberation movements---in our time. Moreover, in light of the accent on self-emptying or self-deflation (*anatman*, *anatta*), this impulse seems to be relatively free of the modernist conundrums regarding anthropocentrism or a self-constituting agency (or subjectivity). On closer inspection, however, things are more complicated; in fact, the very denial of self-nature (*svabhava*) appears to obstruct any viable conception of concrete human liberation. For, one may ask: in the absence of self or self-nature, who or what would be the subject or agent of liberation? And on the same premises: who or what is going to be liberated in the process of enlightenment seen as an exit from delusion?

Questions like these, to be sure, are not new and have prodded Buddhist reflections for centuries. In fact, one can safely assert that Buddhist reflections on the topic provide some of the most innovative and stimulating contributions to contemporary liberation debates.[2] Nevertheless, practical considerations or concerns not infrequently override the task of theoretical elaboration. Under the impact of (post)colonial struggles and/or the pressure of modernizing agendas, many non-western societies in recent times have witnessed the emergence of Buddhist-inspired and Buddhist-led movements dedicated to the goal of social change and the removal of oppressive inequities. In their study on *Engaged Buddhism*, sub-titled *Buddhist Liberation Movements in Asia*, Christopher Queen and Sallie King have assembled impressive evidence testifying to a widespread stirring of social and political consciousness in Asian societies, a stirring which flatly contradicts Buddhism's reputation of social escapism or world-denial. A crucial ingredient of this upsurge is a redefinition of the traditional Buddhist notion of suffering (*dukkha*) and its overcoming: a redefinition which shifts attention to social and political causes of human suffering and the possibility of their correction or removal. In the words of Christopher Queen, it is precisely a "new awareness of the social and institutional dimensions of suffering and the liberation from suffering" which has provided fuel for the rise of contemporary Buddhist liberation movements.[3]

Yet, caution is indicated at this point. As Queen fully recognizes, the phenomenon of "Buddhist movements" investigated in the text does not merely affect Buddhist teachings in a marginal or tangential way. The idea of such movements, he acknowledges, amounts in fact to a "profound change in Buddhist soteriology," namely, a change from "a highly personal and other-worldly notion of liberation to a social, economic, this-worldly liberation". In its trail, this change implicates other traditional features of Buddhism, including the conceptions of "*karma*" and "rebirth", the veneration of the "*bhikkhu sangha*" (monastic community), and the focus on "ignorance and psychological attachment to account for suffering in the world". Under the auspices of the new movements, these traditional features have taken "second place" in favor of a concentration on "the institutional and political manifestations of greed, hatred, and delusion" and on "new organizational strategies for addressing war and injustice, poverty and intolerance."[4] The question which arises here concerns the Buddhist character of these movements. For clearly, if liberation movements become completely embroiled in "this-worldly" struggles and activities, what happens to the liberating transcendence of such embroilment? If Buddhist "engagement" means the wholehearted pursuit of worldly ends by any means, what happens to such traditional virtues as non-attachment, non-violence, and compassion?

To illustrate some of the issues involved in Buddhist modes of liberation, I turn now to two prominent intellectual initiatives, one taken from the context of Japanese Zen Buddhism, the other from the Theravada school in Thailand. Apart from being a major voice in Buddhist-Christian conversation during recent decades, the Japanese philosopher Masao Abe also has made important contributions both to the praxis and the theoretical clarification of "liberation" in the Buddhist context. On the level of praxis or practical engagement, Abe has been actively involved in a loosely structured lay movement called the "F.A.S. Society" (dedicated to the "awakening of the formless self" everywhere), a movement which had been initiated by one of his teachers, Hisamatsu Shin'ichi. As conceived by Shin'ichi, this lay movement was meant to transgress the traditional Zen focus on monastic practices and private-individual illumination in the direction of a concern for social transformation (on both the domestic and global levels); in order to promote this transformation, more concretely: the liberation of people from oppression and injustice, lay Buddhists had to be ready to serve as emancipatory agents---without, however, embracing the modernist premises of anthropocentrism or sovereign self-constitution. Faithful to central Buddhist teachings, Hisamatsu thus was led to champion liberation in a loosely "post-modern" sense, namely, by embracing the double gesture of affirmation and transcendence manifest in the liberating role of an unattached or "formless self" (that is, a self-liberating people both from oppression and self-delusion).[5]

On a more theoretical or philosophical plane, Abe has made significant strides toward the formulation of a liberating, yet not substantializing (or essentializing) agency. In an exchange with Christian and Jewish theologians, Abe developed the intriguing notion of an affirmative and dynamic *sunyata*, that is, of an emptiness that transcends or transmutes itself in the direction of a compassionate social engagement. As he noted at the time, *sunyata* cannot be conceived as a mere vacuum or pure negativity hovering outside plenary being, that is, as an antithesis standing "somewhere outside of or beyond one's self-existence". For, construed in this manner, emptiness quickly turns into a distinct, though negative entity or substance juxtaposed to the array of positive (ontic) substances. In the tradition of Mahayana Buddhism, efforts have always been made to guard against this substantializing danger. Abe perceives here a parallel between Mahayana Buddhism and strands in recent western philosophy. "Following Martin Heidegger," he writes, who put "a cross mark X" on the term "being" (*sein*), Buddhists are well advised to put a cross mark on *sunyata*, thereby highlighting its intrinsic ambivalence (without erasing it). Once this is done, *sunyata* can be perceived as being located neither inside nor outside of being or "self-existence", that is, as occupying a terrain which is "neither external nor internal, neither transcendent nor immanent". This insight, in turn, allows *sunyata* to be seen as a dynamic process of transformation, as a continual transgression of self-being toward (non-external) otherness.[6]

Viewed as a mode of dynamic-existential engagement, *sunyata* clearly has implications for human agency and its role in (social) liberation. Given the close entwinement of insight and outside, liberation for Abe cannot be confined to solitary enlightenment but must include struggle against (avoidable) social ills. At this point, self-awakening and enlightenment reveal their intimate connection with social service and the still broader arena of compassion (*karuna*) with all living beings. In Abe's words, *sunyata* properly understood harbors within itself a deep compassion in the light of which existing forms of oppression or domination can be "freely turned over" or at least alleviated. Invoking the classical doctrine of "dependent co-arising" (*pratitya-samutpada*), he interprets emptiness as a pathway not to solitary self-withdrawal but to an understanding of existential mutuality, that is, to the realization of "the sympathetic universality and the cosmic solidarity of *karma*". Regarding the notion of human agency (as a corollary of *karma*), Abe boldly proposes a "kenotic" rendering of human willing and acting---a reformulation which both preserves and transcends human initiative, namely, by embedding the latter in the framework of emptiness. According to Abe, the connection of willing and non-willing (or unwilling) forms the basis of the Buddhist "vow" or engagement in the world (*pranidhana*). At its core, this is the pledge "to save others, however innumerable they may be, as well as one's self," a pledge in which "the mind to seek enlightenment and the desire to save all sentient beings are dynamically one."[7]

In many ways, Abe's initiatives find a parallel in the context of Thai Buddhism, particularly in the life-work and teachings of Ajarn Buddhadasa, also known as Buddhadasa Bhikkhu. Like Abe, Buddhadasa has always insisted on the need to (re)connect theoretical insights with the domain of lived praxis. Reflecting this conviction, one of his central efforts has been to render Buddhism meaningful to ordinary people, an aim which put him at odds both with clerical monastic hierarchies and with ruling power structures and prevailing state ideologies. To further the goal of radical renewal, Buddhadasa in 1932 established a center (or rather a forest retreat) for the study and concrete practice of Buddhism, a center which came to be known as *Suan Mokkh* or "Garden of Liberation". It was at *Suan Mokkh* that Buddhadasa first articulated some of his more overtly social-political ideas, ideas which subsequently were promulgated on lecture tours throughout the country. Foremost among these ideas is the notion of a Buddhist or "Dhammic Socialism", a formula meant to stand in contrast both to western capitalism, with its celebration of private profit, and to Soviet communism, with its glorification of totalitarian state power. For Buddhadasa, "Dhammic Socialism" can be seen as a form of democracy----but a democracy respectful of the spiritual authority of *dhamma* (or *dharma*) and mindful of the continuous need of human self-transformation.[8]

In terms of religious-philosophical teachings, Buddhadasa recognizes the centrality in Buddhism of the four "noble truths" with their focus on suffering (*dukkha*) and its removal. As previously indicated, suffering is commonly traced to wanton desire and self-delusion. Deviating from traditional construals, Buddhadasa views desire as including both individual wantonness and the craving for social-political status, power or dominion---a craving which Buddhism is meant to cure. To this extent, the Buddhist striving for enlightenment and liberation from suffering extends from private life to the arena of social or "worldly" arrangements. Although trained in the Theravada tradition, Buddhadasa's thinking on liberation is quite flexible and freely embraces a number of Mahayana and Zen conceptions, including the notions of no-self-nature (*anatman* or *anatta*) and emptiness (*sunyata* or *sunnata*). As in Abe's case, emptiness here is not a static entity but carries dynamic transformative connotations: precisely by virtue of no-self-nature, individuals as well as societies can detach themselves from stifling habits or ingrained power structures and embark on the process of moral experimentation and liberating renewal. Again, like Abe, Buddhadasa recognizes the role of agency in this process, while giving it a Buddhist or *dhammic* cast. Although taken by itself agency is not properly liberating (but only *karma*-producing in a confining way), non-attached or self-transcending action can pave the road to genuine freedom (or *nibbana*). In this context, Buddhadasa also reformulates the concept of "dependent co-arising" (*paticca-samuppada* in its Pali version) by extricating it from a doctrinaire *karma*-wheel. Inserted into concrete social life, "co-arising" means that removal of oppression cannot occur through private self-withdrawal but only through cooperative struggle and reform (which is the heart of "Dhammic Socialism").[9]

II

Among the great world religions today, none seems less hospitable---at a first glance---to liberation than Islamic civilization. In fact, in the eyes of many observers, Islam is almost completely identified with a fanatical and "illiberal" kind of fundamentalism, that is, with a "totalizing" political agenda fueled by unexamined religious dogmas or beliefs. Despite tendencies in this direction, this identification is nevertheless mistaken or unfounded, at least when placed in a historical context. Although urging human "surrender" to God or the divine, Islam in its long history has never counseled blind surrender to the "powers that be"---whether these powers are wielded by clerical or political elites. On the contrary, precisely by differentiating between divine and merely "worldly" rule, Islamic thought has nurtured a suspicion of human power and its proclivity to unjust oppression---a suspicion which can be a motive for liberation. Both the suspicion and the motive are amply evident in the Qur'an, especially in suras 1 and 90. While the former exhorts people to pursue the path of justice or righteousness (*zirat al-mustaqim*), the second spells out the direction of this path, now called the path of the "steep ascent". What is this steep ascent? the Sura asks, and responds:

> To free a neck
> (from the burden of debt or slavery,
> Or to feed in times of famine
> The orphan near in relationship,
> or the poor in distress;
> And to be of these who believe,
> and call upon one another to persevere,
> and urge upon each other to be kind.[10]

Today, in the eyes of many observers, this legacy of Islamic liberty is under siege in many parts of the Muslim world. Due partly to global pressures and partly to internal-political restrictions, the spirit of liberating and enabling practice seems to be less prevalent than in the past. In the account of Annemarie Schimmel---certainly a sympathetic student of Islam---there is today a disturbing tendency of intellectual closure. "In a civilization whose traditional greeting is *salam* (peace)," she has stated, "we observe at the moment a great narrowing and stiffening of dogmatic and legalistic positions." Thus, in lieu of the search for spiritual enrichment and a closer union with the divine, "we are confronted in large areas with sheer power politics, with ideologies which utilize Islam more or less as a catchword, and have very little in common with its religious foundations."[11] Nevertheless, despite this troubling tendency, the potential of liberating faith (here Islamic faith) is by no means vanquished or extinguished today---although it is often sidelined or put on the defensive; as Schimmel would be the first to recognize, there are still important voices in contemporary Islam testifying to the continuing legacy of both religious and philosophical renewal. For present purposes I select two such voices: one from a Sunni context, the other from the context of Shiism. The first voice is that of Mohammed Arkoun, an Algerian expatriate living and teaching in Paris; the second is that of Ali Shari'ati, an Iranian opponent (and final victim) of the Shah's regime.

A professor of Islamic history and philosophy at the Sorbonne, Mohammed Arkoun is author of numerous books and essays on the contemporary significance of Islam. By all accounts, Arkoun is one of the most subtle and sophisticated interpreters both of Islam and of the present-day intellectual scene in the West. In his writings and lectures, Arkoun has placed himself in sharp opposition to clerical dogmatism and elitism, exhorting Muslim intellectuals to become active participants in debates concerning the present condition and future prospects of the evolving global village. At the same time, while adopting a "liberal" stance of open-mindedness, his writings have also been critical of certain routinely (or dogmatically) held liberal predilections, especially the predilections for an agnostic secularism and a market-centered politics. According to Robert Lee, one of his English translators, Arkoun's life-work has always addressed a question crucial to both Muslims and non-Muslims in the contemporary world: the question of the proper relation between self and other, or (differently put) of how people "can be thoroughly themselves without isolating themselves, by virtue of this identity, from their neighbors and the rest of humanity?" In wrestling with this question, Arkoun's thought is situated at the crossroads of (western) modernity and postmodernity, of tradition and renewal, and also of (philosophical or scientific) reason and faith. While challenging the presumed self-sufficiency of modern reason, he also refuses himself the comfort of a self-enclosed religious particularism. Rekindled as a partner in the conversation of humankind, Islam re-emerges here as a "liberal" or liberating faith—provided that (western) liberalism itself sheds its imperial or triumphalist aura.[12]

For English language readers, Arkoun's views are most readily accessible in a stimulating volume published under the title *Rethinking Islam: Common Questions, Uncommon Answers*. In his "Introduction" to this volume, Arkoun very lucidly profiles his general intellectual stance. As he points out, his basic aim has been, and continues to be, to "liberate" discourse on Islam from dogmatic limitations and contradictions, and especially from an approach that tends to "enclose and marginalize Islam in 'specificity', particularism, and singularities". Although largely ignored in the West, such a liberating impulse is by no means lacking in Islam. In fact, alongside the fundamentalist tendencies "so obligingly observed, reported, and echoed in the western media," there exists also a "liberal, critical Islam open to change, an Islam still little known and rarely taken into consideration". Venturing into this hidden Islam requires an effort to stir up frozen or congealed thought patterns; as Arkoun writes (in a phrasing vaguely reminiscent of Heidegger), it requires a retrieval of the "unthought" in traditional Islamic thought. Such retrieval, in turn, is predicated on an emancipatory premise; for, he adds, breaking new ground not only in Islam but in the three monotheistic religions depends on "the liberation of thought from all theories, dogmas, and imageries bestowed by the self-founding and self-proclaiming theologies of each community against its rivals". Reflecting on recent intellectual trends in the West, Arkoun sees the need and the opportunity to shift the understanding of Islam from the purely epistemic level---what Foucault called the "historico-transcendental theme"---to "the level of postmodern reason which has become critical of Enlightenment reasoning itself." As he remarks pointedly: "I believe Islam will not escape the upheavals of post-modernism."[13]

The implications of this emancipatory perspective are fleshed out in subsequent chapters of the volume (of which only brief glimpses can be offered here). For Arkoun, liberating faith---especially a socially and politically engaged faith---needs to be carefully distinguished from the vogue of "fundamentalism" marked by the indiscriminate fusion of religion and politics and the ultimate surrender of faith to power objectives. To highlight this issue, the volume differentiates between a properly religious of "mythical" discourse and a purely "ideological" discourse bent on instrumentalizing religion. As Arkoun notes, contemporary fundamentalist movements owe their partial success to the availability of impoverished and frustrated masses of people "still sensitive to Messianic promises and eschatological expectations". In enlisting these sentiments fundamentalist strategies tend to have corrosive and even "devastating effects" on religious faith: namely, by promoting "ideological" platforms which slyly substitute "unrealizable political programmes" for the "millenary, transhistorical hopes" of the past. This substitution was particularly evident in Khomeini's so-called "Islamic revolution" in Iran; here the confusion between "mythical religious discourse" and a "mobilizing, desanctifying ideological discourse" reached the greatest height of "mobilizational efficacy", while also spreading its destructive impact on the "semantic ordering of the community"

As opposed to ideological-fundamentalist mobilization, liberation for Arkoun must tap deeper religious resources located beyond, and even repressed by, sheer power politics. Here, the notion of reflective retrieval becomes crucial. In his words, "the *unthought* and the *unthinkable* in Islamic thought have been accumulating ever since ideologies of struggle for political liberation took over the *whole* of the social arena". What is needed to regain access to these repressed domains is a critical awareness capable of critiquing itself (in a kind of double gesture). In Arkoun's terms, we need to enter a new phase where critical thought—a thought "anchored in modernity but criticizing modernity itself and contributing to its enrichment through recourse to the Islamic example"—would "accompany, or even for once precede, political action, economic decisions, and great social movements."[14]

As these comments indicate, liberation in Arkoun's sense is at odds both with religious fundamentalism and an agnostic power politics, a politics often wedded to a dogmatically affirmed "secularism". Focusing on the latter issue, *Rethinking Islam* calls attention to the emergence of modern Turkey under the leadership of Atatürk. As will be recalled, Atatürk sought to enact a radical rupture with the past: by replacing the sultanate with the nation-state, the Arabic with the Latin alphabet, the turban and fez with the hat, and the *shari'a* with the Swiss legal code. In Arkoun's view, however, Atatürk's understanding of both Islam and western modernity was highly defective, and in fact reflected the "naïve state of consciousness" prevalent among Muslim intellectuals during the heyday of colonialism. The consciousness was naïve, he writes, "because these generations believed naïvely that it was enough to take the 'prescriptions' for the success of western civilization and apply them to Muslim countries". Among other nostrums and panaceas, secularism was then perceived as one of those "effective prescriptions" designed to cure backward societies of their religious traditions. Emulated later by many nation-builders in the Third World, Atatürk's "revolution" in effect installed an ideological elitism disdainful of sedimented symbols; for Arkoun, it signaled "the triumph of positivist, historicist reason, radically cut off from the mythic consciousness in which the great mass of believers, ulema and illiterate alike, continued to move". In its long-range repercussions, it opened a breach between revolutionary leaders and the masses they claimed to emancipate, a breach that severely "impaired the symbolic capital cultivated by the living tradition".

As one should note, Arkoun in this context distinguishes carefully between an "open-minded secular thought" and a dogmatic "secularism" and agnosticism. While the former can be valuable in preserving the integrity of both religion and politics, the latter is liable to yield indifference and even illiteracy regarding important well-springs of popular culture and belief. In Arkoun's words, it is "secularist thought" which, "on the pretext of neutrality," has eliminated from public schools all instruction in "the history of religions understood as a permanent and universal dimension of human societies". As a result, the general public has become "illiterate in all that touches religious life and expression" and thus been disabled to think about "myth, symbols, symbolic capital."[15]

In our time, the liberating potential of Islam has been articulated not only by expatriate scholars (like Arkoun), but also by Muslim intellectuals active in their homeland---where their work has often exposed them to political ostracism or persecution. A prominent case in point is the Iranian intellectual and sociologist Ali Shari'ati who lived and struggled---often from a prison cell---during the Shah's reign and who died in 1977 shortly before the Iranian revolution (presumably at the hand of the Shah's agents). Educated both in Iran and in Paris, Shari'ati was an astute observer and critic both of modern western and of traditional Muslim society and culture. Although appreciating the freedom of inquiry and individual initiative promoted by western modernity, he was appalled by, and fiercely attacked, the western propensity toward materialism, consumerism, and secularist anthropocentrism; at the same time he held no brief for clerical traditionalism, and certainly not for any kind of "fundamentalism" bent on exploiting religious beliefs for purely mundane objectives of political power. Against these diverse tendencies or temptations, Shari'ati invoked the liberating energies of a critically self-reflective Islamic faith—energies which, in his view, were alone able to move people and to effect genuine human and social transformation. In the words of one of his biographers, Shari'ati fought "on two fronts simultaneously". "He opposed the extreme traditionalists who had spun a web around themselves, separated Islam from society, retreated into a corner of the mosque and the madrasa, and often reacted negatively to any kind of intellectual movement within society." But he also challenged the "rootless and imitative intellectuals" who had made "the new scholasticism" their stronghold (where scholasticism means a combination of positivism, secularism, and materialism).[16]

For Shari'ati, genuine liberation can only proceed from spiritual or religious impulses—provided they are not corrupted for worldly aims. Among the major world religions, he finds the great virtue of monotheism precisely in its liberating or emancipatory élan. Whereas the founders of other religions almost immediately turned to secular power in the hope of propagating their message by means of that power, the story of monotheism runs differently: "All the prophets of the Abrahamic line," he asserts, "from Abraham down to the Prophet of Islam, proclaim their missions in the form of rebellion against the secular power." As Shari'ati realizes, even in monotheistic religions this liberating élan was subsequently subdued and muffled through policies of compromise and accommodation. Thus, in Judaism, the original message of Moses came under the spell of "rabbis and Pharisees" aligned with worldly elites, just as Christianity—after an initial period of persecution—succeeded to "the throne of the Roman Empire," thereby "perpetuating the imperial order". Even Islam, after a time of struggle, was reshaped later by imperialistic caliphates when it turned into a "rationale for the acts of the most savage conquerors" and a cloak for the "feudal order of the Saljuqs and Mongols". In Shari'ati's account, the basic reason for this decay or contamination is the transformation of religion from a path or highway into a fixed doctrine or destination. As he notes, religion is nothing but a path "laid down from clay to God," that is, the path of "an infinite migration" and inner transformation. Historically, all the ills afflicting religious societies arise from the fact that "religion has changed its spirit and direction" by becoming a destination rather than a path or road.[17]

Shari'ati's strongest affirmation of Islam as a liberating message (or a theology of liberation) occurs in an essay titled "The Philosophy of History: Cain and Abel". In Shari'ati's view, the story of Cain and Abel provides the key to a profound "philosophy of history," a history propelled by the conflict or confrontation of two opposing elements in the form of an evolving "dialectic". The drama begins with the killing of Abel by Cain—where Abel represents "the age of a pasture-based economy" and of "the primitive socialism that preceded ownership," whereas Cain represents "the system of agriculture and individual or monopoly ownership". Following this opening event, history evolved as a struggle involving economics, political power, as well as religion. In the initial event, Shari'ati notes, Abel the pastoralist was killed by Cain the landowner; with this murder, the period of "common ownership of the sources of production"—which was the age of pastoralism, hunting and fishing and also an age of "brotherhood and true faith"—came to an end and was replaced by the establishment of the system of private ownership "together with religious trickery and transgression against the rights of others". As he comments, in a quasi-Rousseauan vein, with the rise of agriculture and private ownership human and social life were "exposed to a profound revolution which, in my view, constitutes the greatest revolution in history". It was a revolution that "produced a new man, a powerful and evil man, as well as the age of civilization and discrimination."[18]

Over time, the revolution carried in its train a radical and far-reaching change in moral and religious attitudes. With the advent of property, the earlier ties of kinship were replaced by "bonds of servitude" while equality was sacrificed to discrimination and brotherhood to fratricide; likewise, the earlier spirit of "humanity, conciliatoriness, and compassion" gave way to the passions of "hatred, rivalry, oppression, and self-worship". Shari'ati perceives this change also as the upsurge of two different human personality types---with Abel as "the man of faith, peaceable and self-sacrificing" opposing Cain seen as "the worshipper of passions, the transgressor, the fratricide". The conflict of personalities is ascribed by Shari'ati not to a difference of "human nature," but rather to the difference of social and moral contexts. Abel was a man of "sound disposition" because an inhuman social and economic system had not yet "alienated, disfigured, perverted or polluted him"; though being of the same progeny, evil propensities were by contrast unleashed in Cain by "an anti-human social system, a class society, a regime of private ownership that cultivates slavery and mastery and turns men into wolves, foxes or sheep". During ensuing centuries, history testifies to the struggle between the descendants of Abel---those oppressed people who throughout history have been "slaughtered and enslaved" by power---and the "system of Cain" which has always been upheld by the ruling classes. Contrary to Marx's theory, this conflict involves not only a class struggle but a struggle of morals and religions. For Shari'ati, the crucial historical battle is not that between religion and irreligion or between knowledge and superstition but "the war of religion against religion." Here is a passage which ably captures Shari'ati's point:

> There has existed throughout human history, and there will continue to exist until the last day, a struggle between the religion of deceit, stupefaction and justification of the status quo and the religion of awareness, activism and revolution. The end of time will come when Cain dies and the "system of Abel" is established

> anew. That inevitable revolution will mean the end of the history of Cain; equality will be realized throughout the world, and human unity and brotherhood will be established through equity and justice.[19]

III

The preceding discussion has focused on a number of "new" or recent voices in Buddhism and Islam, voices bearing affinities (in many respects) with strands in western liberation theology. As I need to emphasize, focus on these voices was not meant to suggest that freedom and liberation are new inventions or discoveries in these contexts. On the contrary, as indicated, freedom in a soteriological sense has always been a cornerstone of these religious traditions. In the case of Buddhism, the notion of a universal Buddhahood (*tathagata-garbha*) has always stood as a challenge to traditional forms of caste and status hierarchies. This oppositional stance brought Buddhism into conflictual relation with the established practices of Hindu society on the subcontinent (no matter how compatible or incompatible these practices were with Vedic teachings). After the transplantation to Asia and especially to China, the same oppositional or non-conformist stance was a major motive in the successive waves of persecution suffered by Buddhism at the hands of ruling elites. In the Japanese context, critical or non-conformist attitudes can be found in at least some branches of the Nichiren school and some practices of traditional Zen Buddhism.[20]

In the case of Islam, students of history cannot fail to remember the story of the great Muslim mystic Husain ibn Mansur, better known as al-Hallaj, and his opposition to worldly power. Of modest Persian origins, al-Hallaj came to live and work in Baghdad which then was the seat of a sprawling empire under rule of Abbasid caliphs. Moving in the inner circles of public life, he experienced with growing dismay both the effects of political corruption and the growing ossification of religious faith at the hand of orthodox clerical elites. Adopting the stance of a prophetic critic, al-Hallaj challenged with increasing vehemence both governmental oppression and clerical dogmatism—a challenge for which he was finally executed or martyred (in 922 A.D.) on charges of heresy. Basically what heresy boiled down to in his case was his insistence on cutting through legalistic formulas in search of a more direct and intimate union with the divine. In the words of Herbert Mason which ably pinpoint the gist of the saint's outlook (in broadly postmodern language): "Clearly the Hallajan way implies a certain surrender of self, an expatriation of mind, an absorption with the life and spirit of another than oneself."[21]

In various forms, the heresy attributed to al-Hallaj has been embraced and practiced by sufi mystics and other followers of sufism down through the ages to our own day. In its insistence on a closer union between humans and the divine, coupled with the strengthening of inter-human brotherhood and sisterhood, Sufism's mode of religiosity also implies a liberation from the shackles of religious sectarianism, and hence an openness to inter-religious dialogue and understanding. This openness is amply illustrated by the ecumenical symbiosis of Muslim sufism and Hindu *bhakti* religiosity through the centuries. An outstanding example of this symbiosis is the famous weaver and "poet-saint" Kabir—whose "voice" I invoke as a concluding testimonial to the legacy of soteriological freedom. Although presumably (or possibly) of Muslim background, Kabir lost no time to alienate himself from the clerical Sunni establishment; and while living among Hindus in Benares, his lifestyle did not endear him to Brahmanic elites either. This alienation is clearly reflected in one of his poems where we read:

Hindus, Muslims—where did they come from?
    Who got them started down this road?
Search inside, search your heart and look:
    Who made heaven come to be?
Fool, now
    Throw away that book, and sing of Ram [God] alone.

The intended impact of Kabir's poetry is liberating or emancipatory---but not in a modernist or secularist sense; for liberation here works through and for faith. Here is one final poem:

> If caste was what the Creator had in mind,
> Why wasn't anyone born
> with Shiva's three-lined sign?
> If you're a Brahman,
> from a Brahman woman born,
> why didn't you come out some special way?
> And if you're a Muslim,
> from a Muslim woman born,
> why weren't you circumcised inside?
> Says Kabir: No one is lowly born.
> The only lowly ones are those
> who never talk of Ram.[22]

Notes

1. See Jan Nederveen Pieterse, "Emancipations, Modern and Post-modern" and Ernesto Laclau, "Beyond Emancipation," *Development and Change*, vol. 23 (1992), pp. 6-7, 19, 23-24, 121-123, 136-137. The latter essay is reprinted in Laclau, *Emancipation*(s) (London: Verso, 1996), pp. 1-19.
2. Compare in this context David Loy, "Freedom: A Buddhist Critique," *Journal of the Faculty of International Studies* (Bunkyo University), vol. 6 (1966), pp. 25-34.
3. Christopher S. Queen, "Introduction," in Queen and Sallie B. King, eds., *Engaged Buddhism: Buddhist Liberation Movements in Asia* (Albany, NY: SUNY Press, 1996), p. 10.
4. Queen, "Introduction," p. 10.
5. Regarding Hisamatsu's writings compare, e.g., *Zen and the Fine Arts* (Tokyo: Kodansha International, 1971); *Nothingness* (Kyoto: Association of Self-Awakening, 1957); "Postmodernist Manifesto,"

FAS Society Newsletter, No. 1 (1976), and "For the Postmodernist," *FAS Society Newsletter*, No. 2 (1977). For a general discussion of Hisamatsu and his relation to Masao Abe see Christopher Ives, *Zen Awakening and Society* (Honolulu: University of Hawaii Press, 1992), pp. 69-90.

6. Masao Abe, "Kenotic God and Dynamic Sunyata," in John B. Cobb, Jr., and Christopher Ives, eds., *The Emptying God: A Buddhist-Jewish-Christian Conversation* (Maryknoll, NY: Orbis Books, 1990), pp. 27-28.
7. The Emptying God, pp. 32, 50, 57-58.
8. For some of this background see Santikaro Bhikkhu, "Buddhadasa Bhikkhu: Life and Society through the Natural Eyes of Voidness," in Queen and King, eds., *Engaged Buddhism*, pp. 147-179. Regarding "Dhammic Socialism" Santikaro writes perceptively (p. 170): "Ajarn Buddhadasa seemed to try to accomplish two things here. First, he legitimated socialism as an issue and an approach appropriate to Buddhism, Thai culture, and the current situation. Socialism is not something to be shunned as western or foreign, for it can be found in Thailand's cultural and religious heritage. In fact, it is more appropriate for Thailand than the western forms (capitalism, consumerism, technocracy, etc.) currently being mimicked. Socialism as he understood it, would allow Thai society, as well as Asian culture as a whole, to preserve and further develop those elements of their heritage that are superior to what is being imported from the West. Finally, he argued for a more religious understanding of socialism, one based in Dhamma principles."
9. See Buddhadasa Bhikkhu, *What is Paticcasamuppada?* (Bangkok: Group for the Propagation of Excellent Way of Living, 1974). Buddhadasa has also been active in the Buddhist-Christian dialogue for several decades. Paralleling Abe's "kenotic" reading, he interprets the Christian sign of the cross as the simultaneous affirmation and crossing out of the "I." See his *Buddhadasa's View on Buddhism and Christianity* (Bangkok: Tianwaan Press, 1984). On the above points compare also Suwanna Satha-Anand, "Religious Movements in Contemporary Thailand: Buddhist Struggles for Modern Relevance," *Asian Survey*, vol. 30 (1990), pp. 395-408. In a concrete manner, Buddhadasa's teachings are continued today by the Spirit in Education Movement (SEM) in Thailand, and

especially by Sulak Sivaraksa, one of SEM's chief promoters and a key figure in the "International Network of Engaged Buddhists" (INEB). Among Sivaraksa's publications see *A Socially Engaged Buddhism* (Bangkok: Thai Inter-Religious Commission for Development, 1988); *Religion and Development* (3rd ed., Bangkok: Thai Inter-Religious Commission, 1987); *A Buddhist Vision for Renewing Society* (Bangkok: Thai Inter-Religious Commission, 1994); Sivaraksa, ed., *The Quest for a Just Society: The Legacy and Challenge of Buddhadasa Bhikkhu* (Bangkok: Thai Inter-Religious Commission, 1994). Compare also Donald K. Swearer, "Sulak Sivaraksa's Vision for Renewing Society," in Queen and King, eds., *Engaged Buddhism*, pp. 195-235.

10. Al-Qur'an: A Contemporary Translation, by Ahmed Ali (Princeton: Princeton University Press, 1984).
11. Annemarie Schimmel, "A Good Word is like a Good Tree" (speech delivered in October 1995 on the occasion of the bestowal of the German Book Trade's annual Peace Prize); reprinted in English translation in *JUST Commentary*, No. 21 (March 1996), p. 4. As she added (pp. 4-5): "The fundamentalists try to recruit followers from among the unemployed, rootless youth whom they supply with a few simple formulas to manipulate them easily. But such a politically misused Islam is something completely different from lived Islam; it is, as Tahe Ben Jalloun writes, a caricature of true Islam."
12. Robert D. Lee, "Foreword," in Mohammed Arkoun, *Rethinking Islam: Common Questions, Uncommon Answers*, trans. and ed. R. D. Lee (Boulder, CO: Westview Press, 1994), pp. viii-xi. In Lee's words (p. xi): "Arkoun follows contemporary analysts in suggesting that liberalism depends upon a religious tradition and not, as Mustafa Kemal (Atatürk) seems to have thought, upon a radical separation of politics and religion; he embraces liberalism on the condition that liberalism itself be reinterpreted."
13 Arkoun, *Rethinking Islam*, pp. 1-3. Arkoun is well aware that his "postmodern" reading of Islam will be resisted not only by traditional Islamicists but also by western modernists wedded to western supremacy (p. 4): "The West has not accepted the challenge---or even the objection—that arises from within its own culture; even in the midst of a generalized crisis such as that opened by the end of Marxist eschatology, western reason has

maintained its pressure on the rest of the world and its refusal to entertain forms of thought coming from the outside.... In this fashion the history of the hegemonic world rolls on, perpetuating a sovereignty over human beings that was once attributed to God, while secondary actors exhaust themselves in imitating, adapting, reproducing and confirming the productivity and insuperability of that world."

14. Arkoun, *Rethinking Islam*, 12-13. In Arkoun's presentation, the merge of faith and public power is not the invention of contemporary fundamentalism, but can be traced back in part to the classical age of Islamic civilization, the period of the Umayyad and Abbasid caliphates.
15. Arkoun, *Rethinking Islam*, pp. 20, 24-26.
16. See Gholam A. Tavassoli, "Introduction: Biobibliographical Sketch," in Ali Shari'ati, *On the Sociology of Islam*, trans. Hamid Algar (Berkeley: Mizan Press, 1979), pp. 20-21. Although committed to human liberation, Shari'ati questioned the modern western paradigm of liberation in both its liberal-capitalist and its orthodox Marxist forms. As he wrote at one point, modern humanism "which all post-Renaissance humanitarian intellectuals hoped would take over the task of human liberation from religion," has in fact become a scholastic doctrine, a "sacred article of faith for all the atheistic schools of recent centuries." See Shari'ati, "Humanity Between Marxism and Religion," in *Marxism and Other Western Fallacies: An Islamic Critique*, trans. R. Campbell (Berkeley: Mizan Press, 1980), p. 91.
17. See Shari'ati, *On the Sociology of Islam*, pp. 66-67 ("Approaches to the Understanding of Islam"), pp. 93-94 ("Anthropology: The Creation of Man"); also *Marxism and Other Western Fallacies*, pp. 37-38 ("Modern Calamities").
18. "The Philosophy of History: Cain and Abel," in *On the Sociology of Islam*, pp. 98-99. While emphasizing the role of the ownership of the means of production, Shari'ati disagrees with Marx on the precise sequence of events. In effect, he says (p. 100), "the exact opposite of Marx's theory applies: it is not ownership that is a factor in the acquisition of power, but the converse. Power and coercion were the factor that first bestowed ownership on the individual."
19. *On the Sociology of Islam*, pp. 102, 106-109. In Iran today, Shari'ati's legacy is ably continued and further deepened by

Abdol Karim Soroush, a philosopher trained both in Iran and England. An opponent of the Shah's regime before the revolution, Soroush in recent years has emerged as a highly articulate defender of a "liberal," open-minded Islam and a trenchant critic of the Iranian clerical establishment—a stance which has made him the target of repeated abuse and persecution.

20. The above comments are implicitly at variance with recent arguments advanced by some Japanese writers to the effect that "buddha-nature" is inherently discriminatory and that Zen is not a genuine form of Buddhism. See Jamie Hubbard and Paul L. Swanson, eds., *Pruning the Bodhi Tree: The Storm over Critical Buddhism* (Honolulu: University of Hawaii Press, 1997).
21. Herbert Mason, *The Death of al-Hallaj: A Dramatic Narrative* (Notre Dame, IN: University of Notre Dame Press, 1979), pp. xiv, xix.
22. See John Stratton Hawley and Mark Juergensmeyer, eds., *Songs of the Saints of India* (New York: Oxford University Press, 1988), pp. 52, 54. Compare also *Songs of Kabir from the Adi Granth*, trans. Nirmal Dass (Albany, NY: SUNY Press, 1991); Muhammad Hedayetullah, *Kabir: The Apostle of Hindu-Muslim Unity* (Delhi: Motilal Banarsidass, 1989).

Chapter Six

Culture and Development: Lessons from Swadhyaya

Ramashray Roy

I

For more than four decades now, discontent with the dominant paradigm of development has been voiced all around the world. Strenuous search for solutions to its deficiencies is on for sometime now. The main complaint against this model of development is its primary, if not exclusive, emphasis on escalating economic betterment. Technologically induced and sustained economic growth is sine qua non for it, but it causes personal, social and ecological problems. Production and productivity that once used to be the synonym of the assertion of individual autonomy and efficacy have now given way to commodity fetishism in the non-Marxian sense with all its ill effects. What is more, its promise to establish a paradise on this earth has turned sour and has dotted this troubled planet with black holes of deprivation and destitution. Inequality, exploitation and oppression, both within and across nations, have not only persisted but also become more widespread, wicked and injurious.

Economism has induced and exacerbated mal-development. It has led to violation of human dignity, autonomy, and rights. More importantly, it has played havoc with cultural heritage of different peoples submerging it into the vile sea of homogenization. As a reaction to this and in order to cure development of its ills, it was hoped that tagging it with the preservation and promotion of such values as human dignity, individual autonomy and human rights would rid it of distortions. However, for various reasons, even this has failed in stemming the tide of mal-development and promoting benign development. This shift in position was doomed from the very beginning insofar as the reignant model of development does not respect or obey any externally imposed values except those that are organically ingrained in it.

The unworkability of this shift has now made it imperative to introduce another modification. This would, it is hoped, bring culture and development together and make them work together to stop the decimation of cultures of different peoples. Culture would, then, exert its benign influence on development which, in turn, would enrich culture. No doubt, this is a subject worthy of serious consideration and concerted pursuit. The World Decade for Cultural Development of the United Nations and the UNESCO is the recognition of this approach. This is also the recognition that different cultures should be preserved and promoted not only because they are unique expressions of particular societies but also because they belong to the whole mankind. However, the important question is: Will this coupling work?

To satisfactorily answer this question, we must raise and answer other questions. What, for example, does the term "culture" signify? And, for that matter, what is understood by development itself? There is yet a third question that needs to be explored. Also, what does the coupling of culture and development concretely mean? Insofar as this coupling signifies some kind of relationship, the form and content of this relationship have to be specified and elaborated. Broadly speaking, two kinds of relationship between culture and development can be envisaged. One kind of relationship subsumes development to be the dominant element which shapes the form and content of culture and uses it as a resource for clearing the path of its own onward movement. In this perspective, culture is not immutable; it does not belong to a realm which, if it is not transcendental, is, at least, trans-individual. Culture is some thing that is subject to laws governing the process of genesis, growth and decay of human civilization. As a product of the process of the self-making of man, culture is changeable and transient. On this view, the relationship between culture and development can, for the sake of convenience, be envisaged as "culture at the service of development".

In contradistinction to this, there is entirely a different perspective on culture. In this perspective, culture, even as a human artifact, acquires a trans-individual character and attains the authority of prescribing human goals and regulating the use of means for realizing these goals. In this sense, culture, even while subject to the laws of growth and decay, rises above the vicissitudes of the phenomenal world and becomes a reliable means of coping with these vicissitudes. As a prescriptive and regulative force, it determines what development should mean and how it should be implemented. In this sense, it is culture that determines the form and substance of development. It is in this sense, too, that development becomes subservient to culture. This would be an instance of "development at the service of culture".

In view of this, it is necessary to specify the relationship that is visualized between culture and development. What follows is an attempt to elucidate this relationship by exploring, first, the meaning of the reignant model of development and the role of culture in it. The discussion, then, moves on to examining an alternative formulation of the relationship between culture and development. And, finally, a concrete example of development governed by indigeneous traditional cultural values is discussed in order to demonstrate the workability of this mode of development.

II

The birth of the dominant paradigm of development took place almost three centuries ago, although it emerged in its full force only after the Second World War when the United States rose on the world scene as a colossus to save the mankind from the red menace. The panacea it offered was Fordism projected on the world as global Keynesianism, that is, a system of mass production and mass consumption by relatively well paid industrial workers in order to achieve a non-inflationary Keynesian virtuous cycle ensuring prosperity, banishing austerity and minimizing governmental intervention. The war ravaged and war-weary Europe and the expectant peoples of the Third World were ready to accept and use it for coping with their own respective economic and other ills. It is true that it was in the interest of the United States to globalize Fordism.[1] But, then, what was good for the United States was good for the world, it was persuasively argued.

The infant out of which the giant Fordism grew over time was in Hobbes' apt phrase "the search for felicity", that is, the quest of happiness through satisfying one desire after another.[2] This was the resting place man found after he cut himself off from the larger cosmic order of which he was an integral part and jettisoned the extra baggage of a higher life purpose distinct from the fulfilment of ordinary life needs in the process of production and reproduction.[3] The pursuit of felicity is the natural outcome of the disenchantment of the world in which, as Max Weber argues, the meaningfulness of a meaningful cosmos centres around interest, particularly material interest.[4] The ground of the meaningful cosmos is, Weber insists, rationalization, the capacity to control the world through calculation.

The pursuit of felicity in the sense of satisfying one desire after another entails the rise of what Taylor calls the self-defining subject who derives his purposes from his own nature. To derive purposes from one's own nature, in essence, entails the assertion of autonomy from the external world—social institutions, traditions, customs, etc.—and the exercise of self-determination. As Taylor points out, "nature" becomes internalized in the modern period. On this view, the free subject becomes someone who follows an internal purpose and who owes to *apriori* allegiance to a pre-existing order but only to structure that one has created by one's consent.[5] The prominence of self-determination in modern times signifies not only the crucial importance of equality both as a value relevant for the status of the autonomous individual and as a defining property of social order and the consequent break down of a hierarchical society. It also signifies the central role of efficacy in supporting and sustaining the status of the self-defining subject.

To lack the capacity to realize self-determined purposes is to nullify the status of the individual as a free subject. That is why efficacy of man as *homo economicus* is a factor that is highly valued in modern times. Efficacy in this respect signifies essentially two things. First, since the pursuit of felicity involves basically the fulfilment of material needs---of wealth, power and prestige not only the access to material goods and services has to be ensured but also their quantum must be progressively increased. This means transformation and/or manipulation of nature in order to force her to yield her hidden treasures. Second, efficacy also signifies the central importance of reason in the realization of individual purposes. What is striking about persons in modern times is, as Taylor suggests, their ability to conceive different possibilities, to calculate how to get them. To choose between them and thus to plan their lives. The striking superiority of man is in strategic power. The various capacities definitive of a person are understood in terms of his power to plan.[6] This means, as Taylor suggests, higher control over oneself besides nature in terms of meeting ordinary life needs in "a sober, disciplined, clairvoyant, and rational way."[7] Two things become essential for enjoying, coaxing or coercing nature to spill its treasures. First, man's attitude towards nature must change; instead of nature being significant in its own right, it must be seen as simply a concourse of casual interactions. Second, proper and adequate means must be developed to transform/manipulate nature. The former became possible when the rejection of the notion of intelligible essence led Galileo to treat the universe as composed only of isolated physical bodies, destitute of life, altogether a dead matter. Also, the rejection at his hand of the organicity of the body, led him to view both human body and nature as a bundle of mass and motion inscribed in the language of mathematics. Initiating a scientific trend that took "soul" out of both man and nature, Galileo provided for "the frame for a depersonalized world picture within which mechanical activities and interests took precedence over more human concerns..."[8]

With this, science and technology were freed from their subjugation to philosophy and morality. They took rapid and astonishing strides and cleared the way for the unrestrained transformation and manipulation of nature. In the dynamic interaction between man's needs and technological advancements not only did man's needs proliferate but also the way for technologically induced economic growth with emphasis on bigness was paved. Insofar as reason is concerned, it signifies only prudential, calculative reasoning joining ends and means. Reason, in this perspective, is defined less in terms of a vision of true order of things or an integral part of the soul enabling man to transcend the contingencies of his own particular existence; it is defined more in terms of instrumental reasoning that seeks the satisfaction of ordinary life needs in an effective way. However, the assumption of the pursuit of these needs under rational control was thrown to the dogs when Romanticism emphasized the fulfilling of true impulse of nature as not simply meeting a biological need but also the satisfaction of a higher aspiration, a moral fulfilment.

With this infusion of what Taylor calls the expressivism perspective, "the life according to nature involves a fusion of the biological and the moral instead of their hierarchical ordering as with traditional moralities, or their setting in a relation of rational control..."[9] This fusion as well as the technological advances has been instrumental in making needs endless in two important senses. They get detached from the pursuit of a higher life purpose and become their own ends and they proliferate endlessly.[10] However, the satisfaction of endless needs has, from Vico to Marx through Hegel, been treated as the ground not only of personality development in the sense of actualization of potentialities, but also of social evolution and civilizational progress.[11] It is in this process that the individual, it is claimed, acquires distinctive personality, involving the creative use of man's faculties in transforming nature, creating institutions as well as the development of faculties themselves and in the process, changing human nature itself. It is no wonder, then, that Lord Keynes observes that "economic development is the possibility of development."[12]

The conjunctions of all these factors have meant a very strong emphasis on accumulation, production and consumption. But achievement in this sense is not just a matter of meeting quantitative targets. More importantly, it is significant in a psychological sense as an important prop to the modern identity of man. To quote Taylor:

> Increasing production originally became a value in our civilization, against all the temptations to sloth and all the blandishments of traditional ethics because in producing we came to see ourselves as not just meeting our needs but also as realizing our status as autonomous, rational agents. Continued accumulation bespoke a consistent, disciplined maintenance of the instrumental stance to things; it was a realization of our spiritual dimension. Far from being an obsession with things, an entrapment in them, as it might be stigmatized on a Platonic conception, it is an affirmation of our autonomy in that our purposes are not imposed on us by the supposed order of things. The instrumental stance towards nature is meant to be a spiritual declaration of independence from it.[13]

It is evident from the discussion above that the dominant paradigm of development is rooted in a worldview that considers man simply as a bundle of desires which must be satisfied if individual felicity, social well-being and civilizational progress are to be assured. For this, man is supposed to be endowed with immense capacities to create the conditions of his own living modifying and changing the external world in the process. The modification of the external world on the scale we have been witnessing for decades now would not be at all possible if man did not adopt an instrumental stance towards it, stand outside it, and become, in essence, disengaged. The rise of subjectivity both as the ground of knowledge construction as well as apprehending and dealing with the world is another characteristic of the modern times. It is a natural attribute of the self as what Robert C. Soloman calls the "transcendental ego" or "transcendental pretence".[14] Since the self as "transcendental ego" is the resident not of the realm of actuality but of possibility,[15] its true nature can develop and take a definite shape only in history and by removing all limits and constraints. Since virtue now consists in the satisfaction of ever-prohibiting desires, all limits on time and space must be lifted or abolished. Abolition of limits is a drive towards bigness engendered by science and technology themselves in so far as underlying them is the common belief that "there are no desirable limits to the increase of knowledge, of material goods of environmental control, that quantitative productivity is as end in itself, and that every means should be used to further expansion"[16]

The reality of limitless needs and the assumption of limitless powers of man have certain disastrous consequences for man and his relationship with the external world. First, it has led to a strange combination of masochism and what Richard Sennett calls, "narcissistic vision" on the external world.[17] Since the satisfaction of desires is central in human existence, every one must try to get a privileged access to social resources. However, in the absence of any substantive criterion of contentment,[18] the individual is unable to decide what desires to satisfy and when and where to stop in satisfying decision. As a result, "life-corroding competition" for scarce societal resources, as Gandhi calls it, pervades social relations. In a condition of perpetual scarcity made operative not only by escalating needs but also by physical and social limits to growth[19] as well as by unequal distribution of resources, the tendency towards self aggrandizement takes roots and becomes stronger. And since individual purpose can be realized only through the exploitation of the external world---both society and nature---the individual comes to think of them merely as something that exists to fulfil the self. This tendency is further reinforced because of the erosion of what Theodore Lowi calls "autocontrol"[20] and progressive attention to external controls and with the sharpening of individualistic perspective, the world becomes what Sennet calls "a peculiar mirror of the self". As he notes:[21]

> It exists to fulfil the self, there are no "human objects" or object relations with a reality all their own. The peculiarity, and the destructiveness, of the narcissistic vision is that the more the environment of the human being is judged in terms of its congruence with or subservience to self needs, the less fulfilling it becomes at once so vast and amorphous, the possibilities of fulfilment are distinguished.[22]

The paradigm of development sketched above no doubt generated wealth and raised the level of living all over the world. However, it has also brought havocs: alienation, social unrest and conflict, severe loss of traditional indigeneous knowledge, erosion of different cultures, ecological degeneration, and many others. What is most distressing is that it has reinforced those structures and tendencies that it had promised to weaken and neutralize, if not completely abolish. It has increased inequality, deepened exploitation and institutionalized oppression. The hope that these malign features of the reignant model of development would be controlled, if not completely eradicated, by yoking it in the service of individual autonomy and human rights is futile since both of them are integral components of the dominant paradigm of development. As such, these are also responsible, if not wholly then assuredly partially, for maldevelopment. If this is so, can the intermeshing of culture and development be expected to put development on a proper keel?

Undoubtedly cultures of different peoples must be protected against incursions and erosions from outside. But, the coupling of culture and development signifies something more. This "something more" cannot be those cultural properties that sanction and support those values, structures and processes that militate against the spirit of development we prefer. Of course, one can think of weeding out those components of culture that do not conform or are antithetical to the model of development of our preference. This may, however, prove a case of treatment worse than the disease. If we attribute organicity and wholeness to culture, it is, then, difficult to separate favourable and unfavourable properties and successfully weed the latter even if we are able to identify and separate them. And, if we deny organicity to culture and treat it as a human artifact that comes into being, grow and then decline or pass out in the process of the self-making of man, we are, then, referring to a situation which was earlier characterized as "culture at the service of development".

Perhaps it is expected that since culture pertains to the realm of values, values that enter into the structuration of attitude and the regulation of behaviour, the intermeshing of culture and development will enable the individual to exercise self-restraint in need satisfaction and resource utilization. Or, alternatively, it will train individuals to judge the merit of their own actions in the light of the consideration of the good of others. Needless to say that these are the two sides of the same coin. However, to expect culture to play these beneficial roles is to visualize it as qualitatively radically different from the one the reignant model of development creates, sustains and reinforces. Today, culture means a ceaseless search for novelty and is equated with entertainment rather than enlightenment. That is to say, culture has, for all practical purposes, lost, its intellectual, chiefly educational, vaguely perfective and, above all, the evaluative significance. This was what the classical humanistic version of culture signified.[23]

With the waning of the classical tradition, culture took on the overtones of historicity and materiality.[24] It came to be treated as an artifact, the creation of human will, and subject to change influenced, on the one hand, by the change in the way of looking at things and, on the other, with particular stages of social evolution. This paved the way for treating culture not as a personal, but a collective, trait. It is no wonder, then, that culture came to be identified with civilization. That is why Tylor defines culture as "that complex whole which includes knowledge, belief, art, morals, law, customs and any other capabilities and habits acquired by man as a member of society."[25] The equivalence of culture with civilization denotes a progressive quality of both the material and the moral states of mankind as a whole. As equivalent to civilization, culture acquired a singularity assuming the universality of human nature. This is, as Solomon shows, the outgrowth of the self as the "transcendental ego".

The transcendental pretence is the unwarranted assumption that there is universality and necessity in the fundamental modes of human experience. It is not mere provincialism, that is, the ignorance or lack of appreciation of alternative culture and states of mind. It is an aggressive and sometimes arrogant effort to prove that there are no such (valid) possible alternatives. In its application the transcendental pretence becomes a priori assertion that the structures of one's own mind, culture, and personality are in some sense necessary and universal for all.

It can be argued that the modifications that Herder introduced in the conception of culture can very well take care of adverse cultural ramifications of the transcendental pretence. It is quite true that Herder gave culture a new connotation which initiated the search for the typical but unique in history by emphasizing the variety rather than the uniformity of human nature.[26] With it culture lost its singularity and became plural; it came to be considered as an integrated whole, a Gestalt, instead of being hierarchically ordered. As such, culture as *Volksgeist* is animated and shaped by a central tendency of growth, a *telos*. In this sense, culture refers to a particular pattern of life, with a focus on specific meaningful historical products rather than on general capabilities. In this perspective, culture, since it is now a collective trait, sheds off its individualistic attribute; it emerges as "collective instead of personal, expressive and empirically given instead of ideal normative."[27]

Despite some basic differences between the two versions of culture, it must be noted that the development of culture in both the senses is inextricably linked with the process of self-making of man. This means that it is man's interaction with nature for need satisfaction that imprints on culture distinct characteristics.[28] The revolutionary advances in the instruments of production bring about changes in relations of production and, along with them, in social relations and institutional arrangements. In this perspective, culture ever evolves; its particular stages signify the nature and the level of historical evolution denoting a structurally interrelated whole unified by some inner principle. And since this inner principle may undergo change, sometimes a radical change, from one age to the next there may usually be a succession of fundamentally different possibly unified cultures. Even while cultures may be varied and plural, they do not escape the over all homogenizing influence of industrial civilization. The universalization of values encompassed by industrialism leads Gellner to observe that "genuine cultural pluralism ceases to be viable under current conditions."[29] He argues that "the industrial order requires homogeneity within political units at least sufficient to permit fairly smooth mobility, and precluding the 'ethnic' identification of either advantage or disadvantage, economic or political."[30] For him, there are three crucial factors that impinge on the making of modern society: (i) centralized control with a distinction between power holders and the rest; (ii) pervasive high culture (having standardized; literacy and education-based systems of communication; and (iii) identity (as opposed to diversity) of culture.[31] All these factors lead to cultural homogenization promoting and institutionalizing everywhere similar ways of looking at things.

This homogenization process is what Toffler calls "the bursting of boundaries,"[32] and the growing interpenetration and interdependence in the world today. Also noteworthy is that modern culture enjoys, as Bell points out, "the extraordinary freedom to ransack the world store house and engage any and every style it comes upon. And in its search, there is denial of any limits or boundaries to experience. It is a reaching out for the experience; nothing is forbidden, all is to be explored,"[33] and, perhaps, assimilated. One need not stress the fact that it is symptomatic of the tendency to lift all limits in the sphere of culture as in other spheres of life. The increased interaction and the breaking down of traditional societies have supposedly paved the way for syncretism, the mingling and cohabitation of strange gods. Thus, even traditionally distinct cultures are losing their distinctiveness and are becoming more and more alike as homogenization proceeds unabated.

Culture has, thus, come to denote, in modern times, simply an ensemble of human capabilities that man develops in the process of interacting and dealing with the external world, the world of objects and object relations. Whether culture symbolizes "the cosmos of civilization" or the cosmos of *Volksgeist*, culture is a domain where man, no longer a discoverer of truth or of values, indulges in religion, philosophy and art. It is true that by this transmutation, culture has come to symbolize the victory of sensibility over social conventions and contrivances.

However, by achieving this victory, it lost its authority. It is no longer concerned with or responsible for setting norms and affirming a moral and philosophical tradition against which action could be measured and, if necessary, censured.

If this analysis has any validity, how can it be expected from culture, whether that which pretends to be universal or that which is supposed to be indigeneous and particularistic, and therefore parochial, to play the role of the saviour of development. The former cannot play this role because it represents a problem to be solved, not a panacea to be adopted. The latter is also an unfit candidate for this role inasmuch as it has itself incorporated some of the key elements of the universal culture. We are, therefore, back again to the need of reformulating conceptions of both culture and development and rethinking the relationship between them.

III

If the goal as well as the course of development is to be influenced, if not completely determined, it is obvious, then that the substantive concerns of development must be closely scrutinised and changed, if necessary. It is true that that the dominant paradigm of development has evoked a lot of discontents and stimulated a plethora of suggestions to remove the constraints that handicap development in its career. The removal of constraints is usually understood in terms of changing its socio-political environment. For example, as Hettne puts it: "Development to my mind necessarily involved structural transformation which implies political, social and economic changes."[34] The implication of this perspective is clear: there is nothing wrong with the concept of development as such; what distort it are certain external factors related with socio-economic and political dimensions of man's existence that are either totally inappropriate for or deeply distortive of development.

But when attention is focused on the externalities of development, i.e., the environment in which it has to occur, it is assumed that there is nothing wrong with the idea of life according to nature. What matters are the consequences of individual actions undertaken in an uncoordinated way for realizing given purposes. These purposes cannot be judged either at the bar of reason or anywhere else. However, these actions, in their concatenation, assume certain structures and initiate certain processes which, in many cases, distort or derail development. That is why occasional structural transformations are required to keep development on its feet. Obviously, structural transformations pertain to the public realm of social order, its institutional structure, to be more precise, which needs to be fashioned and refashioned so that it can prove a better instrument of serving man's purposes. This structure is accepted and respected not for what it expresses, but for what it gets or can get done. Thus, the social institutional arrangement is treated, in this perspective, as a neutral, objectified domain, to be organized and reorganized for maximum effect. The institutional structure is man-made; it is there to serve man's purposes. If it fails to do so, it must be altered or replaced by a new structure.[35]

Such a perspective, it need not be stressed shifts attention from what man is or should be and focuses on the consequences of what he does. As a result, it becomes difficult not only to articulate what development must mean but also to overcome the unwanted and adverse consequences of what man does. *The point of departure for a fresh thinking on development is man himself.* It is not to deny that the dominant paradigm of development lacks any conception of what man is or should be. It is only to stress that the conception of man it celebrates is too lopsided and incomplete and therefore unacceptable. It projects, in Murdoch's words, "a broken totality,"[36] signifying not only a split between reason and sentiments. It also signifies repression or rejection of the claim of the spirit and the installation of what Gandhi calls "bodily comfort" as the pivot of human existence. The import of the "broken totality" is that we know man is valuable but why he is, is not clear. As a result, the Renaissance focus on individuality and the dignity of man and the Enlightenment emphasis on human freedom and self-expression remain attractive but prove unattainable.

The reasons for this unattainability can be traced to the conception of the self as "transcendental ego" or "transcendental pretence". It is this conception that is at the root of "broken totality" which is sought to be mended with the help of commodity fetishism. Since felicity of the transcendent ego cannot be ensured without privileged access to material and social resources, the endeavour to ensure access to resources makes man, as Wood argues,[37] an externalized creature. Man becomes, in essence, then, only a receptacle of interests. By this same token, it is also symptomatic of the inner split between spirit, reason, and sensibility. The split elevates reason to the status of a monarch, to be sure. However, it is like that monarch who can play only a puppet to his subjects[38] because it has neither the authority to pass judgement on the merits of individual desires nor the power to punish if they seem to be whimsical or capricious. As such, reason is unable to provide any standards for discriminating between desires. Nor can the idea of felicity do so, because, in the lack of a substantive criterion to order desires, felicity remains an elusive but very tantalizing goal and when coupled with calculative, prudential reasoning, the pursuit of felicity makes life a desert where only the cacti of alienation flourish.

This interior split has its external counterpart. This takes two concrete forms: separation between man and man and that between man and nature. Given the acute scarcity of resources and given the prime importance of privileged access to societal resources, the life-corroding competition pits individuals and groups against each other.[39] The economic system is avowedly designed to meet demands for goods and services. However, additions to the material goods that can be expanded for all does, in itself, increase the scramble for those goods and services that cannot be so expanded. And, as Hirsch observes, taking part in this scramble is fully rational for any individual. But, he never confronts in his actions "the distinction between what is available as a result of getting ahead of others and what is available from a general advance shared by all".

This introduces a mismatch between private and public morality. Competition among isolated individuals in the free market leads to a situation where the edifice of society—the obligations and cooperation as a basis of social order—collapses. This creates a situation where the possibility of war of each against all is ever-present. It is this situation to which Rousseau refers to when he observes: "...what must be the state of things when all men are forced to care and destroy one another at the same time; and when they are both enemies by duty, and knaves by interest."[40] Again, this situation is responsible not only for eroding the distinction between good and right but also for generating conflict between what is good for the individual and what is right for the collectivity. It is, again, this situation that is responsible for the split between man and nature paving the way for increasing transformation/manipulation of the latter by the former.

What is most perturbing about this situation is that while it eviscerates internal control and relies on external control to keep man on the path of virtue, it makes these controls extremely ineffective. The modern state, even while it was installed to keep under control the adverse consequences of man's endeavour to satisfy private passions, faces a dilemma in resolving the conflict between freedom and order that the dominant paradigm of development generates. If it does not curb individual freedom, it threatens order; if it does attempt to curb it, the likelihood of striking at the very root of those factors that give the system its dynamism is accentuated. If the state is unable to reconcile the interest of the individual with the good of the collectivity and ensure compatibility between the pursuit of happiness by one person and by other persons, the rule of law, too, proves to be ineffective and therefore incompetent. The rule of law signifies today not any substantive vision of society but simply a procedure of making and implementing public decisions. As such, the rule of law is itself involved in the power game of politics. Also, the factors that necessitated rules and their coercive enforcement also explain the fascination for terror and violence unlimited by law as a device of social organization. As Unger argues: "The less one's ability to rely on participation in common ends, the greater the importance of force as a bond among individuals. Punishment and terror take the place of community. Moreover, when they view everything in the social world as a creation of the will, men come to believe that there is nothing in society that will sufficiently violent cannot preserve or destroy."[41]

In view of the incompetence of external controls in keeping man on a straight path, it is necessary to restore auto control as an antidote to transcendental pretence. This requires to jettison the Cartesian concept of man as "a body mind complex" and go back to the traditional notion which treats man as incomplete without the soul as the sensorium of divine. It is this soul that, both in the Platonic and the traditional Indian perspectives, constitute the master principle that can install order in man's interior. When attuned to the divine ground of being, the soul develops the capacity to resist attempts by passions to rule over it and to become the ground of order in the psyche. This attunement transfers the individual being with diverse faculties tending to work at cross purposes into an ordered being, it becomes a kind of corporation in which the several members of community work together each in its own way, and such a vocational society is an organism, not an aggregate of competing interests and consequently unstable "balance of power".[42]

The ordering of the psyche through the attainment of the soul to the divine ground of being also constitutes the ground of ordering society. Once internal transformation takes place, outward forms automatically change. What, according to Gandhi, is therefore necessary is "...a radical change more in inward spirit than in the outward form. If the first remains unchanged, the second, no matter how radically changed, will be like a whited sepulore."[43]

But this inward change as a consequence of the soul's attunement does not automatically translate itself into principles that should govern the ordering and the conduct of pragmatic affairs of life. Attunement provides only an insight into the truth of order; it does not provide a ready made blue-print for ordering society, it only provides tentative guidelines for ordering pragmatic affairs of life.[44] These guidelines are by no means something that can be taken hold of and possessed like things, they only determine the direction in which the self must develop. It is in the process of development that certain dispositions and attitudes take shape. The disposition, for example, to treat others as distinct but not different, the awareness of a shareable commonality (the Heraclitan *xynon*), and the perception of the need to respect the integrity of others (non-violence), it is these that constitutes the rock bed of right-mindedness and like-mindedness.

The development of the self on these lines yields no general principles (in the Kantian sense) of yea and nay but trains the mind to decide what would be worthdoing in a particular situation. This is what *sanskriti*, a conjunction of *samyaka* (proper) and *kriti* (action), the equivalent of culture in Indian tradition, signifies. It is as the ground of determining right and wrong course of action that culture assumes prescriptive and regulative authority. It is, again, in this sense that culture determines the substance and direction of development. In this perspective, development is yoked in the service of culture.

IV

That the perspective on culture sketched above is neither utopian nor anachrionistic is well illustrated by the Swadhyaya movement in India now in operation for more than four decades.

It is also very active in Gulf states, some pockets of Africa, England, the USA and Canada. In social terms, its adherents are, quiet diverse and heterogeneous coming from quite dissimilar backgrounds and experiences. The main spring of this movement is Sri Panduranga Vaijanath Athavale Shastri who guides its destiny. Its objective is to transform people so that they reorient their individual life and reorder collective existence. This transformation is to instil in the people a sense of brotherhood among the children of God, improve the conditions of their earthly existence, and ennoble themselves spiritually. Swadhyaya values service to society, but is not a service society. It rejects the idea of social service both in the traditional sense, that is *purtadharma*, and its modern version. It rejects the former because it is grounded in charity and formal piety and the latter, because it smacks of superior wisdom on the part of service agents who usually arrogate to themselves the role of doctors of morality (a term coined by Helvetius). This in itself implies denial of equality and dignity to the common man, a denial further compounded by treating the people as ignorant, passive, dependent, and pliable.

Swadhyaya therefore relies on traditional culture to restore the rule of *dharma* (righteousness) as the basis of action and through it, reshape individuality in a way that, whilst it retains its distinctiveness, it acquires self-confidence, values self-reliance and self-effort, manifests sociality, and promotes cooperation. It is true that Swadhyaya draws upon the rich Indian tradition but does not become backward looking. The central idea behind Swadhyaya is the age old concept of *lokasamgraha* (maintenance of the lived world as a unified approach to life) which underlines the desirability of choosing between desires and going about satisfying them in a way that contributes to the maintenance of the lived world. Otherwise, *matsya nyaya* (the law of the shark) would prevail. It does not mean that the individual has to tolerate poverty or practice extreme austerity. On the contrary, he must lead a normal life of duties and responsibilities that his earthly existence imposes on him a normal life that enriches personal life and collective existence. This is possible when the pursuit of *artha* (material well-being and *kama* (satisfaction of desires) is placed under the suzerainty of *dharma*. In this connection, *dharma* itself will have to become an active and dynamic principle in structuring and organizing personal experience and social relations. It calls for the liberation of *dharma* from lifeless rituals so that it once again becomes the regulator of personal conduct and social affairs. Further, it also means the demolition of the artificial division separating the material from the spiritual. But, how can this be done when materiality is tightening its hold on the people? This question has two aspects for Swadhyaya: personal and social. The personal is, however, the key to the social. That people have to relate with each other itself assumes significance. The notion that the good of the individual can be realized either by sacrificing the good of others or by subordinating individual good to collective good is not acceptable to Swadhyaya. It asserts that compatibility between individual and collective good is possible. But, then, it needs a change in the character of *dharma* and the ego. This is necessary because its eradication or suppression will destroy self-identity and self-respect.

The point of departure for this change is the realization that the individual is not self-complete, nor alone, nor helpless. His interior is the abode of God; as such, he is not an ordinary being; he is a spark of the divine. He, therefore, realizes that concentrated within him are all the powers of goal waiting to be discovered and realized. This realization transforms the individual into a self exploring person who, taking stock of his or her passions, appetites and desires directs them towards *bhakti*, devotion to God, by sublimating them and, turning inward, mobilizes his or her internal resources. This awareness produces in him a higher and more effective ego sense and initiates a process first of withdrawal from and them relating once again to the external world. This higher and nobler ego sense generates self-respect, self-confidence, and self-existence. It also induces an orientation that makes the individual realize his or her own limitations and check any self-aggrandizing tendency.

Swadhyaya has both a personal and social significance. Interpreting the first *mantra* of *Ishavasyopanishad* in a novel way Athavale Shastri turns the seemingly descriptive statement, that is this phenomenal world is the abode of God, into a dynamic principle signifying the need of covering this world with the love of God. Interpreted in this way, Swadhyaya signifies, at one and the same time, that a genuine knowledge of the self entails more than a transforming act on the self, it entails the realization that to know in this sense is not only to reflect and comprehend, but also to shape and create. For to know oneself is simultaneously to perfect oneself and help others to perfect themselves. This involves action as a medium not only for self development but also for enriching and ennobling collective existence. But action here does not signify action for action's sake. Action, in Swadhyaya perspective, is an offering to God, an offering "for covering this world with God's love". Since there is nothing that the individual can call his own except perhaps his efficiency and that too is the gift of God, he can offer only this. Thus by offering his *nipunata*, efficiency, the individual acknowledges his debt to God and expresses his gratefulness to Him through action. To offer one's efficiency to God is to perform one's inherited or acquired by worldly vocation with skill, proficiency and devotion. This is what in Swadhyaya parlance is called *Kritisheel Bhakti*, devotion through work. *Kritisheel Bhakti*, then, becomes the foundation of *lokasamgraha* and proves instrumental in removing animality in man, restraining him from seeking pleasure alone, engendering compassion and transforming compassion into virtue. *Lokasamgraha* cannot be ensured through the supposedly natural process of concatenation of individual actions, actions undertaken without any reference to others. It calls for a conscious choice of action which does not ignore or hurt the good of others. In this sense, *lokasamgraha* is an active and dynamic force which stresses personal responsibility. It signifies actions that are instrumental in awakening consciousness, conscience, compassion and vital life forces in man. To be committed to *lokasamgraha* is to accept life envigorating and world sustaining principle of dharma. This means the subjection of the pursuit of *artha* and *kama* to the suzerainty of *dharma*. This subjection enables the individual to rise above his own narrow self interest, relate himself to the social order, and contribute to the enrichment of personal life and social existence.

Kritisheel Bhakti, has, as indicated earlier, a social aspect. The first and foremost element of *Kritisheel Bhakti* in its social aspect is *Bhaktipheri*, making rounds for spreading the love of God, which awakens people, through religious and cultural dialogues, to the need of attuning themselves to the divine ground of being, and thus open themselves up to the possibility of self-development and Lokasamgraha. It is through *Bhaktipheri* that the central idea of divine brotherhood is propagated. At the root of this is the realization that individuals differ not only in terms of personal characteristics but also in terms of their location in the factual order and may have different expectations and aspirations. However, all of them partake in a shareable commonality. Thus there may be distinctions but not differences among them. The creation of the feeling of brotherhood is the stepping stone to community building. The ossification of the individualistic tendencies creating social distances, sharpening social differences and aggravating social clearages----all these factors have dissipated the idea of divine brotherhood. Consequently, social relations are marked with distrust, dissension, discord and disruptions. Community-building therefore receives special attention in Swadhyaya. For that matter, the deprived and wretched of Indian society have been the primary focus of Swadhyaya movement which has, since its inception, been working among such depressed groups as tribals, low caste fishermen, Vagdis and other such neglected groups. Swadhyaya aims at and has achieved remarkable success in breaking the cultural isolation of these groups and, through this, instilling in them a feeling of self-esteem, self-confidence and self-reliance. This also has been instrumental in improving personal conduct and family relations and promoting cooperative corporate effort for improving the economic conditions of these groups. Swadhyaya also seeks to make them rid of their arrogance and disdain towards the depressed and deprived. Swadhyaya thus is making a concerted effort to bring everyone in its fold and lay the foundation of an intimate community based on equality and dignity of the individual.

In order to overcome man's weakness for wealth, Swadhyaya makes a conscious effort to create what it calls *Apauresheya Lakshmi*, literally wealth created by no one person, trans-individual wealth. This signifies that since man owes everything to god, he must pay his debt to him in a suitable manner. This consists primarily in the best use of his *nipunata*, expertise and efficiency in producing whatever he is capable of and good at doing and offering a part of his earnings at God's feet. In addition, Swadhyaya followers engage in certain productive enterprises that are communal (corporate) in nature. Their products do not, therefore, belong to a particular individual since the community, as a whole, has contributed its skill, labour and resources in producing that wealth. It is in this sense that the wealth thus produced is *apaureshaya*. Examples of this kind of collective enterprises are *Matsygandhas* (construction and deployment of mechanized fishing boats), *Yogeshwara Krishi* (collective farming for Yogeshwar), *Upavanas* (orchards for the entire village), and now *Sri Darshan*. *Shri Darshan* has been introduced only recently. The *Apauresheya Lakshmi* belongs to no one in particular but to Lord Yogeshwar, the God of Swadhyaya adherents. One-third of this wealth is used to meet short term requirements of the needy Swadhyaya devotees. The help is neither charity nor a loan; it is given as *prasad* (offerings to God distributed among devotees). The recipient is under no obligation to pay it back; if he chooses to return, he can pay back any amount he can afford without any interest. The remaining two-thirds of the income from the sale of products are deposited in a non-interest earning trust fund called Madhav Raksha Sankalpa, a trust created by each local community. The accumulated fund in this trust is used to buy agricultural and other equipments and meet input needs of different enterprises.

Yet another interesting symbol of community effort and solidarity is the *Amritalayam*, the abode of Nectar. A village where Swadhyaya work has taken deeper roots, measured crudely by the proportion of village population (over 90 percent in this case) being devotees, can build an *Amritalayam*, a temple of simple structure built with locally available materials, which serves as only as a place of worship for all, but also a community centre where people assemble to deliberate on their problems, debate ways and means of solving them, and arriving at consensus decisions. *Amritalayam* also functions as a centre of transmitting traditional culture. It is here that the individual ego sheds its aggressive I-ness and merges into the larger order. It is also here that persons of both genders and all age groups receive essential religious and cultural education. Space does not permit to discuss other aspects of Swadhyaya movement. But, this is enough to indicate how the relationship between culture and development can be made useful and benign.

Notes

1. Worth perusing in the vast literature on this subject are David P. Calleo and Benjamin H. Rowland, *America and the World Political Economy: Atlantic Dreams National Realities* (Bloomington: Indian University Press, 1973) and Walter Russell Head, "The

World Economic Order: Perils after Bretton Woods", *Dissent* (Summer, 1990), pp. 383-93.

2. Thomas Hobbes, Leviathan (New York: E P Dutton, 1950), p. 79.
3. See Charles Taylor, "Growth, Legitimacy and the Modern Identity" *Praxis International 1*, 2 (July 1981), pp. 111-125.
4. Max Weber, "Science as Vocation" in *From Max Weber*, eds. Girth and C. Wright Hills (New York: Oxford University Press, 1958), p.139.
5. Taylor, op. cit., p. 112.
6. Charles Taylor, *Social Theory as Practice* (Delhi: Oxford University Press, 1983), p.55.
7. Taylor, "Growth, Legitimacy, and the Modern Identity", p.112.
8. Lewis Mumford, *The Myth of the Machine* (New York: Harcourt Brace Javanovich, 1970), p.51.
9. Taylor, "Growth, Legitimacy and the Modern Identity", op. cit., p.113.
10. See Sheldon Wolin, "Post Modern Politics and the Absence of Myths," *Social Research* 54(1987) pp. 238-39.
11. On the point see Maurice Mandelbaum, *History, Man and Reason: A study in Nineteenth Century Thought* (Baltimore: The Johns Hopkins University Press, 1971), p.142.
12. Quoted in Ignacy Sachs "Gandhi and Development: A European View', in Ramashray Ray, ed; *Contemporary Crisis and Gandhi* (Delhi: Discovery Publishing House 1986), p.192.
13. Taylor, "Growth Legitimacy and the Modern Identity", p.116.
14. Robert C. Soloman, *The Rise and Fall of the Self* (Oxford: Oxford University Press, 1989), p.619.
15. On this point, see Stanley Rosen, "Man's Hope", *Social Research* 48, 3 (Autumn 1981), p.619.
16. Mumford, op. cit., p. 165 Even before Mumford made a reference to this, Mahatma Gandhi had already drawn attention to it "I detest this desire to destroy distance and time, to increase animal appetites and go to the ends of the earth in search of their satisfaction." Collected Works of Mahatma Gandhi (Delhi: Publications Division, Government of India) Vol. 33 Appendix 1, p.486 (to be hereinafter referred to as CWMG).

17. For a discussion of its implications for the self see my "The Concept of Development: Its Implications for Self and Society", Psychology and Developing Societies 3.2 (1991), pp.133-155, included in my *The World of Development: A Theoretical Dead-End* (Delhi: Ajanta Publications, 1993).
18. On this point see Roberto M. Unger, *Knowledge and Politics* (New York: The Free Press, 1975).
19. For a discussion on social limits to growth, see Fred Hirsh, *Social Limits to Growth* (London: Routledge & Kegan Paul, 1972).
20. Theodore J. Lowi, *The End of Liberalism* (New York: WW Norton & Co, 1979), pp. 20-21.
21. For a discussion on the evisceration of control mechanism both internal and external, see my "One True World or Many? A Gandhian Perspective" in *Captive Vision: Ideas as Weapon* (Delhi: Ajanta Publications, 1993).
22. Richard Sennet, "Destructive Gemeinschaft" in N Birnbaum. ed., *Beyond the Crisis* (London: Oxford University Press, 1977), p.177.
23. For a discussion on this, see Merquior, *The Veil and The Mark:Essays on Culture and Ideology* (London: Routledge & Kegan Paul, 1979), p.39.
24. See Govinda Chandra Pande, *Bharatiya Parampara Ke Mool Swara* (Fundamental Tenets of Indian Tradition) in Hindi (New Delhi:National Publishing House, 1981), chap.1.
25. E.J.B. Tylor, *Primitive Culture* London: Murray, 1871, I. pp 2-3 are the considered culture as reasonable of knowledge, customs tradition characteristics of a certain people.
26. Solomn, op.cit., p.7.
27. See Donald R. Kelley, *Foundations of Modern Historical Scholarship* (Columbia: Columbia University Press, 1970), p.4.
28. Merquior, op.cit., p.43.
29. Ernest Gellner, *Nations and Nationalism* (Oxford: Basil Blackwell, 1984), p.55.
30. Ibid., p.109.
31. Ibid.
32. Alvin Toffler, *Future Shock* (New York: Bantom Books, 1971), p.15.
33. Daniel Bell, *The Cultural Contradictions of Capitalism* (London: Heinemann 1979), pp. 13-14.

34. Bjorn Hettne, *Development Theory and the Third World* (Stockholm: Swedish Agency for Research Cooperation with Developing Countries 1982), p.7.
35. Even A.H. Maslow falls a prey to this wide spread view point as he says "A good environment is one that offers all necessary raw materials and then gets out of the way and stands aside to let the organism itself to alter its wishes and demands". *Motivation and Personality* (New York: Harper, 1962).
36. Irish Murdoch, *Sartre: Romantic Rationalist* (London: Fontana, 1968.
37. E.M. Wood, *Mind and Politics: An Approach to the Meaning of Liberal and Socialist Individualism* (Berkeley: University of California Press, 1972), p.111.
38. Cf S. Freud, "Our mind is a peacefully self-contained unity. It is rather to be compared to a modern state in which a mole, eager for enjoyment and destruction, has to be held down forcibly by a prudent superior class." Quoted in P. Rieff, *Freud: The Mind of the Moralist* (New York: Anchor, 1961), p.63.
39. Fred Hirsch, *Social Limits to Growth* (London: Routledge & Kegan Paul, 1977), p.10.
40. Jean Jacques Rousseau, "A Discourse on the Origin of Inequality," in *Social Contract and Discourses* trans. J.D.M. Cob. (Every man's Library), p.275.
41. Roberto M. Unger, *Knowledge and Politics* (New York: The Free Press 1975), p.150
42. Ananda Coomaraswamy, *What is Civilization*? (Delhi: Oxford University Press, 1989), p.5.
43. CWHG, XXXIV, p. 18.
44. Commentary by Pandurang Shastri Athavale (Bombay Sadvichar Darshan Trust, Samvat 2042), p. 158 and Gita Pravachana (Bombay: Sadvichar Darshan Trust, 1983), p.17 These are now available in several collections of Athavale Shastri.

Chapter Seven

Integral Education: The Vision and An Experiment

Chitta Ranjan Das

"The first principle of education is that nothing can be taught", thus goes Sri Aurobindo's first of the three hypotheses about education. "Mind has to be consulted in its own education" is his second adumbration; and he concludes in the third principle that "all education has to proceed from near to the far." Sri Aurobindo had enunciated these principles during the first decade of this century. His ideas about education took shape when he was actively involved in the Bande Mataram Movement and at one time had become the principal of the Calcutta National College. The National College was itself a protest against education as it then prevailed in India and sought for an alternative. The very nature and import of the three principles clearly indicate that Sri Aurobindo was very much aware of the contemporary movements of thought in the field of education in Europe. In fact, he had then perhaps a better acquaintance with the heritage of the West than of the East. The three principles suggest the key psychological insights that then saturated all educational endeavour. Those were the days of many experiments, asking questions that had never been asked before. The very attitude about what a human child is and would be was changing radically.

Sri Aurobindo left Indian politics and came to Pondicherry in 1910. An altogether new phase began in his life and in his quests. Though many in India will fondly describe him as a yogi, his yoga was very much different from the traditional Indian path. The latter stood for renunciation of world and life, it took the world for a place which was full of suffering and explained human nature as condemned to remain what it always has been. There was, as it were, no prospect of a change or a betterment. All human effort at an improvement was proclaimed as useless. The only way out was to run away from here, seeking for a bliss only hereafter in a heaven. All real redemption was a fight from this condemned state. It is astounding to know that almost all the excellent pieces of wisdom has been uttered in ancient India by sages who had renounced the world. Indian mythology and religious lore is replete with stories to convince the human fool about the futility here and the promises over there.

Sri Aurobindo said, "God has not created this world. He has become this world, He is this world." This really changed the very axioms. "The Divine is infinite possibility," Sri Aurobindo declared, and the possibilities have to be realized here by us as individuals and in the collective. The aim of yoga is spiritualization of society, or of humanity if you choose to say so. The entire tone is one of affirmation. Ancient Indian wisdom had of course sung of the soul that is within in everyone of us, but it had imagined it as imprisoned waiting to be released of the thralldom. There had been moral codes, prescribed religions and the like, but the utter aim was an escape; all this was recommended to be undergone to qualify yourself for the release. There was no emphasis upon changing the world to make it worthy of the Divine in you. One has only to live out one's stigma of *karma* and then get away into the contemplated supreme bliss.

Even the many sages of the enlightenment of the 19th century India, though they so much and so often sounded affirmative and radical, had held out renunciation and release as the ultimate goals. It seems Sri Aurobindo was an exception and spoke with a totally different emphasis. "We have not to lose ourselves in God, but to find ourselves in God"—was what he said as the aim of all yogic pursuit, it had altogether a different appeal and called for a different kind of readiness. He has said several times that many of the world religions have dreamt of the kingdom of heaven come down to us upon this earth, but very little has been accomplished in actuality. We may perhaps add, the mundane powers that be have used religions to their own benefits and have been instrumental in bringing in most of the manmade sufferings and miseries to which most of the people of this world have been persuaded to accept as ordained by fate. Religions or the agencies that have manned religion through the ages have been responsible for much of the inertia that has kept people fettered. Ego has had the mandate, both individual and the collective varieties of it and in the very process of the insinuations, people have almost forgotten that the real power and truth are within. They have been led to believe that they are helpless and unable. Tyrannies flourish when we forget our own inner worth and begin to depend upon icons and idols.

Sri Aurobindo believed in evolution. No religion has ever abided by the evolutionary logic. God as being has always overshadowed our inquiries into God as becoming. From Charles Darwin to Telihard de Chardin and Sri Aurobindo is really a robust story, revealing to all who care how life and phenomena have followed an ascending curve not at all pre-determined, but unfolding unendingly the many possibilities. The Divine is the truth and the agent behind the unfoldings, and its counterpart in the human individual is what Sri Aurobindo calls the psychic being. To say it figuratively with him, the Divine is an eternal child playing an eternal game in an eternal garden. And all of us are the media through which the game is being played. Once you decide to believe in evolution, you say good-bye to all the myths fabricated around heaven and hell. You feel responsible, you begin to feel that you have an errand to deliver through living your life and decide no more to lecherously pray and pine for your own salvation. The feeling really elevates you to what Abraham Maslow would have called the peak. You feel you are now ready to live for something, no more languishing in your ignorances and abstract obsessions, never giving room to that self-destroying propensity called alienation.

Consciousness, according to Sri Aurobindo, is the criterion which will explain evolution. Consciousness has been the prime mover and consciousness is the capital with which we shall come to collaborate with the world process of evolution. Looking back, we have matter as the first station where consciousness was latent and dormant; then in the ascending scale we have the vital energy (*prana*) and the mind respectively. To quote again, the divine is sleeping in matter, wakes up and moves in prana and becomes conscious at the level of the mind. Man, the mental being, is at the acme of the march of evolution now, but man or mind for that matter is definitely not the last station. Evolution after Darwin has made all kinds of speculation about the next stage after mental man. Chance and environment can never entirely explain this universal theme. Man, the conscious being, conscious of past and the present, conscious about himself and what is more, always speculating about the shape of things to come and arranging the present accordingly, cannot just be a creature of chance and environment. Man as has been made and equipped, is also the creator of his environment and circumstances; he can choose between several chances seemingly present before him. He can choose, opt and decide. In fact he has been all the time taking decisions and choosing. False gods have appeared and have coaxed him to believe that he is only a creature and just a coping paltry thing. But the major happenings of history and culture have been always negating it. Man has to be adequately educated to work, act and have his being according to the dictates of this consciousness. The consciousness that is within him is not in any essential way different from the consciousness that pervades the universe and also, if you will, beyond the universe.

The mundane conditionings have kept the human person small and cramped. Collective suggestions and obligations of habit have conspired as it were to compel him to live and think reconciled to his immediate destinies and loyalties, geography, religion, state and even the national idea have all contributed to keep him content with his diminishment. Yoga is the way that can bring you out of these fixations and liberate you from the false finalities that have kept you bound to that original sin. The psychic being in man is the collaborator which will show you the way, provide you with the appropriate clues and give you a real chance to be what you really are by your right of a divine predilection. Man, being a conscious being, can always hasten the process of further evolution by a concentration of consciousness and its channelization to facilitate the descent of the next state. This concentration of consciousness is what Sri Aurobindo would define as *tapashya*. The latter has traditionally meant all odd sorts of austerities and religious orders all through the ages have been indeed very innovative in catechizing those austerities. These have been, alas, more exhibitionist than serious and genuine. The means have very ably derogated the end.

In keeping with the three steps in nature, Sri Aurobindo has spoken of a three-fold life. At the base is the bodily life, the area of our physical and emotional beings and their eventual becoming. The second step is the step of man, the mental being. The advent of mind has added dimensions to life as could not be thought of before man appealed and took the reins. Science, civilization, the myriad's of artefacts that go together to describe our culture, the discovery of the wide world which has rendered the human race to feel as a single neighbourhood, all these devices that have made modern life comfortable, less full of drudgery and highly increased the level of our aspirations, all these are the gifts of mind that has sustained us. But all this is only the first birth, the very necessary infrastructure upon which the second birth has to be actualized and lived. Hidden within this first birth is the psychic being, the seed that will lead man on to his further excellences. Mind acts on the principle of division, compares, has a hunger that seeks to devour, is precariously ensnared by I-nesses and my-nesses. This state has to be transcended, by choosing to get beyond the present parochialisms. There will be a further ascent at the ladder of our consciousness—life as it is will then voluntarily aspire for the life that might be. This renewal in the life of the human individual will result in the renewal of the community. The divine community will be born, and life will be a life divine. It will further translate itself in changes in all walks of our lives—economics, political arrangements, art, culture, literature—these will function at a new key and for a new end.

The psychic comes to the forefront and takes change. The mind abdicates in favour of a consciousness which is beyond mind. This ascent or going deeper with does not however mean that one has to relinquish the life of the body, of the vital or of the mind. The higher consciousness will come down and use body, life and mind for purposes which are not exclusively of the ego. The process will be an expansion of the consciousness to a state where you are not alone, where your good is intimately knit together with the good of the world, where you learn to rejoice in living for the Divine only, living for this world. Interests will not compete with one another, they will be sublimated or transformed in such a way that they fulfil and complement one another. Greater fulfilment will be the end of life. Because we are now led away by what we ludicrously call our own good, our body, our life and mind do not get a chance for an optimal functioning and development. They are much less than what they might be, almost morbidly occupied with their own little goals, intentions and fears. When the psychic becomes the decision-maker, body, life and mind also attain to their excellences.

When one begins to look at life as this totality, Sri Aurobindo would say, body then becomes the base and the foundation of whatever you have opted to become. Assuming that the world was an appearance and an illusion, sages of old have always advised in India to neglect the body, to look down upon it as it were a barrier to our further attainments. Especially in India we have made little use of our highest wisdom because we have derided the body as abominable something which has to be spurned in order that we can give our sole attention to what we have held up as our real pursuits. India has been more often than not a land where otherworldliness, indifference and heartlessness have been exalted. The best people have chosen to run away in a sort of righteous disgust from everything that stands for this world. World-hate has got the better of being drawn toward the world with a love and with a determination to change it.

What has all this discussion to do with education, one may wonder. Education has always meant exactly what we really wanted to do with education, in all our intents and purposes. The state has, as a rule, need for obedient citizens and hence frames out a scheme in the field of education. Whenever the aim has been to use only a part of the human being, an appropriate education has meant addressing itself only to a part of him. Right from Athens and Sparta, along the many religious and idealistic orders, that has always been the rule. Even the Nazi regime in Germany had an appropriate mechanism of training up young people which it called education. As long as you happen to be in power and intend to use man for your designs, you are cursed to see only a part of man. That is a sacrilege. Man is here not to be used by tyrants, he is here to flower up as a fully functioning entity, fully functioning and fully aspiring, so that he may be fit to give himself fully in the fulfilment of the evolutionary scheme that this world is. Somebody or some situation has to tell him that he is full of possibilities and it is his foremost job and *dharma* to try at locating and developing those potentials, grow to his full bloom freely, without let or hindrance. Because, the more one grows up in freedom and with a joy that is yours, if you are free to invest yourself at your fullest, the more you can be of use for the world that needs you, the more you can collaborate with the presiding forces of evolution.

It is only very recently that education has come to mean being occupied with the whole human person. A human being is just not a body, a life and a mind (you may add, a soul, if you like) put together. He is veritably a whole. Pico della Mirandella's "An Oration on Man" in the 14th century during the days of the Italian Renaissance was perhaps the earliest document proclaimed on behalf of man defined as full of potentialities. Subsequent discoveries of the geisteswissenschaften and particularly the study of man as a total gestalt brought before us an entirely different image of man. The people who have wielded power did always look upon man through their glasses, darkly, and the homo humanus has always refused to submit to that fragmentary definition. To look at the human being straight and as a whole is to deal with the spiritual realm. If by science we understand the willingness to look straight and without inhibitions, then we can come to realize how several modern findings by the science of man tend to project and present him as a whole as a spiritual entity understood by the totality of its connotations.

"Education of the Whole Man" was the title of a book written by L.P. Jack sometime during the early decades of this century. The debate about how education ought to be has been gathering momentum as our definition of man has tended to become more and more holistic. Man is at once a body, a being with appropriate sentiments and emotions, a mind interpreting the world around him and also interpreting himself and his relationships upon an appropriate context, and finally a soul or a psyche. He is all these and yet a whole, a unique psychophysical organization living and having his being with other human beings. Thus, education has to be designed and imparted in a way which can never afford to overlook the totality that the human being is. There ought to be physical education for the body, vital educations for the emotions, mental education for the proficiencies of his mind and psychic education so that whatever a person learns and becomes through his education of the body, vital being and the mind can be integrated and used for a goal that subserves the evolutionary goal. Body, the vital being and the mind have to be prepared and should form the base upon which the edifice of a person's psychic potentials can be erected. The methods have to vary as the goals. The child has to be approached as a store-house of possibilities, as a soul that carries the divine within it. Whatever education he receives by way of a schooling ought to nourish the soul that is waiting to grow and unfold itself.

Hence, it should follow, all education should be imparted in an atmosphere of freedom, should be built upon the belief that a man is basically good and willing to co-operate in his own education and unfoldment. The approach has to be one of invitation, not of command. The relationship between the pupils and their teacher will be one that inspires joy, unreserved participation and a mutuality that respects and recognizes the learner on either sides. Not everyone can be a teacher in a school that has decided in favour of such an education. He or she should have made a decision and moulded himself and herself accordingly. No traditional hierarchy should find a room in these schools to vitiate the design. The school should be a community where everyone is just everyone else's equal in respect of being recognized, irrespective of age. Nobody should feel superior, and what is more, nobody should feel inferior either. He or she who is really more and knows as well as understands more can always afford to give precedence to those others who, they think know and understand less. The approach has to be essentially individual, dialogical, based on an I-Thou relationship. No person, including the young ones, should be treated as a thing. These are not utopian ideas, they can be real if we really mean it; they have attained a near-real level whenever an educ ationist---Pestalozzi, Kristen Kold, Korchak, Neil and many others like them, has decided upon leaving the old rut and experimenting something new. It is very hard to be different, yet it is not impossible.

The first integral school was started at Sri Aurobindo Ashram, Pondicherry already in 1943 and began almost from scratch. The vision of course was there, but the structures were worked out as experiences created a need for them. The Sri Aurobindo International Centre of Education was formally opened in 1951 and has been functioning ever since. It provides education right from the kindergarten level up to that of the college. No rigid syllabus is followed, no text books are prescribed and no examination decides the fate of a student who has studied there. No certificates are given; because perhaps what is given can never be expressed through a certificate. The inspiration has been in the meanwhile carried over to other states in the country, by mainly enthusiasts who thought an alternative has to be found out to the imbroglio that education has come to be now in India. They have a large-size school in Delhi and states like Andhra Pradesh, West Bengal, Gujarat and Rajasthan have embarked upon experiments, each in their own ways.

The first Institute of Integral Education was started in Orissa in 1970, in the state capital. During the past quarter of a century, the number of these type of schools has gone to more than one hundred and fifty. These schools are no longer confined in the urban areas only. There are now more schools in remote rural and tribal areas than in the cities and towns. These are of course, each marked out from one another by characteristics of the milieu that is involved. At the moment, there are about twenty-five schools who run education up to the secondary level. New schools keep springing up every year and the number keeps increasing. The urban schools are as a rule bigger in size. Several of the rural schools provide hostel facilities. Every school is free to choose its own staff, its own style of functioning and the management of its finances. Barring a very few, all the schools have the mother tongue as the medium of instruction. But English, Hindi and Sanskrit are also given due weightage. To make an educational coordination among these schools possible, there is a Trust which is constituted of representatives from all of them. Educational coordination includes sharing of experiences among teachers, programmes of teacher training and zonal and state level periodical meets where real issues are discussed collectively. Besides, there are also occasional workshops on themes like child psychology, teaching methodology and school organization. Parents play a pivotal role in the running of these schools, more so in those situated in rural areas. At times and at a few of these schools mothers meet separately to discuss the progress and problems of their children.

The Trust has framed a base syllabus. The individual schools have always the option to make their own variations of it according to local needs. The teachers meet frequently to discuss issues of mutual concern and try to find out solutions. The principal of the institution is more a leader than a boss or big brother. The management looks after procuring the wherewithals of running such a school. To facilitate better sharing and exchange of experiences, there are teacher exchange programmes between the schools and at times also, pupils exchange programmes. Annual meets of the teachers are real occasions for small group discussions which always arrive at a workable consensus and this is how new strides are taken. The pupil teacher ratio is much better than is obtained in the regular schools run by the state department of education. We do have examinations in the schools, but they are never a horror. Grades are given instead of marks. There are periodical, half yearly and annual tests; and promotions are a result of a cumulative performance by a child throughout the year. If a child lags behind, he or she is given special or remedial assistance. And what is more, every child has more than one way of proving his/her worth and hence the so-called academic performance is not a bully.

Physical education is given equal importance. There are provisions for music, drama and dance education. The school library gives constant company. Debates, amateur performances and the like are regular auxiliary programmes. No child is ever compared against another, so that feelings of superiority and inferiority do not get a chance to pollute the interrelationships. And painting is a must for every child. The aim is not to produce skilled artists who have mastered the familiar art techniques, but to study the total progress of the pupil through how he has expressed himself through his paintings. A child's painting can also render therapeutic assistance. Not everyone can be happy as a teacher in schools like these. If you yourself also do not grow along with the children who surround you, you are sure to feel very much out of place all the time. When children get a chance to grow up in freedom and affection, their expectations from the teachers also rises high and you can never afford to remain merely a respectable school master for them. And then, discipline should also mean different things; when there is nobody eyeing upon you as a policeman to find out your mistakes. A sense of self-respect gets a chance of forming itself from within the child and it learns to conduct itself with dignity. It is then as if one has found out one's own centre within and does not need any policing. The moment the child has reasons to be convinced that the teacher is very much on his own side, he throws away much of his built-in inhibitions and does not find any interest in any guilt consciousness.

It is always a pleasure to participate in an experiment like this. You have only colleagues and fellow-travellers around you, a kindred group with whom you can always share your difficulties and take counsel. Whenever there is a problem, they sit together and arrive at a solution. And when nobody is there to censor you for a fault of yours, there is also no need for you to smartly show up that you are faultless and to put on holier than thou countenances. So much unnecessary suffering is overcome in a group situation when you assume that there is always a room for further improvement and hence it is indeed your good fortune that you are together with others. There have to be hurdles if we are out to do what others are not doing, and if you are struggling upstream all the time, integral education is in many ways a conspiracy, not only against the education system run by the establishment, but against the present society. It challenges the established mores and values and wants to do away with the age-long distances. You can endure only when you have spiritual convictions, when you are not autocratic and will not like to force things on people. Nevertheless, you have to take the society with you, always convincing it you are more than a breaker of old idols and you have definitely many things better to offer. Our links with the society that we wish to see changed are our children and if we can show real results or at least real honesty, the new is sure to strike a root.

How do the integral education centres manage themselves financially? They have an army of teachers, both young women and men, who do not work against any real salary. It is true that one does not live by bread alone, but without bread, you run the risk of not living at all. Most schools do not have the resources to provide enough in terms of emoluments. Yet, if you can make possible a community that comprises the teachers who run the school, you can perhaps solve many of the problems. There has been a Sri Aurobindo Study Circle Movement all over the state since about the sixties, and it is no wonder that most of the teachers who come to join the integral schools are more often than not those who have been associated with these circles when they were students. Hence, it is often a personal decision with them and they are emotionally prepared for the pecuniary situation that obtains in the schools. Moreover, a few other non-economic incentives may also play a role. If you get other satisfactions from working in such a school and have a sense of fulfilment that you may never get in the other schools, that helps you to stick on with a bare minimum. And, when you do not happen to have those props that give you the needed strength to continue, you are very likely to feel out of place and seek better places that will pay you more. Hence, some teachers always leave, yet others also keep coming. That does create difficulties, yet one has to be reconciled with it.

The experiment has already caught the notice of the state government. The very high ups keep coming to see what all goes on in these out of the track educational endeavours; as individuals they are very happy to see that many things which are not possible in the state schools are possible here, they encourage us by saying that such experiments ought to go on. But as people serving a government they say that they cannot do very much for the schools unless these throw in their lot with the prescribed patterns. The latter will of course mean losing your own soul in order to gain the whole world. Negotiations go on all the time and a few makeshift reapproachments are also made now and then. Some financial aid is now given to some schools and possible departures are also made. But, gradually, more and more schools seem to be convinced now that you cannot do justice to an experiment making compromises with people who represent the establishment. Schools in the rural areas have, in the meanwhile, started searching for other sources of income. They have farmlands, fishponds, orchards and whatever local conditions may provide in the way of earning something so that you may self-sufficiently plan and run your experiment. The urban schools do not have these opportunities. The only way to earn more is by increasing the school fee. That is never a very happy solution. And what is most unfortunate, in this way you begin to restrict your school only to a few definite strata of society and foolishly drive out perhaps the more deserving ones.

Sometimes, an experiment, an experiment in education included, starts with a lot of enthusiasm. One very sincerely wants an experiment to succeed, is willing to help it with all the externals needed; yet one somehow wants to see it run as it were by proxy. It sounds so preposterous, but it does happen nevertheless. While you start a school and wish to have an experiment in education made through that school, you and a few others of your category procure the initial requisites, land, money and what not, and then hire or engage teachers who will work it out. You thus belong to the management, you throw out a blueprint which you have fancied out in some of your best moments; you stand out and simply supervise. You and your teachers represent two different tribes. You never share, you are too high and mighty for sharing and therefore your dream and your teachers are called upon to fulfil that dream. Whenever such paradoxes begin to contaminate an experiment, they bring about into ruin, expectations are always high one side and the other side has all the time to labour under an excruciating feeling that he is simply there to feed a horse that somebody else is meant to ride. And the moment such a feeling gradually takes possession of you, you are no longer yourself and you can no longer give yourself with dignity. That also becomes a problem at times in the experiment with which we are dealing here. The worst victim in this case is spontaneity, on which so much has to depend in the area of educational pioneering.

No homogeneous school community is possible as long as the organizers and the teachers function as two different groups though it is formally professed that both have the same end. The organizers belong to the old society, they are somewhat successful in the old society and are people who matter in the old order of things. But, there has been no personal revolution in their lives though they may sincerely wish a change and show sufficient gesture in favour of a change. One has to be very much in the very process of change if one realizes that there should be a change. Integral education in Orissa has yet to be freed of this dichotomy and come of age. Most of our problems are to a large extent those ensuing from this distance. It appears, a solution will come when both the sides really decide to grow. It is self-growth that engenders better understanding and annihilates the distances. The ideal will be when a whole group of people who have made a decision to take up an experiment live together on the spot very much in the pattern of an intentional community. All of them will be involved both in the managing and teaching aspects. In fact in an educational experiment undertaken by people who live in a community, management will be the least sophisticated and management issues will always give priority to issues of education and innovation. Only in event of a dichotomy, the managers are tempted to act as fault-finders and insist on paltry routine and conformities.

Integral education in Orissa has the educational experiment in Sri Aurobindo's Ashram at Pondicherry as its source of inspiration. Sri Aurobindo's vision about the next future promised to mankind if the latter so wills will always be before it as the beckoning catalyser. Nevertheless, the international centre of education at the Ashram can never be a model for it. The Ashram School is after all an island experiment. It is indeed an excellent laboratory for controlled experiments. The persons who do the teaching there have all renounced the world responding to a call from within. They are all *sadhakas*, spiritual aspirants, and teaching in the educational centre is a part assignment in their *sadhana*. How far has the appeal to integrality gone into the lives of those who pass out of the centre is yet to be assessed. Integral education outside the Ashram can never function with such island assumptions. The insights gained at the Ashram can however be extended to the greater laboratory that our world is and there have to be modifications in the very process of extension. After all, it is the world that will change and humanity that has to prepare for it and therefore, a green house experiment will never be adequate, with whatever solemnity and seriousness one may wish to say that it is so. The experiment outside in the world has to reckon with its own specific challenges and work out its own models. That needs much more courage and collaborative endeavour, the courage to be in spite of.

One can conclude only in an optimistic vein, because the experiment and the adventure to date have been very enriching, confidence-giving and hope-inspiring. It is perhaps an inevitability that the more one gives oneself heart and soul to an effort larger than oneself, as one learns to live more for something higher than oneself, one gets the requisite strength and the guidance verily from within. Something or somebody keeps prodding you on. And it seems to be more so with a group than in the case of a solitary individual. Most of the integral schools in Orissa have very little to show you outwardly. All arithmetic will tell you that nothing will be possible with so little to depend upon. Yet, as you spend about a day in one of these schools, silence begins to speak out as it were and you begin to see great strides being taken principally because people in committed groups know how to depend upon and keep confidence in one another. No jealousies, no hypocrisy; that seems to be the secret. Even a rough calculation will tell you that there are quite a thousand young men and women in these schools in Orissa at the moment, who are not ascetics and yet can be so happy with so little. Sharing gives you that spiritual strength which no ceremonious austerity in isolation will be able to give. To be one in a common mission while honouring the individual differences, even recognizing one another's shortcomings and fond idiosyncrasies, that is perhaps the quickest way to achieve an elevation in your consciousness.

And what do you think the children in these schools be like? They are a happy lot, always at home in those schools, in many a sense more happy and more at ease here than in their customary homes. They, more than anything else, have helped their teachers to remain young and ever willing to give more and more of themselves. Mistakes are of course made, but there is always a mutuality that finds workable solutions. Education, and integral education for that matter, is not a goal fixed somewhere there to which you have to drudge under a compulsion. Maybe you will never reach any goal to everyone's satisfaction. Yet the idea will survive and surge ahead because of what you have been able to contribute. One liberates oneself by collaborating with a liberating process and that is perhaps how we all collaborate in the march of this world of ours.

Chapter Eight

Cross-Cultural Conversation and the Making of a Global Community

Anindita N. Balslev

The contention of this paper is that even if curtailing of the "geographical distances", irrespective of cultural differences, is a distinguishing mark of the contemporary technological civilization in which we live, the sense of what it really is to be members of a global community is yet to be achieved. We need to probe into the question, how to build and foster such a community more authentically than what we know it to be at present? In fact, this is one of the challenging projects that the advent of the twenty-first century places before us. One of the most effective ways of accomplishing this, I am inclined to believe, is by promoting cross-cultural conversation on issues that are perceived to be of global concerns, both for theory and practice. This calls for new ways of exploring the potentialities that are present within various cultures that would have ramifications in overt and subtle ways on the making of a global community.

The participants of this conversation---if the project is to succeed---must be educationists coming from an array of disciplines, activists, politicians, journalists, etc., as well as men and women from various walks of life belonging to different cultural traditions. Consequently, these participants are those who are fully aware of the fact that the complex and many-faceted question of diversity of cultures cannot be brushed aside either by glorifying a sense of abstract, homogenized unity or by highlighting a sense of radical difference. In other words, what I see cross-cultural conversation as seeking to achieve is the bridge-building task, a process that needs to gather momentum if we must learn to perceive ourselves as members of a multi-cultural global community----a project which is still in its inception.

In order to sketch a scenario with a broad brush, let me say that by a sense of community is meant here, minimally speaking, a sense of partnership that members cherish for various purposes----social, political and others. They recognize that there are shared bonds, shared interests despite their divergent perceptions, even conflicting opinions on various strategic issues. To speak of a possibility where the partners must engage each other in conversations does not imply that all in the long run, would get to hold the same views with regard to specific issues, or recommend the same public policies or even approve of the final decisions. In short, the sense of community, understood in this open formulation does not mitigate against the possibilities of differences, disagreements among its members just as it does not outrule that on occasions demands may be made for the employment of devices for arriving at a consensus. Note that whenever and in whichever context this sense of community has been attained by various human aggregates, it is perceived as something which needs to be guarded against all possible disruptive forces that seek to destroy the bond of civility that binds the members.

What does it take to strengthen and sustain this sense of community? Experience points to that it requires among other components setting up of various institutions----educational, social, political, etc. It is obvious that these are mutually re-enforcing processes----the community at large sets up and supports the institutions and the latter empower the former.

Living in a technological civilization, as we seek a higher level of critical understanding by placing ourselves in a progressively larger context it inevitably involves an encounter with the "otherness" of other cultures and eventually we cannot stop short of the global context. The fact that technology has "killed the distance" does by no means entail that we need to seriously ponder over the fact that today when the distances between the remotest corners of the globe can be covered with such incredible speed, when some have even begun to describe our planet as the "global village" why have these not furthered the cause and promoted the sense for what it is to be members of a global community more than it actually has. This could be ascribed to various reasons of which perhaps one of the principal ones is that we are not yet genuinely comfortable with the notion of a community which is pronouncedly multi-cultural in character. The existing structures of our educational, social and political institutions have not lived up to the challenge that living in a technological civilization demands. We are still not quite at ease with the thought that human solidarity does not ask for a homogenized or a forced cultural unity. The myth of monoculturalism legitimatizes more often than not actions that are geared to bring about human suffering. In our present situation, it seems to be of singular importance that we learn to see where lies our ultimate allegiance and recognize that this sense of community does not ask for an obliteration of diversity nor does it seek to generate a sense of fictive oneness that in no way seems feasible. However, what needs to be insisted upon is that we perceive the interconnected and the overlapping character of the membership, that we seriously take into account that all of us are members of multiple groups---cutting across the dividing lines of gender, race, nationality, religion, profession, etc., and most of all, we candidly acknowledge that countries of documented events here witness to the fact that given the mortal frame of life, most of human suffering is man-made suffering. It is, therefore, important that we recognize that the present environment of sophisticated resources, which no doubt is opening up a wide range of opportunities, could be utilized creatively and fruitfully or be simply abused. A rich diversity of thinking is needed to examine the options available to us and the consequences of our choices. One of the hardest tasks before us is to identify the forces that lead to the formation of power structures that is destructive of diversity of liberty in no matter which arena of our thought and action for this is what paves the path for oppression and exploitation.

Constructing such a community is a task for all those institutions which regulate our social practices, primarily of course of our educational institutions. I specially mention the educational institutions as it seems to me that in the long run lasting and effective changes can be brought about predominantly through the educational channels. To promote cross-cultural conversation in the university campuses, let us note, is not to introduce a totally separate field but to give a new direction to academic enquiry by attempting to bring together the expertise that scholars of various disciplines already have about numerous cultures and sub-cultures. It is rather to be considered as a program having decidedly a contemporary slant in so far as it invites the cooperation of scholars of different disciplines, recruiting them from diverse cultures for correcting some of the oddities resulting from certain configuration of power and knowledge. This programme has to draw from our past and must yet be forward-looking. It is born of an awareness that our academic curriculum needs to reflect the realities that the technological civilization has created for us.

The complexity of the present situation is such that it is no more possible for any one or any group to deal with it singlehandedly. An active participation of a community of scholars of different cultural traditions and of various disciplines, to repeat once again, is required to start with, gradually incorporating into the program the input of men and women of other walks of life. It is only then that we can hope to get a glimpse of the real world to become capable of registering the tremors all around us and to get a feeling for what really are the options available to us. To the extent a social theory ignores or glosses these features of our current situation that are increasingly making our interconnectedness prominent it loses its explanatory power. The call for a New World Order is getting more and more audible as the balance of forces is shifting. This idea of a New World Order, however, is neither simple nor clear. It seems to acquire shift in meanings and implications depending on who is using the phrase. To those of us for whom if cultural diversity is a key concern, and yet the emphasis on our shared bonds is all the more vital, it means---minimally speaking---working to create a new cultural environment that allows for the emergence of a new civil society that consciously strives for a more critical self-understanding in a global context, which is willing to acknowledge the past mistakes, confess ignorance and is fully supportive of new ways of thinking about the "otherness" of others. It seems to me that as cross-cultural conversations continue, it will be possible to ascertain the overlapping contents of cultures without underplaying their differences and that in and through this process would emerge a partnership which does not get put off by the vocalization of "radical difference" or gets thwarted by musing over the highly unlikely possibility of a dissolution of cultural identity. A sense of community need not bank on the melting-pot metaphor, it is decidedly a multi-cultural configuration. Conceived thus, this conversation is about creating an intellectual space opening up new ground that allows us to rectify some of the gross asymmetries in cross-cultural exchanges. It is prompted by the awareness that the sort of technological civilization in which we live calls for a thinking that can serve a powerful critical function. We need cosmopolitan thinkers who can teach us "to think globally" without demolishing local differences, who can fill in the gaps where our culture theorists have been deficient, who can weave stories of the interactions between cultures and how these have shaped their destinies. In short, to be able to perceive ourselves as members of the multi-cultural global community is to discover that cultures are not merely juxtaposed in a public space but are related to each other in multiple ways, more than it ever has been.

Dissemination of stories of cultures and sub-cultures, of their successes and failures, of their pain and hope and to what extent the plots and sub-plots of these stories interweave with those of other human aggregates who otherwise happen to claim a distinct, separate identity of their own, may well turn out to be one of the most effective ways that our educational institutions can render service to our plural world. More than theories what we need are these narratives. May be, as members of multi-cultural community, we will then begin to perceive how the exploitation and humiliation of a people or a tradition has been considered as the story of glory and success by another. We will become aware that the game is still going on when "otherness" of the other is used to legitimize oppression and subjugation, be that in the name of group identity where membership is not even voluntary such as that of race and gender or where perhaps there is a possibility of choice such as that of religious denomination or secular fold of divergent political ideologies. The tensions and anxieties that we bear as members of distinct groups are to be seen in their interconnectedness. A deeper level of sensitivity that registers the overlapping, interdependent character of our present multi-cultural situation needs to be cultivated. Carried out in earnestness, I am inclined to believe, that it will be appreciated as an indispensable aid for improving the quality of national and international debates. The politicians who are now the major players in the "cross-cultural games" will have to live up to the challenges of the better-informed academic communities that will raise new political issues which demand greater proficiency to handle. We are bound to arrive at a critical consensus that will help us better perceive what our common options are, where ought to be our priorities and how do we stop the wastage of intellectual and economic resources that serve the cause of violence.

The aim of this conversation is not to seek a vision of an ideal world community but to reflect on issues relevant for theory and practice-so that we may eventually break the silence about all those themes regarding which we have hitherto felt uncomfortable to speak, even when we knew that this silence implied nothing but complicity with the status quo. The participants in this conversation can only hope that this will eventually dismantle some of the obstacles in the context of meeting of cultures, facilitate communication and promote a sense of togetherness that various groups have always missed. The scope of such an endeavour is naturally wide and allows for an exploration in many directions.

At this point let me consider a few possible objections that may be raised against the possibility of cross-cultural conversation. It may be argued, for example, that conversation is out of the question since here we are speaking of radically different communities between which no communication is possible. It seems to me that this idea of "radically different conceptual worlds" advocated by the exponents of an extreme form of cultural relativism is a purely theoretical construct, an artificial problem. To assert that there is an incommensurability among the diverse cultures to the point of denying the possibility of communication which is needed for fostering a sense of community is to bargain for a position which is obsolete. Practice does not corroborate it and it is self-defeating on theoretical ground. We are not prisoners of our cultures since no living culture erects such obstructing walls or as I have put it elsewhere, set up a boundary in the hard sense of the metaphor. I have urged that the metaphor of boundary in the context of a plurality of cultures must be understood in its soft sense, where boundary means a border, a separating line which allows us to distinguish one from another and not in its hard sense, where the metaphor of boundary signifies a barrier, an insurmountable obstruction.

The opponent may still argue that conversation between cultures is not feasible as there is no single, universally agreed upon concept of rationality or morality or whatever else may happen to be the issue under consideration but that there are alternate, competing modes of understanding that separates one major culture from another. My response to it is as follows: Granted that it may well be the case that we have to opt for pluralistic interpretations of such concepts and admit that a forced unanimity is in no way fruitful or even desirable, I would still maintain that the participants can be truly said to have arrived at a consensus, through conversation, about how to conduct affairs in the public space.

Moreover, given the difficulty that is undeniably there, the task will not perhaps seem so unbearable if one candidly faces the fact that no major culture is really monolithic, that pluralistic modes of perceptions are very much present as well within any given major culture. This is precisely why cross-cultural conversation---as I see it---entails not only the exchange between major cultures but also among the sub-cultures within the major cultures. It is a conversation which seeks to mediate the marginalized and the dominant groups—pertaining to race, gender, religion, ethnicity, class, etc.---in the context of a single culture. We tend to forget that very often the seeming uniformity of a major culture is achieved by ignoring those who are at the margin, whose visibility is often hazy, whose voices are not particularly clearly heard, or at least so was the case until recent times. The practice of projecting a simplistic picture of a culture, the refusal to take into consideration the inner divergences, the conflicting traits that are present have not always been fortunate as this has lead to such vain efforts that seek to describe large complexes of cultures such as the East and the West either in terms of the forces of emancipation while ignoring those which are geared to oppression and the "other" culture quite as simplistically in a contrasting or opposite manner. Let me give a few examples; the most extreme form of contrasts bearing on the East and the West echo Kipling's famous line "Never the twain shall meet". At the end of the nineteenth and the beginning of the twentieth centuries, it was commonplace to describe the East as spiritual and the West as materialistic, then after the era of colonialism a self-critical posture of some western thinkers (such as Roger Garaudy) the contrast sounds something like the West is "sick" and others are "deceived", and recently a well-known American philosopher (Richard Rorty) has expressed the contrast as "one is a culture of hope and the other is a culture of endurance".

Note that based on any of these formulations each of which tends to overemphasize certain traits of one culture by contrasting it with the other, as if the latter traits are totally absent in the former-the idea of a global community seems like a farce. What we need is a more nuanced understanding of both ourselves and of others. At a time when neighbours and strangers are interchangeable verities, it seems that this practice of describing cultural differences in terms of elegant externism or the tendencies to create an evaluative hierarchy while speaking of cultures in a global context needs to be soon behind us. Instead, it will be more useful to redescribe these cultures and bring into focus those aspects, trends which can contribute toward fostering a sense of partnership but which have been so far, very largely, pushed to the absolute periphery of our discourse on cultures in our eagerness to project them as diametrically opposed. I am inclined to believe that emancipatory forces and sinister designs are present in overt or rudimentary manner in all major culture-forms. It seems to me worth a try to see closely in what way through our mutual cooperation and collaboration we can reduce and reject some of the undesirable components. We need to realize that the challenge before us is not to validate a heritage or a culture at the cost of another but to perceive cross-cultural conversation as a mutually empowering enterprise that raises the consciousness of all the participants involved and to appreciate that this is immensely helpful in checking the grotesque asymmetry in cross-cultural exchanges of all sorts. Only then will we be in a position to protest and condemn in one voice ruthless practices such as wars, genocides, planned famines, planned holocausts etc. no matter where these take place.

It is precisely to draw attention to this situation where asymmetries and disparities reign that rhetorical devices are needed. The New International Economic Order, for example, is a rhetorical device that seeks to highlight the utter disparity in the global economic context. As participants of this conversation, it is not enough that we occasionally come across analyses done by a conscientious individual from the North or the South which show that a further impoverishment of some of the LDCs (less developed countries) are sustaining the prosperity of some of the richer countries. If it is so, let those participants, who are more qualified in economic matters than some of us, relentlessly search for what can be done to remove some of the structural inequities that exist in the world trade, in control over resources and raw materials and in acquisition of technological expertise, which have lead to this immense gulf. Let there be more vigorous analysis first in order to comprehend and then to check the forces that allow hunger, malnutrition and diseases of certain kinds especially when we know that some of these are consequences of such inhuman practices. Let the members of an emerging global community find out why such ideas as world food security based on a global grain reserve, accepted by the United Nations in 1974, do not work out in actual practice and what can be done to make such international undertakings a success.

Cross-cultural conversation, let me emphasize, is indispensable not only for arriving at a consensus about what sort of goals need to be incorporated into the global agenda for the next century but more poignantly for finding out how proper measures can be taken to rectify the lapses which prohibit the actual implementation of the recognized goals. In order to exemplify the complexity of the situation, let me draw your attention to a real life scenario in order to make my point. Recently the Supreme Court of India has recommended punitive actions against some large industrial concerns for industrial pollution in West Bengal. As a consequence of this court order, some of the big industries are seeking to move to other states where environmental issues are not yet on top of their list. This in turn, has caused---quite understandably---tremendous anxiety among the trade-union leaders as such decisions can affect the lives of thousands and thousands of workers.

The point I am seeking to make is that it is much easier to state that there must be an end to the greed for profit at the cost of ecological damage than to find out through social negotiations how can such situations be effectively handled. Environmental activism cannot thrive in a vacuum, it must incorporate into its projects the know-how to resolve these crucial problems. This calls for a deeper understanding of the power-structures of a given society where the court and the industry, politics and trade-union all have to be adequately dealt with. We need to figure out why those who should in principle---like the workers and the trade union leaders---be actively involved and interested in the matter of implementation of environment-friendly policies get second thought and eventually may seek to back out from such enterprises.

In other words, we need a more complex, a more nuanced and intricate understanding of the relations that exist among large human aggregates. We need new stories about our collective past where success and defeat, growth and poverty, hunger and affluence will be told in a manner that their interconnectedness will come into focus, where concerns of economics, politics, ethics and philosophy will intersect each other. A search for this sort of complex understanding will gather momentum when we will not try to bypass these questions. If all these still seem to be a bit far-fetched, that is because it is never an easy task to change the trends in thinking, to examine questions that are yet outside the ambit of our intellectual self-consciousness. It is tempting to observe that it is unlikely that there will be any final answers to any of these questions but then, final answers are not what we are seeking. However, it does not seem altogether implausible that as we continue to struggle with these questions, we will in this process eventually learn to overcome the latest forms of tribalism. It is a call to promote a sense of togetherness that the technological civilization alone can promote. No living culture today unfolds its life by maintaining a pristine distinctness without vigorously interacting with the "otherness" of the other cultures. If understanding the other need not be construed as an unwarranted attempt to reconcile differences, it also does not entail an advocacy for overemphasizing differences that are trivial. It is possible, in the name of human solidarity, to imagine a posterity which will know of new ways of resolving conflicts and which finds it obscene to waste intellectual and economic resources serving the cause of violence.

The challenge before us is how do we enlarge our sense of loyalty and sense of social responsibility that we no longer feel inhibited to perceive the overlapping contents, the interconnectedness of the destinies of traditions and cultures or to assess the countless ways in which these nourish and impoverish each other. We need to ask together, no matter what sort of group affiliations we otherwise have: How communal passions are whipped up in the name of ethnicity, religious denominations and why governments fail to protect their victims? Why a specific nation's survey data shows that inequalities keep increasing? What to do when public distribution systems lie crippled and when a nation's health infrastructure fails to function even at the nominal level? There are many such questions.

In order to launch a program for achieving this, it is vital to mobilize support from many quarters. When those of us who are involved in this enterprise, even though ordinarily we are not trained to see ourselves as serving a single cause, will begin to do so and operate in unison to the extent that if required we are ready to withdraw our support from some of those narrowly drawn-out projects, labelled as serving so-called national interests but are geared to retain the existing socio-political and economic scenario in a global context, we can truly claim that we have achieved what we set out for. A globalist has to be an internationalist at heart. Global institutions will have to be in a position so that these can perceive clearly which issues and events are pushed to the periphery and which are projected more in the media, drawing more public attention and why? Given the multi-national composition of the political setting, global institutions must question to what extent issues that are projected as being of national importance---in specific national contexts---really are so and when these are due to elite politics or even due to the manipulation of an oligarchy? In brief, the question of social development in a global context is as much a moral issue as it is that of political economy.

I would like to welcome the rhetoric of the New World Order or for that matter any other rhetorical device, if any of these or all of them together can help correct the present configuration of power, wealth and knowledge and which can act as a force for creating a better environment by fostering a sense for a global community.

Before I conclude, let me emphasize that the sense of a global community must not be perceived as something which has been already accompanied and actualized by the very fact that technology has brought us physically nearer to each other nor is it an obvious corollary of the fact that today we have at last begun talking among ourselves about those who were previously ignored for some reason or other. Granted that all these are helpful contributions, we still have a long way to go. The point is that to perceive ourselves as members of a multi-cultural global community is not merely a way of thinking about ourselves but it is a mode of being and acting in this world. It is our deeds that new options are today at hand which were previously not available to us.

Creating a New World Order calls for a tough confrontation with the status quo on many fronts and multiple levels---be that in political, economic, educational, moral or cultural spheres of life. It is indeed so, if this rhetoric is meant to be perceived as insisting on bringing about a real change in the human psyche, as urging to open up hitherto untired possibilities for new ways of educating and socializing the next generation than the way we were. It is an incredibly difficult project, for its eventual goal---as I see it---is not to oppress, exclude or defeat one party for the sake of another but to gradually innovate and create a global community across diverse cultures which can wage a battle against the "system"---the system that produces the oppressors and the oppressed, the exploiters and the exploited, the winners and the losers cutting across nationality, race, religion, gender or any other form of collectivity. While we get ready to engage ourselves in such an enterprise, in small and big ways, alone and in groups, we know that countless obstacles will try to thwart the process. However, while struggling to change the environment in which we live at present and facing the seemingly insuperable opposition to this project, it may be wise to keep in mind the Gandhian slogan that could be heard all over the sub-continent of India during the Freedom Movement, now almost half-a-century ago: "Hate the system, do not hate the people."

Chapter Nine

The Calling of a Transformative Politics: Criticism and Creativity in the Work of Roberto M. Unger

Prakash C. Sarangi

Democratic governance has always fascinated both scholars and activists. However, there has been no consensus regarding its organization or function. It is like the proverbial hat which fits into any head. Its problems get aggravated when its wearer becomes aware of the consequences of an ill-fitting garb. Since the shape of the head cannot be changed, the hat gets the flak from all possible sources. Fashion designers come forward to tinker with the design of the old hat. Or, someone may design an altogether new style. Roberto M. Unger belongs to the latter category and presents a blueprint of a radical democracy.

There has been several assessments of democratic theory and action during the last few years.[1] While most of these works question various aspects of liberal democratic framework, there is no serious attempt to present a radical alternative. Unger's transformative approach presented in his *False Necessity*[2] is therefore refreshingly different. He presents an explanatory theory of society and a programme for social reconstruction. He consciously departs from both orthodox Marxism and western liberalism. He seeks to free social explanation from its dependence upon the denial of our freedom to resist and to remake our forms of social life. His programme of social reconstruction shows how we may carry forward the radical project of freeing our practical and passionate dealings from the constraints imposed upon them by entrenched social roles and hierarchies.

Unger develops an antinecessitarian approach[3] in order to solve a particular explanatory problem. This problem is the origin and the basis of cycles of reform and retrenchment that characterize both the western democracies and the communist countries. We find that partisan conflicts and attitudes about the uses of governmental power with respect to major issues, such as the direction of economic policy, move among a small number of familiar options. "The stubborn, mysterious cycles represent a permanent insult to societies whose official culture claims to base fundamental social arrangements upon the wills of free and relatively equal citizens and rightholders rather than upon blind drift or coercive authority" (1987: 5). Unger tries to solve this riddle of policy cycles by studying the influence and the character of what he calls "the formative contexts, structures, or frameworks of social life: the basic institutional arrangements and imaginative preconceptions that circumscribe our routine practical or discursive activities and conflicts and that resist their destabilising effects" (ibid: 6-7). He wants us to recognize the influence of these contexts. This would enable us not only to rebel against these contexts, it would also help us to diminish or intensify the force with which they constrain us.

However, Unger admits that these explanatory theories have inherent limitations. They cannot help us understand how these contexts are internally constituted, how they get remade, and how they inform a richly textured life of practical and argumentative routines. Unger, therefore, feels that there is also a need to devise a set of critical and constructive practices carefully crafted and militantly wielded to preserve their antinecessitarian power. His programme of empowered democracy is an attempt in this direction.

Notion of Empowerment

Unger presents a programme of social reconstruction as a radical alternative to social democracy. It is a programme of empowered democracy whose implementation would realize more effectively both liberal and socialist commitments. He suggests how to reorganize governments and economies in ways that further a non-statist socialism and give more effective form to liberal aspirations. The aim is to carry forward the radical project of establishing institutions that empower us more because they divide us less.

Unger describes his notion of empowerment thus: "The empowerment that the programme is meant to foster is in part the development of our practical productive capabilities. But it is also the freedom resulting from what we most prize even in current versions of democracy and community: the promise of forms of social engagement that save us from having to choose between isolation from other people and surrender to them and that describe modes of attachment that are also exercises in self-assertion. Finally, it is the empowerment that consists of conscious mastery over the institutional and imaginative contexts of our activities" (1987: 9). Thus, Unger's programme seeks the individual and collective empowerment that can result from the creation of institutional arrangements that undermine the forms of dependence and domination.

Unger is both a visionary and a realist. He provides both the types of justifications for his programme of empowered democracy. The vision offered by this programme is that of a society in which people are more fully empowered through the development of institutional arrangements that "both diminish the gap between framework-preserving routine and framework-transforming conflict and weaken the established forms of social division and hierarchy" (ibid: 362). Unger's goal is to subject social life to democratic participation and conflict. He visualizes a society in which individuals are freer to deal with one another as individuals rather than as placeholders in the system of class, communal, role, or gender contrasts. He expects individuals to imagine and defend a certain change in the quality of their experience of subjectivity and sociability. This change consists in the interaction among three varieties of empowerment:

> One variety consists in the development of our practical capability through the openness of social life to the recombinational and experimental activities of practical reason. Another type of empowerment is the exercise of a more complete and deliberate mastery over the imaginative and institutional contexts of our activities. And still another lies in our success in escaping both submission and isolation and in diminishing the conflict between the enabling conditions of self-assertion: between our need to participate in group life and our effort to avoid the dangers of dependence and depersonalization that accompany such engagement (ibid: 363).

Though these varieties of empowerment have convergent or overlapping institutional requirements, no necessary or permanent conflict exists among these. It is up to us to discover in our historical situation which conditions of each variety of empowerment also satisfy the other varieties. While Unger's vision includes the idea of enabling individuals to develop and pursue their life projects, it emphasizes "whatever in the experience of the individual enables him to treat others and himself as an original, to fashion practical and passionate attachments less vitiated by dependence and depersonalisation, and to move within his social contexts with the heightened self-consciousness and engagement of a context-revising agent" (ibid).

The realist in Unger prompts him to provide several internal justifications of empowered democracy. He starts with a minimalist version of democratic ideal that it is a regime where the social relations is subject to the wills of free and equal citizens. The goal is to prevent the state from becoming hostage to a faction, irrespective of whether a faction of a class, a community, or a party.[4] Unger feels that the single most powerful source of the gap between the minimalist democratic ideal and the realities of democratic politics is the reliance on absolute property rights as the primary device of economic decentralization. These rights provide the institutional shell within which those who act as delegates of property owners are entitled to organize work on non-democratic principles.

Secondly, Unger feels that the basic arrangements of social life in a democracy should be chosen by the will of free and equal citizens. Unfortunately, in the contemporary democratic social order one is trapped by the logic of majority rule. No majoritarian choice destroys the framework that enables new majorities to emerge and to change or reverse earlier decisions. Democratic politics is caught in the midst of reform cycles in which a small number of policy options alternate that are almost no party's favourite solutions. The question of social transformation is overlooked. Such a situation strengthens the idea that "privilege becomes stable only by being insulated from the effects of routine conflict" (ibid: 376).

Thirdly, Unger argues that in the contemporary regimes there is constant frustration in the fulfilment of party political programmes, no matter whether it is a classical liberal programme of governmental decentralization and economic competition, a centrist programme of corporatism and community, or a social democratic programme of redistribution and participation. Political parties face two horns of a dilemma. On the one hand, if the proponent of a programme continues to accept the existing institutional framework, he finds himself repeatedly frustrated in accomplishing his objective. On the other hand, if he tries to reform the current institutional structure for better realization of his goals, he discovers that they require of him a revised understanding of his programmatic aims and their relation to the aims of his adversaries. In either case, there is a distinct gap between the party platforms and the corresponding institutional arrangements in a democracy.

In order to overcome these problems in the contemporary polities, Unger presents his blueprint of empowered democracies. It has two components which complement each other:

ideal models of human association and the institutional arrangements that realize these models in fact. Institutional ideas have to be realized by social activities that might establish them. Unger argues that a programmatic vision that cannot rely on a corresponding style of practice remains unstable. Therefore, his proposal for institutions of empowered democracy is preceded by his vision of transformative practice in quest of empowerment.

Transformative Practice

Unger argues that the most important task of transformative movement is to maintain the connection between grassroots mobilization and the contest over governmental power (ibid: 407). He expects the collective mobilization to be non-partisan in character; but there is also scope for taking help from political parties and bureaucracy. While political parties are simply electoral syndicates which take for granted current definitions of group interests, collective identities and social possibilities and which are much less likely to defy these contexts which sustain them, support can be taken from those political parties which are closer to the vision of an empowered democracy. Similarly, bureaucrats and professionals with social commitments can help in the process of grassroots mobilization.

Secondly, Unger wants the transformative movement to be an experimental model in anticipation of the empowered democracy. Such a movement should succeed in establishing small-scale, fragmentary versions of the future the programme advocates for society. An experiment arises from the very nature of collective mobilization which defies established hierarchies and roles. "The relations between the superior and the subalterns, or between centralised collective decision and individual and factional initiative, the merger of democratic and communal ideals with each other, and their extension to ordinary practical dealings, must all turn the movement into a living icon of its programme" (ibid: 413).

The third task of transformative practice, according to Unger, is recruiting and managing the cadres of the movement. The cadres are distinctly different from the leadership and the rank and file. They are the activists or militants whose relatively privileged social circumstances and intimate psychological identification with the movement enable them to devote themselves to its task. Theoretical enlightenment of this cadre is necessary to remove the inadequacies of cadres of sectarian or consensual types. If necessary, a new cadre may be created with proper understanding of transformative practice.

The fourth task prescribed by Unger is recognizing and devaluing the logic of group interests. By group interests he means "the overall constellation of positive and negative aims that seem to inhere in the distinct places that every system of social division and hierarchy generates" (ibid: 420). The activist must respect the constraints that group interests impose on collective action, and yet he must act in the spirit of one who sees these collective interests as dependent upon institutional frameworks that are not themselves guided by higher order laws. His aim is not merely to replace one set of collective interests by another but to change the sense in which society making remains at the mercy of a pre-existing system of group interests, whether of classes or communities. Transformative politics must embody the dissolution of classes and communities, while at the same time not lapsing into a Hobbesian search for pre-emptive security. Such dissolution should result in alternative institutional arrangements ensuring vital security of the individual.

Unger's fifth suggestion is that the transformative movement must learn to identify and exploit opportunities for practical and imaginative destabilization even when the current formative context seems most stable and entrenched. The stability is exemplified by "the close connection between the perceived group interests or identities and institutional arrangements, the failure of any institutional or imaginative framework to accommodate all emerging opportunities for practical or passionate human connection, and the irrepressible ability of context-preserving activities to escalate into context-transforming struggle" (ibid: 424). Any minor crisis or disharmony may provide a transformative opportunity in the form of disturbance in the existing institutional arrangements. "The transformers must recognise the initial opportunity. They must master the practice of the disturbance-maximising response. They must turn each success in the pursuit of this response into an example of the fragmentary anticipation of their programme" (ibid).

Finally, Unger argues that there is a need to formulate a visionary language of transformation. The forms of discourse now available to radical transformative movements are largely unsuited to the programme of empowered democracy. "In a very real sense the movement must talk itself into power, and its talk, like its more worldly stratagems, must be both a tool of persuasion and a device of discovery" (ibid: 430). A suitable discourse enables people to reflect upon the interplay between the definitions of group interests and successive adjustments of the institutional framework within which these interests get defined and satisfied. The language of the movement must repudiate the exclusive contrast between reformist tinkering and all-out revolution. The discourse must be both prophetic as well as institutional. "It must achieve a visionary freshness and immediacy to enlist energies on the side of the institution-challenging forms of interest satisfaction and to maintain the instructive and encouraging connection between present experiences and ultimate programmatic aims" (ibid).

Organization of Government

Unger's programme of empowered democracy is primarily a plan to empower people. He criticizes the established version of democracy because it places much of its institutional order beyond the effective reach of democratic politics. Therefore, he proposes multiplication of the number of branches in government, all elected by a general electorate. "The multiplication of powers in the state should obey two overlapping criteria: first, that when the total system of powers and functions has been established, it will work to prevent any section of society from gaining a lasting stranglehold over the material or human resources that can be used to generate the future form of society; second, that the same system provide an opportunity for the exercise of every major variety of transformative activity, practical or imaginative" (ibid: 449-50). By subjecting governmental institutions to mass politics Unger aims at loosening the oligarchy effect that is prevalent.

Unger criticises the principle of checks and balances as a mechanism to resolve conflicts of power among different branches of government. This principle has "proved both an intolerable insult to popular sovereignty and a superfluous guarantee of social stability" (ibid: 454). Because of the system of checks and balances, a faction with an ambitious programme must capture more or less simultaneously the different branches of government. Hence, any political project of transformative nature would face obstacles from this constitutional machinery. Unger presents three principles which may concurrently govern the conflict of powers under the reformed constitution. The first is the absolute restraint one power may impose on another. Second, priority among different branches should be fixed. The third principle is the use of the immediate or delayed devolution of constitutional impasses to the general electorate.

Unger proposes for an identifiable decisional centre within the constitution of empowered democracy (sovereign power?). The instruments at the disposal of this decisional center must be more effective than those available to the ruling parties in traditional democracies. They must be proportionate to the intentions of collective movements capable of linking struggles at the height of state power to the rivalries of everyday life. "The powers forming this decisional centre are those most immediately responsible for the implementation of a partisan programme that may address the overall structure of society and for the ultimate control over the state's dealings, in peace and war, with other states" (ibid: 458). Unger argues that those governmental institutions that stand closest to the citizenry and that provide the broadest scope for popular decision must also be the ones to make the choices that involve most dramatically the lives and fortunes of the people.

Instead of a comprehensive constitutional scheme as it prevails in the contemporary democracies, Unger supports the idea of mini-constitutions. He argues that there should be opportunity to establish special constitutional regimes for limited contexts and aims. At the most modest level, the party in office may have flexible powers to set up institutions in particular sectors of society. At the highest level, the leaders of a party may appear before the universal electorate requesting some special regime of power that can be reconciled with the constitutional safeguards for individuals, minorities and oppositions. In such a case, the election becomes a conflict over the form of the state and the identity of the highest officeholders.

Unger's constitutionalism of permanent mobilization seems to have an apparent problem of political instability. It looks as if the state and society would be reduced to bitter strife and paralyzing confusion. Unger, however, is very optimistic about the integrative aspect of such partisan conflict resulting in political stability. He feels that emancipation of society is possible by dissolving social classes into parties of opinion. In fact, he goes further and pleads for aggravation of the destabilization effects of partisanship. He thinks that partisan rivalry is safe when the principles and interests to which each major party is committed do not fit into a single cohesive vision. A multiplicity of crosscutting factions would lead to the prosecution of particular goals. The citizens would find themselves divided in many contradictory ways rather than over two or three bases of organization of society. As a result, "partisan conflict would rarely seem to be about society's formative institutional context or its enacted imaginative scheme of association. It would be largely about the marginal advances of certain groups within that context. Any change in the defining institutional arrangements or the embodied vision of social life would normally come about as a by-product of the struggle over fragmentary goals and interests" (ibid: 463-64).

Unger favours decentralization of political power. At the same time he leaves room for major swings in the emphasis different political parties may give to either greater centralized authority or more decentralized experiment. But such swings should be within a framework that upholds the broader commitments of empowered democracy. Such a framework must prefer the forms of centralization and decentralization that are less likely to immunize privilege against effective challenge. Individuals and groups would have a right to opt out of norms established by higher authorities. At the same time, any devolution of power should not help to entrench old or emergent privileges.

The programme of empowered democracy includes a scheme to facilitate the self-organization of society outside government. "The negative aim is to organise a parallel state or even an antistate. It is to form a set of institutions that, without canceling the opportunities for government sponsored social experiments, diminishes the risk of despotic perversion: the danger that the governmental arrangements of the new-model democracy may be used to initiate a concentration of power unrestrained by independent social organisations. ...The affirmative point is to turn the organisational instruments of non-governmental association into better means of discovering, questioning, and revising each formative institutional and imaginative context of social life" (ibid: 476-77). People may organize themselves where they work and live. A host of other associations may flourish free from governmental control. Legal opportunities, public resources and free access to the means of communication support these additional groupings. These voluntary associations help keep the state humble and the people proud, inquisitive and restless.

Organization of Economy

Unger's programme visualizes an alternative institutional definition of the market. He is highly critical of the current version of market institutions. It jeopardizes freedom by increasing the authority of centralizing forces and by generating inequalities of wealth. He argues that within the established regime of the capital, economies of scale seem to require the consolidation of property rights over large amounts of capital in a single decisional center. Its move towards plasticity of economic arrangements loosens the predetermination of exchange and production relations by rules and regularities that remain unavailable for revision in the light of emergent practical opportunities. Further, the present market system imposes a constraint upon macro-economic policy by making it growth-oriented with no focus on redistribution (1987: 480-91).

Unger's alternative economic order seeks to minimize these constraints on the current economic systems. He wants to use it in the effective success of his experiment of empowered democracy by increasing the freedom of economic relations from predetermination by a challenge-resistant scheme of social life. The key idea of his institutional proposal is the break up of control over capital into several tiers of capital takers and capital givers. The ultimate capital giver is a social capital fund controlled by the decision center of the empowered democracy: the party in office and the supporting representative assemblies. The ultimate capital takers are teams of workers, technicians, and entrepreneurs, who make temporary and conditional claims upon divisible portions of this social capital fund. The central capital fund does not lend money directly to capital users. Instead, it allocates resources to a variety of semi-independent investment funds, each specializing in a particular sector of the economy. Effectively a competitive capital market emerges among these investment funds. These funds in turn allocate resources to the primary capital takers. they profit from successful enterprise and suffer from business failure. But they never acquire permanent individual or group rights to the capital they receive. Success merely increases their income.

"Thus, the proposed regime provides three tiers of capital givers and capital takers, the second tier being both a taker and a giver. The precise balance of economic power among these levels represents a major topic of political conflict under the empowered democracy" (ibid: 492). The basic legal principle of this alternative economic order is the disintegration of property. It offers an institutional framework within which the principle of deliberate social control over the forms and consequences of economic accumulation can be reconciled with decentralized economic decision making. "The economic order of the empowered democracy is both more a socially responsible economy and more a market economy than the system it is meant to replace" (ibid). It is more of a socially responsible economy because the means for collective review of the arrangements and results of economic life are deeply integrated into the institutional order rather than dependent upon a relatively haphazard pattern of governmental intervention. It is more of a market economy because it promises to increase both the absolute degree of economic decentralization and the revisability of the organizational settings of production and exchange.

System of Rights

Unger attempts to redefine the system of rights. "By a system of rights I mean simply an institutionalized version of society, which is to say, a form of social life acquiring a relatively stable and delineated form and generating a complicated set of expectations. The stability and the expectations are not merely those of the prison camp: a system of rights defines arrangements that many people treat as the expression of a defensible scheme of human association" (ibid: 508-9). Unger extends the boundaries of rights beyond the legalistic vocabulary which limits it to the state-described and state-enforced law. He suggests two generative principles of a reconstituted system of rights. First, "the security of the individual should be established in ways that minimise both the immunity of institutional arrangements to challenge and conflict and the ease with which some individuals can reduce others to dependence" (ibid: 513). This principle commits to establish the individual's position of immunity in a way that minimizes both the rigidification of the institutional order and the risks of personal subjugation. The second principle is the effort to affirm legal rights that, by their form and content, suit the obligations of interdependence that characterize communal life. These rights should embody and promote a certain prescriptive vision of communal relations. "At the center of this revised approach to direct personal relations stands a conception of community as a zone in which the increased acceptance of mutual vulnerability makes it possible to multiply ways of diminishing the conflict between attachment to other people and the claims of self-consciousness and self-possession. Overcoming this conflict represents but another facet of the project of human empowerment" (ibid: 518). In Unger's reconstruction of the system of rights, therefore, the operational characteristics of entitlements cease to be seen as the inherent features of rights, just as rights themselves are no longer thought to mark the built-in structure in an institutional type of governmental, economic and communal organization.

Unger presents proposals for several rights which are in their distinctive ways quite novel (ibid: 520-39). First, *market* rights are to be employed for economic exchange in the trading sector of society. Existence of such a right becomes inevitable within a fully realized version the reconstructed economy where teams of workers, technicians and entrepreneurs gain access to the social capital. Second, *immunity rights* protect the individual against oppression by concentration of public or private power, against exclusion from the important collective decisions that influence his life, and against the extremes of economic and cultural deprivation. They give him the confidence to participate fearlessly and actively in making collective decisions about the organizations of society. Immunity rights would include not only freedom against governmental and private oppression, but also the guarantees of access to material and cultural resources through welfare entitlements. Third, *destabilization rights* protect the citizen's interest in breaking open the large-scale organizations or the extended areas of social practice that remain closed to the destabilizing effects of ordinary conflict. The destabilization entitlement ties the collective interest in ensuring that all institutions and practices can be criticized and revised to the individual interest in avoiding oppression. This right is a necessary condition for protecting the individual from the structures of domination and dependence. Lastly, *solidarity rights* give legal form to social relations of reliance and trust. The aim of this system of entitlements is not only to bring about institutional transformation, but also a cultural-revolutionary transformation of personal relations that goes hand in hand with the plan to empower democracy. People can experiment more freely with ways to achieve self-assertion through passionate attachments. The situation calling for the exercise of such entitlements include family life, continuing business relations and various types of fiduciary relations. The trust such relations require may be voluntary and reciprocal or half-deliberate and unequal, usually in the setting of disparities of power or advantage.

An Evaluation

A basic premise of the empowered democracy is that reduction of the differences between context-preserving routine and context-transforming conflict cannot be achieved either by throwing out the state altogether and putting a pure system of human coordination in its place or by submerging fixed institutional arrangements in personal charisma. Nor, on the other hand, can it result from solutions imposed by a self-appointed vanguard upon a recalcitrant population. Empowered democracy attempts instead to change the relation between large-scale and inclusive institutions and noninstitutionalized collective action. Unger's goal in a nutshell is to search for individual and collective empowerment through the dissolution of the prewritten social script.

It is not clear therefore whether Unger's project is an extension of the liberal doctrine or a replacement of it. The programme of empowered democracy shares with the libertarian the aim of freeing individual experience to the greatest possible extent from the overbearing influence of predetermined collective categories class, community or gender. But, the disruption of communal bonds is sought to be remedied by the organizations intermediate between the individual and the state. Unger's programme is centrist in that it characteristically emphasizes the improvement of hierarchy through loyalty and self-restraint rather than through the radical subversion of hierarchical bonds. It is sometimes corporatist because the intermediate bodies, which may be productive enterprises as well as territorial entities, are to occupy a recognized place in the organization of the society.

Unger himself claims that his blueprint is a leftist programme. Like all leftist views it holds that only by an institutional transformation we can realize in practice our ideals of freedom and community. It seeks to undermine forms of dependence and domination. But it also differs from the mainstream radical leftist programmes. Its explanatory ideas are different from traditional Marxist theory. Further, it refuses to equate, as a leftist does, the market economy and the representative democracy. On the contrary, it sees in the development of alternative forms of democracies and markets the best hope for the accomplishment of leftist as well as liberal aims. Finally, it draws heavily upon a tradition of institutional thought and experimentation to which the main current of leftist theory and practice has been hostile: the tradition of petty bourgeois radicalism.

Both liberals and the leftists would perhaps be uncomfortable with Unger's championing of the cause of the petty bourgeoisie. But he supports his argument from historical research that the radical challenge to the dominant forms of governmental and economic organization comes from skilled workers and artisans, technicians and professionals, shopkeepers and petty manufacturers, rather than from the proletariat. He feels that the attempt of these utopian socialists to establish a different form of industrial society was rarely put to test that would make it possible to assess their advantages and drawbacks. But there could be many practical objections to petty commodity production. It may be economically regressive because it does not permit the economies of scale and the market organization that would encourage technological dynamism. Second, petty commodity production is economically unstable. The more successful petty entrepreneurs would drive the less successful ones out of business and would reduce them to the condition of wage labourers. Only a corrective system of redistribution can prevent such an outcome. But such a system would then become the real economic order, and it would disrupt the economic calculations of small-scale producers. Third, petty commodity production is politically unstable. The national governments capable of supporting such an economic regime would always be either too strong or too weak. The government, resting on a population of independent proprietors obsessed with their personal interests, might be starved of resources that would enable it to administer and defend the society. On the other hand, if the government did obtain these resources it would soon overpower a social order without large scale organizations capable of counterbalancing its own authority.

A major problem of transformative politics has to be with the relation between the effort to reconstruct social arrangements and the attempt to change the nature of personal dealings among individuals. It is not clear whether Unger has been able to integrate these two endeavours. The human sense of institutional proposals depends ultimately on its implications for the social microcosm. It is possible that anticipatory experience of transformed personal relations would encourage self-restraint. Unger's programme may not provide enough guarantee to contain the disruptions of transition. For example, redistribution may exercise a mobilizing effect by granting larger numbers of people the security that enables them to give themselves wholeheartedly to institutional reconstruction. But both rapid distributive and institutional change could disrupt routines of production, exchange and administration. The crucial test is whether there would be enough cushions to push the conflict beyond the instrumental struggle over material advantages to a commitment for social transformation.

There could also be a tension between the importance and the dangers of using governmental power in order to transform society in the image of a programmatic vision. The use of centralized, coercive state power to impose a plan of social life is likely to be futile if it aims at changing habits and sentiments. The rulers of the state may find themselves waging war against a resistant society. The results of the interplay between the transforming will and the social resistance may bear little relation to the initial programme. Therefore, the commitment to carry the programme might become secondary compared to the struggle to hold on to the state power.

Unger admits that his proposals are designed primarily with the contemporary western democracies in mind. Though a Brazilian himself and one who had worked as a political activist to develop a democratic leftist party in his native country, he does not attempt to develop a specific design of empowered democracy for third world countries. His cynicism regarding the politics in these countries is evident from his statement that "in the absence of the great accidents of war and invasion many of these countries can expect to attain western levels of economic equality and democratic pluralism only through the militant organisation of the oppressed, the excluded, and the angry. It is not enough for these sectors of society to mobilise; they must remain mobilised. They and their leaders must use the favouring circumstances of crisis, revolution, and radical enthusiasm to establish economic and governmental institutions that help perpetuate in the midst of humdrum social routine something of the transitory experience of mass mobilisation" (1987: 394-95). Unger feels that many third world countries need very bold initiatives to achieve the status of social democracies and therefore have a long way to go to reach the stage of the radical alternative that he proposes. They need a more radical thrust than what the western democracies require. Here, Unger unwittingly falls into a trap of necessitarian logic which he intends to avoid.

Unger's ambitious design to reconstruct the western liberal democracies cannot be simple and straight forward either. Human beings are not modules of a machine. They are self-defining animals: they differ from other animal species precisely in their ability to constitute for themselves their own identities. Human beings are full of miscellaneous diversities with which they present themselves to each other. Their personal identities are not natural facts, but cultural artefacts. Unger does not take into account the socio-psychological consequences of his reconstruction of institutions. One should not ignore the contributions of public culture on the personal autonomy and the fact that it is impossible for the state to be neutral in respect of promotion of virtue and the realization of human capacities.[5] If Unger is genuinely interested in empowering people, then he has to view his programme as one among a variety of orders in which human beings may flourish.

Unger's concept of power has a positivist connotation, though he himself questions positivist social theorization. Concept of power is an essentially contestable concept depending on the opposed conceptions of human interests.[6] The essential contestability of the concept derives from the fact that rival applications of it embody conflicting value commitments. Hence, any study of power becomes a normative exercise. The problem of locating power in society is to fix responsibility. Fixing responsibility involves making a moral appraisal. One has to distinguish exercises of power from structural determination of social happenings. Though opportunities for action are structurally constrained, the subject matter of the theory of power is human agency rather than the workings of social necessity. Understanding the exercise of power therefore inescapably involves the application of moral notions connected with responsibility and with the nature of persons who constitute a "civil association".[7]

In spite of Unger's long description about the transformative practice in the empowered democracy, one does not get a clear picture about the nature of civil society he expects to emerge. Collective mobilization in a postliberal society with incommensurable values is not going to be easy.[8] Imposition of a collective plan in a society with diversity of views, both religious and political, might push it to the limits of toleration. Any decision procedure to reconcile the rival and possibly incommensurable conceptions of the good would inevitably occasion conflict. In such an event, restraint imposed on the omnicompetence of the government by the rule of law is crucial. It is not clear from Unger's analysis whether his plan to empower people is matched by effective limitation on government's power by rule of law.

Unger's programme of empowered democracy is based on a radical theory for action.[9] Theory of action is in the domain of strategy and organization. But, unlike a mere manipulative politics, a radical theorist is acting in the name of and for the sake of principles, ideas and aims which claim universal validity. This is the domain of moral legitimacy. Though Unger's goal is to be anti-contextual, any radical politics has to risk itself in a specific context and a particular conjuncture of history. An action has to get strategic legitimacy by being effective in a particular context. "Being a principled politics, a radical theory has always the problem of a double transformation. Such a theory has to so orient its actions that their strategic legitimacy also gets the dimension of moral legitimacy. Its contextual interventions must also have a non-contextual authority, such that its politics could be both vindicated by its context and validated by its principle."[10]

Notes

1. A sample of this work is: Brian Barry, *Democracy and Power* (Oxford: Clarendon Press, 1991); Frank Bealey, *Democracy in the Contemporary state* (Oxford: Clarendon Press, 1988); C.J. Berry, *The Idea of a Democratic Community* (New York: St Martins, 1989); S. Bowles and H. Gintis, *Democracy and Capitalism* (London: Routledge, 1986), especially the chapter on Postliberal Democracy; F. Cunningham, *Democratic Theory and Socialism* (Cambridge: Cambridge University Press, 1987); Robert Dahl, *Democracy and its Critics* (New Haven: Yale University Press, 1989), especially the chapter on Sketches for an Advanced Democratic Country; G. Duncan (ed.), *Democratic Theory and Practice* (Cambridge: Cambridge University Press, 1983); Carol C. Gould, *Rethinking Democracy* (Cambridge: Cambridge University Press, 1988); David Held, *Models of Democracy* (Cambridge: Polity Press, 1987); Alan Hunt (ed.), *Marxism and Democracy* (London: Lawrence and Wishart, 1980); Rajni Kothari, *State Against Democracy* (Delhi: Ajanta, 1988); G. Parry and M. Moran, *Democracy and Democratisation* (London: Routledge, 1994).
2. Roberto M. Unger, *False Necessity* (Cambridge: Cambridge University Press, 1987). Unless otherwise mentioned, all the references in the text are from this work.
3. This style of analysis criticises an evolutionary stereotype, such as the identification of a simplified view of economic growth associated with modernisation or capitalism. Given a theory's

presumed necessity, a critic would hesitate to reject it entirely. Therefore, he would reinterpret it against a background of forgotten conflict or of repressed alternatives.

4. Unger's argument is similar to Michel's 'iron law of oligarchy'. Also, see Joseph Schumpeter, *Capitalism, Socialism and Democracy* (New York: Harper, 1942).
5. See the argument given in this respect by Joseph Raz, *The Morality of Freedom* (Oxford: Clarendon Press, 1986).
6. Despite the differences among the scholars on the notion of power, there is broad agreement on this issue. See, for example, Steven Lukes, Power: A radical View (London: Macmillan, 1974); and W.E. Connolly, *The Terms of Political Discourse* (Oxford: Basil Blackwell, 1983).
7. For a discussion on the civil association, see Michael Oakshott, *On Human Conduct* (Oxford: Clarendon Press, 1975), pp. 108-84.
8. John Gray, *Postliberalism* (New York: Routledge: 1993), p. 314.
9. A distinction is made between a theory of action, for action and in action. See, for example, R. Sundara Rajan, *Towards a Critique of Cultural Reason* (Delhi: OUP, 1987).
10. Ibid., p.17.

Chapter Ten

State, Market and the Voluntary Sector: Agragamee, Social Criticism and the Contemporary Dialectics of Transformations

Vidhya and Achyut Das

State, Market and the Tribal Situation

The context of Agragamee's work is the tribal situation. So it might be well to begin with a brief look into the tribal heritage that provides the backdrop to the organization. Tribal communities were once a fiercely independent people. Reports indicate that though early rulers did often claim large tracts of forest land for timber, they met with guerrilla resistance. Thus, the rulers from the Ashoka period through the Gupta and Mughal periods left forest dwellers in peace. Further, it is also found that tribal communities that maintained forest oriented self-sufficient economies were best able to prevent outside political domination.

Much of this changed with the arrival of the British colonial interests, with their excessive demands on forest resources. The relative isolation of the tribal people ended, their egalitarian social order was destroyed and in time they were reduced to agricultural labourers, bonded slaves and sharecroppers and tenants. The tribal people, spread over large parts of the country, organized hundreds of militant outbreaks and insurrections during the 19th century. These outbreaks were marked by immense courage and sacrifice on their part and brutal suppression and veritable butchery on the part of the rulers. The uprisings were broad based, involving thousands of tribals, often the entire population of a region. Ethnic ties formed a basic feature of most of these movements, the rebels as themselves not as a discreet class but as having a clear tribal identity. Fellow-tribals were never attacked, unless they had collaborated with the enemy. Also, there was hardly any violence against the non-tribal poor who had social relations with the tribals, often, the rural poor formed a part of the rebellious band of the tribals.

Needless to say, the warfare was completely unequal. The tribals brought together on their dislike of foreign rule were fighting with their bows, arrows, axes and spears a trained regiment armed with the latest weapons. The tribals died in lakhs. The biggest of these uprisings against the colonizers was the Santhal uprising of 1877 in which more than 60,000 tribal people were mobilized against the outsider or *dikus* by the leaders Sido and Kanhu. The colonial government declared martial law, and mobilized their regiments under the command of a major general. More than 15,000 Santhals were killed, and by 1866, the rebellion was crushed. The Kols of Chhotnagpur, the hill tribes of coastal Andhra Pradesh, the Mundas of Bihar and Orissa, under the leadership of Birsa Munda, the Kondhs of Kondhmal, rose in revolt. Over the whole period of the 19th century and the early part of the 20th century numerous major and minor tribal uprisings took place which were crushed ruthlessly, as the British government established its regime.

Thus, over the first century of colonial rule, there has been a near genocide of tribals with consequent destruction of tribal polity, culture, tradition and morale. Where tribal people were the lords of their forests and uplands, living by choice and egalitarian life, based on the values of conservation, they were eventually reduced to mere labourers dependent helplessly on the the mercy of government and occasional employment.

With the dawn of independence, all the communities coming under the scheduled and excluded and partially excluded areas were enlisted under the 5th and 6th schedules of the Indian Constitution. Pt. Jawaharlal Nehru's *Panchsheel* was accepted as embodying the essential principles for tribal development. These principles included the right of tribal communities over their land and forest resources, not imposing exotic systems and administrators onto tribal communities and encouraging development planning for tribal areas by the tribal people themselves.

But when development planning was taken up, tribal area development plans had a largely paternalistic and protectionistic attitude. During the first five-year plan a number of problems in tribal areas were attempted to be tackled through the community development programmes. In the second and third five-year plans, special tribal blocks were identified and specific programmes taken up for them. In 1979, an evaluation of the programmes revealed that most of the benefit had gone to the non-tribal community, with the most primitive tribes being completely denied and that the major problems in tribal areas continued to exist.

In the subsequent five-year plans, tribal areas were brought under the tribal sub-plan. ITDAs (Integrated Tribal Development Agencies) were set up, and funds for tribal development from all sectoral programmes were channelised through these. Apart from these, special micro-projects were taken up to address in the problems of the different primitive tribes. During the sixth five-year plan, tribals living in scattered pockets were brought under the Modified Area Development Approach (MADA). Despite this multiplicity of programmes, the project affected people, displaced in lakhs by large scale industries, dams and mines have not been given sufficient attention.

Thus, we see that as far as schemes and planning goes, the government has the best of intentions where tribals are concerned. But, after that things start going wrong. Thus, when work under JRY (Jawahar Rojgar Yojana) is sanctioned, private contractors come into the picture in a big way, and people are never even able to get their due minimum wages. On the other hand, though tribal people have amply demonstrated their abilities in implementing these village level projects on their own, they are never given due recognition, and are harassed to submission if they insist on by passing the private contractor and doing the work through the village committees. The public distribution system, another scheme contracted to private dealers, benefits primarily the local politicians. Schools in tribal areas are maintained mostly on paper, and it is taken for granted that they will mostly remain defunct.

Apart from all this, political and economic forces in tribal regions have led to the increasing marginalization and impoverishment of tribal people. Thus, despite the goals emphasizing tribal development, its actual policies of development have led to huge public sector investments for the creation of large-scale infrastructure for the building up of industry and technology, most of it to the cost of tribal and other marginalized communities. According to estimates, dams, mines and large-scale industries have displaced anything between 1.8 to 2.7 crore people since independence. Out of this 40 percent are from tribal communities. Thus, in the last half century since independence, more than 2 percent of the total population of our country have been forced out of their traditional homes. Of these, less than 30 percent have been rehabilitated. Government records remain silent about the plight of the other 1.8 million people.

Government policies on forest and minor forest produce, land acquisition, landownership and other issues that afflict tribal people are drawn from the laws formulated by the colonizers. Apart from being archaic and outdated these policies deprive the tribal communities of all resource base for survival and render the tribals insecure, fearful and dependent on the mercies of an indifferent government.

Role of the NGOs in Emancipation of the Tribals and the Poor

In order to bring qualitative changes in the lives of the poor and marginalized tribals, the non-governmental response has evolved over a period of time. These responses have been dependent on the tribal situation on the one hand and the "ideological nature of the NGOs (non-governmental organizations)" on the other. The responses by and large have fitted into the socio-economic and political environment of the tribals.

The NGOs working in the tribal areas are broadly categorized as (a) charity and welfare oriented, (b) empowerment and entitlement oriented, (c) support service oriented, and (d) network oriented. Though each of these types are playing some critical role in the tribal situation, the NGOs working for empowerment and entitlement of the tribals need special discussion because of the emancipatory process involved in the relationship. Such NGOs generally work on issues with sharp ideological commitment---the issues related to livelihood access and control of resources, environmental conservations and political empowerment. These NGOs believe that they have a role in confronting the evil designs of the state and the market which are perpetually trying to support the rich and powerful at the cost of poor and the dispossessed. These NGOs by the principles of ethics are non-violent and non-political but the issues they raise are not necessarily the same. Hence, most the time these NGOs are limited and work with a limited perspective.

To confront the state and the market at their worst, the NGOs are often in dilemma. Because of the patronage and co-option, the NGOs get absorbed within the state machinery or in the market mechanism. This is inevitable as the NGOs are dependent on the state and the market for financial support and co-existence. In such a situation, it is only the people's organization that can confront the dominant state and market as illustrated in the experience of the Chipko movement, anti-mining movement in Gandhamardhan hills and the anti-nuclear movement in Baliapal, Orissa. Hence, it is important that the NGOs believing in the process of empowerment and entitlement must build up people's organizations that are self-sustaining in terms of leadership and inner dynamics of taking up relevant issues. By this the NGOs will find the right replacement for themselves if they wish to withdraw from the scene.

Agragamee's Interventions and the Dynamics of Transformations

This being the broader context of Agragamee's work, the organization took up the challenge of addressing the problems of tribal groups in the most interior and backward pocket of the state. It was a conscious choice, as explicitly stated in the first report of the organization:

> The choice is very very conscious. The socio-political and geographical factors were of paramount importance. Orissa has a sizable tribal population distributed over all the 13 districts. But five districts have large concentrations which includes Koraput, Social Work and Research Centre (SWRC) (registered in 1987 as AGRAGAMEE) did make an in-depth study of all these districts by going through various socio-anthropological survey reports and the experiences documented by a number of voluntary groups. In Orissa SWRC was only interested to confine to a Tribal Block when it was aware of tribal problems. Like elsewhere in India, the tribals here are being exploited in a number of ways. Though a major portion of them have converted to Christianity over the years through religious exploitation, the tribal people's plight remains largely unchanged. Administration has also ignored them resulting in isolation from the mainstream. The special agencies launched for the development of specific tribal communities have not delivered the required benefits. Hence, AGRAGAMEE perceived the necessity of addressing the problem at the micro-level.

Kashipur was not only chosen for its problems of poverty but also tribal initiative and struggle against a difficult system. The tribals grow a number of crop where there is not much of plain and irrigated land. He can make mud bunds over the rapids and wild streams to have some irrigation. Despite malaria and wild animals he has to save crops though a large portion of this would go to the money lenders.

And so an extensive survey of the block was taken up and the critical indicators of the tribal situation were studied and their causes sought. The parameters of intervention were mapped out with pragmatism and a determined effort to grapple with the cause. As the 1982-83 report states: "What is the necessity of a theoretical elaboration when one has the perceptions of a set of people who are bonded for a salary of Rs. 60 per month or who survive the ordeal by eating mango and tamarind seeds! One is worried for the exploitations and oppressions existing in every walk of life. To fight them one has to have one's approaches and strategies well-defined. Agragamee has adopted such strategies which can be reflected in the programme contents."

The main strategies which have been outlined are as follows:

(a) to have demonstrations in all related areas to show to the people as well as other agencies that things are possible. This has a lot of bearing upon the delivery system;

(b) to build up pressure groups within the village through certain educational activities to oppose the forces of exploitation. This pressure group is also to see that there is not much outflow of labour as well as produce;

(c) to strengthen the village level organization so as to have well-built infrastructure; and

(d) to have such micro-level activities to have maximum productive employment within the village.

Agragamee believes that the poor and the exploited can be made aware of their situation by taking part in various self-motivated actions to change their lot. Agragamee has attempted to channelize people's initiatives and strengths for a process of change and transformation. In doing all this, Agragamee recognized an essential principle of voluntarism and social change that there is nothing much an outsider group can do unless people themselves take up the initiative and challenge. There has been a basic recognition that even the poorest communities have resources within themselves to initiate a process of change and development. And indeed, Agragamee's stand has been proved right time and again. In fact, during the course of its work Agragamee has found that the poor and more deprived groups are the ones who are capable of taking up the greatest challenges. Agragamee has found that in numerous instances, the women were taking the much tougher stand and that they had taken the initiative for action when the men were still hesitant, unsure.

What in this context is criticism and creativity, where and how does the dialectics of transformation begin and end? In the tribal context in which Agragamee struggles and strives, the preoccupation is with survival. The dialogue with life and death is almost a battle here and who are we to impose such strange sounding concepts on their backs?

And yet, transformation is nothing new to these people. With colonization as described earlier, these societies were transformed from independent self-reliant communities to the status of slaves and bonded labourers, decimated and subdued. And what of the independent state? Does it not continue the process of transformation started by the colonizers, is it not just the same game with different players? The state focuses on industry, power, technology build-up, and millions of families all over the country are forced to change, are forced to give up their existing livelihoods and lifestyles, and take up a life of dependence, entire communities are disrupted and made to disintegrate, disappear without a trace, and in their place the state ushers in modern technology. The state chooses to lease out a forest tract, a commons to an industrial house, and in the entire region, people have to change their economy: bamboo workers are reduced to the category of the unemployed, women have to scrounge leaves for fuel, or start using precious cattle dung, and animals are deprived of their grazing ground. This is the transformation, the poor of the country are up against. Whether one likes it or not the transformation goes on. The forces are too big, the tribal and their other poor brethren too small to push back these forces.

But this force is not a tidal wave, unleashed by a whimsical nature. It is a force unleashed by a government that poses to represent the people, it is a force against people by an institution that is supposed to be of, for and by the people. Social change is inevitable for any community, much more so in the present times, with the break down of geographical barrier, and the giant leaps in communication technology. But what does a state owe to its people in terms of planned change and development, what does it owe to a people, marginalized, and on the other edge of poverty by every indicator; demographic, social or economic? Is it extermination, or should it be a responsible commitment for reconstruction with the involvement and the interests of the concerned communities as its central focus? The state today identifies with the market. The clarion call is liberalize or perish. In a democracy, this is a betrayal of the people. The first allegiance of a state should be to its people, and their economy not to global forces. This is common sense logic of governance, followed by most nation-states, including the greatest proponents of free market, the ever so liberal West. In his essay "Democracy and Markets in the New World," Noam Chomsky underlines this fact:

> The US has been the mother country and bastion of modern protectionism, and further, the United States in particular has been extreme in rejecting market discipline. That is how it developed from the beginning, including textiles, steel, energy chemicals, and gained enormous wealth and power instead of pursuing its comparative advantage in exporting furs, in accord with the stern principles of economic rationality.

Britain had followed a similar course, only turning to free trade after 150 years of protectionism had given it such enormous advantages that a level play field seemed a fairly safe bet, even then relying on the fact that 40 percent of its exports could go to the third world (1800-1938).

For Chomsky, "Britain itself would have been deindustrialized by the cheapness of Indian calicoes if protectionist policies had not been adopted. We all also know that the mills of Britain could hardly have been set in motion had it not been for the sacrifice of Indian manufacture, and that in the process, it was India that was deindustrialized." Free market is acceptable if it is really free. But, in this country, the state supports the capitalists, and the people have lost the battle, even before it was begun. In all this, there is an accompanying rhetoric, which grows increasingly shrill, making one realize that perhaps, that is all the state has to offer---rhetoric. The policies of development-induced displacement may be cited as a case in point. Thirty years back, the rehabilitation and resettlement policies for big dams gave a commitment of land for land. The Rengali Project committed six acres of irrigated and three acres of unirrigated land for the displaced. Now volumes after volumes are being produced on involuntary resettlement, numerous training programmes are being organized and lakhs being spent on just the so-called R&R planning, a draft national policy has been formulated, but with the basic submission that land for land cannot be given to the victims. Why then does the state agree to projects that nudge thousands of families from their land and homes? If this is not a violation of human rights then what is?

Creativity and Social Criticism

Tribal communities are unorganized and politically weak, their very leaders have been co-opted by the other side, and they have no voice. And yet, Agragamee's response in this situation has been to work on political literacy for the tribals which will lead to formation of people's organizations. This has already resulted in tribals taking up issues like marketing of non-timber forest produce (NTFP) and minor forest produce (MFP) and questioning existing state policies. In another case, tribals are asking questions about the proposed bauxite mining and alumina refinery in the region which are huge enterprises by multi-national companies. In recent years, this struggle has intensified as the State has colluded with the multi-national companies and let loose a reign of terror on the tribals resisting mining operations. In December 1998, the Orissa government banned Agragamee along with three other voluntary organizations of the locality on the charge of inciting the tribal population against the developmental policies of the state. Agragamee did not still give in and after two years the state government revoked the ban. But, the struggle still continues. In the course of fight for their rights over the last nine years, the tribals and the other downtrodden communities of the locality have been emboldened which makes both the state and the multinational mining companies nervous. To teach the resisting tribal population of Kashipur a lesson, police came to the tribal village of Maikanch on December 16, 2000 and opened fire on innocent, murdering in cold blood three young people. But, this has not deterred the local population. They are more determined to protect their homes and villages and evict the mining companies which are out to drink their blood.

The present anti-mining struggle in Kashipur has behind it other determined efforts to make a difference in their lives. There are already successful examples of the tribals stopping large-scale commercial plantations like coffee. A new awareness on land use has brought many landless tribals to take possession of surplus government land. To face the state and market, the only way left for the tribals is to articulate on the socio-economic and political processes and decide a course of action to ensure basic food security and living with dignity.

However, realizing the fact that the tribals are unorganized, the state should not and cannot use this as an excuse to exploit the tribal situation without end. In his book *Tending the Earth*, W. Periera talks about the indigenous systems developed by traditional communities for sustainable resource use, he talks about the creativity of traditional farmers in getting the best out of their land. This has also been Agragamee's observation and experience. The state condemns the practice of *podu* (slash and burn agriculture) and formulates numerous scientific options to this traditional form of cultivation in the tribal hinterlands. And yet a viable alternative to the tribal practice has not been found by the state despite its resources, expertise and infrastructure. A government-funded programme for development of Kashipur tried introducing various alternatives, including commercial crops and agro-forestry. None of these programmes were able to take off, or even remotely approximate the tribal people's returns from shifting cultivation, where they practice mixed cropping, growing upto eight or nine crops on the same patch of land in a single season. In another region, the tribal community has found its own alternative by taking up extensive terracing on the hill slopes, a practice meticulously carried out to prevent almost any flow of water on the terraces.

Agragamee's experience shows that when people have been given the confidence to act they have taken the initiative and organized for collective action. What then goes wrong? Why does tribal development not take off? The pointing finger is once again forced towards the state, at state policy and action. In one of his papers, Dr. N.C. Saxena points out that the numerous poverty alleviation programmes of the central and state governments are often nullified by their many anti-people policies and actions. Wherever people have taken the initiative to act, the state machinery has acted to hinder them, and has left the voluntary organizations like Agragamee quite stupefied and gaping. Rural development funding is a large chunk of finances coming into villages and panchayats. Major portions of this are siphoned off before they reach the people, or in the process of reaching the people by the politician-contractor nexus. In some tribal blocks, people decided to break this nexus by taking up work themselves and not allowing the private contractors to take up the work. But, the government departments had a different idea, they were loathe to credit the people with such initiative and took to systematically confusing the estimates, delaying the payments, and making the village committee members run to them times without number. Complaints to higher authorities brought hardly any responses, and visits of district level officials only evoked a lip service that the matter would be looked into.

In another instance, tribal women's groups across Orissa protested the injustices to them in the collection and sale of minor forest produce. The state ignored their plea and continued in its policy of leasing out minor forest product items to private parties. Women formed groups, and applied for the permits to be given to them, but without stating its reasons time and again, the state refused permission. In protest, the women's groups collected the forest items in their regions, and hoarded them. The lease holder took the help of the forest department to wrest the hoarding from these groups.

In February 1995, 5,000 tribal people demonstrated outside the office of a mining unit of the Larsen and Tubro Inc. in Kashipur block and demanded that the state tell them under what terms and conditions the company was allowed to come into their area for mining activities. The state never answered their questions, and instead, tacitly supported the goondaism unleased by the company by ignoring the many cases of violence that the people reported to the police which booked the leaders of this uprising in false cases.

An NGO like Agragamee, perceiving the disparities, the growing injustices, the inhuman dimensions of misery wrought on humans by humans, steps in and attempts to make the people more assertive, the state more responsible, accountable. These efforts may be commendable but all this is always with the understanding and realization that they can not go very far. The very logic of formation of a voluntary organization limits its possibilities. The commitment for resources for people's development should come from the state. If the State fulfils its constitutional responsibility then voluntarism would not be required.

Civil Society and its Role in Social Transformation

Some time back, the World Bank President addressed a group of NGOs in Delhi. Emphasizing the need for a close collaboration between the World Bank and civil society organizations, i.e., NGOs, he observed that development would be meaningless without people's participation and without economic and political development. In stating this fact, the President has not said anything new or profound. People's participation had crept into the development jargon more than ten years back, but what is new is the increased emphasis on civil society organizations, which stands undefined and smacks of co-option. The government has already been scramming NGO involvement, and thereby, finding new methods of debunking its role. Now, the World Bank too catches on. NGOs are a risky proposition. If left to themselves, they might just find the space to make trouble for the World Bank schemes of increasing resource appropriation. It would be best to take them into confidence. And so, in increasing the nexus, the poor may be conveniently forgotten. Civil or uncivil, it is high time, the poor of this country are invited, encouraged and in fact just allowed to play a greater role in the general scheme of things. The state is increasingly becoming redundant, as market forces are allowed greater and greater space. And yet, the state wants to retain essential controls, where its resource sumpts lie: in the rural and especially tribal areas. India is one of the few countries, still with a living and thriving countryside. With the dual policies of the state, this will soon become a thing of the past, because the state is claiming redundancy only on the face of it, but capital-intensive enterprise make inroads into rural and tribal hinterlands, against people's wills using state power. As we said before, this is a great betrayal, and if NGOs get co-opted by the World Bank rhetoric, then they would also be joining in the betrayal.

Chapter Eleven

The Dialectics of Environmentalism

Amita Baviskar

While conflict over the ownership and control of natural resources has been a salient aspect of most political struggles in India, it is only recently that this conflict has been articulated in terms of competing notions of the environment. This paper examines the different meanings attached to the 'environment' by social actors engaged in ecological transformation around a national park in Himachal Pradesh---the Great Himalayan National Park (GHNP). The area around GHNP has been targeted for a World Bank-funded project called 'ecodevelopment' which attempts to wean people away from their dependence on resources found within the park. While the World Bank and park authorities invoke the value of 'conservation' to legitimize cordoning off the park to local communities, local villagers cite their traditional rights of subsistence as guaranteed in the colonial settlement report to defend their continued resource extraction. Yet these competing ideologies---'conservation' as well as 'traditional subsistence rights'---which claim to safeguard natural resources draw upon common constructions of 'traditional community', 'legal rights' and 'development'. On the basis of some exploratory fieldwork in the vicinity of the park, this paper attempts to delineate the dialectical inter-connections between apparently contradictory processes of appropriating nature.

The Area

The Great Himalayan National Park covers an area of 765 square kilometres in Kulu district, Himachal Pradesh. The park largely consists of high mountain ridges rearing more than 5,500 metres tall, divided by the gorges cleft by three streams—Tirthan, Sainj and Jiwa Nala—that ultimately flow into the Beas.[1] These upper reaches of the Beas catchment are covered by moist temperate forests of oak and conifers, high-altitude forests of birch and fir interspersed with sub-alpine pastures, crowned at the highest reaches by alpine meadows, scrub and snow-capped peaks (Kothari et al 1989: 146). The rich flora of the area sustains an equally rich fauna, including several endangered species such as the musk deer, serow, brown bear, blue sheep, Himalayan tahr, western tragopan, chir pheasant and the splendid-looking monal.

Every spring, as the snow starts to melt in the mountains, the high altitude pastures come out of hibernation. When the weather warms, thawing ice moistens the soil and allows the first shallow-rooted annual herbs to sprout. As spring lapses into summer, the pastures change colour as one group of herbs, grasses and sedges flowers, sets seed and dies, to be replaced by another group. The wild herbivores of the area are not the only beings to keenly monitor this succession: for the human inhabitants of the adjoining villages, the seasonal vegetation includes many species of medicinal use, which have recently become commercially valuable too.[2] Besides medicinal plants, the villagers also seek chhunchhru or guchchhi (Morchella esculenta), the morel mushrooms growing in the shaded understorey of the forest, much prized as delicacies abroad.

The pastures provide excellent forage for the herds of sheep and goats reared by villagers on the periphery of the park. In an intricately ordered system of grazing runs, every village despatches its livestock in herds of 500 to a thousand, supervised by three or four fuaal (graziers) and their dogs, into the park. From June to October, the animals graze in the alpine pastures and gain the flesh that will see them through the winter. The pastures also attract herds from villages far south of the park in Ani tehsil as well as migratory pastoralists such as Gaddis. While historical records show that livestock has grazed in this area for more than a century and a half, the extent of grazing in the past is not known. At present, it is estimated that around 35,000 sheep and goats enter the park annually.[3]

The National Park and Ecodevelopment

While grazing is an ancient activity, the park itself is of recent creation. From 1980 onwards, the birds and large mammals in the reserved forests of the region came to be sporadically surveyed by Gaston and Garson (a pair of Canadian and British biologists, respectively), key actors in the Himachal Wildlife Project, an enterprise of international environmental NGOs and the Himachal government. Largely on their recommendation, the initial notification for GHNP was issued in March 1984, specifying a core and buffer zone. However, it was soon realized that the buffer zone contained numerous villages, all of which would have to be evacuated before final declaration of the National Park could take place under the terms of the Wildlife Protection Act 1972[4] (Gaston and Garson 1992:9-12). Since the inclusion of this highly populated zone in the park would make the settlement of rights 'impossibly complex', the Himachal legislature issued a re-notification specifying that only the original core area was to be declared as the GHNP. This left only 24 households spread over four settlements inside the vastness of the park. However, as we shall see later, the redefining of the park boundary did not avert a conflict over villagers' rights to resources within the park; it merely reconfigured it.

From 1987 onwards, the park authorities prepared a ten-year management plan for the area that set forth the following objectives:

(i) to maintain optimal habitats for wildlife,
(ii) to increase populations of endangered species,

(iii) to eliminate factors causing degradation of ecosystems,
(iv) to carry out surveys and research on wildlife,
(v) to provide wildlife viewing opportunities for educational and recreational purposes, and
(vi) to provide employment opportunities for local people (Gaston and Carson 1992: 20).

The sweeping objectives notwithstanding, the only significant activity of the park staff has been to try and control poaching. Hunting was banned in Kulu district in 1982 (except for crop protection) and inside the park it was doubly disallowed. If caught, poachers are liable for fines and imprisonment; teams of forest guards remove snares from the park in preventive combing operations. Trapping for flesh or fowl used to be a common pastime for villagers in the winter when animals would move to lower altitudes. Besides food, snares were also set for two prized quarries---the musk deer for its valuable gland and the male monal for its iridescent crest used as an ornament on caps worn by local men. Hard as it is to get reliable information on a subject that might land the informant in trouble, I would hazard the observation that enforcement by the park staff, combined with greater material prosperity in the agricultural economy, seems to have reduced overall hunting in the park.[5] While the right to set snares and trap animals was evidently extinguished without a collective outcry, a few signs of lingering resentment on the part of villagers against the park authorities could still be detected. After the initial notification, one would have expected the state government to proceed with the settlement of rights to natural resources within the park, as mandated by the Wildlife Protection Act. However, this has not happened and, so far, full-fledged National Park status has not been achieved. However, this state of limbo is by no means unusual; most of national parks and sanctuaries in India have not received final notification. Instead of a frontal assault on villagers' rights, then, the park authorities have initiated a crab-like sidways motion that nibbies away at rights while promising greater prosperity to the dispossessed villagers. This project is called *ecodevelopment*.

Since the park was established with the avowed aim of creating optimal conditions for wildlife, especially endangered species, this entailed eliminating factors causing 'degradation of ecosystems'. By definition, any ecological change inimical to the interests of wildlife, especially the endangered species, became condemned as 'degradation'. Thus, a forest clearing gradually created by graziers may result in increased floral diversity, but would still be described as 'degradation' by the park authorities because, it is argued, livestock disturbs wild animals and deprives wild ungulates of fodder. From the very beginning, the agents of 'degradation' most visible to the park authorities and outside experts were the livestock herds and the herb-collectors. The browsing flocks of livestock, and the graziers and dogs who accompany them, who ascend on the park's pastures from June to November disturb breeding pipits and wild ungulates and compete for food. Not only that, it is claimed that the visitors transfer diseases to the wild animals of the park. The other side of the equation, that domesticated livestock leaves its precious dung behind in the pastures and contributes generously to their fertilization, for the benefit of all---wild or tame, is often underplayed. So also is the collection of herbs perceived as 'degrading the ecosystem' even though it is not clear what the deleterious consequences are.[6] Yet as far as the park authorities are concerned, any human activity inside the park is suspect. And, since grazing and the collection of medicinal plants are the two most significant human activities inside the park, they come in for the greatest censure. While grazing and herb collection are identified by park authorities and conservationists as the two main 'biotic pressures' threatening the conservation of wildlife within the park, the assertion is based only on impressions gained from short treks through the area, and not on any 'scientific study'. I had assumed that the research component of the ecodevelopment project was aimed at monitoring ecological changes brought about by human resource use. But researchers who have been working in the park for more than a year were swift to disabuse me of this notion. Monitoring change, they said, requires baseline information on the species diversity of plants and animals inside the park, and the relationships between them. The process of collecting this data had hardly begun. In the absence of baseline information about biodiversity, how can one track changes in it? Thus, without substantial evidence that human resource use adversely affects park wildlife, the state has initiated measures to curb such use.

However destructive park authorities may consider villagers' activities inside the park to be, villagers have undeniable rights to graze their livestock, to collect herbs and to a quota of construction timber.[7] These rights are laid down in an astonishing document---Anderson's Forest Settlement Report of 1886 which records in minute detail the specific rights of villages and even individuals in the demarcated forests of Kulu (Anderson 1886). There has been no substantial revision of rights since the compilation of this report and it remains the standard reference for present-day DFOs (Divisional Forest Officers). The power of this book over people's lives is enormous and their faith in it unshakeable. Illiterate village elders, who could never have had access to the report, let alone decipher it, when questioned about their rights will say that on such and such page of the *kitab* (book) the names of their ancestors are recorded and that is how they, the descendants, come to have rights. Of course, the rights accorded in 1886 now operate in a vastly changed context where human and livestock populations, land use practices, links with the outside economy and lifestyles bear little resemblance to what prevailed more than a century ago. As the subsequent discussion will show, villagers successfully invoke their 'traditional legal rights' in order to legitimize different present-day resource use practices.

It is unclear why the rights of 1886 have not been gradually revised since. However, it would appear that the notification of the national park made it incumbent on the forest department to proceed with a task it had avoided for decades. Yet the process of settling these rights remains 'impossibly complex' because local livelihoods remain heavily dependent on resources within the park. Even though park boundaries had been carefully redrawn to ensure that only four settlements would be physically displaced by the notification of their lands as part of the park, apparently the authorities had entirely overlooked the problem of 'resource displacement'. That is, more than 150 villages outside the western and southern edge of the park and unnumbered pastoralists from further afield stood to lose a crucial component of their economy, a threat that brought forth murmurs of local protest. Instead of attempting to settle these rights, a hazardous process full of headaches like offering inadequate compensation and facing public wrath, trying to identify alternative resource sites in an already burdened landscape and so on, conservationists suggested that GHNP be adopted for the ecodevelopment approach which would 'wean away' villagers from going into the park by providing alternative economic opportunities for them.

Ecodevelopment on Paper and in Practice

Officially, ecodevelopment is described as a "site-specific package of measures derived through people (sic) participation, which addresses all aspects of land use and other resources, in order to promote sustainable landuse practices, as well as income-generating activities, which are not deleterious to protected area values" (Panwar 1992, cited in WII 1996:8). Ecodevelopment's basic thrust is to divert biotic pressure from the protected area (Kôthari 1996). This attempt could take the form of establishing substitute fuel and fodder plantations to meet villagers' biomass needs and starting cottage industries to provide alternative income sources. Thus ecodevelopment is rather like rural development, but with an added emphasis on natural resource conservation, especially the conservation of wildlife within the protected area. However, ecodevelopment begins with the assumption that wildlife conservation is a priority that overrides people's rights to resources within the protected area. Its underlying philosophy is statist in that it ignores the crucial issue of redressing a fundamental inequity, viz., the denial of rights to local people, a systematic bias begun by the colonial state and continued in independent India (Gadgil and Guha 1992).

The strategy of ecodevelopment for India's protected areas was first mooted around 1990 by international NGOs such as the World Wide Fund for Nature (WWF). The idea gained institutional support during the 1992 United Nations Commission for Environment and Development (UNCED) conference in Rio deJaneiro following which the World Bank creating a special loan fund called the Global Environment Facility (GEF). The World Bank approached the Indian government to identify possible protected areas in the country where ecodevelopment could be tried out. In the first phase, two national parks----GHNP and Kalakad Mundanthurai in the southern Nilgiris were chosen. In the second phase, eight other parks and tiger reserves, including Ranthambhor in Rajasthan, Rajaji in Uttar Pradesh, Gir in Gujarat, Melghat in Maharashtra, Simlipal in Orissa were also targeted.

In the case of GHNP, ecodevelopment was launched in November 1994. The GHNP project consists of a Rs. 6 crore loan from the World Bank to be disbursed over five years, repayable at 4 percent interest. This money to be spent on three heads: (i) improving park management (training, equipment, infrastructure; (ii) research (being conducted by the Wildlife Institute of India); and (iii) actual ecodevelopment. The World Bank loan conditions stipulate that the park authorities must prepare detailed 'micro-plans' for every panchayat with the involvement of villagers as well as local NGOs. However, the exercise was entirely foreign to the Forest Department and, despite a crash course in Participatory Rural Appraisal (PRA) techniques, micro-plans cold not be made before 1994. Research gradually got under way from July 1995. In effect, this meant that research (an input into the planning process), planning and implementation started concurrently!

The present situation is somewhat absurd. Ecodevelopment suffered a temporary setback till mid-1996 with the World Bank rejecting all the micro-plans submitted by the GHNP authorities, on the grounds that, inter alia (i) they did not quantify returns such as enhanced ecological productivity outside the park due to ecodevelopment;[8] and (ii) did not include enforceable contracts between the park authorities and local people in which latter would agree to forego their rights to resources within the park in return for ecodevelopment. Since two years passed without any signs of money coming in, these expectations have become tinged with the suspicion that the park authorities were bent on deceiving and manipulating people. Combined with this were apprehensions about the nature of ecodevelopment itself. The Park Director narrated a story about the absurd fears that villagers entertained about ecodevelopment.

Villagers told the Park Director that they had heard that, under the ecodevelopment programme, a special kind of leopard had been released in their forests. This leopard had been imported from America and its diet chiefly consisted of sheep and goats. The villagers said that they knew someone who claimed to have seen one such leopard and this person had reported that the leopard had an identification tag in its ear which said, "Made in America".

The Park Director had laughed heartily at this story and at the villagers. "Bring me this man", he said, "and I will fall at his feet. He must be extraordinarily brave if, on seeing a leopard, instead of running for his life, he went close enough to actually read what was printed on his ear-tag!"

The Park Director relates this incident to stress that people's doubts about ecodevelopment are baseless. Yet the story can also be interpreted as villagers' use of a telling metaphor of an imported concept, viz., ecodevelopment, consuming and alienating local resources. The apprehensions about ecodevelopment could not be easily dismissed and the park authorities were forced to realize that the atmosphere was too charged to allow the project to proceed smoothly. They played for time by initiating a new approach called TRUCO—Trust and Conference-Building Measures. With the objective of getting villagers to look favourably upon the park authorities, officials undertook public relations activities, including building bridges, repairing bridle-paths, improving water supply and so on. However, TRUCO was perceived by some villagers as a move on the part of the park authorities to insinuate themselves into areas of public life traditionally managed by the village panchayat, and they remained wary of this approach. Villagers also felt, rightly, that the park authorities had to have some ulterior motive for their actions; they simply did not fit the role of fairy godmother. Ironically then, the upshot of TRUCO was a groundswell of opposition to ecodevelopment and a widespread unease about the intentions of the park authorities vis-a-vis local rights to resources within the park. This opposition has been buttressed by an NGO working in the area, as well as by local traders who control the trade in medicinal plants and by local politicians.

Villagers say that the resources within the park are theirs by virtue of their longstanding customary rights, rights which are enshrined in the colonial settlement report. As traditional stewards of the forest and its creatures, they have an intimate understanding of natural processes. Villagers feel that, as managers of the forest, they have certain privileges too. As an elderly man put it, "They call this a park. Park means *bagicha* (garden). And one can pluck flowers from a garden." A grazier said, "Just as God put the bird in the sky and made seeds for it to eat, so He placed our sheep on the earth and gave them pastures upon which to graze." In articulating their opposition to the park and to ecodevelopment, villagers often use metaphors and analogies naturalizing their relationship with nature and attributing to it a timeless quality. The identification of certain spots in the upper reaches of the park as sacred sites endowed with mystic power adds another dimension of cultural signification to the park landscape, an aspect that reinforces the feeling of continuity and timelessness. Such a naturalization and sacralization of the park-people relationship is employed to further legitimize claims to resources within the park. Yet, as we shall see in the following section, this strategy constructs a selective history and a partial present.

Economy and Ecology

For the people living in the ecodevelopment zone immediately adjacent to the park, the area inside its boundaries has several meanings. It is an extremely important element in their resource catchment. Since agriculture and animal husbandry are inextricably linked in the local economy, the former would not be possible without access to the high-altitude pastures inside the park. Besides maintaining the fertility of the agricultural fields, livestock herds provide highland people with wool, meat, leather, and are also assets that can be readily encashed when money is needed. The traditional highland economy consisted mainly of the cultivation of subsistence crops such as barely, wheat and beans, and the rearing of livestock. This economy, however, has been drastically changed over the course of the last two or three decades. With the expansion of the road network and improved transport and communications in Kulu district, horticulture has emerged as a lucrative alternative to subsistence agriculture. Orchards of apricots, apples, plums and pears have replaced the barely fields. More recently, vegetable crops such as potatoes, radish, tomatoes, garlic have also been enthusiastically adopted. The climate of the area has always been suitable for these crops; with improved transport facilities, perishable produce can reach urban markets quickly. Enhanced links with cities have also fostered the collection of medicinal plants. Once gathered only for one's own use and in much smaller quantities, now different species of plants are collected in bulk and sold to traders who meet the rising demands of pharmaceutical companies. A similar situation prevails with respect to cannabis and opium, the most profitable as well as the most risky crops grown locally. Cannabis flourishes in the wild here. Earlier harvested only for self-consumption, it is now grown almost entirely for sale. In the more remote villages where these illicit crops can be cultivated and processed with little fear of punitive action, villagers discuss the economics of their operations with a business-like matter-of-factness. At least two growers approached me for tips about contacting dealers directly in Delhi and Goa!

Consequent upon these changes, there has been a large influx of money into the area and lifestyles have changed too. However, the rise in incomes has not been uniform. Villages closer to the roadhead have been better able to capitalize on market opportunities. Within villages, those with larger land holdings have prospered more than those with less land and the landless, but even the latter seem to have gained more employment locally in agricultural work. The increased profitability of agriculture has weakened the economic relationship between people and the park to the extent in that the livelihood of the better-off households appears to be less dependent on livestock rearing. On the other hand, however, the more intensive collection of medicinal plants has resulted in greater resource extraction from the park. Certain other practices appear to be unchanged; for instance, dalits still harvest bamboo (*Arundinaria falcata*) and bhashal (*Salix wallichiana*) for weaving baskets, their traditional occupation, from the park.

Increased integration with the market, changed cropping patterns and intensity, combined with the higher densities of human and livestock populations in the region, have modified the nature and extent of people's relationship with the park. Yet this vastly changed context is ignored when villagers oppose the park by dwelling upon their 'traditional subsistence rights' as authoritatively guaranteed by the settlement report. It is ironical that what must once have been a configuration of rights with considerable fluidity came to be frozen in colonial law and, over time, acquired an emblematic character, even as resource-use practices continued to change. It is even more ironical that both villagers and park authorities, who stand in conflict over the control and management of natural resources, appear to subscribe to the same notion of 'traditional subsistence rights'.

While the park authorities seek to extinguish these rights through ecodevelopment, their plans are based on the same problematic notion of 'local community' that villagers use to legitimize their continued resource extraction. That is, ecodevelopment plans are aimed only at people living in the immediate vicinity of the park; they completely ignore the equally legal claims of the graziers who come from distant parts of Kulu district. Just as local villagers attempt to discredit these groups by classifying them as 'outsiders', the park authorities too have devised their ecodevelopment plans "with community participation" in a way that disenfranchises the more distant members of the community.

Finally, I would argue, villagers and park authorities share a common vision of 'development'. That is, both seek to increase linkages with the outside world in order to materially enhance their lifestyles. The strongest demand that villagers voice when asked about ecodevelopment is for roads. Roads are the essential prerequisites for development, they feel, a belief that is shared by the park authorities. Regardless of the ecologically disastrous impact of road-building in the hills, both parties to the conflict concur in the importance they give to improved access. In July 1996, the first large chunk of ecodevelopment money, Rs. 1.9 crore, was released to the park authorities. One of the first activities taken up was the improvement of the forest road to Shangarh. Until then, the people of Shangarh had clearly expressed their hostility to ecodevelopment. However, in late September, when the visiting World Bank mission drove up to the village on the newly-built road, they were greeted with garlands, a gesture that took even the Park Director by surprise.

Notes

1. Since 1994, 265 sq km of the Parbati valley have been included in the park.
2. In terms of both monetary value and quantity collected, the most important medicinal plants are dhoop (*Jurinea macrocephala*), kadu (*Picrorhiza kurroa*), patees (*Aconitum heterophylum*), hathpanja (*Orchislatifolia*) and nhaini (*Valeriana hardwickii*).
3. While park authorities accept this figure, it is challenged by those opposed to the park as a gross over-estimate. So far, there is no study that reliably establishes the magnitude of grazing
4. The Act specifies that rights to land or other resources inside the area to be notified as a national park or sanctuary must be acquired by the government, thus effectively displacing villages. In addition, no wildlife can be destroyed, exploited or removed from a National Park, nor can grazing be permitted
5. However, I have just learnt that a census of the musk deer population conducted over the last five years shows an alarming decline (by almost half) in their numbers (Mehra, personal communication). The reasons for this decline may be poaching, disease, drastic changes in food availability or habitat, or some combination thereof. It does seem rather ironical, through, that the numbers of a species identified as 'most vulnerable' by the park authorities should plummet following the 'protection' of its habitat.

6. Only one of the species collected—kauri patees (*Acontium heterophylum*) is listed as endangered in the Red Data book on Indian plants (Anon. 1995)
7. Villages are allocated rights in different forests and each household in a village is entitled to one tree every five years.
8. The World Bank seems to be primarily interested in reducing the situation to a simple equation: quantifying the value of natural resources extracted by people from the park, and investing in ecodevelopment in order to generate the same value outside the park. Such an elegant solution, unfortunately, is a little hard to obtain in the context of an ecological landscape saturated with political-economic and other cultural meanings.

Chapter Twelve

The Trap of Nationalism and the Chittagong Hill Tracts, Bangladesh

Amena Mohsin

The signing of the Chittagong Hill Tracts (CHT) peace accord between the Bangladesh government and the Parbattya Chattagram Janashonghoti Samity (PCJSS)----the political body that had carried on the movement for the CHT----on December 2, 1997, has demonstrated the limitations of the nationalist construction of the Hill people. Jumma nationhood, a construction of the PCJSS for uniting the diverse thirteen groups of the CHT, in its bid to attain political and economic autonomy and above all a recognition of the cultural distinctiveness of the Hill people within the state of Bangladesh, has succeeded to a limited extent but then the state has remained uncompromised on the issue of the hegemony of Bengali 'nation' within the state. The state position is only an extension of its hegemonic nature that has the potential of creating further polarizations and divisiveness in future.

The process of nation construction is naturally divisive and hegemonic. The construction of one identity denotes the separation of the group/community from the other. Besides, the nationalist discourse[1] is inextricably biased towards the dominant/majority community. This results in the hegemony of the dominant identity over the weaker ones. A natural consequence or continuation of the above is the formulation of rationales and development models by the state that alienates as well as marginalizes the weaker communities. Consequently, at a certain period, the weaker communities come to adopt the rhetoric and politics of the former in the form of construction as well as assertion of new politicized identities for themselves. In this construction, 'nation' or 'nationalism' is viewed as a libertarian and counter-hegemonic force, whereas in actuality it entraps human beings within the same divisive and hegemonic groove, due to the discourse's inherent bias towards the majority/dominant community. The exposition in the paper will make this clear.

The paper is divided into four sections. The first section examines the conceptual and practical aspects of Jumma nationhood. In the second section a critique of the above has been made in order to demonstrate the problematic inherent and associated with this construction. The third section, through an analysis of the peace accord, examines the proposition that the peace accord has fulfilled the Hill people's expectations and demands to a limited extent. The last section presents concluding observations. The paper argues that the hegemonism inherent within the state nationalism is the major impediment towards the realization of the demands of the Hill people; on the other hand hegemonism and centralization was integral to Jumma nationalism as well. Nationalism, by its exclusion, only weakens the creation of a humane society that can truly fulfil the aspirations of autonomy of any human community. The paper further contends that the state position is fraught with the dangers and potentials of future contentions between the Bengali and non-Bengali communities of the state.

I

Jumma Nationalism and Autonomy for the Hill People

The persecution of the Hill people in the CHT by the 'Bengali' state[2] led to the demand by the PCJSS for a separate nationhood fcr the Hill people. This party was formed by Manobendra Narayan Larma (the elected representative of the Hill people to the Bangladesh Parliament) in March 1972 in the wake of Sheikh Mujib's (the then Prime Minister and Father of the Nation) refusal to recognize the Hill people as a community distinct from the Bengalis. This indeed is an irony as well as paradox of history that Sheikh Mujib, who had all along fought for the rights of the 'Bengali' nation within the state of Pakistan, and in fact had constructed 'Bengali' nationalism to counter the hegemony of Pakistani nationalism, had himself become a prisoner of the nationalist within him. In this instance, he proved himself to be the Father of the Bengali nation—the dominant/majority community—of Bangladesh, not of the entire population of the state, thereby giving rise to the same hegemonism and divisivism so characteristic of the state of Pakistan, within the new state of Bangladesh also. This, however, was not surprising given the nationalist politics of the state.

Subsequently, the PCJSS added an armed wing the Shanti Bahini (SB) to it. The PCJSS set up its base in Tripura, India and carried out its activities from there. From the mid-1970s till early 1990s the party waged an armed insurgency in the CHT. Besides, since the mid-1980s the party started referring to the Hill people as the 'Jumma nation'. This demand for a separate nationhood was not equated by the PCJSS with statehood. The party insisted that for it the nation is a cultural category.[3] The party's nationalistic agenda too was quite explicit about it (see Appendix 1). Through Jumma nationalism the PCJSS aimed to acquire cultural as well political autonomy for the Hill people, therefore it had a conceptual as well as a practical side to it. The PCJSS maintained that this construction of Jumma nationhood could satisfy the aspirations of self-identity and autonomy of the Hill people within the state of Bangladesh. But this position as the analysis below suggests was beset with problems.

Contours of Jumma Nationalism

(i) The word 'Jumma' has its origins in *jhum*, which has been the traditional mode of cultivation of the Hill people. It was used pejoratively by Bengalis to denote the Hill people as primitive and backward farmers. The state (British as well as Pakistan) had also made repeated attempts to put a stop to *jhum* cultivation as it was considered to be backward, primitive and non-profitable. But, for the Hill people, *jhum* constituted not only a mode of cultivation, but also a way of life. It was integral to their religious, social and cultural ethos. The PCJSS, therefore, invoked this particular nomenclature to infuse the Hill people with a sense of pride in their past, their traditional system and values, which have been the objects of repeated onslaughts by outsiders. It was also a means for the PCJSS to recreate images among the Hill people of their simple and harmonious past, which according to them had been shattered due to exploitations by outsiders. This nostalgia for the past, on the one hand, created images of 'outsiders' and 'insiders' among the Hill people (thereby *nationalizing* people), and on the other provided them with a sense of continuity and unity.

(ii) *Jhum* also denotes the special relationship of the Hill people to their land. It introduced a territorial dimension in this construction, which assumed that the CHT had traditionally been the land of the Jummas or the Hill people and needed to be protected from non-Jummas or outsiders. The possession of this homeland became a core element in this construction of a shared identity.[4]

(iii) An important element of Jumma nationalism was its emphasis on the separateness or distinctiveness of the Hill people from Bengalis. In this context, according to the PCJSS, *jhum* denotes the economic separateness of the Hill people from the plain land Bengalis. Since 90 percent of the land in the CHT constitutes of hilly land, so *jhum* is still the dominant mode of cultivation among the Hill people. This mode is not only completely different from plough cultivation that is practised in the plains, but is also totally absent in the latter parts. This PCJSS held not only sets the Hill people apart from Bengalis, but also creates among the former a common attitude towards life and its values.[5]

(iv) In this construction they also emphasized upon and highlighted their cultural separateness from Bengalis. In linguistic terms they emphasized the fact that Bengali is not their mother tongue. In religious terms they stressed that Islam is not their religion. In this endeavor, the PCJSS made extensive use of the negative stereotype images of Bengalis prevalent among the Hill people. Its circulations on the one hand depicted the Bengalis as rapists, killers, torturers and land grabbers, and on the other emphasized upon the unity and harmonious relations prevalent among the Hill people in the past.[6] Apart from this, one also observes the emergence of a fiery pattern of literature among a certain section of the Hill people. The following poem by Kabita Chakma, a young local poet, is an instance:

Why shall I not resist!
Can they do whatever they please..?
Turn settlements into barren land
dense forests into deserts
mornings into evening
turn fertile into barren.
Why shall I not resist!
Can they do whatever they please...
Estrange us from the land of our birth
enslave our women,
blind our vision
put an end to creation.
Neglect and humiliation cause anger
the blood surges through my veins
breaking barriers at every stroke,
the fury of youth pierces the sea of consciousness.
I become my whole self ... why shall I not resist.[7]

The call to become one's whole self and to resist the oppressor is clearly indicative of the fiery counter-hegemonic thrust of the Jumma nationalist discourse. In April 1996, the Jumma Peoples Resource Centre in Australia (a Hill students network) also started a magazine in the Chakma language—*Jumpada*---to revive among the Hill people their own culture in their own written language which most of them today do not know. The Hill people have also constructed martyrdoms at different places in the CHT to commemorate the killings of the Hill people by Bengalis.[8] These constructions draw the lines between Bengalis and the Hill people where the former emerges as the oppressor and exploiter and the latter as the victim.

(v) Above everything else, the PCJSS maintained that the shared experiences of deprivation and exploitation and the struggle of the Hill people against Bengalis have created an awareness among the Hill people that they share a unique historical past. This has instilled in them a common bondage and feeling of oneness.

The above factors, according to the PCJSS, justified its assertion that the Hill people constitute a separate and single nation, which they have named Jumma. This Jumma nationhood, it maintained could satisfy the identity quest of the Hill people, which apparently is under threat from the hegemony of Bengali/Bangladeshi nationalism.

Autonomy Plan of the PCJSS

With a view to realize autonomy for the Hill people, the PCJSS had put forward a number of demands to the Bangladesh government. The major demands were as follows:

(i) *Territorial*: The Constitution should recognize the CHT as a special administrative unit, with regional autonomy. The three districts of CHT---Rangamati, Khagrachari and Banderban---should be merged into one unit, and the region should be renamed Jummaland.

(ii) *Administrative*: Jummaland should be administered by an autonomous Regional Council (RC). This Council would be elected directly by the people on the basis of adult franchise. It would be responsible for the following subjects: general administration and law and order; local government institutions; police; land; agriculture; education; forestry; health; judiciary; animal husbandry; trade and commerce; small cottage industries; roads and communications; tourism; fisheries; land revenue and taxes; water resources and power supply; markets; cooperatives; social welfare; finance; cultural affairs, information and statistics; youth development and sports; population control and family planning; country liquor; religious institutions; graveyard and cremation grounds; *jhum* cultivation; environment; and jails.

The institutional framework of the proposed RC would be as following:

The RC would be called Jummaland Regional Council (JRC). It would be headed by a Chairman and would consist of 48 members. Membership seats were allocated as following:

35 general seats for the Jumma people;

7 seats for the Jumma minorities, this would exclude the Chakmas, Marmas and Tripuras;

3 seats for Bengalis; and

3 seats for women, who would be elected by other members of the Council.

The JRC would have an Executive Council (EC) too. The Chairman of the JRC would decide the number of members of this body, and it should be formed by the majority party. The JRC would have a term of five years.

The above arrangement would be constitutionally guaranteed, and no change could be brought about in the administrative structure of the CHT without the prior holding of a referendum on the issue, within the region itself.

(iii) *Land and Bengali Settlements*: All lands in the CHT, except the Kaptai power station, Betbunia satellite station, state owned industrial areas and state acquired land, should be placed under the jurisdiction of the Council. A constitutional ban ought to be put on the purchase of land in the CHT by outsiders. Deeds made to lease out land to Bengalis for rubber plantation and forestry should be canceled and the lands ought to be placed under the Council's jurisdiction.

The Constitution must put a ban on Bengali settlements in the region. All outsiders who have settled in the area since August 17, 1947 should be withdrawn from the region.

(iv) *Economic*: Service rules should be relaxed for the Hill people. Special quotas should be reserved in government civil services for the Hill people. The government should set up a special bank in the CHT for the Hill people alone to help them with investments. The Chittagong Hill Tracts Development Board (CHTDB, an economic body instituted in the CHT in 1978 for the economic development of the area) should be put under the jurisdiction of the Council.

(v) *Political*: Parliament seats of this constituency should be reserved for the Hill people only.

(vi) *Security*: An autonomous indigenous Police Force constituting solely of the Hill people should be formed. Quotas should be reserved in the defense services for the Hill people. The region ought to be demilitarized. For the purposes of guarding the borders, only the BDR (a para-military force) could be deployed along the borders.

(vii) *Culture and Communication*: A constitutional recognition should be given to all the small nationalities of the area. A full-fledged radio station should be set up in the area.

(viii) *Relief and Rehabilitation*: All international and internal Jumma refugees[9] should be properly rehabilitated. Members of the SB and all individuals who have been implicated for association with the former should be properly rehabilitated.[10]

Jumma nationalism thus had a conceptual as well as a practical basis to it. But it was best with problematic at both levels. The following is an explication of the problematic.

II
Problematics of Jumma Nationalism: Thematic & Practical

Thematic

The assertion about the threat to Hill people's separate identity was (is) indeed true, but problems existed with the former, i.e., the adequacy or ability of the idea of Jumma nationhood itself to satisfy the identity quest of the Hill people. It is posited here that the perceived hegemony of the 'Bengali' state appeared to be the main strength of Jumma nationalism, but was also paradoxically its major weakness. This is for two reasons. To begin with, the Hill people do not constitute a homogeneous community; instead they are divided into thirteen different ethnic groups.[11] As such they lack the common cultural denominators, viz., common language, religion, culture, history and so on that may mark them off as a single cultural entity as claimed by the PCJSS. The Hill people, however, have shared a common administration since the British colonial period. But, in this context, one can point out that Bengalis have also experienced British colonialism, though the form of administration varied in their respective cases. However, both the Bengalis and the Hill people were part of the Pakistani administrative system. In this light even the factor of a common administration looses much of its salience as a contributing element towards their claim for single nationhood. Thus, in view of the absence of any internal cohesive factor among the Hill people one may question the viability and capability of the above construction to keep the Hill people united once Bengali rule was removed.

At another level one may even raise the more fundamental question, i.e., in view of the existence of thirteen different ethnic groups in the CHT, how far did the idea of a Jumma nation indeed do away with the threat and fear of hegemony? It is true that the overwhelming majority of the Hill people supported the PCJSS's demand for autonomy in the CHT. But this consensus fizzled away when it came to the issue of identifying themselves as one Jumma nation. Members of the different groups, more specifically the Marmas and Tripuras, argued that Jumma is a Chakma word and since the PCJSS was overwhelmingly a Chakma dominated institution, so there existed the very real fear of Chakma hegemony in this construction itself. They therefore, preferred to identify themselves with their own generic names like Marma or Tripura, instead of being identified as a group. However, in the eventuality of such a need, they preferred to be called Paharees (Hill people) or Upajatis (tribals) instead of Jumma.[12] It is important to note here that both Paharee and Upajati are Bengali words commonly used by the Bengalis to denote their separateness from the Hill population of the state. The preference of the Hill groups for Bengali nomenclatures to a Chakma one is indicative of the internal divisions prevalent among the Hill people. It also suggests that for the smaller groups of the CHT little difference exists between the ideas of Bengali/Bangladeshi nation and Jumma nation, as from their perspective both are hegemonic constructions, one of the Bengalis and the latter of the Chakmas. More importantly, it reveals that the Hill people do not perceive themselves as constituting a single nation.

There is also lack of consensus among the educated section of the Hill people, including the Chakmas about the appropriateness and suitability of the term 'Jumma' to describe the Hill people. They point out that the above appellation was given to them by Bengalis. It was a calling name used pejoratively to denote them as backward and primitive farmers. According to them *jhum* is an occupational category which cannot form the basis of identity of a people. They further maintain that the term is more accusatory than descriptive. It conjures up images of primitivism and nomadism about the Hill people in the minds of outsiders. Such conjurations they believe is harmful for them, more so, for they have long been categorized as a backward and primitive people by outsiders.

Apart from the above, one may also point out that the emphasis of the PCJSS upon the unity and harmonious relations of the different Hill groups in the past were a fictitious one. Mackenzie's[13] and Lewin's accounts tell us of the warfare prevalent among the different Hill groups. Lewin informs us that:

> None of the hill tribes appear to have any general term for all the hill dwellers.[14]

Proshanta Tripura, an eminent anthropologist from among the Hill people, has described this as following:

> Earlier, each of the "hill tribes" had their own way of designating ethnic boundaries. For example, the Tripuras used the expression "Wanjwi Shikam" which literally means "Bengalis and Kukis", to mean "other people". From this it may be concluded that the Tripuras in the past felt no closer affinity to the "Kukis" than they did to the Bengalis.[15]

A review of the Hill people's literature during the insurgency period also suggests that divisions and contradictions existed among the Hill people. The literature of the PCJSS and its front organizations bore the message of anger and revolt against oppression. While the general literature emphasized upon the principles of humanism, peace, tolerance and harmony.[16] It is also important to point out here that *Jumpada* was written in the Chakma language. This not only draws the lines between the Bengalis and the Hill people, but also among the Hill people themselves, i.e., between the Chakmas and the non-Chakmas, thereby giving credibility to the allegation that Jumma nationalism is essentially biased towards the Chakmas---the majority/dominant group---in the CHTs.

The above reveals the problems of this construction at the conceptual or thematic level.

At this point one may also point out that by invoking the notion of 'nation' itself to liberate the Hill people from Bengali hegemony and colonialism the PCJSS itself had taken recourse to a form of colonialism. It is posited here that the invocation of this particular concept reinforces the colonial constructions and segregations of human societies into 'tribes' and 'nations' as representing lower and higher stages of human evolution. It also demonstrates the inability or the total colonization of human mind that has made it impossible for it to think independently in terms of categories other than nations.[17]

Here, one also has to be mindful that the notion of 'nation', as invoked by the PCJSS is quite alien to the ordinary Hill people. There does not appear to be an equivalent term for the word in their own vocabularies, so it essentially remained a borrowed and alien concept In this context, the assertion of the PCJSS that Jumma nationalism led to the construction of the 'whole' the 'self' among the Hill people, and acted as a liberating force---both spiritual and physical—does not appear to be much credible.

Practical

Aside from the thematic problems, it is argued here that the autonomy formula of the PCJSS was quite inadequate to provide autonomy and real power to the Hill people. Any autonomy formula entails the devolution of power at the local level. In this context, the PCJSS has made two specific demands, first, the three districts of CHT should be merged into one political unit and the region should be renamed Jummaland. The region would then form a special administrative area with its own judicial and land tenure system. Secondly, Jummaland should be administered by an autonomous RC. There was thus a territorial as well as administrative dimension to this demand.

The territorial aspect of this formulation was a problematic one. In the context of autonomy for the Hill people it was simultaneously unrealistic and illogical. The CHT is not inhabited by a homogenous community, on the other hand, its population consists of thirteen different ethnic groups each having its own conception of justice and property, for instance the valley-living people have acquired a fairly well developed conception of private property while the ridge-top people continue to look upon land as communal property. In this situation, a single judicial and land tenure system for the entire region is quite unrealistic. It has been seen that at the conceptual level disagreement existed among the local inhabitants on the question of being identified as a single nation, or a Jumma nation. In light of the above there was no logical basis for renaming the CHT as Jummaland. Besides, there was no historical basis to this demand. More importantly, the demand to merge the three districts into one political unit worked against the very principle and logic of decentralization. Through this formulation the PCJSS committed itself to the same homogenizing and collectivizing thrust that it purported to fight.

The proposed administrative structure for Jummaland too followed the principle of centralization. It is evident from the institutional composition of the proposed JRC, which envisaged a two-chamber body, the RC and the EC. Members of JRC were to be directly elected on the basis of adult franchise and the winning party was to form the EC. In view of the numerical and dominant position of the Chakmas in the CHT, one can safely infer that the JRC would have been a Chakma dominated institution. Though seven seats were reserved for the minorities, but this did not necessarily ensure equality or justice for them. In the proposed plan power remained concentrated at the regional level, which made the autonomy formula (in the context of the smaller groups) quite weak. It reproduced the majority/minority dichotomy with its attendant elements of domination, deprivation and alienation, which are the characteristics of a nationalist system.

It needs to be pointed out here that the above demands evolved over a number of years through the various rounds of negotiations between the government and the PCJSS. The negotiations started during the Ershad period in the late 1980s and continued through the subsequent regime of Khaleda Zia. The government, however, failed to reach an agreement with the PCJSS largely due to the latter's intransigent position. A peace accord was finally signed on December 2, 1997 with the present regime of Sheikh Hasina. As the analysis below would show the PCJSS has finally compromised on several key issues, this the paper argues the PCJSS had to make since with the change of regime in Bangladesh and the coming to power of the Awami League, the Indian government's attitude towards Bangladesh in general and the CHT issue in specific changed. The Indian government withdrew its support from the PCJSS and gave an ultimatum to the CHT refugees who had been residing in six different camps in Tripura to leave. Gradually, their ration was stopped. Bereft of India's support the PCJSS had little option but to sign a peace accord with the government of Bangladesh.

III
The Peace Accord and the Hill People

One of the major demands of the PCJSS was the recognition of the Hill people as the Jumma nation. But the accord makes no reference to this, instead it recognizes the CHT as a tribal inhabited area. Members of the PCJSS maintain that they had to yield to this under tremendous pressure from the government. It is indeed ironic, for it denied them the equality that they had been fighting for. More importantly, it has set the parameters of the state where Bengalis retain their hierarchy as the 'nation', while the Hill people are relegated as 'tribals'. This politics of nationhood, it is argued here, has only deepened the politics of exclusion that has the potential of destabilizing the system in the future.

The PCJSS demand for political and regional autonomy has been met to some extent but the state has ensured its hegemony in this respect as well. It may be mentioned here that during the course of the negotiations in the late 1980s the government had granted some degree of political autonomy to the Hill people. The Ershad regime through the passage of a Parliament Act on February 2, 1989, had established three District Local Government Councils for the districts of Rangamati, Khagrachari and Banderban. The Councils were headed by a Chairman who had to be a Hill person. It was a 30-member body, of which two-thirds were indigenous and one-third Bengali. The indigenous seats were proportionately divided among the different groups of the districts. The Council was elected directly on the basis of adult franchise and was responsible for the following subjects: law and order; coordination of development works; primary and secondary education; health; public health; fisheries; agriculture and forestry; livestock; cooperatives; small and cottage industries; social welfare; art and culture; non-reserved roads and bridges; recreations, games and parks; rest houses; ferries; implementation of government sponsored development projects; communication facilities; water supply and sewerage; local multipurpose development; religious and moral affairs; and local control over sale, settlement and leases of land. The Council was also responsible for formulating its own budget. At that time the District Councils were rejected by the PCJSS on the ground that the District Council Act had no constitutional basis.

Under the present accord a Regional Council (RC) has been formed combining the three hill districts local government Councils through amending some clause of the 1989 Act. The following is the composition of the RC: Chairman 1, Members: (tribal) male 12, (tribal) female 2, (non-tribal) male 6, (non-tribal) female 1. Among the total male tribal members, five will be elected from the Chakmas, three from Marma, two from Tripura and one each from the Murong and Tanchongyas. In case of female members, one from the Chakma and one from another tribe would be elected. In case of the non-tribal members two persons would be elected from each district. The members of the Council will be elected indirectly by the elected members of the three Hill District Councils. Chairmen of the three Hill District Councils will be the ex-officio members of the council and they will have the right to vote. The elected members of the RC will indirectly elect the chairman of the RC. The Council will be elected for five years.

The Council will coordinate and supervise the general administration, law and order and development activities of the three hill districts. Tribal laws and dispensation of social justice will also come under the jurisdiction of the Council. It will coordinate disaster management and relief activities with NGOs and give license for heavy industries. The government will enact laws relating to CHT in consultation with the Council.

The accord also provides for the setting up of a Tribal Affairs Ministry to be headed by a tribal to look into the affairs of the CHT.

It is evident that the RC is a symbolic institution. Its power and functions are of a coordinating and supervisory nature. Powers and functions of the District Councils have remained the same, though in certain cases amendments have been made to make them more functional. However, the core question that one needs to ask is how representative the RC is, for this would determine the degree of participation of the Hill people in this political body. A look at the composition of the RC reveals the predominance of the majority and dominant Chakma community in this body. Thirteen ethnic groups inhabit the CHT, and only five have got their representation in this body. In other words, the RC is replicating and reproducing the hegemony that it had been purporting to fight.

The government has not acceded to the PCJSS demand of reserving three seats for the Hill people from the CHT constituency. This demand was rejected by the previous regimes as well. Successive regimes have maintained that since three seats have already been reserved for the CHT constituency so there was no justification for this demand. But it needs to be mentioned here that the Hill people had demanded that three seats be reserved exclusively for the Hill people. Under the present situation even a Bengali can be elected from the CHT, and given the demographic composition of the CHT today, when the Bengalis constitute 50 percent of the total population of the region, this is not an unlikely situation. The refusal from the government point of view is also understandable as the constitution declares Bangladesh to be a uni-cultural state. It is, however, pointed out here that even if the Hill people were granted the seats there is very little that the three members could have done to outvote the rest 327 members in the parliament.

Land is the most crucial issue for the Hill people. Closely related to it is the question of Bengali settlers in the CHT, who had been settled there through a state-sponsored policy of settlement. Most of them had been settled by evicting the Hill people, for most of the Hill people do not have titles to land. For them land is communal property. The state evicted them on the ground that they were occupying *khas*, i.e., government owned land. Consequently, the Hill people have been alienated from their most important resource and means of livelihood, i.e., land. This has marginalized and disempowered them. Return of the land to the Hill people and withdrawal of the Bengali settlers is therefore looked upon by the Hill people as a means of empowering themselves, which is so crucial to their survival and was fundamental to their struggle.

Under the present accord, without the prior permission of the RC, no land including leasable *khas* lands in the district, can be leased out, sold, purchased or transferred. However, it will not be applicable in case of the Reserve Forest (RF), Kaptai hydroelectricity project area, Betbunia satellite station area, state-owned industrial enterprises and land recorded in the name of government. The government cannot acquire or transfer any lands, hills and forests under the jurisdiction of the Hill District Councils without prior discussion and approval of the RC. It is, however, important to point out here that with the exclusion of the above mentioned areas from the Council's jurisdiction, the remaining land under it constitutes only 10 percent of the total land area of the CHT.

On the issue of Bengali settlers subsequent regimes had remained uncompromising. The present accord also remains uncompromising on the issue. The government has made it clear that Bengalis would not be withdrawn from the CHT. On the accusation that Hill people have been alienated from their land due to Bengali settlement the accord provides that the land record and right of possession of the tribal people will be ascertained after finalization of the ownership of land of the tribal people. Under the terms of the accord a Land Commission has been constituted under a retired judge for the disposal of all disputes relating to land. To any observer of the CHT issue it is crystal clear that peace in the CHT is largely dependent on the resolution of the land issue. The accord stipulates that land would be returned to the owners once their ownership rights can be ascertained. But in the CHT, in areas where the Hill people practice *jhum* cultivation, there is no conception of private property. Land is communally held and individuals have rights to usufruct only. Under such circumstances it is difficult to envisage as to how the Hill people would produce land documents of land ownership. On the other hand the government had provided land documents to the Bengali settlers and also many Bengalis have been settled in lands left behind by the Hill people who had taken refuge in India as refugees. The accord also stipulates that a land survey would be undertaken in the CHT to ascertain ownership rights. It is important to point out here that a cadastral survey was proposed by the BNP regime in 1992. But, the PCJSS and the Hill people then opposed it on the grounds that the Hill people do not have land documents; and the land records office in the Khagrachari district had been burned down, hence the Hill people were not in a position to prove their ownership rights. The situation has remained unchanged. Yet, the government and the PCJSS have now agreed to go ahead with the land survey. In this context the accord stipulates that in carrying out the survey the local and customary rights of the Hill people would be respected. If this turns out to be the case then it is difficult to see how the government can accommodate the Bengalis, for most of them have been settled in *khas* land, which the Hill people regard as their communal land. The land issue might turn out to be the Achilles' heel for the government as well as the PCJSS!

Regarding the refugees the PCJSS had demanded that all international and internal Jumma refugees should be properly rehabilitated. The previous regime of BNP had promised that a grant of Tk. 10,000 would be given to each returning family. The government promised that land belonging to the returnees would be restored to them; a general amnesty had been declared, besides the returnees were promised educational and employment facilities and opportunities. The present package is not much different from the earlier ones.

The state has also remained uncompromising on the issue of military withdrawal from the area. Its position is that Bangladesh is not a demilitarized state and CHT constitutes a part of Bangladesh; more importantly the region is economically and strategically important. The three hill districts are bounded on the north by the Indian state of Tripura, on the south by Myanmar and the east by the Arakan Hill Tracts and the Lushai hills. Under the present accord the military will remain in the CHT. Permanent cantonments will remain; only the temporary camps of army, Ansar and the Village Defense Forces, excepting the BDR will be gradually withdrawn. The members of the armed forces can be deployed under the state rules and procedures in case of deterioration of law and order situation and in times of natural calamities or like other parts of the country under the control of civil administration. The RC may also request the appropriate authorities for such help and assistance if required.

IV
Conclusion

The mode and nature of the state's interventions in the CHT can be explained by the characteristics of a modern state. At each instance it has sought to impose its hegemony upon the 'subordinate' communities in the CHT. The CHT peace accord is no exception to this rule. What is most disturbing is that it has sowed the seeds of polarization in the region. The state is following the colonial policy of divide and rule. The delay in the formation of the RC and the implementation of the accord with the PCJSS accusing the government of violating the 'unwritten' provisions of the accord are instances of this policy. Such delays are bound to create frustrations and disillusionment among the Hill people about the effectiveness of the PCJSS. This, it is argued here, is the objective of the regime because it aims to posit itself as an alternative and more reliable government in the CHT.

The RC could only be installed in May 1999 that is almost 15 months after the signing of the accord. It is still not clear what those 'unwritten' provisions were and if at all they have been resolved. In the CHT it is widely believed that the PCJSS, which has now emerged as a political party, has become the political opponent of the Awami League that has won all the three seats from the region in 1991 as well as in the 1996 elections. It is, therefore, no wonder that the Awami League MP, Dipankar Talukdar, who is heading the Task Force for the rehabilitation of refugees and the Internally Displaced Persons (IDPs) has proposed to include the Bengali settlers as well in the definition of IDPs. The support of the Bengalis who now comprise almost 50 percent of the total population of the CHT would indeed be critical for any political party in the region. The PCJSS thus is trapped within the number game of the present majoritarian democracy. It can little afford to alienate the Bengalis settled in the CHT nor can it openly acknowledge that Bengalis would remain there.

Disagreements exist on the number of military camps so far withdrawn from the CHT. While the government puts the figure to 75 the PCJSS maintains that it is between 10 and 15. Despite the strong resentment of the Hill people against the military, the government has maintained that the military would be involved in the CHT for infrastructure development. It is plausible to suggest here that the government would want a gradual withdrawal of the military camps, as it is still too early to predict the future attitude of the PCJSS. Besides, the dissident faction of the PCP, HWF and the PGP have floated a political party, the United Peoples Democratic Front in December 1998 and have vowed to carry on the movement for full autonomy.

The accord has also deepened the polarizations within and between the different ethnic communities in Bangladesh. At a national conference held in Dhaka during December 18-20, 1997 on 'Adivasis and Minority Affairs', the smaller communities of the CHT expressed their resentment on the proposed composition of the RC. Members of other ethnic communities (Garos, Manipuris, Saontals and others) also expressed their resentment and demanded representative bodies for themselves also. They further demanded that instead of Ministry of Tribal Affairs, there ought to be Ministry of Adivasi Affairs.

The autonomy demand of the Hill people is indeed a justifiable one, but equally justified is the claim of the other ethnic minorities. Because of the majoritarian democracy it is impossible for members of any ethnic group to get elected in the national parliament. Even when they do so it is on the ticket of the mainstream political parties. This particular provision has created an imbalance situation within the CHT, between the Bengalis and the Hill people, and also among the Hill people themselves. It has also created a dichotomy between the ethnic communities of Bangladesh, and between the Bengalis and the Hill people in general. In order to overcome this divisiveness it is important that strong local government bodies be set up in each division with adequate representation of the minority communities.

The refugees have returned from their camps in India. But they have come back to a very polarized and tense situation. It is important to point out here that India had played the critical role in getting this accord signed. It also gave a one-month ultimatum to the refugees and gradually their ration was stopped. Under the circumstances it is difficult to say that they have come back willingly. A survey carried out by this author among 100 returnees in the Khagrachari district between September 3 and 10, 1999 found that about 92 percent among them felt that the situation was still uncertain and unstable, 8 percent felt that it was bad. Important point to bear in mind here is that none of them felt that the situation has settled down for them. It is posited here that if the state fails to rehabilitate the refugees properly then the disgruntled group from within them along with the opponents of the accord, would provide leadership and manpower for a future movement in the CHT.

Since the signing of the accord the government has consistently maintained that the resources of CHT would be exploited for the economic development of the country and tourism would be promoted. I am sure such naive and insensitive pronouncements remind the Hill people of the Kaptai debacle of the 1960s when the Pakistan government built a dam in Rangamati for the industrial development of East Pakistan. For this purpose an artificial lake was constructed, consequently 40 percent of the prime land of the Hill people went under water and about 40,000 Hill people crossed over to India, where they are still languishing in Arunachal Pradesh as stateless persons. It is, therefore, no wonder that the Hill people regard the Kaptai as their teardrop; while for the Bengalis it is a major tourist site.

It is important to note that the accord has no constitutional basis, the opposition parties have rejected it on the grounds that it has compromised national sovereignty and Bengalis have been turned into second class citizens within the CHT. They also regard the autonomy granted to the Hill people and the formation of the RC as *ultra vire* to constitution of Bangladesh since Bangladesh is regarded as a unitary state by the constitution.

These parties have vowed to abrogate the accord if voted to power. This however seems most unlikely and is used more as a political rhetoric by the opposition to win the Bengali votes. Nonetheless, it does deepen the existing polarizations between the Bengalis and the Hill people on the one hand, and within the Bengali nationalist forces as well, who are divided along the Bengali and Bangladeshi models of nationhood.

It is however evident that the state hegemony in the CHT remains unabated. However, so far as the Hill people are concerned, it is perhaps important to point out here that the way to emancipation, a viable peace and counter-hegemony does not lie in the signing of peace accords or artificial constructions, that draws lines between human populations. Rather in their struggle for emancipation the dominated Hill people should take the dominated adivasis and Bengalis as well and endeavour towards the creation of a non-hegemonic society comprising citizens, not nations.

Appendix 1
Jana Samhati Samiti

(United Peoples Party)
Chittagong Hill Tracts

Guidelines

Ideology: Humanitarianism is ideology of Jana Samhati Samiti.

Principles: Nationalism, democracy, secularism are the main principles of Jana Samhati Samiti.

Aims and Objects: For the achievement of the right of self-determination of the various small nationalities, such as the Chakma, Marma (Mogh), Tripura, Bom, Murung, Pankho, Khumi, Chak, Khiang and Lusai, is the main aim and object of the party, that is:

(1) In order to be free from Islamic fanaticism, expansionism, exploitation, oppression, deprivation and perpetuated rule of Bangladesh and to safeguard the national entity and homeland for the various multilingual nationalities: (a) to ensure the separate entity status of Chittagong Hill Tracts with a constitutional guarantee, (b) to establish Regional autonomy with a Legislative Assembly;

(2) Chittagong Hill Tracts is the homeland of various multilingual small nationalities. Therefore: (a) to do away with difference, oppression, exploitation and deprivation among the various multilingual small nationalities; (b) to develop culture and language of the various small nationalities.

Associate Organizations: The associate organizations of Jana Samhati Samiti are: (1) Shanti Bahini (peace army)—armed wing; (2) Militia (auxiliary force)—armed wing; (3) Gram Panchayat—village council; (4) Juba Samiti—youth forum; (5) Mahila Samiti—women's association.

Strategy and Tactics on External Help: Jana Samhati Samiti irrespective of caste, creed and religion, would welcome and ready to accept unconditionally every help extended from any nation, humanitarian society, UNO, humanitarian and political organizations which are sympathetic to our cause and believe that would accelerate the movement for the right of self-determination. Specially, Parbattya Chattagram Jana Samhati Samiti expect help and cooperation from world humanitarian and democratic states in preserving the national entity and homeland of the Jumma people. It also expects every kinds of help from the UNO along with other world humanitarian organizations, namely, Amnesty International, IFOR, Survival International and Anti-Slavery etc.[18]

Notes

1. Amena Mohsin and Imtiaz Ahmed, 1996, "Limits of the Nationalist Discourse: The Age of Sub-State Nationalism", *Theoretical Perspectives*, Vol. 3.
2. For details see, Amena Mohsin, 1997, *The Politics of Nationalism: The Case of Chittagong Hill Tracts, Bangladesh*. Dhaka: UPL. Also see, Amena Mohsin & Bhumitra Chakma, 1992, "The Myth of Nation-Building and Security of Bangladesh" in Iftekharuzzaman & Imtiaz Ahmed (eds.), *Bangladesh and SAARC: Issues, Perspectives and Outlook*, Dhaka: Academic Publishers.
3. Based on the author's interviews with party members over a period of four years (1992-1996).
4. Willem. V. Schendel, 1992, "The Invention of the 'Jummas': State Formation and Ethnicity in Southeastern Bangladesh", *Modern Asian Studies*, Vol. 26, Part 1, Cambridge, pp. 122-23.
5. Srijagdish, 1993, "Jumma Jatiyatabad", *Jumma Sangbad Bulletin.* No. 14, JSS Publications, p. 18.
6. See writings of the Hill people in JSS published magazines like *Keokradang, Boi Sabi,Radar, Satellite* etc.
7. Kabita Chakma, 1992, *Joli no Uddim Kiteye.*Dhaka: Nari Grontho Prabartana, p. 7. The poem has been translated from Bangla by Meghna Guhathakurta.

8. *Keokradang*, 10.9.93, p. 8, JSS Publications.
9. According to the PCJSS the camps of Tripura and Mizoram shelter 54,000 registered refugees. Another 5,000 are unregistered. See, Samad, 1994, *op. cit.* Another 50,000 are living as internal refugees due to the government sponsored plan of Bengali settlement in the CHT.
10. *Dabeenama*, 1992 (Charter of demands of the PCJSS to the Bangladesh government), JSS Publications, pp. 3-10.
11. These groups are: Chakmas, Marmas, Tripuras, Mros, Tanchangya, Riangs, Bawms, Pangkhoas, Chaks, Kheyangs, Khumis, Kukis, Lushais.
12. The above apprehension was commonly expressed to the author by the local inhabitants during her visits to the CHT in 1993 and again in 1994. It is also important to note that in the 1996 elections the Awami League candidates had won from all the three constituencies in the CHT. This despite the fact that the PCJSS had put up independent candidates for the elections. The party however maintains (interview with the author) that the Awami League has promised a political solution to the issue, that is why the people want to give them a chance, as it became obvious that it was going to form the government.this time.
13. Alexander Mackenzie, 1884, *History of the Relations of the Government with the Hill Tribes of the North-East Frontier of Bengal*, Calcutta: Home Office Department Press.
14. T.H. Lewin, 1869, *The Hill Tracts of Chittagong and the Dwellers Therein, with Comparative Vocabularies of the Hill Dialects*, Calcutta: Bengal Printing Company Ltd., p. 28.
15. Proshanta Tripura, 1992, "Colonial Barriers to Integration in Chittagong Hill Tracts", in Iftekharuzzaman and Imtiaz Ahmed (eds.), *op. cit.*, p. 318.
16. This assertion is based on my personal review of Hill people's literature for over a period of four years. For this, I had chosen three magazines representing the JSS views, viz., *Keokradang, Radar* and *Satellite.* I had chosen two magazines, the *Kheyang* and *Giri Nirjhor*, which publish writings of the general people. Shugata Chakma, a prominent poet of the CHT had suggested to the author (17.9.93) that it is time for the authors to preach humanism instead of nationalism.

17. Ashis Nandy, 1989, "Shamans, Savages and the Wilderness: On the Audibility of Dissent and the Future of Civilizations", *Alternatives*, No. 14, p. 275.
18. The CHT Conference, 1986, *The Genocide Charge: Human Rights in the CHT of Bangladesh. Papers for the Conference on CHT.* Amsterdam: Research Institute of Oppressed Peoples, pp. 129-30.

Chapter Thirteen

Expositions of Illiteracy's Women: The Lessons of Hard Non-Work

Daniel Moshenberg

On Saturday, November 16, 1996, *The Washington Post*, on its front page, ran the following banner headline: "D.C. Control Board Takes Charge of Public Schools". This kind of prominent visual attention usually signifies 'earth-shattering' news, such as 'terrorist bombings' of US federal and military facilities. The most recent banner headline prior to November 16, on November 6, shouted: "Clinton Wins by Wide Margin; GOP Holds Edge in Congress". Prior to that it's been a while. When *The Washington Post*, a newspaper that bethinks itself a national 'organ', portrays the local as of national moment, local community organizers and activists all over the United States stand up and pay attention. When that newsworthy issue is schools, as distinct from education, education organizers and activists likewise pay attention. In this presentation, I want to pay attention precisely to what might be described as the discourses of inattention, the ways in which the political economies of attention and attentiveness are made of exclusion understood and practiced as the public articulation of specified repression; in a Foucauldian sense, the power of the state and parastatal apparati to hold certain members of the body politic up to a public gaze that does not scrutinize, that does not see, that does not acknowledge. This political economy of attention works, schematically, as follows: the 'world' is proferred as a social text; the social text is legible; that legibility entails not only instrumental literacy but clarity of sight and vision; that clarity of sight and vision has an arithmetic of public sacrifice. Some ones, and I hope to demonstrate the socio-categorical, or community, identity of those ones, are presented so as to be eliminated, sometimes gently sometimes brutally, sometimes consensually sometimes coercively. Needless to say, those 'sacrificed' have no say in the consensus; this is representational not representative autocracy claiming itself as democracy. In this scenario, basic 'social text' literacy involves finding the figures of those who are articulated to be disarticulated, who are 'brought forth' in order to be forgotten and ignored. Critical literacy means being-with and being-for those articulated as forgotten and forgettable, as ignored and ignorable and entails attempting to destroy and transform the apparati and agencies of articulation.

In order to clarify and contextualize these trajectories and highsounding words, let us return to the front page of *The Washington Post*, Saturday, November 16, 1996. Beneath the banner headline, a boxed inset reads: "Familiar Territory for New Leader: Retired General Has History of Helping Public Institutions". This is accompanied by a photograph of retired Army Lt. General Julius W. Becton Jr., the new District of Columbia school chief, placed there by a 'financial control board' that was appointed by a hostile Federal Congress to oversee the administration of a city, including its public schools, that, by charter, has no control over its own finances, resources or land. Two long articles describe the new system, complete with organizational charts, thumbnail sketches and photos of the new people in charge, and much discussion of 'our children', 'stakeholders', 'democracy', 'state of emergency', and 'crisis'. Does this sound familiar? 'Ousted' elected officials, peremptorily installed appointed officials, children, parents, teachers, custodians, personnel: everyone is involved. Within the severely circumscribed conditions and terrain of Washington, DC, the 'crisis' is universal, for surely everyone in the district 'cares about *our* children'. In subsequent days, that phrase will be intoned ad nauseam, always stopping, at least momentarily, any sort of debate. It is a social truth that requires neither explanation nor interpretation. 'We' are left to discuss and implement juridical, administrative and therapeutic matters, the technologies of concern and salvation.

But the universe has its own calculus, and some are left out of this state narrative. Nowhere in any of this is there any mention of publicly funded adult education; nowhere do adult learners figure as part of the school system, although their institutions are part of that system's budget. The crisis touches only children, because only children can be at risk, and only children can be spoken for. The economies of caring, as Diane Elson has described them, in a bourgeois liberal state can only operate officially and discursively in the service of adults taking care of children, and thereby asserting their, the adults', adulthood, that is, their majority. So, only children can be educatively at risk. Just as only adults can be illiterate.

Adults in basic education programs suffer history differently. Their non-presence in the Post's Report of Crisis, a master narrative if ever there was one, is no mere oversight. Further, the non-articulation of the gender, race, nation and class of their non-presence is likewise no oversight. In the early stages of the public narrative of this 'crisis', adult education was a key concern. Further, this critical and dramatic concern was visually evoked as a matter of largely Central American and Caribbean women. The site of adult education as a place of working women of color was raised, and then it was dropped. I want to follow the tracings of those droppings, precisely because they offer so familiar, tired and trite an articulation of that space and place particularly inhabited by the public representations of working women of color, and especially immigrant working women, of themselves and for themselves, that is, as women who were not necessarily and constitutively defined and delimited as mothers. I am interested in the discursive spaces of self-referential unoriginal redundancy, the 'evils' of the banal, if you like; of acts and cultures of opposition, resistance, insubordination through a politics of self-definition in the liminal zones; and of the implications of these for the praxes of dialectics and of development, that is, of nation-as-mass and of nation-state.

How do we begin to understand the report, and non-report, of this crisis? Consider this. According to adult basic educator and cultural anthropologist, Wendy Luttrell, "There are no studies of how adult literacy learners view their skills, knowledge, or competencies except for the work of Arlene Fingeret 1983, which ignores the issue of how social differences affect these views. With the notable exception of Kathleen Rockhill's 1987 study of Hispanic literacy learners, there are no ethnographies of adult basic education programs and/or classrooms" (1995: 440). Within the political and scholarly fields of concern, adult literacy learners have neither voice nor image, they make no impression and they leave no traces, and this is, once again, to those committed to a policy and politics of concern that should have predisposed them to some sort of attention to dialogue, presence, and subjectivities. The adult literacy learners are never reported as having views, those who study adult literacy development likewise have no views of the learners either in class or in program. Which adults are constitutively unwritten thus?

In a 1989 interview with *Convergence* magazine, the organ of the International Council of Adult Education, Canada, Paulo Freire was asked, "How would you describe the universe of the marginal population targeted by the International Year for Literacy?" Although, as Secretary of Education for the City of Sao Paulo, his response 'naturally' focussed on the city of Sao Paulo, it covers the 'international' and hence the local universe as well:

> In Sao Paulo, the majority of the illiterate population is made up of migrants coming from the poorest states in the north, the northeast, and also from the countryside of Sao Paulo and Minas Gerais. In general, these are people who make a living off odd jobs or unskilled professions (i.e., construction workers' aides, cleaners, housekeepers). Therefore, their level of income is very low, not even enough to satisfy basic needs like food and housing. They often live in slums, overcrowded tenement houses, and in the self-made shacks in the outskirts of Sao Paulo.... A large part of the illiterate population is made up of women, who have a doubled work load (Freire 1993: 62).

Who are the illiterate, according to Freire? In Freire's response, a kind of phenomenological syntagm is constructed, in which the illiterates are adults (who are migrants, irregular and unskilled laborers, the hungry, slum dwellers)-as-women. However, in the preface to *Pedagogy of the City*, in which appears the interview with Freire, Harold Raynolds, Jr., Former Commissioner of Education, Massachusetts, only writes about children. He writes of making "education work for all children" (9); of how "poor and inadequate schools serve poor and disadvantaged children badly" (9); of the ways in which Freire "nourishes us all in our efforts to make real schooling the birthright of every child" (12). He never, even once, mentions adults, he never ever alludes to women as literacy learners. He describes the "struggle against illiteracy" as a function of the increase "in number and proportion" of poor children "in the United States and all over the world" (9). Why can't educators' policy makers get it right? Why is it so difficult, even with Freire's words right there on the page, to see women specifically and adult learners generally as subjects of public education and public educative concern? How do we explain Raynolds' progressive illiteracies of women's presence? his rigorous inability to read Freire's straightforward description, or census, of 'the universe of the marginal population'?

If a choice of focus is offered, as for example between children and women, the 'educated' will prefer anyone and anything to women. Women will be presented at some point, and then not so much written under erasure as withered under erosion. For example, in, again, a recent article in *The Washington Post*, November 3, 1996, entitled "Boot Camp at the Shoe Factory: Where Taiwanese Bosses Drill Chinese Workers to Make Sneakers for American Joggers", Anita Chan begins her description of the combatzone bootcamp mentality that organizes and operates Taiwanese-owned shoe factories in southern China and South Korean-owned shoe factories in northern China by identifying the labor force as "young Chinese peasant women". Although the pay in these factories is described as not altogether intolerable, the cultures of labor and management are horrendous. In one of the the Korean-run factories, for example, "a woman worker was locked inside a dog cage with a large dog and placed on public display in the factory compound". However, by the end of the article, 'the universe of the marginal population' has shifted from peasant women to migrant workers. Chinese partners and officials are described as "eager to make money by overworking and underpaying the migrant workers". Later, "conversations with government and trade union officials in China reveal that.... they too see military-like control as a quick fix to the problem of a migrant labor force."

While Chan's piece is written with a fair amount of sensitivity to many elements of the social text, the articulation of gender is almost mystifying. Chan never indicates that maybe 'we' should wonder about the mass availability of women for these posts. The preponderance of women as labor-intensive factory and sweatshop workers is 'naturalized' as it is spoken, and so gender is folded into, submerged, and finally rendered invisible: rural peasant women become migrant labor force. In the language of Sherry Ortner's new book, making gender is the politics and erotics of culture. Making gender here means making women become invisible through seamless subsumption; and that act of enfolding itself becomes the pleasure of the social text. As Jacklyn Cock, Cynthia Enloe, Saundra P. Sturdevant and Brenda Stoltzfus have suggested in their writings on sexuality, military culture, and national and state cultures of masculine militarized sexuality as male and men's violence against women, the programs of militarization that Chan notes, in which military control is viewed as a mode of population control in the context of economic development, are directly linked to the normalized and normative abuse perpetrated against those workers as women. In other words, the 'social semiotic' of that woman worker in that cage with that dog is less about her 'rural origins', although that is there, or about her 'migrancy', although that too is there, than it is about her being-woman, a phantom in the juridical-administrative-therapeutic apparatus of state and thus of attempts to radicalize state as distinguished from attempts to transform state, according to Jacques Derrida, for instance, in Specters of Marx.

Derrida first states, "But a radicalization is always indebted to the very thing it radicalizes" (92). He then, in a long endnote, interrogates this obvious oedipal dialectic: "But what does 'to radicalize' mean?....It does indicate a movement of going further, of course, and of not stopping. But that is the limit of its pertinence. The point would be to do more or less than 'radicalize,' or rather something other, for the stakes are precisely those of the root and its presumed unity. The point would be not to progress still further into the depths of radicality, of the fundamental, or the originary (cause, principle, *arkhe*), while taking another step in the same direction. One would try instead to go there where the schema of the fundamental, of the originary, or of the radical, in its *ontological* unity and in the form in which it continues to govern the Marxist critique, calls for questions, procedures of formalization, genealogical interpretations that are *not* or *not sufficiently* put to work in what dominates the discourses that call themselves Marxist..." (184).

In any social category in which gender distinction is not explicitly articulated, the question of ontological unity is precisely the genealogical operations of the sight-invisibility and the site-invisibility of 'illiteracy's women'. Through a reading of minor texts of local interest, I am proposing an interpretive and political methodology that pushes for critical transformation, rather than radicalization, through a feminist antagonistics that sees dialectics as, in Derrida's sense, radicalizing, always insufficiently invested in disrupting the originary unity, interpellated as neutral, enacted as male. Beyond Derrida's methodology, however, or across it, I am further suggesting that we reject his 'hauntology' and seek not the specters that operate an economy of mourning within an international articulation of debt. Instead I suggest that we trace the moments in which women, and particularly in my locale working women of color, are raised as subjects in order to be shelved and forgotten as objects of inattention, and, 'of course' those women's movements of going further and not stopping.

In order to understand this interplay as appropriate, even necessary, to a discussion of regional and national and global development, I turn to the work of Naila Kabeer: "Along with the dominant paradigms within the development field, there have always existed alternative ways of viewing development which have evolved out of grassroots experience. What distinguishes alternative views is that they are based on close, face-to-face interaction between organizations and their constituencies so that ideas and policies are shaped in the crucible of everyday practice rather than in the upper echelons of remote and rule-bound bureaucracies. Empowerment is one such contribution from the grassroots." Kabeer opens her essay, "Empowerment from Below: Learning from the Grassroots", with what promises to be a straightforward and even easily perceptible politics, which is as well a moment of intriguing marxist feminist geography. We are presented with Marx's and Derrida's scene of haunting: the dominant paradigms within the development field are always already not so much inscribed as circum-scribed by the grassroots. Somehow, the field is surrounded by grass. Likewise, paradigms within are accompanied by ways of viewing. This geography entails a drama, a scenography, to which we shall return. This geography of site becomes rhetorically marxist when it depicts the alternative views as a superstructure with base of 'close, face-to-face interaction'. What is produced are ideas and policies. A dialectical material analysis then will follow the production and distribution of those products, the production of production and the consumption of consumption. Thus is born a kind of cultural materialist analysis of development studies and processes. Empowerment, as concept and praxis, is a name for the counter-hegemonic political and economic labor of the grassroots. In the end, the map is re-oriented so that the alternation between inside and out has become, or been translated, into an explicitly articulated 'upper' and an assumed mass below. This is an admittedly crude and schematic reading of the dialectics of Kabeer's introduction to her primary essay on popular development.

I offer an alternative reading of this passage, through a series of anecdotes and readings, to appreciate the *insufficiencies* and construct them as the base for development. I want to re-examine the base, which I see as a double articulation. First, again, "close face-to-face interaction". I want to talk about how complicated the politics of intimate space and of spatial intimacy are "down here on the ground, among the grasses". Likewise, I want to attempt to describe the complexities of knowing the face, holding the face, facing the face. As chicana activist-scholar Gloria Anzaldua has suggested, the politics of 'making face' is a perilous and necessary road we make by walking, or dancing, for it is a moment and tableau of explicit ontological disunification. If, for example, we are operating at the spatial level of imagined communities, if our politics exceed our physical grasp, and if, as we have already seen, the face of woman and the faces of women are articulated in the public sphere only to be subsumed, only to be actively forgotten into the invocations of children and of migrancies, then how do we construct any kind of macro-politique that will effectively resist, smash and transform this political economy of development? How do we teach 'readers', even sympathetic ones such as Harold Raynolds, Jr., to engage with and respect women's faces as constitutively permanent? How do we secure the faces?

Further, I want to try and understand 'the crucible of everyday practice'. Where is this everyday practice located? What is not everyday practice? For example, under what circumstances do the olympian bureaucracies so extricate themselves from history that they can be posited, as Kabeer does here, as not having everyday practices? How thin the layer of everyday practices is when Naila Kabeer suggests that the bureaucracies, metonym for state, are exempt therefrom and, on the other side, theorists and activists of women's liberation, such as Angela Davis, Maria dalla Costa and Fatima Mernissi, suggest that the failure of western models of women's liberation derives in part from its inability to see women's domestic labor as an everyday practice, to see women's liberation as an economic and material issue of 'free kindergartens and canteens', in Mernissi's terms.

In the bourgeois state, modern and post-modern, industrial and post-industrial, it is customary law and traditional practice to articulate women so as to evacuate and evict them from the site of discourse. In the Euro-American states, this is especially the case with working women of color. We have seen, briefly, expressions of this 'illocutionary evanescence'. While this disappearing act does involve the relationships and interactions between women and men, certainly, my interest here is in the systematicity of the disappearing: where women are publicly dissolved, patriarchy as a system of practices and cultures endures and is written as enduring.

In the following stories, minor stories of local interest, I suggest from examples that when worker women of color argue, struggle and labor for a politics of permanence, they are struggling against the disposition of the entire language and culture, which would and does allow 'them' to speak, even to talk back, just so long as they remember afterwards to vanish 'without a trace'. Alas, these will not be triumphant nor triumphalist reports from the front of how women gathered together and in struggle, in the words of Monique Wittig constructed an 'exultant unity'. Not yet. Instead, I consider, through the ongoing experiences of women in struggle at the local level the implications of sympathetically interrogating the apparent simplicity of Kabeer's urging close, face-to-face interaction in order to find, through it, a practical way of rendering the social ontological unity, as imposed and enforced by state and civil society, however complicated those terms have become, insufficient to transformative praxis now.

But where? The problematics posed by re-reading Kabeer's politics of close face-to-face interactions threaten that the site of discourse from which women are evicted, and hence the struggle for permanence, will be construed and metaphorized into a 'purely' discursive site. At issue here is the politics of place. I propose that we read 'literally' terms such as 'close' and 'face-to-face' and think through the crises of proximity, intimacy, and face, so that the base for our own critical analyses and politics is always the struggles of those who are bodily denied secure presence of place, as workers, residents, agents, people, adults, human beings: that is, women. In this, I rely on Doreen Massey's conceptualization of place as fluctive, interactive, specific site of multiply imbricated conjuncture: "Each 'place' can be seen as a particular, unique, point of... intersection. It is, indeed, a *meeting* place. Instead then of thinking of places as areas with boundaries around, they can be imagined as articulated moments in networks of social relations and understandings, but where a large proportion of those relations, experiences and understandings are constructed on a far larger scale than what we happen to define for that moment as the place itself, whether that be a street, or a region or even a continent. And this in turn allows a sense of place which is extroverted, which includes a consciousness of its links with the wider world, which integrates in a positive way the global and the local. This is not a question of making the ritualistic connections to 'the wider system'---the people in the local meeting who bring up international capitalism every time you try to have a discussion about rubbish collection—the point is that there are real relations with real content---economic, political, cultural—between any local place and the wider world in which it is set..." (154-5).

So, I want to talk to you about Washington, DC, not because of the World Bank and the IMF and USAID, though they are indeed there, but rather to engage in a narration of the close face-to-face development processes that are constantly, and actively, disarticulated precisely because the faces engaged are those of working women of color (and one can neither draw near to nor move away from spectral bodies), and that this disarticulation can be understood as an ongoing campaign, in the military, political and etymological sense. That is, the establishment of control of the field of operations through ownership of the field itself. In Armand Mattelart's sense, a critique of the global positionalities of Washington must examine the transnational direction of flow of information, technologies, culture, capital, armed forces, national debts, warm bodies. Instead of 'seeing Washington' exclusively as the sum of its outpourings and emissions, I want to look at those whom Washington has 'taken in', in every sense of that phrase. I want to look at those, and the representations of those, who have come to Washington and who refuse to be written as the shadowy nonbody embodiments of ignorance, as illiteracy's women.

In April 1996, the District of Columbia, in its special circumstances of having no control over its budget, governance or economy, was forced by the US federal government to shrink its budget drastically. This was supposed to be in the juridical-administrative-therapeutic pursuit of public moral health, i.e., breaking the district free of its 'bloated' services. This version of public ethos ignores the relatively high numbers of low-income and indigent people and crushes any reference to the logics and rationality of their histories and present condition. The District School Board decided to close seven schools. Of these, the vast majority were adult education centers. This is how adult education gets spoken: closure and eviction.

Staff, students, learners, and supporters rose in anger and protest against these closings. *The Washington Post* dutifully reported the events, complete with photographs of predominantly Salvadoran predominantly women carrying placards. Likewise, the local television stations covered the news, also interviewing, or showing at least, predominantly Salvadoran predominantly women in action. This was the first time ever that the local print and electronic media represented the population of adult learners, and it was furthermore the first 'public' articulation of their social, political, economic identities as well as their national, class, race, gender positionalities. How was this narrative constructed? What happened then? How was the construction of that narrative related to the later events of the D.C. Control Board effectively closing down the School Board itself? Finally, why should anyone outside of Washington care about these specific faces in this specific place? Although of course it is a story without beginning and without end, I will present it as three reports.

On April 25, 1996, *The Washington Post* reported "Seven Schools are Targeted for Closing in D.C.; Superintendent's List Focuses on Adult, Career Programs" (A1). According to staff reporter DeNeen L. Brown, the "closing list generally spares schools with traditional programs.... Instead it focuses on adult education and career centers.... The closings recommended... are the first batch of an eventual 12 closings, the largest retrenchment by an area school system in nearly two decades." Of the seven schools, two were 'career senior high schools' and two were 'adult education centers'.

"These are very difficult times, and unfortunately some very painful decisions have to be made,' said school board

President Karen Shook... 'Our city's population has declined, and consequently our school system's enrollment has declined. Frankly, we have too many buildings. With the fiscal crisis, we can't afford to operate all the buildings.'" This statement was the first salvo in dissolving the articulated presence of adult learners, whose population was in fact growing, not decreasing. But 'we' need the space, and so 'they' will feel the pain. The plan was to sell five of the school buildings and to move adolescent students, middle schoolers, from two buildings into the Carlos Rosario Adult Education Center, which would be closed. This concerns the the political translation of place into space, ostensibly 'in the name of the children'. In a script you could not have improved upon for irony, Fillmore and Hardy take the space and smash the place of Rosario. Exactly.

The report of the plan was followed by many numbers, comparing present enrollment with past enrollment, and present DC enrollment with those of the surrounding jurisdictions. In all of this, despite the clear and obvious presence of adults, since it is adult education centers which were being threatened, there was not a single word about adult learner enrollment. Instead of numbers, readers were offered the narratives of bathos:

"At Rosario Adult Education Center, where 2,000 immigrants attend English classes each day, students and staff members greeted the news of its probably closing with outrage, bewilderment and sadness.

" 'I was trained as an engineer, but here I will never be a professional until I learn English. I'll be cleaning offices the rest of my life,' said Max Guevara, 28, a janitor from El Salvador who was signing up for classes yesterday with several dozen other people. 'A lot of Anglo-Saxons think we can't reach their level, and only a place like this enables us to.'

"Sonia Gutierrez, Rosario's combative principal, who staved off budgetary doom for months by organizing protests and fund-raisers for the school, remained defiant. 'It's not over till it's over. We are not going to roll over and die,' she said in a brief interview outside her office."

What are we told and not told? We are told there are 2,000 immigrant students in English classes alone each day. We are not told how this compares with past periods, we are not told of the rest of the curriculum. In fact, the numbers of immigrant adult learners in formal programs in Washington, as everywhere in the US, have been rising precipitously as anti-immigrant fervor and exclusionary nativist nationalism grips and is grasped ever more tightly by America and its various legislative bodies. Likewise, while English classes did make up a large percentage of the curriculum at Rosario, in terms of student enrollment, there were certainly other offerings as well, ranging from automotive mechanics to parenting to citizenship classes.

If Max Guevara is 'significative', 'we' are told that the learners are largely Central American, Latino, relatively young, presently employed in professions that are largely women-dominated occupations, low-income, articulate in English, politically critical of what might be called the racial and cultural capitalisms of Anglo-Saxon American, presently not so much desperate as profoundly frustrated and, pardon the pun, alienated, and filled with determination and hope. We are also reminded of the oppressive monolingual politic of the United States. What options are available for Guevara other than public adult education? Of this we receive no word.

Finally, we are informed that the Latina principal of Rosario, whose 'national' or 'ethnic' origins are left at the generic Latina level, is 'combative'. We return in that word to the campaign mentality. We do not know, of course, if Gutierrez's combative nature is a function of her 'hot-blooded' predisposition or of her being, in fact, as we are told, under attack. It is important to note that Sonia Gutierrez not only organized demonstrations but also raised private funds for a public school, not a common occurrence in the district, and yet the school still must go.

In the end, "Rosario... was recommended to be closed as an adult education center because adult education is not mandatory and its students could attend adult education classes in other city schools." The histories of Carlos Rosario Adult Education Center, as a physical site, as a meeting place for people who carry specific histories that they bring together in a specific place, as a geographical site with relatively easy access to the largely Latino communities of Washington: all this is discounted. In the listing of the schools to be closed, each school had a category, 'capacity'. Under Carlos Rosario Adult Education Center, as under Armstrong Adult Education Center, next to 'capacity', the words 'not applicable', 'n/a'. Under what circumstances would the capacity of that center be applicable? How does capacity, in all senses of that word, become not applicable to any site of education?

The next day, Saturday, April 27, 1996, *The Washington Post*, in the Metro Section, continued its report: "Latinos Want D.C. School to Stay Open; 400 Protest Plan to Close Adult Education Center That Teaches English" (B3). In an accompanying photograph, mostly women, mostly Central American women, were shown demonstrating. In the article, however, the only woman who speaks is School Board member Ann C. Wilcox, who proclaims, "It's heartening, and it opens my eyes to support for this program." 'It' is the protest, the dialogue, the conversation. However, it is also clear that the School Board members themselves know virtually nothing about the adult education programs within their own jurisdictional responsibility. Meanwhile, the article quotes Arnoldo Ramos, director of the Council of Latino Agencies: "This is the only adult education center serving Latinos. By closing this program, they are sending a message that Latinos don't matter and that we should continue serving tables, continue picking up garbage and having the lowest positions in society."

When do adult learners 'enter' into the public forum? When do working women of color as adult learners 'enter' into the 'public forum'? One might as well ask when are working women of color as adult learners interred into the public forum. Do they enter as speakers, as full participants, or do they enter as visual objects, as floating signatures of the power of the inscribing and authorizing gaze? If the latter, how does one describe the workings of that gaze, of the apparatus of that gaze, and how do the women, and the learners, learn to write their own names? At this point, the manner of public evacuation of loudly silenced working women of color becomes specific to education, to school, and to the notion of responsibility of state and of welfare state.

In the report of the event, again, we are actively not told anything contextual about the learners. We hear that 400 people picketed the D.C. Board of Education, but we don't hear that this was one of the rare, perhaps even the first, public demonstrations by adult learners in the District of Columbia. We further don't read, as is the case, anything about the 'public quiescence' of urban adult learners generally in the United States. As I have discussed elsewhere, where tertiary education learners, mostly college and university students, are marked by their activism, adult learners are constituted as an absent and silent sector, as 'passive citizens' and worse.

In this article, the only pretense of contextualization is the reiteration of Smith's proposition that Rosario be closed because adult education is not mandatory and because students could attend classes in other parts of the city. Speaking of the Salvadoran community, how 'newcomer' students whose first language is Spanish and whose origins are rural are meant to navigate the streets and information highways in order to find out about the schools, to find their locations in distant neighborhoods, populated by predominantly African American and White English speaking often hostile residents, and to actually get to those distant schools both for registration and on a regular basis is never explained. Again, I am not proposing that the adult learners are helpless. Rather, I am suggesting that the public schools implicitly represent them as minors. Otherwise, transportation would be provided or at least increased community outreach and education would be installed. Of course, none of this happens. Instead, the state policy is that they can make it if they want to; if they don't, well, that's their problem, or better that's the problem of their 'backwardness'.

The report meanwhile leaves the majority of the learners absolutely speechless and spoken for, represented by outside, sympathetic agencies or by male learners, who constitute a minority of both the population at Rosario and the 400 or so who showed up to demonstrate. What we likewise do not read about are the political traditions of protest, predominantly Salvadoran, that underwrite the shock of their presence. All that goes unsaid and, ultimately, unseen. These are the sorts of details we must linger over in order to understand both the Control Board's 'seizure' of the public school system, and its reports.

I suggest that the 'dialogue' between Superintendent Smith and the predominantly female Central American learner-protesters concerns the status of 'free spaces' within the public school system, and even more within the notion of public education. Repeatedly, Smith contends that adult education is not mandatory. What does that mean? It means that the reason adult learners lose their sites of education is because they come out of free will and free choice; children 'deserve' schooling because they have no choice. The responsibility of the state, then, to educate its populations is administrative, juridical and, explicitly, anti-democratic and anti-popular, that is therapeutic. Not elitist so much as anti-popular. This is what Nancy Fraser means when she suggests that the politics of needs interpretation in late capitalist societies is organized essentially into three modalities: oppositional, reprivatization, and expert. Adult learners generally are oppositional, and the School Superintendent, in shutting down the school, is actually reprivatizing it, "articulating entrenched needs interpretation that could previously go without saying" (171).

But within this facing off, there is another scenario being written. The wordless women who populate the photographs that accompany the articles, each time, who carry the placards, who constitute the mass, are seen but rendered invisible. Everytime someone in authority speaks with them, the authority expresses surprise, not at the learners' 'articulateness,' as the racialized codes of the United States would have it, but rather at their very existence. When Smith proposes closing Rosario because adult education is not mandatory, he paves the way, ideologically, for his own removal. As Fraser notes, the third modality of politics of needs interpretation discourse is expert discourse: "linking popular movement to the state" (171). In the conditions of Washington, however, in ways that redound to conceptualizations of colonial cultural and administrative practices, the popular movements are precisely absent and above, the Federal Government. Meanwhile, the women of Rosario Center were arguing, and continue to contend, that adult education was a right, not a need, and therefore should be protected and even supported. They were arguing for the right to self-determination in and through schooling and education. They were visually acknowledged and discursively evicted because they misread their roles. Again, according to Nancy Fraser, they were meant to be clients, "abject dependents,.... *the negatives of the possessive individuals*". As Fraser goes on to note, low income women of color are "largely excluded from the market as workers and as consumers" (152). These women were demonstrating the ideological operations of these public, and patriarchal, operations. They were working, they were consumers, and, most significantly and most 'dangerously', their negation of possessive individualism did not result in abject non-identity but rather in cooperative collectivist subjectivities. The women were arguing that the issue at Rosario Center was a rights issue, their right to be a part of the social text. The Superintendent insisted, by various routes, that the issue was one of needs, and that adults by definition, of state and nature, do not need education or schooling. Practically, from slightly different perspectives, Smith and Raynolds speak the same language. None of this ever made it into the public discussion. The point, you see, is distribution of information as a rights issue and as a needs issue: what information do we 'need', what information do we have a 'right' to demand, in order to construct a progressive policy and praxis of social transformation?

On May 16, 1996, the axe fell, as reported in *The Washington Post*, May 17, 1996, by DeNeen L. Brown in an article entitled "Board Votes to Close 7 D.C. Schools; Protests Are in Vain; Officials Plan to Keep Buildings in System" (D1). Again, the ostensible justification was that of "the school system's aging and underutilized schools". Again, this has nothing to do with the reasons Rosario was closed. Again Karen Shook is quoted lamenting the 'painful', now a permanent trope in the political imaginary of the bourgeois liberal sectors of the city. Basically, nothing new occurs, except for the intensification of the elimination of Latinas. Of the School Board members interviewed, all three, Karen Shook, Erika Landberg, and Valencia Mohammed, are women, none, surprisingly, Latina. The only first-language Spanish speaker, or Latino, to be interviewed is Luis Vasquez-Ajmac, spokesman for the Latino Civil Rights Task Force, who exclaimed, "It was like losing a child after 25 years." No adult learners are interviewed, though one, a male named Dennis Williams, is partially described.

The public eviction of Salvadoran working women intensifies in a word-and-picture conjuncture. First, Karen Shook states, "They are all in terrible condition." Once again, this takes Rosario off the table for discussion, for if they are all in terrible condition, then Rosario is not part of this conversation, of this totality. The Carlos Rosario Center was not in terrible condition, it was in the condition of being perfectly adequate to adult learners. This is unnecessary information. The closings of spaces and of places gets conveniently folded into one another, and place gives way to space. Then, in the photograph accompanying the article, a young Latino bends over a Latina, with the following caption: "Ruben Smith tries to comfort Isabel Valencia moments after they learned that the D.C. Board of Education voted to close Rosario Adult Education Center, where they are students." Never a word is spoken by, only for and of. Isabel Valencia is named as a wordless icon, the long suffering 'unfortunate' woman, the body of pain and sorrow, the client of comfort. To date, this is the last chapter, and the last word, on adult learners in *The Washington Post*. They served their purpose, now let's move on.

But what happens if 'we' stay, once the 'story' has ended, with those who inhabit a different tale and remain? What happens if we submit the 'neat' narrative (of) closure to other stories in which, for example, the race, class AND gender of adult learners is acknowledged? Unless we end up in a politics that concentrates on, and fetishizes, the local as exclusively local, where is the critical methodology by which we might read the events, reported and unreported, of adult learners in Washington, DC, in such a way that we might engage in close face-to-face interaction? The first step is already bifurcated. First, remember that the populations of adult learners remain after the schools are closed, if the interpellation of learners as students is adequately rejected. Their bodies do not go away, and their ambitions and hopes do not dissolve. So, those populations are engaged in developing new strategies for the ongoing promotion of their own education, learning, and literacies. Second, in alternative 'cultural' representations, adult learners speak or at least the questions of adult learners' speech is raised. Again, the adult learner population is not a homogeneous sector. We must study the ways in which the male minority among the adult learners are encouraged, and taught, to speak, and what sorts of oppositional programs might be installed. Once having done that, we can begin to locate Washington in some sort of alternative, progressive international and even global political economy. This is the site and task for development policy from the ground up.

That international political economy is inscribed in the historical context that likewise never gets spoken. Five years earlier, almost to the day, that the School Board closed Rosario, on May 5, 1991, two Washington, DC police officers shot a thirty-one year old recently unemployed construction worker, Daniel Enrique Gomez. For the next two days, the predominantly Latino barrio of Mount Pleasant was a war zone. Predominantly Salvadoran youths not only 'rioted' and 'looted', they attacked police specifically. In the first day of the uprising, for example, the youths drove the police out of six square blocks. This too was previously unheard of in Washington.

According to Jon Liss, "During the 1980's, eight million people immigrated to the United States, more than in any decade since the 1900's. Almost one million of these immigrants were Salvadoran. Over 150,000 Salvadorans settled in the Washington, D.C. area. (Only Los Angeles and Houston have larger concentrations" (20). For the Public School system, these new immigrants brought a precipitous rise in demands and costs: bilingual education, rural/urban multicultural education, documentation. But they also brought enriching and empowering radical political traditions particularly appropriate to progressive adult education. Liss argues that the Salvadoran populations brought traditions of popular education and of cooperative economics: "Popular education, building on Latin American traditions, has two distinguishing pedagogical components which have positive political implications. First, there is the democratic collective character of popular education.... Second, popular education makes explicit the relationship between learning and action. Learning English will not eliminate the learners' oppression as immigrants, people of color, workers, or women. Therefore popular education sees oppression/powerlessness as the central contradiction, not the inability to speak English" (23). Popular education operates, internally, dialectically, seeking out the contradictions and, if not resolving, refining them through action. This is well known. But to understand Washington, specifically, you must also know that this is forbidden knowledge in Washington, and even more so when articulated by (a) women, (b) women of color, (c) Latinas, (d) Salvadoran women, who are presumed to be undocumented residents and the vast majority of whom are domestic workers, and hence should simply shut up. Thus, the field of discourse in which Central American modes of popular education occurs is explicitly antagonistic. Liss concludes his analysis of the Salvadoran uprising with an assessment of the potential contributions of Salvadorans to revolutionary struggle in the US: "years of mass revolutionary practice, insights developed by colonial and racial oppression, and most important at this juncture in history, youthful verve and vigor" (24).

When Salvadoran women, represented as seen but not heard, showed up at the School Board meeting, they visually resuscitated the specter of the uprising five years earlier and the specter of uprising generally, and their articulated 'elimination' by the press speaks to the women's national and women's cultural traditions of popular education as a mode of struggle. I am suggesting that the tableau constructed by the press, that of non-dialogue between anyone in authority, male or female, White or Black, and these women, represents Salvadoran women as the very dangerous bodies of 'true' popular education and articulates the international in the local. Not because individual women are Salvadoran, but rather because the entire women's culture of which they are a part is under attack.

At the moment in which Central American adult learners in formal and popular education cultures and programs in Washington, DC, are radically excised, a kind of map extends chronotropically to culturally appropriate and pertinent experiments in national and regional democratic and critical education in distressed places and times. At the international level, the national literacy campaigns of Cuba, Guinea-Bissau, Nicaragua and El Salvador, Sao Paulo speak to the struggles of adult learners, who in Washington are either Central American, Caribbean, or African American. At the national level, the examples of Black Liberation and Chicano Nationalist struggles' educational experiments, such as the Freedom Schools, are cherished. 'Domestically', adult learners study the education work of Black, Latina, Filipina, Asian working women's struggles to try and understand the lessons of popular education for mass mobilization in which the 'positionalities' and the bodies of women are respected as human beings. In the context of the participants in the specific projects and struggles in the Washington metropolitan area, these are the necessary cultural resources of hope and critique, and provide a curriculum for transformation that offers technical as well as critical training and insight, a fire in the heart and the hearth, as it were.

Consider, as an example, the following poem by local DC poet Ethelbert Miller:

only language can hold us together
only language
can hold us together

i watch the women
bead their hair
each bead a word
braids becoming
sentences

she would
never comb her hair
it was always wild

like new poetry
it was difficult
to understand

she would enter
rooms where old women

would stare & mumble
& bold ones would say

"where's her mother"

she never understood why
no one ever understood the
beauty of her hair

like free verse
so natural as conversation
so flowing like the french

or spanish she heard or
overheard thought she knew

"i want to go to
mozambique" she said one day

combing her hair
finding the proper beads

after so long

"i want to go to
mozambique" she said

twisting her hair
into shape the way her
grandmother made quilts
each part separated &
plaited

"i want to go to
mozambique or zimbabwe
or someplacc like luanda

i need to do something
about my hair

if only i could
remember

the words
to the language
that keeps

breaking in my
hands"

In this poem, Miller constructs an indigenous vision of popular education: African American women gather together and study language and in so doing make new languages. Only language can hold us together, and that language insists on the primacy of historical memory, remembering the words, and of diasporic geographies, Mozambique and Zimbabwe and Luanda. These are not accidental references. They speak to the cultural ambitions of African American women in Washington for social plenitude, a dream that is articulated in the desire for not so much a return as a journey to the Mother Continent, Africa, and to its traditions. The question for adult educators becomes the scope and identity of 'us' who are held together only by language. In Washington, however, with its majority African American and Central American population, these transnational cultural ties, the ties that bind as Bernard Magubane wrote, matter. It is not merely the progressive penchant for international linkages that suggests the cultural appropriateness of the literacy campaigns and movement educational projects; it is the way we talk, the language that does in fact hold us together, in Washington.

At the instant where we start discussing what holds us together, practically, the question methodologically becomes one of dialectics. In popular education traditions, the educator as activist organizer thematizes histories and geographies. With this in mind, I turn to the difficulties radical educators have articulating our practices in the context of any Marxist or neo-Marxist theory. Consistently, Marxist and neo-Marxist educators have made literacy promotion and development a matter of good will, political exigency, responding culturally to workers' demands, or tactics and strategy. These are liberal, as distinct from Marxist/neo-Marxist, positions maintained, ironically, by Marxists and neo-Marxists engaged in adult education. Why? I suggest that the very notion of dialectics within the Marxist and neo-Marxist traditions presumes a certain kind and level of literacy always already inscribed within the mass, or at least among the vanguard leadership of that mass. Thus, the educational work, as dialectical, is always directed towards that leadership. I propose, as alternative to dialectics, antagonistics, as suggested by Antonio Negri and the Italian Autonomia movements.

Negri argues that the logic of capitalist domination has been to construct two subjects, capitalist and proletarian, that are antagonistic to one another, and that the development of communist antagonistics, as distinct from dialectics, points towards the historical and ethical requirement on the part of the dominated and oppressed classes to struggle for separation as a means of attaining self-valorization, first, and ultimately full and complete subjectivity. This struggle for complete and full subjectivity can only occur if a full and radical critique of the proletarian subjectivity, as proposed by Negri, occurs within the articulations of working women's subjectivity. As Negri suggests, "the emergence of the other subject, of the proletarian subject, can't but extend itself to the whole sphere of circulation." In so doing, this emergent subject as proletarian must be interrogated, likewise, antagonized and rewritten... into the everyday lives of those whose work does not count as such, into the living bodies and spaces and days of working women.

According to Marx, in the *Grundrisse*, "the only thing distinct from *objectified* labor is *non-objectified* labor, labor which is still objectifying itself, *labor* as subjectivity" (272). According to Negri, this "is the first time that we encounter this characterization of labor. With that we have entered into a central phase of Marx's analysis. The separation capital-labor was the first moment; here now is the second---*labor as subjectivity*, as source, as potential of all wealth" (69). Negri traces labor as subjectivity through the Grundrisse until he arrives at communist subjectivity. For Negri, the socialist subject as produced by capital, is "the highest form, the superior form of the economic rationality of capital, of the rationality of profit" (166). It is the partner in the dialectics, having no autonomous independent subjectivity of its own. On another hand, for Negri, "communism has the form of subjectivity, communism is a constituting praxis" (163). It insists on the auto-determination of the proletarian, collective, social, multilateral, differentiated subject. And, and here is where we return to the narratives of the closing of Carlos Rosario, "beginning with the refusal of work... the subject pose(s) its own self-constitution. The *refusal of work* constitutes the subject----in that it projects into the world, in that it *constitutes a mode of production*" (167). For Negri, it all comes down to this: communism as the abolition of work, communist history as "the enormous pain of the struggle to abolish work" (166), and "worker and proletarian auto-valorization (as) the planning of the abolition of work" (166-7).

Within this production of communism, of worker subjectivity become revolutionary class, Negri insistently presents the social as critical: "The *Grundrisse* is in advance of *Capital* because *in it the social character of the categories appears immediately as fundamental*.... Where the *Grundrisse* goes far beyond the (earlier) efforts... is... around the definition of *social antagonism.... Marx's insistence emphasizes here the union of the theory of socialization and the theory of surplus value*. The latter makes it possible to consider the former in antagonistic terms. The first allows us to carry the second to universal levels. 'To universal levels' means that the work of modernization and the refounding of Marxist categories must be able to grasp in its object the *development of capital managed by the state* and that the *increasingly impetuous multinational mode of production is growing to the international level*. The critique of political economy can't but be, simultaneously a critique of the political, a critique of socialism, a critique of the multinationality. But these universal levels are nevertheless levels of real antagonism" (187-8).

These levels of real antagonism are 'at work' in the reporting of the protests against the closing of the Carlos Rosario Adult Education Center in Washington, DC. I suggest the following 'antagonistic' conclusion. I take the social character literally, as in the characters of the social. In this instance, *The Washington Post*, as the publication of the master narratives of Washington, DC, by excluding repeatedly Salvadoran women, who were both in the majority and quite voluble in their protests, from speech, demonstrates the real antagonisms at work when those particular characters articulate precisely their independent subjectivities. In the context of Negri's argument, the question posed by exclusion is the following: Why do a bunch of Salvadoran women workers, most of whom are already employed, need or want further education? That question of capital, patriarchy, and, according to Negri, dialectics would lead us to a standard analysis of the contradictions of workers' aspirations for improved wages, living conditions, and, to close the circle, a better life for our children. But what the women were proposing, what made them dangerous, was that learning itself is work. To the same extent that the Salvadoran youths in 1991 transformed an urban riot into a zone of urban guerilla warfare for two brief days, these Salvadoran women were transforming a protest into a picket line. They were calling the question of work itself. I propose that this as their lesson for us, the transformation, rather than radicalization, of work entails as well the transformation of non-work, and hence the politics of refusal to work.

A recent piece by Patricia Williams, entitled "The Saints of Servitude" begins with these words: "There's a lot in the press these days about 'the lessons of hard work'." This is public education in America today, the lessons of hard work. The Salvadoran women who protested against the closure of Carlos Rosario Adult Education Center were trying to teach the counter-lessons of hard non-work. As every woman knows, the social category of non-work is neither leisure nor privilege, and it certainly is a site of deep and real social antagonisms. That's why those women were presented silently, to render their antagonistic tendencies 'merely' dialectic. Close face-to-face interactions must be constructed against the ethos of 'real work' and 'real value'. For this, we must follow the example of the women of Carlos Rosario. I mean that literally. We must learn to read antagonistically, knowing that in every narrative of State, there are suppressed counter-narratives of women-in-struggle that can form the basis for a transformative politics.

Meanwhile, back in Washington, on Saturday, November 30, 1996, *The New York Times* reports that the new School Chief, retired General Becton, is considering placing armed guards in the DC Public Schools.

References

Brown, DeNeen L. (1996a) 'Seven schools are targeted for closing in D.C.', *Washington Post*, 25 April.

Brown, DeNeen L. (1996b) 'Latinos want D.C. schools to stay open; 400 protest plan to close adult education center that teaches English', *Washington Post*, 27 April.

Brown, DeNeen L. (1996c) 'Board votes to close 7 D.C. schools', *Washington Post*, 16 November.

Chan, Anita (1996) 'Boot Camp at the Shoe Factory: Where Taiwanese Bosses Drill Chinese Workers to Make Sneaker for American Joggers', *Washington Post*, 3 November.

Derrida, Jacques (1994) *Specters of Marx: The State of the Debt, the Work of Mourning, & the New International*, trans. Peggy Kamuf, New York: Routledge.

Fraser, Nancy (1989) *Unruly Practices: Power, Discourse and Gender in Contemporary Social Theory*, Minneapolis: University of Minnesota Press.

Freire, Paulo (1993) *Pedagogy of the City*, trans. Donaldo Macedo, New York: Continuum.

Greene, Marcia Slacum (1996) 'Familiar territory for new leader: retired general has history of helping public institutions', *Washington Post*, 16 November.

Kabeer, Naila (1994) *Reversed Realities: Gender Hierarchies in Development Thought*, New York: Routledge.

Liss, Jon (1991) 'Salvadoran immigration and the DC rebellion', *Forward Motion* 10:4, 20-4.

Luttrell, Wendy (1995) 'The Teachers, They All Had Their Pets: Concepts of Gender, Knowledge, and Power' In Barbara Laslett, Johanna Brenner, Yesim Arat (eds.), *Rethinking the Political: Gender, Resistance, and the State*, Chicago: University of Chicago Press.

Marx, Karl (1973) *Grundrisse: Foundations of the Critique of Political Economy*, trans. Martin Nicolaus, New York: Vintage.

Marx, Karl (1977) *Capital*, Vol. 1, trans. Ben Fowkes, New York: Vintage.

Massey, Doreen (1994) *Space, Place and Gender*, Minneapolis: University of Minnesota Press.

Miller, E. Ethelbert (1986) *Where Are the Love Poems for Dictators?*, Washington: Open Hand.

Negri, Antonio (1991) *Marx Beyond Marx: Lessons on the Grundrisse*, trans. Harry Cleaver, Michael Ryan and Maurizio Viano, New York: Autonomedia.

Vise, David A. (1996) 'D.C. Control Board takes charge of public schools', *Washington Post*, 16 November.

Williams, Patricia (1996) 'The saints of servitude', *New York Times*, 13 October.

Chapter Fourteen

Transformation in the Sri Lankan Tamil Militant Discourse: Loss of the Tamil Self, Violence and the Hermeneutics of Recovery

Chitra Sivakumar

> The Eelam Movement is the cry of the spirit of the Sri Lankan Tamils to live in freedom, self-respect, and dignity, and not in subjugation and slavery.
>
> —A Sri Lankan Tamil militant leader

In the recent issue of *Daedlus* (Winter 1996) devoted to the theme of social suffering in the twentieth century, various scholars have explored its hues in different societal landscapes of the world. While some of these scholars have attempted to unearth the reasons for immense suffering and pain in a gamut of social forces ranging from political violence to economic deprivation (made worse sometimes by the play of certain foreign agencies' interests conflating with certain local interests), some others have dwelt on issues such as cultural appropriation of suffering, and professional and public debates on death itself, in countries such as the USA and Japan.

But, curiously, what is missing in this concern with social suffering, is the possibility of a reversed situation, where violence itself can be an expression of unfathomable pain and anguish. In other words, while violence often is the villain of various forms of suffering and pain, in other terrains the villain can be a hero, being itself the bearer of such anguished experiences. An illustration for the latter is the nearly a decade and quarter armed struggle of the Sri Lankan Tamils for 'liberation' from the "Sinhalese cultural and political oppression and violence". They wanted others to awake from the slumber of their comfort and take cognizance of them, and spread the message of their suffering across the world! "Won't India do something about it? Won't mother Tamilnadu do something about it? Won't the world do something about it?"

The critical threshold for the transformation of the Sri Lankan Tamil struggle from being non-violent to violent was the bloody and gruesome riots of July 24, 1983, when all forms of brutality were unleashed on thousands of hapless and innocent Tamils by violent Sinhalese mobs, though the former had little or no connection with the event of the killing of 13 Sinhalese soldiers in Jaffna by some Sri Lankan Tamil militant youth, a few days earlier to the riots. The riots saw hundreds of innocent Tamils killed, thousands of them loosing their homes, livelihood and property.

Soon a spate of literature followed on the ethnic conflict in the island nation, focussing broadly, on the sources of the conflict and of the July riots. But hardly any of these studies have attempted to explore the inner logic of the Sri Lankan militants' themselves, regarding the predicament that led them to opt for an armed struggle and accept violence, or their perceptions pertaining to the impact of the struggle on their society and themselves or other militants. The present paper attempts such an exercise, through the personal narratives of some militant leaders belonging to the major Sri Lankan Tamil militant organizations such as the People's Liberation Organization of Tamil Eelam (PLOTE), and the Liberation Tigers of Tamil Eelam (LTTE). Embodied in the militant discourse is a theory of violence and social transformation, whose broader validity I have sought by resourcing on various works in the field, and other writings such as those of Morleau-Ponty (1988) and Castoriadis (1987).

The three narratives presented here are based on the fieldwork I carried out among the five major Sri Lankan Tamil militant organizations----besides the PLOTE and the LTTE Tamil Eelam Liberation Organization (TELO), Eelam Revolutionary Organization of Students (EROS), and Eelam People Revolutionary Liberation Front (EPRLF)----and many ordinary Sri Lankan Tamil refugees from the mid-80's to the early 90's. Though the narratives relate to the voices of the three militants from the PLOTE and the LTTE, yet at a certain level---subjective dimensions apart----they echo the deep aspirations, concern, anxiety, anguish and frustration of many other militants and the refugees whom I had interviewed during the course of my fieldwork. The fieldwork not merely meant witnessing and sharing their suffering and agony, but also putting my life into jeopardy on certain occasions: given the animosity and internecine warfare among some of the militant organizations, I could well have been one of the untargeted victims along with the cadres or the leaders of the militant organization (whom I was interviewing at a certain juncture), if those who were antagonistic to them had decided to shoot them dead on that occasion. In fact, I was aware that many of the militants I interviewed carried their personal weapons or if they were leaders had also weapon wielding personal bodyguards during my interview sessions with them. There were also occasions when I interviewed them at my home, which meant that members of my family were also exposed to the risk. But this happened rarely and later I desisted from doing so, since I felt that it was unfair on my part to expose my family to such a danger. I thought "during the course of my fieldwork, if I get killed, it is understandable given the nature of my work, but why should my son and husband pay the price for my commitment?" Of course, this is not to say that I was the acme of courage and had no fear of the prospect of death that my work entailed. But often I carried on with suppressed tremulousness, for I wanted to know why people became rebels accepting violence as an instrument to achieve their goals? I suppose, it is this quest, which kept me at it, pushing aside the fears to some corner of my being. Besides, as I pursued my dialogues with the militants and refugees, I found myself involved with their cause as much as themselves. Often I found my emotions swaying with theirs: for instance, if I found them jubilant that the Indo-Sri Lanka accord would bring peace to their hearts and land, I was jubilant too. On the other hand, when they told me in rage and pain that many civilians in Jaffna lost their lives during the IPKF (Indian Peace Keeping Force) disarming operations against the LTTE, I felt anguished, ashamed and angry.

The paper has drawn on the burgeoning tradition of ethnography in social anthropology, where much focus is sought to be placed on the interpretative selves (Clifford and George 1990) for getting glimpses of the "structuration" of societies (Giddens 1979). While I am referring to my informants, whether the militants or the Sri Lankan Tamil refugees, in most instances I use pseudonyms, with the exception of some leaders of some well known militant organizations, where camouflaging their identity would have proved futile.

Arasu Nityan (PLOTE)

Arasu Nityan is a Vellala Christian, hailing from a village in Kaytes---a small island situated in the north-western direction of the Jaffna peninsula and the journey from the coast to the island takes just about ten to fifteen minutes by a boat or a launch. He was in his thirties at the time of my study in 1986. His family, he said, may be considered well-to-do, as they owned paddy land, coconut orchard, etc.

Arasu Nityan narrated his story of transformation to militancy and acceptance of violence, the intra- and inter-militant groups' conflict, the impact of the armed struggle on his society, etc., as follows:

"I am the youngest of the three sons of my parents. My father passed away in the late 70's. My old mother who is in her mid-70's manages all our property, since none of us live in the village. One of my elder brothers is working in England and the other is in Germany. The wife of my England brother lives with my mother along with her children. But my other brother in Germany has his wife and children with him. My brothers left Sri Lanka during mid-80's due to lack of proper employment opportunities.

Now, looking back, it was my father who was the greatest influence in my life during childhood and adolescence. I was a lonely child, since my brothers were away pursuing their college education in Colombo, and my mother forbid me from playing with children of low castes and low economic background. She used to say, "it is beneath our respect to inter-mix with these children".

"My father was a radical and member of the Tamil Federal Party. I often used to see him discussing with his political friends, various issues relating to the Tamils---their political demands for a measure of autonomy, Sinhalese chauvinism, etc. I wanted to be more radical than my father and be a revolutionary. I am a revolutionary.

"During my high school days in Jaffna, i.e., in the early 70's, my friends and myself used to listen to the speeches of Mr. Amirtalingam, the leader of the TULF (Tamil United Liberation Front). Oh! what fiery speeches they were: the Eelam cry was the prominent theme in these speeches. They did rouse antipathic feelings against the Sinhalese dominated Sri Lanka government and lit the fire of Eelam and Tamil nationalism in the adolescent minds and hearts. An independent sovereign Tamil Eelam was projected as the only solution to the unjust and repressive policies of the Sri Lankan government.

"The government's policies in the field of language, education and land colonisation scheme were given as instances of the discriminatory policy of the government against the Tamils. It was also pointed out that these and other government policies had reduced the Tamils to secondary citizens in their own land. The future of the Tamil youth was portrayed as very bleak, with few avenues open for their bread and survival.

"All this naturally created a great anxiety in the young minds about their very survival. I wanted to be a revolutionary and came to champion the cause of Tamil nationalism. This was in the early 70's.

"I joined the nascent and small group of Tamil New Tigers (TNT), which later came to be rechristened as the Liberation Tigers of Tamil Eelam. V. Prabhakaran (currently, the top leader of the LTTE), Uma Maheshwaran (now, the top supreme leader of the People's Liberation Organisation of Tamil Eelam or PLOTE), others and myself all worked together in the TNT. I received training to be a guerilla fighter. I also took part in fighting against the Sri Lankan government's security forces. I know Prabhakaran very well and we were friends. Do you know how often we have walked along the Marina beach (in Madras), discussing various issues of our armed struggle?

"My father was very perturbed about my political activities. One day, when I was back home in my village in Kaytes, my father and myself had a big argument over my political involvement. He wanted me to leave Sri Lanka and go to England to pursue higher studies. Ultimately I had to oblige him. I left for England in 1978. There I joined a course in Electronics Engineering. I, however, continued with my political activities there too.

"But soon fissures began to emerge in the LTTE. You remember the shoot out that took place between Prabhakaran and Uma Maheshwaran in the Pondy Bazaar area in Madras in 1982? The reasons for the clash between the two were partly political and partly due to a woman who worked in the organisation. The woman and Uma Maheshwaran fell in love with each other. I think Prabhakaran also liked her. But he was very piqued with Uma Maheshwaran's romantic proclivities, for one of the crucial conduct codes in the LTTE then was that no member should get engaged in romantic entanglements with women. Such distractions were viewed as non-conducive to stringent guerilla training and discipline and a total involvement in the movement. Another factor of conflict between the two was rivalry for power. The question was who was the supreme leader of the organisation? The issue was settled with a split in the organisation. Uma Maheshwaran, along with some of his staunch supporters in the LTTE, quit it and started the PLOTE.

"I joined the PLOTE, for I did not like Prabhakaran's attitudes to leadership. He wanted to be recognised as the supreme leader in the organisation with the concentration of all power in his hands. He wanted everybody to obey his commands and would brook no difference of opinion. You know how he started? He did not do well in school and used to hang around with some drop-outs from school. This gang spent most of its time in the streets of Jaffna.

"From then on, he became increasingly politically ambitious. In fact, in the LTTE, any member expressed as much as a whisper of dissent, he is physically eliminated. Prabhakaran is ruthless, he has eliminated so many young men in his organisation. You must have also known about the way the late TELO leader Sri Sabaratinam and nearly 150 of his comrades were massacred in Jaffna in 1986. That is how Prabhakaran is !

"Oh! this intense rivalry for power and egotism that is its concomitant, have been the bane of the Eelam struggle. Why do you think there are so many groups—PLOTE, LTTE, TELO, EROS, EPRLF and then the TULF.

"While in England I continued to work for the PLOTE, collecting funds, recruiting members, etc. During my stay in England, I visited Madras a couple of times in connection with political work.

"The divisiveness in the Eelam struggle is because each one wants to assert his importance and power over the other. Each one wants to be viewed as the hero of the Tamil cause. We can trace this to Indian philosophy, with its numerous schools of thought, caste system, etc. We need to have a different philosophy when we are involved in a movement---a philosophy that unites the people as one nation. Marxist philosophy offers such a possibility, with its emphasis on the struggle of the oppressed against the exploiter. Of course, it is a modification of Marx's theory of dialectical materialism. In contexts such as the Tamil struggle, we need to substitute class with ethnic group. The Sri Lankan Tamils are the oppressed group, and the exploiter is the Sinhalese government and the dominant Sinhalese classes that the government represents. But in our Marxist theory, we include the oppressed Sinhalese too, who also need to be liberated from the upper-class Sinhalese government. That is why, we are not against the poor Sinhalese masses, and we shall not engage in any violence against them. In fact, we consider them as our fellow sufferers.

In the initial stages, we all, viz., Prabhakaran, Uma Maheswaran, myself and others worked together, though we hailed from different castes. We were a small group then and caste considerations did not figure in our association. But, as the movement started gaining in strength after the 1983 riots, new leaders emerged from other regions, especially in the eastern Batticoloa province, which to a certain degree also changed the contours of the movement. Prabhakaran started mobilising support among the youth of the Karaya community from Velvettithurai (i.e., the fisherman community he belongs to, and the place he hails from). He gathered increasing number of followers from this community from other areas of Jaffna peninsula also. When the split occurred in the LTTE (in the late 70's), a large number of followers from his community joined him. Dr. Balasingham, the political advisor to Prabhakaran is a Christian convert from the Karaya caste. In fact, many of the top commanders of the LTTE army are chosen from his caste and many of them like Krishnakumar alias Kittu, are his close Kinsmen. It is said that Prabhakaran mainly reposes faith in his castemen and more particularly kinsmen from his caste.

"But in regard to recruitment for the militant organisations, certain significant changes took place after the July 1983 riots. LTTE, for instance, got recruits from various castes, and caste as such diminished in importance at this level. Even in other organisations, the recruitment pattern underwent similar changes. Caste increasingly became less important. In fact, at the lower cadre levels, all the militant organisations have recruits from various castes.

"As you must be aware, PLOTE itself underwent a split, with the dissidents constituting a different group. I am one of the members of the latter. This happened because, we did not subscribe to Uma Maheshwaran's policy in regard to some of our boys who wanted to leave the organisation for various reasons. These boys were bored stiff---they had received military and guerilla training, but had been kept idle. There was no opportunity for them to use their skills. Uma Maheshwaran had held a surveyor's post, before he started working for the new Tamil Elanger Peravai (Tamil Youth Organisation, the youth wing of the Tamil United Liberation Front or the TULF). He had no experience in field situations, that is in the battlefield. According to his theory, the people need to be mobilised first for support to the Eelam cause, and then the armed struggle launched. Meanwhile, the LTTE was making rapid headway, fighting the Sri Lankan army in the battlefield.

"Uma Maheshwaran's punishment to the young boys who expressed their desire to leave the organisation, was too severe---physically eliminate them! Nearly 60 to 70 boys were tortured and killed ! Some of us strongly objected to such cruel punishment, and were asked to quit. So we quit and formed the dissident group. I feel death is too severe a punishment, and need not be resorted to in cases such as the above. If the boys were not willing to be in the organisation, they should have been given the option to quit.

"TELO (the Tamil Eelam Liberation Organisation) became unpopular among the people, because it engaged in thefts, murder etc., among its own people. These are all mayhem type of activities. They should not be encouraged.

"The LTTE in the beginning did the same, but now it is a very disciplined organisation, does not engage in murder and theft of its own people.

"In regard to EROS and EPRLF, I do not subscribe to their form of leftist ideology. They are anyway, small organisations and have few recruits. They are not that popular among the young. PLOTE dissident group subscribes to Tamil nationalism and a certain form of socialism. Tamils are a different nation and there is something called Tamil nationalism."

Arasu Nityan made the following observations on the ability of the militant organisations to fight the Sri Lankan Army, and the impact of the 1983 July riots on the Tamils:

"But I do not think, with our military strength (i.e., combined military strength of all the Tamil militant organisations put together), we can ever defeat the Sri Lankan Army. The latter is stronger and militarily more powerful. They can erase to the ground all the Tamil areas in just one week. If the Sri Lankan navy attacks us on all sides with the help of air cover, where are we? I blame the TULF for all the suffering that the Tamils are facing today. They had no notion of the consequences of their fiery speeches or the cry for Eelam. The TULF MPs are all sitting in Madras today and issuing press statements. It is the boys who are sacrificing their lives in hundreds, against the mighty army of Sri Lanka. Their strategy should have been different.

The 1983 riots, I mentioned to you earlier, brought about a great transformation in the militant struggle—how thousands of youth started knocking on the doors of the militant organisations for entry. The riots on such a scale of horror, we had never experienced. Thousands of our people were killed—massacred with swords and knives or burnt to death alive with burning rubber tyres hanging around their necks—lost their homes, jobs, and number of our women were raped, all by the Sinhalese thugs and mobs. Our very physical survival was at stake!

"Such enormous violence was perpetrated by the Sinhalese for nearly a period of four days against the unarmed Tamils. The Tamils were terror struck and thousands of them left their homes and property in Colombo and elsewhere, and fled to Tamilnadu for refuge—many of them had fled with just their clothes on and some money they could somehow collect! You understand how it is, when your life itself is at stake?

"What the July 1983 riots did was to brutally severe the few flimsy threads of hope that still lingered somewhere in the corner of a Tamil's mind, of living a life of dignity, honour, self-respect and equality, without being reduced to slavery. We never even dreamt that the Sinhalese are capable of such horrifying brutality.

"Do you know that the Sinhalese' violence against the Tamils had evoked little response from the government for almost till the end of the four days of riots? At the end of the Tamil massacre, when President Jayawardene chose to speak his comforting words were only for the Sinhalese! The government, which is supposed to be the protector of life and property of all its citizens, had displayed such partiality at this cruel hour of crisis among the Tamils. It was clear that the government is for the Sinhalese, and not for the Tamils!

"In a crucial sense, more than the Sinhalese violence, it is this government's non-chalance to the Tamils' agony and plight that had decided their mind for them: how could one repose any trust in such a government to protect them? The Tamils felt that they had been repeatedly betrayed by the successive Sri Lankan governments, by abrogating promises for autonomy, and the response to the riots was literally the last straw.

"The Sinhalese common folk too did not say a word during the riots. Their silence revealed that the majority of the Sinhalese leant their silent approval to the massacre of the Tamils. This response of the ordinary Sinhalese was another major factor that made us decide that we can no more live again with the Sinhalese.

"In this context I must mention to you the remarks of an elderly Tamil friend of ours, who said: 'It is true that the Sinhalese are nice, sociable and hospitable people. I was brought up by a Sinhalese ayah, who was nice and gentle with me. Now, it is different. As a community, somehow, they never seem to perceive the justness of our demands: they are not prepared to approve of them. Even such a well-known scholar historian as W.F. Rahula, smacks of Sinhalese chauvinism. What do we do? Our plight may be compared with an ill-treated daughter-in-law who has no where to turn for succour.'

"It is under these circumstances that the Tamil nation decided that violence is the only means for our survival and recovery of our Tamil selves. Violence of the Sinhalese has to be met with violence, otherwise the Tamil race will be eliminated from the face of the earth. The Sinhalese have been engaging in various forms of genocide of the Tamils. Their strategy is to either drive us out of our homelands or kill us. They want us to be subjugated to them and accept second class status.

"Why should we? We have been as ancient settlers in this land as the Sinhalese. The Sinhalese think that the whole of Sri Lanka belongs to them, and that we are intruders. Generations of Tamils have lived in the northern and eastern provinces. Many have contributed to the growth of the Sri Lankan nation. But yet, the Sinhalese refuse to recognise all this. What do we do under these circumstances? The only way is to wage a war for our right to live as self-respecting human beings.

"If blood needs to be shed, we will shed it. Most crucially, it is a question of being alive, and then to be able to live in self-respect and dignity as Tamils. Instead of getting killed by the

Sinhalese, we would rather fight and die. If we don't like to engage in violence, what is the option? We subject ourselves to being killed by the Sinhalese and let the whole Tamil race be erased from the soil of Sri Lanka."

Arasu Nityan spoke about the impact of the armed struggle on his society as follows:

"As to the impact of the struggle on my society, the less said the better. Some time back I went to see my aged mother in Kaytes. Do you know what she said to me? She mentioned of our neighbour, a woman in her 40's with four children, having an affair with a young boy of eighteen! My mother said that this has what our Eelam struggle has done to the people. There are quite a few cases of this sort she said: my own sister-in-law, my mother complained has started wearing short shirts which do not even cover the knees, and visiting movie theatres often. My mother was very bitter. In fact, there seems to have been a breakdown of the moral norms of the society.

"In Jaffna today, the main pre-occupation of young boys is to see blue movies and take drugs. Sexual licentiousness has also increased. Many young wives have either their husbands away or dead, and many a young woman is unmarried. These are naturally very sexually frustrated and go in for extra-marital and pre-marital relationships. This is what is Sri Lankan Tamil society today, which just a few years ago had such rigid sexual norms. Besides life itself has become so uncertain----one is not sure whether one will be alive tomorrow. The young men are also very frustrated and bitter----their whole future is in doldrums. Their attitude to life is: 'Kick it up today, for you may not be alive tomorrow.'

"On the economic front, the whole economy of Jaffna and other Tamil areas is in a shattered state. What does one do under such circumstances? The Sri Lankan government led by Jayawardene is responsible for all this. They want to wipe us out from the surface of the earth.

"My own life is in a mess. I fell in love with a girl who was a member of PLOTE. The whole thing started this way. I used to take some classes in Marxist theories to the members of the organisation. On a number of occasions she was critical of my views regarding the role of the family, women, etc., in society. She espoused strong feminist views. In fact this led me to wonder whether marrying such a girl would not result in intense conflict in the family. I feel that one of the most important aspects of one's life is to have a peaceful and harmonious family life. But, the girl was playing a game with me. After intense discussions in the class, she would send me a note expressing her love for me. So finally, I asked her whether I could visit her parents and extend my proposal. She was, however, rather reluctant. She kept postponing it. She ultimately said that I have to wait for three years to get married to her. I got fed up and sought my elder brother's opinion on the matter. My elder brother strongly advised me against marrying the girl. So, I have dropped the whole idea. The truth is, no girl wants to marry a revolutionary with neither career nor future! I am a broken man. I do not know what the future has in store for me."

Sarveshwaran (PLOTE)

Sarveshwaran is about twenty-eight years old and hails from a village in the eastern Batticoloa district of Sri Lanka. He belongs to the Karaya caste. His father originally hailed from Ramanathapuram district in Tamilnadu and was an illiterate. His mother, however, is literate and studied upto fourth standard. She is a 'Ceylon Tamil'. Sarveshwaran's family owns about 1.5 acres of dry land, which was cultivated by his father, before he died in 1981. His father also did coolie work to supplement the family's income. About his attitude towards caste, Sarveshwaran said: "My father was a conservative man. He stuck to the members of his own caste and did not mix with members from lower castes. But as far as I am concerned, I do not subscribe to any casteist notions. I have had and have friends from upper and lower castes, as well as rich and poor. I eat in anybody's house."

Sarveshwaran has two brothers and two sisters, and is second in the order of birth. One of his sisters studied upto class seven and was married off. The other sister is studying in class five. His elder brother studied upto eighth class, after which he gave up his studies. He too became a coolie labourer along with his father. He is married and fled to Tamilnadu during the army atrocities following July 1983 riots. He is now living in a refugee camp near Madurai in Tamil Nadu.

Sarveshwaran's another brother is younger to him and was studying in twelfth class when he had to discontinue his studies, as the army kept creating problems for their family.

Sarveshwaran himself completed his secondary school education in 1976, at the age of seventeen. He studied in Tamil medium. Since he could not obtain admission to any college, notwithstanding a distinction in science subjects, he had to discontinue his studies. Further, the family too did not have the economic wherewithal to support him in college education.

Sarveshwaran's interest in the Eelam problem was kindled when he was around fifteen (1974-75). He was an avid reader of Tamil newspapers such as Veerakesari and Dinamani, which reported on the bombing and other activities of Sivakumaran and Kasianandan (considered the pioneers of the militant movement) belonging to Tamil Manava Peravai (Tamil Students Organisation).

Sarveshwaran narrated his decision to work for the 'Eelam cause' and engage in the armed struggle in the following manner:

"Tamil Manava Peravai was constituted in 1972 by Sivakumaran. He was an Engineering student studying in Colombo, when he decided to start this organisation. He hailed from Jaffna and belonged to Vellala caste. Kasianandan hailed from the Eastern province. I used to get information from my friends about Kasianandan's activities. He was also a poet. He wrote a number of poems on Tamil Eelam and I was an avid reader of his poems. Oh! you should read him poems. It was full of powerful patriotism and also sang about the resilient spirit of the Tamils. Sivakumaran died in the late 70's by swallowing cyanide when the police were about to capture him.

"Even while I was studying, I started working for the cause of Eelam. I used to distribute and paste pamphlets concerning Eelam. I was around fifteen-sixteen then. I was incensed at the discrimination meted out to the Tamils in every field. The whole future of the Tamil youth was so bleak: the opportunities to receive higher education and employment were highly restricted. Further, employment in agriculture was also highly restricted for a sizable majority of the Tamil youth who hailed from poor agrarian backgrounds. In the Tamil areas, industries too were few and far-between. The Tamil youth faced a blind wall wherever they turned. There was not even a ray of hope about any improvement in the situation, with Sinhalese dominated Sri Lankan Government getting increasingly discriminatory and hostile to the Tamils. What could the TULF do in the parliament? Being a minority, they had to witness silently the spectacle of the ruination of the Tamils.

"Further, in school, we were forced to study Sinhalese since it was made a compulsory subject in 1974. I do not think anything should be forced down the throat of the people. If there is acceptance, it should be voluntary and spontaneous. Anything forced will not work.

"I became a member of the Tamil Elanger Peravai (Tamil Youth Organisation), which was started by Santhathiyar, Senadhiraja, Vasudeva etc., in 1973. Around the same period. Tamil Eelam Vidudhalai Eyakkam (Tamil Eelam Liberation Organisation) was established by Kuttimani and Thangadurai. Both hailed from Velvettiturai, a coastal town situated in the northern part of Jaffna peninsula; the town was largely constituted by people from the Karaya caste, and both Kuttimani and Thangadurai were from that caste. They had been captured by the Sri Lankan Security forces in the early 80's and lodged in the high security Welikade jail in Colombo. During the 1983 riots, the two, along with some other Tamil freedom fighters, were massacred in the jail by violent Sinhalese prisoners.

"Prabhakaran also was close to Kuttimani and Thangadurai for a while, before he along with some others established the TNT (the Tamil New Tigers). It was first started in Jaffna and later established branches in the Eastern Provinces of Batticoloa and Trincomalee. Even at the village level, branches were established. In my village, a student studying at 'O' level (i.e., equivalent of plus two), called Saravanabhava, established it.

"As I told you, I had to give up my studies after GCE, due to lack of finance. There were no scholarships either. I very much wanted to go in for higher studies in science. Since I could not continue with my studies, I started working as a coolie along with my father (1976-77). Later I got a job in a grocery shop in Chettikulam (in Vavuniya district) as a salesman with a salary ranging from Rs.150-200 a month.

"It was around this time that Alford Doraippa, the Mayor of Jaffna was assassinated, since some of the members of certain youth political organisations felt that he acted as an informant to the police, viz., identify the youth working in Tamil political organisations. Santatiar and seven others were implicated in the 'crime' and arrested. But after a while Santatiar was released, as the court found that there was no sufficient evidence against him. He resumed his role as the secretary of the Elangar Peravai.

"Around 1976, Elangar Peravai established its branches in Vavuniya. Sentantiar met me in the shop where I worked and solicited my help in mobilising support for the organisation. I was only too pleased to do something.

"In 1977, there were these riots in the plantation areas where the Indian Tamils worked. The latter were assaulted and their property looted by Sinhalese mobs. Many of them fled to Vavuniya, Jaffna and Mullaitivu. It was for them that the Tamil

Refugees' Rehabilitation Organisation was established. In the beginning it was the church fathers who were involved in rehabilitation work. Later on, other persons from various walks of life joined them. Meanwhile, the Gandhiam Society also got involved in the work of rehabilitation. The President of Gandhiam Society was S.A. David. Another prominent and active member of the society was Dr. Rajasundaram, who was later arrested (around 1982) by the government under the PTA (Prevention of Terrorist Act) and lodged in the Wellikade jail. He was killed by the Sinhalese mobs in the Wellikade Prison massacre during the July 1983 riots.

"Other prominent persons who were involved in refugee rehabilitation work in Vavuniya were Uma Maheshwaran (PLOTE leader), Santatiar and Mr. K.V. Nityanandan (a lecturer in Jaffna College). Uma Maheshwaran was working underground. As I mentioned to you earlier, I was working as a shop assistant in a small town in Vavuniya. Santatiar who kept in touch with me, one day asked me to give up the job and do whole-time rehabilitation work. I did as he bid, since I considered him my guru (teacher). I started doing rehabilitation work under the auspices of the Gandhiam Society. I gained new experience while engaged in rehabilitation work. I was a witness to the acute plight, despair and agony of the Tamils in Sri Lanka. Do you know what it is to be unwanted and treated like dirt in your own country, where you have lived and toiled for generations? The Sri Lankan Tamils and the plantation Tamils have lived for generations here. In fact, the former are as old settlers as the Sinhalese, yet the Sinhalese behave and act as though they are the sole proprietors of the land and that only they have the right to be there. The Tamils' plight is horrible. They can do little by way of peaceful political protests to obtain a rightful share in the country's governance and equally importantly have equal opportunities in all fields as the citizens of Sri Lanka. The Sinhalese, being the dominant community, attempt to thwart any efforts by the Tamils to assert their rights. It is this increasing sense of hopelessness and alienation which posed great threat to the erosion of their identity and in fact their very survival. These have been responsible for the emergence of militancy among the youth.

"Besides doing rehabilitation work, I continued with my political work being a member of the Tamil Elangar Peravai. The latter had to be done secretly. In fact a number of times, the army had come to Gandhiam Society in search of me. But Dr. Rajasundaram protected me, and told the police that I was not a member and I was not there. This was around 1979.

"Somewhere around 1982, the LTTE split into two, viz., the LTTE and the PLOTE. The former was led by Prabhakaran and the latter by Uma Maheshwaran. The causes of the split were mainly due to the struggle for power supremacy, and a woman. You must have heard about the Pondy Bazaar shoot out incident between Prabhakaran and Uma Maheshwaran in 1982---that was an expression of their settling the scores.

"After the split in the LTTE, Sanitatiar, Kannan, Sundaram, myself, etc., joined Uma Maheshwaran's PLOTE. This we did since Prabhakaran was a very dominant character, who wanted to be acknowledged as the party's supreme leader, without anybody expressing any difference of opinion with him---he wanted everybody to accept his rule as the law. He is a man of moratu swabhavam (rough temperament), who would not think twice in eliminating any dissident member.

"I continued with my party work moving from one area to another, from one village to another. We were trying to mobilise the masses at the grassroot level for the Eelam cause. Of course, this had to be done secretly. In 1982, I was arrested in Vavuniya by a CID. I was lodged in Jaffna prison and tortured. I was kept for a month in the prison and then moved to Jaffna army camp. I could not eat and my health started waning. Then Mr. Sivasithamparam's (a TULF leader) brother, a lawyer fought my case in the court. I was released since the CID had no proof that I was engaged in any 'terrorist' or underground activity when he arrested me.

"After I was released, I started my political work again. This was around 1983. I got a government job in the irrigation department. Some person I had known got me the job. I worked for three months and gave it up. I took up the job to misguide the CID. I came back again for party work. After the 1983 riots, I came over to India.

"The 1983 riots marked a crucial turning point in the Eelam struggle. You know, thousands of Tamil youth spontaneously came to join our organisation. The riots had in one stroke transformed them: thousands of Tamils massacred, loosing their homes and property, raping of Tamil women, had brought about a radical transformation in their minds. While earlier, i.e. before the riots, the militant organisations were small, and each could boast of just 20 or 30 members. It was very hard to persuade the youth to join us. Besides their parents were unwilling to allow them join us. The riots changed it all: not only the youth came in hordes, many parents even encouraged their sons to join the struggle. The riots had posed two options, i.e., either die at the hands of the Sinhalese or fight back to protect your life, home, property, self-respect, and dignity. The Sinhalese had killed us, violated everything that we held dear, because we were Tamils. The riots made clear the Sinhalese hatred of the Tamils.

"Armed struggle was the only option open to Tamils. The Tamils for nearly three decades had been engaged in non-violent struggle for the realisation of their rights. The Federal Party leader, the late Chelvanayagam had led those struggles, but everything was in vain. The Sinhalese government broke every promise of redressal of our grievances. Every accord that was made---the Bandaranaine—Chelvanayagam accord of 1957, and the Senanayake---Chelvanayagam Accord of 1967---was respected only in its breach. Besides the Tamils (both the estate and Sri Lankan Tamils) had to face the brunt of every riot (e.g., 1958, 1972, 1977), when many of them lost their lives, property and homes. The Tamils asked for a federal solution and autonomy, because of all this and the discriminatory policies in education and employment, land-colonisation programmes pursued relentlessly by the successive Sinhalese governments' over decades.

"Armed struggle for the restoration of our rights seemed the only plausible option. We are Tamils, we have grit and resilience to fight the atrocities of the Sinhalese government. Let us see."

Sarveshwaran then reverted to talking about his organisation, the PLOTE:

"I was one of the central committee members of the PLOTE. The committee consisted of a total of twenty-five members. I became the secretary of land action committee, a top body of the organisation.

"Around early 1986, differences in our organisation began to grow. Santatiar who is one of the senior members of the committee, asked Uma Maheshwaran some uncomfortable questions in one of the committee meetings. For example, he asked him for the accounts regarding financial expenditure, the amount of money contributions from abroad, etc. As a result he came to be disliked by Uma Maheshwaran.

"Then arose the question of a number of young cadres who were physically eliminated (around 100 of them) by Uma Maheswaran, because they wanted to leave the organisation. Some of the recruits after receiving arms training found themselves idling away without being in the field. So they wanted to leave. There were some others who could not take the hardships of military training, etc., and hence wanted to quit. Uma Maheshwaran suspected them to be informers of the LTTE, EPRLF, etc., and also feared that they were plotting to kill him. So he tortured them and eliminated them.

"This upset a number of the central committee members. Sentatiar was the most vocal of the lot. We thought that the boys did not deserve that punishment and we told this to Uma

Maheshwaran. But Uma Maheshwaran was unrepentant. Consequently, we parted company and told him that he has been suspended from the PLOTE. After sometime, Uma Maheshwaran eliminated Santatiar also. Oh! what a transformation he has undergone! He was such a gentle soul when we were all working together in refugee rehabilitation programme, but now he has assumed a ruthless abominable form!

"In the LTTE, it is worse. Even before you utter a word, you are eliminated.

"I don't like to join Prabhakaran or anybody who follows an 'unjust' (*aneethi*) path. I have never been afraid of death. I may be shot by Prabhakaran or Uma Maheshwaran or the Sri Lankan army any day. My policy is to do proper work by adopting the right means. That is all. That is why I move around alone, I have no bodyguards.

"Uma Maheshwaran has killed so many. What is the punishment for him? What he himself deserves is death?"

Sarveshwaran talking about the Sinhalese people said, "It is the government which is against the Tamils, not the Sinhalese people." They are nice and simple people.

He further remarked: "Till now we have hardly achieved anything through talks and non-violent means. It is this that had convinced me that violence had to be met with violence. But if talks and negotiations can help in getting a substantial portion of our demands met, we do not mind participating in it. But, my strong skepticism persists."

Sooryan (LTTE)

Sooryan hails from Mullaitivu province, one of the northern provinces of Sri Lanka. He is twenty three years old and hails from Vellala caste. His father is a middle peasant owning around ten acres of land: out of the ten, six acres are dry land and the remaining four wet land. His father also owned a small grocery shop. Sooryan was one of the five children of his parents, being third in the order of birth. He has two brothers and two sisters, and the latter had been married off.

Sooryan narrated his involvement with the LTTE, the nature of the organisation, and his perceptions of other militants organisations as follows:

"I have studied upto secondary school in Tamil medium. My father was very keen that all his children received higher education, which he was not able to pursue himself. I too was very keen to pursue higher education. I had been doing quite well in my studies, but the 1983 riots decided the future for me. What the Tamils suffered during the riots, made me give up my plans and join the LTTE. The riots symbolised the closure of every door for the Tamil---even our very physical survival was at stake!

"I realised that to survive one had to fight, use violence against violence. The logic was, it is better to die fighting for your rights, than to be massacred by the Sinhalese. At the least we can die cherishing the hope of Eelam, and if lucky to have survived, then live in Eelam breathing free air, with self-respect and dignity. What is the use of living like slaves under the Sinhalese hegemony? I am not afraid of death---every human being has to die, if not today, tomorrow, so what difference does it make if I am dead today or tomorrow?

"I joined the LTTE, because it is the most committed organisation. Total commitment to the Eelam cause. It is Tamil nationalism, Tamil, Tamil, Tamil all the way.

"Anna (Prabhakaran) is warm and nice to us. If any of us is wounded or sick, he himself comes and comforts us! But any sluggishness or indifference, he is a task master. Why he himself is ruthless on his own self.

"For us all that matters is our Eelam struggle. It pervades every iota of our consciousness and being. Nothing else exists for us. We are mentally and physically trained to be tough like steel. We can make do with any food, we can even survive in the harsh environment of jungles. You know to be like this, it is the mental state that matters.

"Religion doesn't figure in our consciousness. We are taught to understand every aspect of our mind and body in a rational framework. It is the rigorous training that we receive that makes us powerful beings. Once you are not afraid of death, nothing else matters. I told you I am not afraid of death, I mean it in every sense of the term. To die for the Tamil cause, is an assertion of we being Tamils, a proud and self-respecting nation and race. What is the meaning of living without either self-respect or dignity, or being proud of being a Tamil.

"Do you know in our organisation, the members are not allowed to see Tamil movies produced in Tamilnadu. That is because it corrupts the young people's mind—the romances, the gyrating sexual dances, it is all so vulgar and crude. Such romantic movies oozing with sexuality distract the mind. To be committed to the Eelam struggle, the mind has to be pervaded with that only thought of winning the Eelam, setting at liberty the spirit of the Tamil nation. Of course, we do see other movies on war (minus romance), on martial arts, etc. It is Tamil, Tamil, Tamil in every ounce of our blood and every breath that we take.

"The other militant organisations are false—their commitment to the liberation struggle is only skin-deep. Who asks them not to jump into the battle-field? We are mainly operating in Jaffna, well they can do so in Trincomalee, Batticoloa, Mullaitivu, etc. Their interest is only in looting the public—they steal and extort money and valuables from the public, sometimes they even murder for such gains. They are an undisciplined lot. We cannot join hands with them in our struggle for Eelam If they cannot engage in battle, the least they can do is to give up their pretensions, and pursue ordinary life. Who prevents them from pursuing their careers, education etc.?"

Talking about the LTTE's perpetration of violence against civilian Sinhalese, Sooryan said:

"Sinhalese are our enemy, whether they are adults, children or old. Haven't they perpetrated violence against thousands of

Tamils? Many thousands of Tamils have been massacred, deprived of their homes, livelihood, property, etc. The Sinhalese have engaged in ethnic genocide of Tamils—they do not want us in Sri Lanka.

"Well, generations of Tamils have lived in the northern and eastern provinces. We are as ancient residents of Sri Lanka as the Sinhalese. Our homelands are ours. We will fight for our homeland until our last breath."

About how the LTTE guerillas could bring themselves to massacring even helpless, defenceless sinhalese children, women and men, Sooryan said:

"You know these guerillas are in a state of frenzy, their mind pervaded by a state of consciousness, which does not distinguish between helpless/armed, children/adult, women/men, sick/healthy. For them, they are all just Sinhalese, representatives of the Sinhalese race, who have perpetrated unimaginable atrocities on Tamils for decades—massacred them because they demanded a certain measure of autonomy, deprived them of their homes and livelihood, children killed and orphaned, women raped, thousands of young men jailed, tortured and eliminated. The frenzied state is pervaded by a consciousness, where all that matters is a question of their survival versus mine. It is natural that for them it is Tamil, Tamil, Tamil, one-fourth all the way, to eternity if need be.

"There are limits to tolerance in any being. You must have heard of the famous Tamil proverb that, 'Even a timid being can be provoked to violence under unbearable circumstances'. The Tamils had been reasonable for long with the Sinhalese. The former had been asking for autonomy because of the discriminations and violence perpetrated on them, by the latter. Are we human beings or scum of the earth? Are we slaves of the Sinhalese? Don't we have self-respect and dignity? Don't we have the right to exist as Tamils? The Sinhalese throughout have been trying to cow us down into submission through violence and repression in every domain of life.

"The Tamil spirit then asked: Do you want to be a slave or a human being with self-respect and dignity? Do you want to live in slavery or freedom? Will you transform yourself to a Sinhala, so that you can enjoy the comforts of being so?

"Well the response of the spirit was: "I would rather die protecting my honour, self-respect and dignity, I would rather die as a Tamil, then be a slave."

The Bitter Memory and the 1983 Riots: Denial of the Self, Betrayals and Survival

All the three narratives recount the emergence of the militant movement for substantial political autonomy, if not a sovereign state of Tamil Eelam, in the context of discriminatory policies pursued by the successive Sinhalese dominated governments since independence (1948) against the Tamils.[1] These policies concerned language, 'land colonization' (i.e., of 'Tamil lands' by Sinhalese settlers), education, employment and the domain of culture.[2] Then there were the betrayals of accords (1958 and 1967) which incorporated elements constituting a measure of political autonomy for the Tamils---between the then ruling Sri Lankan governments and the Tamil Federal Party leader, the late S.J.V. Chelvanayagam, who had led non-violent struggles for the redressal of Tamil grievances during the period.

But most crucially, the narrators said that such experiences (*anubavangal*) had led to deep disenchantment and bitterness with the Sinhalese dominated Sri Lankan governments and loss of faith in non-violent struggles. Fuel was added to the fire in the ambience, when the late Amritalingam, the fire-brand leader of the Federal Party, gave fiery speeches on various occasions denouncing the Sinhalese government for practicing discriminatory and oppressive policies against the Tamils, which held serious threats to their very physical and cultural survival---it was a systematic annihilation of the Tamils to be reduced to a position of second class citizens, if not abysmal slavery.

The situation seemed alarming and there was a deep sense of despair among the Tamils all around. It is in this situation that the militants said: "Some of us perceived that the only option was an armed struggle to free the Tamils from the shackles of oppression and indignity." The period was the early 70's: as though hailing the only option came the violent acts of Sivakumaran and Sathyaseelan, the two educated youth of Jaffna, who blasted bombs in the police station of Jaffna city---the first violent act of defiance of the Sri Lankan government. They were arrested and jailed. Sivakumaran committed suicide by swallowing cyanide in the jail. Sathyaseelan, however, was released after some months. As one of the narrators said: "The two were hailed as the heroes of the Tamil cause."

But it was only very few Tamil youth who joined the newly constituted militant organization, the Tamil New Tigers (TNT). As a militant leader recalled that "they had to hunt for new recruits" during this early period of the militant movement. In other words, the Sri Lankan Tamils in general were in a liminal frame of mind, pondering and still hesitant about the armed struggle option and the violence it entailed. This is how a radical Tamil leader, characterized the Sri Lankan Tamil society of the early 70's: "You know the Tamils were a security conscious people. It was security and order that constituted their lives. A majority of the Jaffna people preferred government jobs to anything else. Education was the major industry in Jaffna. They were peace loving and religious people, and very traditional in their outlook. Violence of any form was abhorred." In short, in the 'social imaginary' of the Sri Lankan Tamil society, violence hardly figured as a 'magma' of signification (Castoriadis 1987:343).[3] The experience and knowledge (Morleau-Ponty 1988:27) was rooted in the traditional social imaginary (Castoriadis 1987) and the rhythm and flow of life concretized it.

The liminal pondering frame of mind, met with a shattering experience in the blood-curdling, terrorizing 1983 riots. In the experience was born a new imaginary and a new knowledge (Morleau-Ponty 1988:70) and a new ontic being.[4] The post-liminal frame of mind witnessed thousands of Tamil youth knocking on the doors of the recruit starved militant organizations, to be recruited. Many parents too approved the decision, with some even encouraging their children to be brave sons of the Tamil cause.[5]

The 1983 spectral episode, was a trauma (Young 1996:245-59) for the Tamils, which marked the transformation to a new magma of signification, acceptance of 'violence against violence'.

The narrators and many other ordinary Sri Lankan Tamils had recalled that the riots had induced a strong fear in them about loosing their very lives: "Our lives were threatened, our very physical survival was in question." Besides the spectre of homelessness, the prospect of loosing livelihood and property haunted them.

Valentine Daniel (1997) in his highly poignant and 'soul-nibbling' study of the anthroposemeiosis of the victims of violence in Sri Lanka and Indian Estate Tamils (in Sri Lanka and India) has given us portrayals of the stunning, silencing, searing and shattering effects of violence on beings. Many of these victims trapped in the pain's qualisign and sinsign (a sign embodied singularly and uniquely), in their firstness and secondness, had great difficulty in entering semeiosis, a sign of being human (ibid:152). Consider, for instance, the case of Benedict, a young Sri Lankan Tamil from Batticaloa in eastern Sri Lanka, who was arrested by the Sri Lankan army (in 1983) for alleged militant links (who professed to the author of his innocence) was most brutally tortured and incarcerated in jails for nearly four years. While being interviewed by the author after his release (in 1987), he would go into meticulous details of the varied brutal tortures perpetrated on him and the food they ate and the kind of mat on which they slept, or show the 'invisible' scars on his wrist or elsewhere on his body to the author, was however was silent on his experience of the pain of the tortures (ibid.:139-40; 147-52). It was after nearly three months that he could bring himself to expressing to the author what pain meant to him: "Even now, sometimes, like the other day when the BBC man was interviewing me, my body felt like a bubbling candle, filled with pain, inside and out, all over the skin and all over inside. One pain" (ibid.:140).

But the embodied pain of violence seem to come in varied hues. The case is that of Kamalam, a Tamil refugee, in her mid-thirties, whom Valentine Daniel interviewed in 1990, in the Mandapam refugee camp situated on the southern shores of Tamilnadu in South India. Kamalam, hailed from Vavuniya in northern Sri Lanka, having migrated there along with her Indian estate Tamil parents, who originally worked on the tea plantations of the hilly tracts of Sri Lanka. Kamalam's pain of her lost son during a Sri Lankan army raid in the region in 1985, and the fact that she was unable to recollect his face having lost every album containing his photograph—when her house was consumed by flames in one of the airforce bombings of the area---had transformed the comportment of her being into a phantasmagoric world of waiting her son's arrival. She would sit staring at the sea for hours on end, nonchalant to the world around her, waiting for her son's arrival. She would say, "I don't say, 'Tomorrow my son might come'. I say, 'Here he comes. Here I see his face? That is the way I see. That is how my life is" (ibid.:108-9).

Four years later, in 1994, the author tried to track her in the same refugee camp. But he couldn't find her. An Indian fisherman who new her told the author, "the hours that Kamalam spent looking at the sea began earlier and earlier and lasted later and later until toward the end she spent all night and day by the ocean's edge. She did not know one day from the next. She said that she was waiting for her ancestors who had left to work on the hills of the tea estates. Not for her son---she never mentioned her son---but for her great-grandfather and great-grandmother. "They went for the 'parade' (*perattu*), she would say, 'Behold, they will come! (Itovantiruvara)'. For her, neither death nor distance had consumed them" (ibid.:134). In other-words, Kamalam's sepulchral silence now regarding her son, seemed to be the intensity of her pain trapped in the anthroposemeiotic sinsign.

Young (1996:245-59), in his fascinating account of the various studies of the effect of traumatic experience on people, points out how such experiences could bring about a drastic transformation in their cognitive affective and ontic selves. On several people, Young points out, such traumatic experiences had resulted in permanent mental disorders.

Lawrence Langer (1996: 47-65), in his insightful and moving study of the holocaust testimonies of the Jews---many of whom had survived the horrifying and terrifying experiences of the Auschwitz's torture and killing fields, provides portrayals of the disastrous effects of the experiences on the psyche and the social being of the survivors. For instance, some of the survivors, after many years since the holocaust experience, having reformulated their lives---having a career, marrying and having children---yet relieved those moments of unbearable helpless anguish as nightmarish dreams, or just existing as 'living dead', or with a deep knawing guilt for having survived while their loving ones had met another fate. Of course, the experience of the Jews had also inspired them to seek a solution in having a homeland of their own (Israel) promising safety and security of their being.

Durkheim (1970:241-57), in his classic study of suicide, mentions how sudden affluence or sudden impoverishment, results in a substantial spurt in suicide rates. His exigesis is that people find it difficult to cope with such sudden transformation in their life circumstances, and hence decide to end their lives.

It is, perhaps, of little surprise then that the Sri Lankan Tamil collective consciousness responded to the 1983 'magma' of experience by opting for violence for its recovery. As many Sri Lankan Tamil refugees recalled: "We can no more trust the Sinhalese or the Sinhalese government. We can never live with them again." Violence and death became metaphors for Tamil recovery. As an LTTE militant put it: "It is more honorable to fight and die for the Tamil cause, than to live in slavery or get killed by the Sri Lankan army."

Violence in Praxis and the Transformative Hermeneutics of Death

Violence in praxis involved training the body and mind for engagement in an armed struggle. In a short time, hundreds of military training camps were established by the major militant organizations in 'their Tamil homelands' in Sri Lanka, and in neighbouring Tamilnadu and elsewhere in India. Consequently, thousands of young Sri Lankan Tamils went through the rigors of military training for many months.

Some of the militant organizations such as the PLOTE and the LTTE also held classes in Marxist and nationalist ideologies for the young recruits, to re-frame their mind in accepting violence as an instrument for achieving 'liberation'. The LTTE is known to show war and martial art movies to its cadres, as a part of their military training programmes. A measure of the success of the training can still be witnessed in the ongoing war between the LTTE and the Sri Lankan armed forces. In fact, of all the militant organizations, the LTTE had earned the name as the toughest, most disciplined, and the best trained guerilla army. Their famous cyanide capsule, which almost every LTTE guerilla sports around his or her neck, is considered a symbol of their highest sacrifice for their Tamil nation, their lives.

The radical cognitive transformation that acceptance of armed struggle had entailed and meant, not only waging an armed war in the battle field, but a transformed hermeneutics of death. Death, at least, cognitively, did not invoke a sense of fear as it did under ordinary circumstances. We have noted how the PLOTE leader Sarveshwaran commented on the meaning of death for him: "I am not afraid of death. I may die today, tomorrow or any day." Many LTTE cadres had commented: "Why should one be afraid of death? All people have to die one day, if not today, some other day. It is just a matter of time. Instead of just dying due to some natural cause, it is better to die for the Tamil cause. Death assumes a meaning in the Tamil cause. It symbolizes the supreme sacrifice of an individual for a great cause. It justifies the meaning of existence. Every body marries, every body pursues some career and earns money, every body dies. What is so great about it? To be a 'tyagi'[6] for a great cause has no analogy in ordinary existence. To die for the Tamil cause is to die for Tamil glory." Indeed, the LTTE is known to celebrate annually the 'Mavirarnal' (Great Heroes' Day or Great Martyrs' Day), has cemetries for its martyrs on whose tombs are etched epitaphs and the battle in which they died, and has cassettes singing martyr and Tamil nationalist songs.[7]

Indeed, the LTTE has, since 1989, been celebrating annually the Mavirarnal spread over ten days in the month of November. The celebrations commence ten days ahead of Prabhakaran's (the LTTE chief) birthday on the 26th of November. During this period essay competitions, debates dramas, etc., are held in schools and colleges revolving on the theme of martyrdom, freedom, the struggle for the achievement of Tamil Eelam (the motherland), etc. Patriotic songs on martyrs and freedom are played on loud-speakers. The celebrations culminate on the 26th—the day of Prabhakaran's birthday. This is how the celebration on this day was narrated to me by my informant from Jaffna:

"At 12 o'clock midnight, the bells go chiming in all the temples, and all the churches in Jaffna. In some of the famous temples such as the Nallur Kandasamy temple (temple dedicated to the deity Kandan or Murugan, the son of God Siva), elaborate worship and prayers are offered to the deity. Almost every house too is awake in Jaffna at this time, lighting lamps in front of the images of deities in their homes and in front of their houses, and offering prayers for relief from suffering and success in their liberation struggle. In the meanwhile, at that time (12 o'clock midnight) the parents of the mavirar are taken to the mavirar cemetry accompanied by some LTTE members to light lamps and offer prayers at the tomb of their martyr son or daughter. It is a very solemn occasion."

Another crucial aspect of the LTTE's hermeneutics of death and martyrdom, is the notion of the 'ever-living' martyr. According to the LTTE it never 'buries' its dead martyrs, but plants them as 'seeds' to be re-born again (Peter 1997:66).

Let alone for the LTTE and other militants, even for ordinary Sri Lankan Tamil civilians, death seems to have assumed a transformed meaning. This is what one of them said: "When a close kin (husband, wife, son, daughter, mother, father, etc.) dies in the war situation, if it is the first time it is happening, you are totally shocked and shattered. But next time it happens, you take it in your stride. You say 'that is what happens in a war'. By looking at others who have also lost many close kin in the war, you draw some solace. Do you know, whole families have been wiped out in this war in Jaffna. In fact, death has become such a common occurrence that people conduct very few death rituals in a cursory fashion with just a handful of family members present on the occasion. Sometimes they just dig a pit, bury the dead, and come away. What to do? That is the nature of war." In other words, death gets reformulated as an ordinary occurrence and a phenomenon of an extraordinary situation—death assumes normality in an extraordinary situation. The collectivity placed in a situation of shared tragic experience, the burden of the tragedy is lessened by a collective solace.[8]

In other words, death, for the Sri Lankan Tamils, became a polysemic emblem, signifying not merely the recovery of dignity, honour, self-respect, nationhood and freedom, but also an instrument for the recovery of the Tamil ontic self in its 'hiddeness'.[9] The anxiety and tremulousness of the Sri Lankan Tamils was for a recovery of this 'hiddeness' which had been scotched by the nothingness of the Dasein[10] born in the spectral episode.

In the Nietzschean's *The Birth of Tragedy* mould, death in the violent struggle for the militant combatant assumed the soul-stirring, comforting quality of the Dionysian dithyram-bic Greek chorus (Nietzsche 1968:61-73), anthroposemeio-sising (Daniel 1997:121) a recovery of the tattered Tamil self. In the Nietzschean genealogical mould (Nietzsche 493-599), death for the combatants represented the victory of life over it, for death, a means of recovery of life.

The militants, especially the LTTE's hermeneutics of death, seems a part of the Tamil cultural 'magma',[11] where death under certain circumstances, is an emblematic representation of supreme sacrifice for a cause, which not merely represents the intense fervour and commitment to the cause, but also a matter of 'honour' and 'glory' to the martyr. Consider, for instance, the number of Tamils who immolated themselves during the anti-Hindi agitation in Tamilnadu in the late 60's.[12] The immolations constituted the emblem of the passion of a Tamil for his cultural identity. Similarly, when the former Chief Minister of Tamilnadu, M.G. Ramachandran, passed away in 1988, a number of people immolated themselves, not being able to bear the bereavement of their *hridaya deivam* (God of the heart), their *puraktchi talaiver* (revolutionary leader) their *makkal tilagam* (symbol of the people).[13] These immolations symbolized the passion of their commitment to the cause that M.G. Ramachandran represented, the 'protector' and the 'saviour' of the poor and the destitute.

The Other Faces of Violence

The militants' episteme[14] also unravels the other dimensions of violence, the way the emblem of the liberation struggle, transforms and transfixes the being of the militant, sequelling intra-militant or inter-militant killings and bloodshed, calling forth characterization of the actor and the act as ruthless, heartless, cruel, etc. Consider, for example, the remarks of Arasu Nityan and Sarveshwaran of PLOTE regarding the elimination of nearly fifty to sixty cadres of their organization by Uma Maheshwaran, the chief of their organization. Arasu Nityan had remarked that it was horrendous to do so, for such an innocuous reason as their wanting to quit the organization. He had felt that the cadres did not have to pay such a heavy price, for their mere wish to quit. He, in fact, justified the cadres' wish to quit especially when they had been bored stiff being trained for months and kept confined to camps, without ever having a chance to test their skills in the battlefield. In fact, this event had upset Arasu and many other influential members of the organization to such an extent that they had decided to part company with their long-time comrade-in-arms and leader, Uma Maheshwaran. Sarveshwaran too echoed the same sentiments regarding the event. In fact, he said that the punishment to Uma Maheshwaran for killing his own cadres, was death. The former was also disenchanted with the way the latter got Santatiar (one of the founding members of the PLOTE), eliminated since he had questioned him about the state of funds in the organization. For them, Uma Maheshwaran had been transformed into a monstrous being, in contrast to his earlier idealistic, amicable self. Uma Maheshwaran, himself had earlier worked for some years in the Gandhiam Organization, in resettling and providing succour to the Indian Tamil[15] refugees many of whom had fled to the northern Tamils provinces during the 1971 and 1977 riots perpetrated by "Sinhalese against the Tamils". Such intra-group violence also occurred in other militant organizations, but on a much smaller scale---the leadership of these organizations seemed to have been more circumspect about the consequences of large-scale dissent provoked by such "ruthless unjust acts", held to the unity and the very survival of the organization.

Another telling instance of the ensnaring quality of violence is the case of a young camp commander in one of the Sri Lankan Tamil militant training camps operating in 1984, in southern India. For this 21-year-old camp commander and some of his lieutenants torture of the chosen cadre victims, invariably began as an amusement, but suddenly got transformed into unbounded power fantasy, whose 'throwness' (Heidegger 1962:295-310) assumed forms of shearing sadistic delight in seeing the victim "cower and shrink in pain". What started as a mere amusement, would end up as a "pretense of its having been an attempt at information gathering or punishment for some vague infraction" (Daniel 1997:141). An instantiation of such sadism of the commander was witnessed in the case of Guhanesan, a young senior cadre in the camp, who was subjected to horrendous torture for defying the orders of the commander not to visit his young wife and newly born son in Mannar---it may be noted in this connection, that in this militant organization, a much brandished part of its manifesto was that a genuine revolutionary forsook all his family connections; but this ideal was honoured more in its breach than in practice. Guhanesan had promptly returned after a week from Mannar to prove he is no mean traitor deserter, only to be subjected to the torture of having a nail hammered on his sole, and legs broken which had left him paralyzed below his hips. He dragged himself in the camp's ground with a tire tied to him like a beggar. His condition was meant as a 'living example' to the rest of the cadres, for what awaited them if they dared to disobey the commander's orders. For the outside world, however, he was to be spoken of only as a beggar. Guhanesan often complained of excruciating pain on the point of the sole where the nail had been hammered (but had been removed subsequently)---this inspite of his lower half of his body being totally paralyzed. Some of his comrades' attempts at locating the pain on the sole of his foot had been in vain (Daniel 1997:141-2).

In other words, cases such as those of the late Uma Maheshwaran and the above commander and his lieutenants, demonstrate the enormity of violence in bringing forth such radical transformation in the being of people.

The acceptance of violence had also entailed perpetration of violence by the militant organizations on each other, especially between the LTTE on the one hand and the other militant organizations, viz., the TELO, PLOTE, and EPRLF on the other. A telling example mentioned by the PLOTE narrators was the ruthless massacre of Sri Sabaratinam (TELO's chief in command) and 160 of his cadres in Jaffna peninsula around April 1986.

Another aspect of the magma of violence in the Sri Lankan Tamil armed struggle for liberation, was the massacre of civilian Sinhalese population by the LTTE guerillas. As the LTTE narrator mentioned, for them, "a Sinhalese is a Sinhalese' irrespective of their age or sex". In his words: "They have occupied our land. They want us to be driven out and decimated. Why should the Sinhalese government engage in systematic 'colonisation' of our land? Spontaneous migration of people is one thing, systematic colonisation is another. Since Independence, successive Sinhalese regimes have been relentlessly engaged in 'colonisation' of the Tamil lands. The government and the Sinhalese settlers need to be taught a lesson. The only fear they understand is death. So when we go on a assault of Sinhalese colonised areas, it hardly matters which age or sex they belong to. They are all just Sinhalese who have occupied our land to decimate us." Many ordinary Sri Lankan Tamil refugees, didn't seem to disapprove of the LTTE's elimination strategy. When asked how could the LTTE bring itself to killing helpless Sinhalese children and women, and old men, one of the refugees said: "The boys are in a frenzied (veri) state. In such a state children, women etc., doesn't make a difference. They are all just Sinhalese who have occupied our lands. They need to be removed from our soil. We have been subjected to violent assaults during various riots since independence. Then there have been so many Sri Lankan army operations against Tamils in our land. We are driven out of Colombo and when we come to our land in the north, they try to drive us out from there too. What more illustrations does one need for the genocidal intentions of the Sinhalese?"

In other words, violence as the emblem of the Sri Lankan Tamil armed liberation struggle, constituted the transformed social imaginary of the Sri Lankan Tamil society. But, the consequences of this transformative logic had other dimensions as well: for certain sections of the militants, violence was not merely a weapon of the liberation struggle, but also a tool in the internecine conflict for supremacy within and among the organizations, and for keeping dissidence in check within the organization. We have noted how within the PLOTE, Uma Maheshwaran, the chief of the organization, eliminated Santatiyar (a senior much respected founder member of the organization), when he interlocuted him about funds and other issues pertaining to the organization. Similarly, the former eliminated 50-60 of his own cadres, since they complained of the futility of their training (being not put it to use in a battlefield) and boredom being confined to camps, and wanted to quit on that count. This action of Uma Maheshwaran, had so much upset some senior members that they had quit the organization in utter disgust.

In course of time, PLOTE saw many more killings and torture of its members, at the behest of its chief. In fact, many had come to liken Uma Maheshwaran to a mafia-don. Such developments had ultimately led to the disintegration of the once powerful and popular organization. The case of militant leaders such as Uma Maheshwaran, bespoke the tragic irony of the leader and his organization, whose goal of liberation through armed struggle, had left such trails of ignominy and annihilation. The internecine conflicts among the militant organizations for supremacy, was no less awesome in its magnitude of tragedy and bloodshed---the massacre of the TELO leader Sri Sabaratinam and 150-160 of his cadres, by the LTTE was one such instance. The killing, in course of time had witnessed the disintegration of TELO from a considerably powerful, popular organization to a toothless entity. These illustrations, are instances of the construction of the new episteme of the armed struggle for liberation and their ontic expressions in the lives of the militants and their struggle.

The Armed Struggle and Transformation in Other Domains

Arasu Nityan sorrowfully spoke about the nature of erosion of traditional sexual norms, destruction of families, the new drug pornography culture among the youth and the mayhem ambience pervading his society under the impact of the war between the militants and the Sri Lankan army. The new sexual norms were reflected in married women with children cohabiting with teenaged young men, either because their husbands were away abroad making a livelihood or were dead. What Arasu was shocked about was that these married women were cohabiting (not with other adult men) but with 'boys' who were 18 or 19 years of age. Such sexual behaviour, according to him, rarely occurred in pre-armed struggle Tamil society, and if ever occurred it evoked stringent stigma from the rest of the society. His own sister-in-law with children (her husband away abroad), now wore short skirts, which had provoked censorious comments from his mother not only about her daughter-in-law, but also the militant struggle. There were other refugees, who in sadness spoke about numerous instances of young Sri Lankan Tamil girls taking to prostitution in cities such as Colombo, either due to sexual frustration (being unable to find a match, since a large number of eligible young Tamil males had joined the armed struggle) or for making a living.

Many young men in Jaffna, whiled away their time taking drugs, seeing pornographic movies, etc. Their philosophy was "kick-it-up today, for you may not be alive tomorrow". This was the upshot of the war conditions in Jaffna, where the educational system and other establishments could hardly function. There were also instances of young men taking to robbery and killing for gain and making a living.

The families were in a disarray. Husbands, fathers or sons, if they had not joined the armed struggle, had left for other destinations abroad to make a living. Or families could face still worse situations, with their adult earning members dying being caught in cross-fires in the war between the militants and the Sri Lankan army. In many instances, whole families were wiped out in the bombing operations of the Sri Lankan army.

Another critical consequence of the armed struggle was the phenomenon of orphaned children and people suffering from mental disorders. Quite often in the latter case, reconstitution of the lives of the victims and of their kith and kin, meant living the rest of life in anguish and agony.

Many refugees talked in dismay about the destruction of the Sri Lankan Tamil culture. In the words of one of them: "Do you know, there are thousands of Sri Lankan Tamils who are living abroad. Can you imagine the demise of our culture in such a context? There are many instances of brothers who live in different countries—one in France, another in Germany, another in Denmark. When their children meet, they cannot communicate with each other. One speaks French, the other German, the third Danish. Their grandmother who lives in Colombo, when is visited by her grandchildren, stretches her arms to hug them, the grandchildren run away, for she is a stranger to them! Can you comprehend the anguish of the grandmother?" Another Sri Lankan Tamil academic told me: "You know, I want someone to take a project on the Sri Lankan Tamil society in 2020 A.D. What would it be like then?" In the question seemed embedded his vision of his society in two decades from now: A howling void replacing all that defined them as Sri Lankan Tamils? Or a new society with a new social imaginary, the offspring of the decades of the struggle for liberation? Or no Sri Lankan Tamils in their 'homelands', a referral of their very definition and being, once upon a time.

To be a militant involved not only defying death and construction of a new hermeneutics of it, but also denial of the self in some of its fundamental hues. Arasu Nityan's narrative of his unconsumated love for a girl, and his interpretation of it in terms of his being a militant brings out the pathos of the situation---the girl had rejected him because he was a militant with no career or prospects of a career. He had remarked that no girl would like to marry a militant, "who had nothing to offer but his revolutionary zeal". Indeed, many other militant youth shared the predicament of Arasu Nityan. Being a militant meant a reconstitution of the self, altering the very premises of one's pre-militant self. The emergence of new social definitions in the society?

Another interesting dimension in the narratives (except that of the LTTE narrator) is the comments made by the narrators about the Sinhalese in general: they said that they had nothing against the Sinhalese people, but they were only against the Sri Lankan government. In fact, Krishnan one of the top leaders of EROS, mentioned that Sinhalese as people were more hospitable and friendly than Tamils, and that the Sinhalese society a more enlightened society, with no pernicious institutions such as dowry and rigid caste hierarchy. In fact, he said that he took part in the Janata Vimukti Peramuna's (People's Liberation Organization) rebellion of 1971, along with thousands of Sinhalese youth. For Krishnan and many other militants and ordinary Sri Lankan Tamils, the ordinary Sinhalese people were hapless, while it was the Sri Lankan government which manipulated them for its own political expediency. In short, it is the Sri Lankan government, and Sinhalese politicians who were actually the villains of the Tamil tragedy.

Even to this day, after nearly a decade and a half, the armed struggle for liberation is still being waged by the Liberation Tigers of Tamil Eelam. Much water has flown under the bridge since the militants' narratives. To note only a few critical developments since then, for instance, the 1987 Indo-Sri Lankan Accord which envisaged a peaceful settlement of the Sri Lankan Tamil ethnic conflict, saw another bloody war this time, most unfortunately between the Indian Peace Keeping Force and the LTTE, in the formers mission to disarm the latter (Singh n.d.; Bhaduri and Karim 1990). Besides, due to unwilling-ness on the part of the Sri Lankan government to implement all the provisions of the accord (for various reasons), the accord became confined to the dustbin or history. Negotiations between the then Sri Lankan government headed by the late President Premadasa (United National Party) and the LTTE to reach a settlement on the Tamil demands, also ended in a failure. So also has been the negotiations conducted between the current SLFP (Sri Lanka Freedom Party) led alliance government, headed by President Chandrika Kumaratunga and the LTTE, held with a similar agenda, during 1993-94. The Sri Lankan government in the meanwhile, has opted for a double-pronged strategy to settle the conflict---a military operation to cow-down the LTTE to submission, and a political package for a certain measure of devolution to the Tamil dominated northern and eastern districts of Sri Lanka. But the latter itself is in doldrums, with strong objections raised by the other major Sinhalese party, the United National Party (UNP), and certain other sections of the Sinhalese 'majority community' to certain provisions in the package (the reasons alleged, being 'Sinhalese chauvinism', fear of dismemberment of Sri Lanka, etc.).

Under these conditions of war and uncertainty, there has been another spurt of exodus of the Sri Lankan Tamils to other parts of the world, extending the canvas of their diasporic homelessness. A further erosion of their Tamil selves and a deepening of the void?, as remarked earlier by the Sri Lankan Tamil refugee and the Sri Lankan Tamil academic, respectively.

As a Jaffna Tamil woman academic commented on the exodus and the misery and anguish of her people under the current war ambience in the 'Tamil homelands': "Thousands of Tamils have left Jaffna to safer places such as Colombo or other parts of the world, if they could afford to migrate. The Sri Lankan army's operations 'Riviresa' and 'Sat Jaya' in 1995 have left thousands of Tamil civilians dead thousands of others taking shelter in LTTE controlled jungles, and thousands of refugees in refugee camps. It is in the army's bombing and shelling several Tamil civilians get killed, many homes are razed to the ground. The army also engaged in looting the houses of people. There have been instances of the army raping girls and killing them. In the search operations, the army has taken away many male youth from Tamil homes, and with no information about their whereabouts. People fearing for their lives and safety have migrated to other safer places. Such conditions prevail not only in Jaffna, but also in Killinochi, Mullaitivu, Batticoloa, etc.

"You know it is only Jafna town that is occupied by the army. The rest of the Jaffna peninsula is under the control of the LTTE. Many Tamils have lost all their furniture and other household articles in the bombing and shelling by the army. People just sleep on mats. Many homes have no windows and doors, and bear numerous shell marks. Jaffna University is not functioning, and many of its rooms are taken over by the army, to be used as their office premises."[16]

During this period, the Sri Lankan Tamil society has seen certain other transformations too. Increasing number of young Sri Lankan Tamil women have joined the armed struggle of the LTTE. This has caught the attention of the media too. Some of the Colombo based Sinhalese owned English popular dailies, in some of their stories pertaining to possible LTTE's 'terrorist' attacks on the capital's targets, carry cartoons of women tigers, dressed in a tiger's garb (a tiger's face and tail), with a begging bowl in hands. The latter signifying the possibility of even women tigers being 'terrorists', and assuming such innocuous garbs as that of a beggar. People, were thereby warned and cautioned to be ever vigilant of such wily strategies being employed by the LTTE in achieving their goals.

Young Tamil women joining the armed struggle in ever increasing numbers, is an illustration of the transforming imaginary pertaining to the conception of the 'feminine' in the Tamil society. As some of the Sinhalese and Tamil women remarked while looking at a picture published in some dailies of nearly 150 women tigers killed in a recent battle (all the killed were placed in a row): "These young girls whose soft hands should have worn bangles, now carry rifles. Oh! it is so terrible, I can't bring myself to even looking at the picture." To be 'feminine' is to be soft and non-violent, whereas to be "masculine" is to be hard and capable of violence. For a female to cast off the bangles and hold a gun instead, calls for a substantial radicalism of the self, a magmic transformation of no mean magnitude. On the other hand, these women tigers draw kudos and admiration from the rest of the Sri Lankan Tamil society, for their courage and valour. To quote a Sri Lankan Tamil refugee: "These *pen puligal* (girl tigers) are no less courageous than the boy tigers. Look, how they fight the Sri Lankan forces. Many of these women brigades have fought shoulder to shoulder with the boys in many battles against the Sri Lankan army. They are *veeranganais* (courageous warrior women)fighting for the liberation of Tamils and their homeland. When it is a war for life or death, well every Sri Lankan Tamil has to be prepared to do his or her bit. If not slavery or death are the only options under the Sinhalese hegemony. We Tamils are a proud nation, we will never submit ourselves to abysmal subjugated status. We would rather die than live such an existence."

Even for many young Tamil children in their early teens (14-16), growing up in the midst of war, death and suffering of varied sorts, gun has become the symbol of existence and survival. The option even for these kids is either to be frisked away by the Sri Lankan army and "never be seen again" or join their own army, the LTTE, and fight for Eelam, and death if it comes is an 'honourable' one—a 'martyrdom' celebrated with hosannahs by their own people. As a Sri Lankan Jaffna Tamil woman said: "Even to this day Sri Lankan army conducts midnight searches in houses and take away male youth, even those who may be just 15 or 16 years of age. They are never heard of again. This is one of the major causes for the people wishing to flee to India or elsewhere. The army wants to arrest the recruitment to the LTTE so that militarily it gets weakened. A majority of the Tamils support the LTTE. This is not to say that they are not critical of it on certain occasions. Consider for instance, the case of the LTTE blowing up the Sri Lankan navy ship when the 'negotiations' were going on between it and the Sri Lankan government last year (1995). The people disapproved of the LTTE's action in the midst of negotiations. But the LTTE explained, 'The Sri Lankan government is not serious about offering a meaningful devolution package to resolve the conflict'. The government's flippant and non-serious attitude is reflected in the kind of people they send to represent the government. It is a bishop, a social worker or someone, and no proper official representative of the government. They fly in helicopters, descend on Jaffna, are taken to the LTTE's office. The LTTE has got everything of its agenda and papers properly worked out and placed before them. The government's 'representatives', sit, sip tea, chat and leave. Such 'fake' meetings have taken place any number of times. So we understood that the government doesn't mean business and are not serious about a proper settlement of our demands. It is then that we decided to attack the navy's ship and cease the ceasefire!"

The Tamil women further remarked: "The recent operations 'Riviresa', 'Sat Jaya', etc., by the Sri Lankan army against the LTTE has led to extensive displacement and misery of the people. Many Tamils have died in the bombing operations. One thing is clear about the plans of the Sri Lankan government: they want to decimate the Tamil race. They want to either kill them or make them leave the country."

Acknowledgment

I acknowledge with deep gratitude all the Sri Lankan Tamil militants and many other Sri Lankan Tamil refugee friends for sharing their experiences and perceptions during the course of my field work. I had learnt with anguish that since my field work, some of my Sri Lankan Tamil militant informants had died a bloodied death in the inter and internecine conflicts among the militant organisations and in the on going war in Sri Lanka. I dedicate this paper to their memory and for peace for the Tamils and the island nation. I am also grateful to Dr. Ananta Giri, for the concern and avidity he showed in egging me to write this paper. I acknowledge my sincere thanks to all the participants of the Silver Jubilee Seminar, for their unstinting comments and criticisms. Needless to say, the errors that remain are wholly mine.

Notes

1. See, for instance, Tambiah (1986), Ponnambalam (1983), Manor (1984), and Alagappan (1985).
2. See Sivakumar (1989), for a substantiation of their above views.
3. Castoriadis defines the term 'magma' as follows: "What we seek to understand is the mode of being of what gives itself before identiary or ensemblist logic is imposed: what gives itself in this way in this mode of being, we are calling a magma. It is obviously not a question of giving a formal definition of it in received language or in any language whatsoever. The following statement, however, may not be unhelpful:

   "A magma is that from which one can extract (or in which one can construct) an indefinite number of ensemblist organisations but which can never be reconstituted (ideally) by a (finite or infinite) ensemblist composition of these organisations" (1987:343).
4. I use the term 'ontic' in the Heideggerian sense of the 'everydayness' of living. See Heidegger (1962:322-23).

5. It needs to be noted here that the then Indian government (1983) led by the late Indira Gandhi had decided for whatever 'foreign policy' considerations, to assist the armed struggle of the major Sri Lankan Tamil militant organisations, by providing military training, arms, etc. In fact, this response of the Indian government was considered to have been one of the major motivating factors for the massive enthusiasm of the Sri Lankan Tamil youth to join the militant organisations soon after the 83 riots. See in this connection, Narayanaswamy (1994:93-115). The Indian government's response, perhaps was a moral brooter and reinforced the option of the armed struggle.
6. The term 'tyagi' is Tamil means renouncer of life itself or all the trappings of life such as economic well-being, status, power, family-bonds, kin-bonds, etc., for the sake of a cause.
7. Also see in this connection, Schalk (1997:61-84).
8. This, of course, is not to contend that all Sri Lankan Tamils prefer to stay in battlezones and die. The fact that the 83' riots witnessed thousands of Sri Lankan Tamil refugees fleeing to Tamilnadu and to elsewhere in the world, to "protect their lives" reveals the "instinctual" propensity of most (if not all) living beings to try to save their lives when threatened.
9. I have used the term 'hiddeness' in the Heideggerian sense of the first and second levels of the hiddeness of the phenomenon. See Heidegger (1962:59-60).
10. Heidegger uses the term Dasein (Being there) for that entity of the Being which is Being-towards death, or "nothing and nowhere". See Heidegger (1962:228-311).
11. I am here referring to the Tamil society in general encompassing the Tamils in Tamilnadu.
12. The agitation was launched by the then Dravida Munnetra Kazhagam (DMK) government, headed by Annadurai, against the 'imposition' of Hindi by the Indian government on Tamilnadu.
13. In fact, currently, the rumors going round in Tamilnadu are that the DMK regime headed by M. Karunanidhi is some what apprehensive of bringing the former AIADMK Chief Minister, J. Jayalalitha to book for various acts of corruption—though this constituted one of the major planks of the election campaign of the DMK-TMC (Dravida Munnetra Kazhagam and Tamil Manila

Congress) etc. alliance during the 1996 elections held in May for the Tamilnadu Legislative Assembly and Indian Parliament, as such an action may result in immolations by the AIADMK followers, besmirching the government's reputation. Another critical dimension of the Tamil social psyche is the proneness to suicide, when she/he feels dishonoured under certain circumstances, such as a father insulted by a son, a girl jilted by a lover, or a wife insulted by her husband. This information is based on the field work conducted by S.S. Sivakumar in some Tamilnadu villages during the mid-70's.

14. Foucault (1970:p.XV).
15. These Indian Tamils constitute the bulk of the plantation labour (tea plantations) in Sri Lanka. They migrated to Sri Lanka around the last quarter of the 19th century during the British colonial regime. They are distinguished from Sri Lankan Tamils who consider themselves ancient settlers on the island, with their history of settlement in the northern and eastern provinces being traced back to around 5 A.D.
16. Also see in this connection the report published by the organisation called the University Teachers for Human Rights (Jaffna) on the trenchanting travails of the Sri Lankan Tamil civilians under the repressive rule of the Sri Lankan army in the northern Tamil dominated areas. Report of the University Teachers for Human Rights (UTHR): 1996. Also see report of the University Teachers for Human Rights: 1994.

References

Alagappan, M.V.M., *Tears in Teardrop Island*, Sterling Publishers, Delhi, 1985.

Bhaduri, Shankar and Karim, Afsir, *The Sri Lankan Crisis*, Lancer International, Delhi, 1990.

Clifford, James and Marous E., George (eds.), *Writing Culture: The Poetics and Politics of Ethnography*, Oxford University Press, Delhi, 1990.

Castoriadis, Cornelius, *The Imaginary Institution of Society* (trans. by Kathleen Blamey), Polity Press, Cambridge, 1987.

Daniel, E., Valentine, *Anthropography of Violence: Sri Lankans, Sinhalese and Tamils*, Oxford University Press, Delhi, 1997.

Durkheim, Emile, *Suicide: A Study in Sociology* (trans. by John A. Spaulding and George Simpson, and ed. by George Simpson), Routledge & Kegan Paul, London, 1970.

Foucault, Michael, *The Order of Things*, Tavistock, London, 1970.

Giddens, Anthony, *Central Problems in Social Theory: Action, Structure and Contradiction in Social Analysis*, Macmillan, London, 1979.

Heidegger, Martin, *Being and Time* (trans. by John Macquarrie and Edward Robinson), Basil Blackwell, Oxford, 1962.

Langer, Lawrence, L., 'The Alarmed Vision: Social Suffering and Holocaust Atrocity', Daedlus, Winter, 1996: 47-65.

Manor, James (ed.), *Sri Lanka: In Change and Crisis*, Croom Helm, London and Sydney, 1984.

Maurice, Morleau-Ponty, 'Philosophy and non-philosophy since Hegel', in Silverman, J., Hugh (ed.), *Philosophy and Non-Philosophy since Morleau-Ponty*, Routledge, New York and London, 1988, pp.9-83.

Narayanaswamy, M.R., *Tigers of Lanka: From Boys to Guerillas*, Konark Publishers, Delhi, 1994.

Nietzsche, Friedrich, 'On the Genealogy of Morals', in Walter Kaufmann (trans. and ed.), *Basic Writings of Nietzsche*, The Modern Library, New York, pp. 451-599.

Nietzsche, Friedrich, 'The Birth of Tragedy Or: Hellenism and Pessimism', in Walter Kaufmann (trans. and ed.), *Basic Writings of Nietzsche*, The Modern Library, New York, 1968, pp.31-144.

Ponnambalam, Satchi, *Sri Lanka: National Conflict and the Tamil Liberation Struggle*, Zed Books Ltd., London, 1983.

Report of the University Teachers for Human Rights, November 2, 1996, Jaffna.

Schalk, Peter, 'Resistance and Martyrdom in the Process of State Formation of Tamililam', in Pettigrew, Joyce (ed.), *Martyrdom and Political Resistance: Essays from Asia and Europe*, VU University Press, Amsterdam, 1997, pp.61-84.

Singh, Depinder, *The IPKF in Sri Lanka*, Trishul Publications, Noida, n.d.

Sivakumar, Chitra, 'Social Origins of the Sri Lankan Tamil Militant Movement', *Sociological Bulletin*, Vol.39, No.1, March 1989.

Sivanayagam, S., 'The Phenomenon of Tamil Militancy', in Suryanarayan, V. (ed.), *Sri Lankan Crisis and India s Response*, Patriot Publishers, Delhi, 1991.

Tambiah, S.J., *Sri Lanka: Ethnic Fratricide and the Dismantling of Democracy*, Oxford University Press, Delhi, 1986.

The University Teachers for Human Rights (Jaffna), Someone Else War, published by the Movement for Inter Racial Justice and Equality, Colombo, 1994.

Young, Allan, 'Suffering and the Origins of Traumatic Memory', *Daedlus*, Winter, 1996:245-59.

Chapter Fifteen

Documenting Dissent: A Study of Contesting Memory

Badri Narayan Tewari

I am the voice
crying in the night
that cries endlessly
and will not be consoled.

—Dennis Brutus[1]

The Problem

Four caste riots had taken place in central Bihar centred round folk memory of Chuharmal between 1970 and 1990. Chuharmal is a hero and god of the lower castes in the region. The folk myth represents the symbol of victory of Dusadh[2] (a lower caste) on Bhumihar (prabhu jati) in the region. While feudal forces are trying to erase this memory by the barrel of the gun, lower caste people struggle to save and preserve it. This paper focuses on the 'folk memory' of Chuharmal which is cause of tension in an Indian society. Here a case study of Ekauni Kand reveals these phenomena. Ekauni is a village in the Aurangabad district of Bihar where a killing of theatre artist had been taken place due to only he was performing the role of Chuharmal.[3] In the continuation of this incidence many clashes had taken place in the village.

The methodology of this paper is based on observations and field studies in the Aurangabad, Patna and Bhojpur districts of Bihar at identified places whose oral rendering, symbols, texts, rituals used in the contemporary life of common people as well as political and religious discourse going on in that society have been collected. An attempt has been made to analyze the protest ballad and relate it to the contemporary socio-political context.

In this work I build upon the following propositions:

(a) Memory is remembrance in Hegelian sense that extents to the concept of collective remembrance.[4] Remembrance is not a mechanical act, it contains some interchange with creative imagination. So one finds many versions of one text during different time frame.[5] Collective memory is the basis of social order and it ought to lie at the centre of our historical investigations (Halbawachs 1992).[6]

Memory is a social phenomena and selectivity of memory lies in the processes of remembrance. Remembrance is an act not of mere recollection but rather of repetition (Michelet 1939).[7] Memory tends to disappear unless they are rekindled through repetition, whether or not memories are repeated depends on whether or not the social framework of memory imbues them with a collective function.[8] To me collective memory is not an innocent, univocative and unified domain. It is contesting and fragmented whole.[9] It is contesting because the way in which the past is recalled depends upon the power of the group that frames its (Collective, traditions) memory (Halbawachs 1975).[10] Memory (historical memory) is the constitutive element of the identity (Erinnerung) of the group. Commemorative monuments, religious rituals, folk tales, family lore are the vehicle of collective memory.[11]

(b) Power and elite forces make use of folk memories but are equally frightened of it. They try to erase some of those social memories which threaten their power.[12] But forces of resistance want to save and preserve these memories. During this process, the elite capture the memories, reconstruct them in accordance with their convenience and interpret them according to their interests, visualizing their forms according to their own aesthetical sense.[13] Thus, power attempts to erase the true memories from the people's mind and instead transplant false memories, to suit its political ends. For this it uses all available as much as creates new forms of communication, *shabd* (words), *vakya* (phrases, sentences), army of intellectuals, education and other means of mass communication. Colonial power in India as well as in Africa transplanted new memory through these media. In Kenya, literature written in colonial language is a potential weapon to transplant false memories (Thyongo 1994). So is true of India. W. Smith and others tried to build Indian history from colonial angle to create colonial memories.

Massacre of Memory: A Narrative of *Ekauni Kand*

It was of June 19, 1978. Near Daudnagar of Aurangabad district of Bihar, a marriage party (*barat*) had arrived at the house of Nonu Sahu in Village Ekauni. Dance-*nautanki* (drama) was being performed in the *khalihan* of village. Just as, the love scene of Reshma and Chuharmal started, a bullet, was fired from the spectators which entered the chest of actor playing the role of Chuharmal. A roaring sound echoed, "Stop this nonsense", and there followed a stampede among the spectators.

This is not part of any fiction, it is a real event which occurred in the interior area of Aurangabad on 19 June, 1978. Subsequently, two groups were formed in the village. One was led by Bhumihar and other group comprised lower castes; viz., Bania, Koiri, Chamar, Dusadh and others. This escalated tension and conflict between the Bhumihar Tola and the Purvi Tola (populated by the lower castes)of the village. In fact, the bullet was fired by a youth of Bhumihar caste because Reshma, heroine of the play belonged to this caste. Bhumihar, a feudal upper caste of this area perceived this memory as an insult to their caste, on the other hand, lower caste adopted the same memory as a memory of protest against feudal and elite class of this region.[14] Five murders have taken place during this prolonged tension and conflict besides many minor conflicts and factionalism.[15]

At first, we came to know of this astonishing event from the files of Bhojpuri local daily *Tatka* (2 February, 1978). We attempted to understand intra-social dynamics of this society. How could memory get transformed into caste and class tensions? How and why some people want to preserve a memory while some other people try to erase it?

Police (Daudnagar *thana*) maintained that event is simply a murder and a result of long continuing recorded caste tension. By conversations with villagers that cause of the caste tension in village is the drama of Chuharmal and the memories that the ballad sought to preserve and retrieve. While agreeing that Chuharmal was the cause of tension, noted that the drama was an insult to them.[16] This is imprinted as 'Ekauni-Kand' in the memory of people. Kand is an event that contains flashing elements, and the memory of which is long lasting.[17]

About 40 percent of total population in Ekauni village belong to Bhumihar caste and the remaining 60 percent include Bania, Koiri, Yadav, Chamar, Dusadh and some other castes. This is a high-caste dominated village and region in which Bhumihars have major landholdings. The lower castes possess very little land. These castes are either small businessmen or involved in traditional occupations. The Dusadh and Chamar landless labourers work on the lands of the Bhumihars.

Of service-class people, major number is from high castes and fever from the middle and lowered castes. Ekauni is a high caste dominated village although the majority of the population is from other castes. This is a region of Magahi culture, e.g., Aurangabad, Jahanabad, Patana and Gaya with Magahi dialect. Magahi term emerged from 'Magadhi' which denotes the Magadh region. To understand the folk consciousness of societies like Magadhi, Angika, Bajjika, Bhojpuri, etc., of Bihar, we have to understand the differences in the structure of their memories. Till the emergence of Buddhism, memories flowing through Vedic and Sanskrit languages were prominent here. But after the emergence of heterogeneous sects like Buddha, Jain, Nath and their popular attempts at deconstructing Vedic memories, memories of Buddhism, Jainism and Nath beliefs[18] became influential in these folk areas. This resulted later in the predominance of linguistic memories of *Pali*, *Prakrit* and *Apbhransh*. Many folk heroes in popular folk lores in these areas are described as related with Nath sect, e.g., Bharathari, Sorathi and Brijbhar.[19] Pali which was the language of Buddhist discourse previously called Magadhi only, although now, there are major differences between contemporary Magadhi and Pali. Yet, the degree of similarity also greater.

As in other parts of the country, Bihar's society is divided and fragmented on lines of caste, class and religion. So the social environment is not favourable for any master narrative of culture, politics and society. This division, fragmentation and inequality in the socio-economic domain provides the condition of the remembrance of local narratives. The caste dimensions and polarisation are very much evident here.

Bihar's caste divisions are based on the traditional landowning structures and the division of wealth and occupations in society. The so-called 'forward' castes predominantly consist of the Brahmin, Bhumihar, Rajput, Bania and Kayastha communities. Of them, the Bhumihars and the Rajputs are the dominant landowning castes who once ruled various parts of the state.[20] They constitute about 15 percent of the population. The middle castes, namely, Yadav, Kurmi and Koeri form about 18 percent, while lower castes comprise 32 percent of the population. The middle and the lower castes together are classified as Other Backward Classes (OBCs). The OBCs thus constitute about half the population of the state.[21] The proportion of Scheduled Castes (SCs), Scheduled Tribes (STs) and Muslims in the population is 14 percent, 9 percent and 12 percent respectively.

If we juxtapose the above demographic data with the pattern of land ownership across the different castes, we get a picture of a society in which land and, consequently, a disproportionately large concentration of agricultural wealth, continues to be owned by a relatively few landlords and large farmers. A majority of the people experience material deprivation. Their long history of subjugation and discrimination and their growing aspirations, restlessness and assertiveness in the face of upper caste groups unwillingness to relinquish their power and privilege, explain, to some extent, the growth of violence in Bihar.

Only 5.7 percent of the upper castes own no land. It can safely be assumed that those who do not own land are professionals belonging to the Brahmin and Kayastha castes or Bania traders.[22] The latter group includes big landlords. For instance, 85 families spread across 18 districts of Bihar who own more than 500 acres of land. Additionally, 89.5 percent of the upper castes belong to the landlord and rich peasant category, while only 2.9 percent and 5.5 percent belong to he middle and poor peasant categories respectively.[23]

At the other end of the spectrum are the *dalits* and tribals, (60.9%) of whom own no land at all. They are often landless agricultural and urban labourers and artisans of perform some menial jobs. An overwhelming majority are marginal farmers who also work as part-time agricultural labourers, while a small proportion owe less than 5 acres of land. Many are also seasonal migrants who travel as far as Punjab and Haryana in search of work. Dalits and tribals own as more than 10 acres of land are almost negligible.

Between these two ends of the spectrum lie the middle and lower castes, the OBCs. Among the middle castes (Yadav, Kurmi, Koeri and others) 25.9 percent are landless, 66.4 percent are small and farmers operating less than 0-5 acres. This is indicative of the differentiation in the peasantry among these caste groups. Of the lower castes (Barhi, Dhanuk, Kahar, Kumhar, Luhar, Tatwa, Teli) a little more than two thirds are landless lower castes work as agricultural labourers, artisans, small traders or in the service sector.

Among the Muslims, 58.6 percent own no land. This section of Muslims consist of professionals, artisans, agricultural urban workers and small to medium traders. Once again, a large proportion of them are marginal and small farmers (35.4%).

In these oppressive and unequal conditions of social existence, the protest of the people are reflected not just in one way. Multiple forms of protest imprint the social memory of oppressed people.

When we attempted to acquaint ourselves with the memory of the people related to the events of Ekauni (Nautanki) and the protest that emerged from it, we were amazed that in the whole Bhojpur-Rohtas region, another region of Bihar characterized by caste tensions and land struggles, similar events have taken place so extensively that they have been preserved and expressed in the form of social memories perpetuating many social conflicts. Another such event took place in Khutahan Bazar in the Tarari police station of Bhojpur.[24] During the drama in Dusehra in which a derogatory song sung by Sutradhar provoked elite class of this region, leading to caste conflict and class tension in this Qasba.[25] Many people-theatre groups are active in this area. These are often way, types of cultural expression of the Naxalite politics that has emerged during the last decade. The banning of performance of such plays by these groups and their arrests has not succeeded in stopping it. Although the political party to which these groups are affiliated once went underground, now they participate openly in parliamentary politics. In fact these theatre groups were often imprinting memories in people's psyche that were inconvenient for the ruling powers.[26] Some incidence of the local and state power oppressive attack on the cultural actions of people theatre groups in the Bhojpur district of Bihar (1979-82) are tabled below:

Group	*Place*	*Date*	*Oppressive Forces*
Yuva Niti	Khawaspur	5.6.79	Kunwar Sena*
Yuva Niti	Virampur	7.8.80	Feudal Caste LandLord
Jan Natya Manch	Kesath	3.9.80	Supporters of Feudal Criminals
Jan Sanskriti Manch	Bagain	16.8.82	Supports of Feudal Criminals

* Kunwar Sena is the Army of Local Landlords in the Bhojpur Region.

Sources: Morcha Lagta Natak, Rajesh Kumar/Arvind Kumar, Bhagalpur, 1990.[27]

These cultural representation of the people play a significant role in the shaping social memory of the society.[28] So, power (both local power and state power) tried to prevent the theatre groups from performing resulting in people retaliation processions and political actions. Such dramas by way of as 'Reshma and Chuharmal' performed by theatre groups are flowing in people's memories in autonomous form since centuries.

Many clashes occurred around this social memory, in the villages like Mahendra Bigaha (1976), and Phoolari (1988) in Aurangabad district of Bihar.[29] Usually lower castes are involved in *natyamandali* and *nautanki* companies. As a result, consciously or unconsciously, they select dramas of such content and context which somewhere assault feudal castes and their values. The irony being that they have to perform their programmes in the ceremonies of higher caste people. They earn their livelihood from those people only, who are opposed to the content of their plays. They entertain those only, against which their consciousness is having resistance. At some places, when they play their dramas without considering the social structure of the villages, they have to face opposition. They are able to conclude their overnight programmes properly wherever the population is not high-caste dominated but at places where feudal castes are in dominance they have to counter physical threats. Nagesar dance troop is the most famous dance troop in Bhojpur. The manager of this dance group says, "Now we do not play drama of Reshma and Chuharmal. Feudal lords fire bullets at it." Even then the memory of Reshma and Chuharmal is becoming popular through these dance-troops. Particularly, the north-eastern part of Bihar is significantly is influenced by this social memory, although it is perceived by different classes in different ways. Lower castes and class glorify this social memory, and perceive it as a part of their 'tradition'.[30] According to them, this was a real event that happened sometime the past in their society.[31] This is the historical memory of the group which they perceived as real. One might observe here the transformation of memory into history in the collective mentality.[32] The other class consisting of feudal lords and forward castes feels insulted by this social memory and want to escape from this. They do not want to return back to this realm of social memory.

Orality, Festivity and Recurrence

The background of this social memory is the 'Tal' area (Tal is the name for vast stretch of uninhabited cultivated land) of Mokama and Badha Badhaiyya situated at the boundary of Patana, Begusarai and Nalanda district of Bihar. As per the narration of this drama, Reshma-Chuharmal hailed from this area. This drama is banned without any declaration in this area.[33] It is the zone of most intense influence by Bhumihars, the land owning caste of Bihar.

The reasons for the ban of this drama are the following: First, it degrades the upper castes, especially the Bhumihar caste (feudals of this area). Second, there is a Vardan (blessing of Devi) that whoever will sing the song of Reshma-Chuharmal, ladies of this area will go with him.[34] There is a belief even today, that there are descendants of Reshama-Chuharmal in that region. Reshma belongs to a rich family of Bhumihar Kshatriya of Mokama village and Chuharmal belongs to a Dusadh family in a village named Anjani.[35]

Narrative location of characters of this drama may be shown as below:

Character	*Area*	*Original Caste*	*Ancestral Link*
Reshma	Mokama	Bhumihar Kshatriya	a. Ajab Singh (Brother) b. Ranjit Singh (Father)
Chuharmal	Anjani Village	Dudhvanshi	a. Bihari (Father) b. Bansiram Surma (Dudhvanshi) c. Chuharmal (Dudhvanshi)

There is an interesting aspect in the caste titles of these folk characters. Those who were called Bhumihar Kshatriya now call themselves Bhumihar Brahmins, and those who were called Dudhvanshi, now call themselves Dusadh.

On visiting Mokama for the study of this phenomenon, I was told by a middle-aged couple who was travelling with me, that it is the fair organized by Dusadh where only lower caste people go. When I asked as to why the upper caste people do not go there, the man became irritated. Further conversation with the couple revealed that they were of Bhumihar caste, and an owner of many trucks.

This incident reveals as to how a social memory has become an identity of a caste or community and how higher caste psyche has received and retained it. This social memory is the memory of Reshma and Chuharmal. Folk tale of Reshma-Chuharmal, is not a dead folklore for the people, but is alive even today. Its hero is alive in the memories of people. A sacred complex of Chuharmal is in Mokama Tal area where there is a fair every year for 2-3 days in the month of Chaitya after the name of Chuharmal.[36] People in lakhs come here to worship the Dusadh Hero.[37] The place is located to the south of Mokama Station at about 10-12 km distance. In a nearby village named Mor, a large statue of Chuharmal without the neck is erected. During this season of crop cutting the harvest of the first crop is offered to Chuharmal. This is a standard ritual in the worship of Chuharmal.[38] People come here and pray for the fulfilment of their wishes (Manauti). Particularly, the lower castes have a faith that the wishes expressed during the worship are fulfilled. They also show their commemorative spirit here. They beat the *danka* (a large drum) and some of them dance, jump and play *gadaka* (a play of stick).[39]

The hero of the love story of Reshma and Chuharmal is also the caste hero of the Dusadhs and other lower castes of this area. It is mentionable that Loric (Yadav) Sahales, Chuharmal (Dushadh), etc., the folk heroes, are also the heroes of concerned castes. While studying the making of their heroism, we can also understand the structuring of the consciousness of these castes, as well as the outlook of the hegemonic castes towards them. Understanding the social meaning of this myth, in its various details, and its popularity in local society and in the vicinity of Mokama, one can understand the social composition of this area as well as the rich details of the social processes and their impact on this society. Due to these factors, the composition of the symbol of these folk heroes becomes a record of social history also. By composing the myth of Reshma and Chuharmal, Dushadh caste has built a protest against feudal hegemony and their oppressive differentiation.

Multiple Texts

A social text, like rumour and gossip multiplies many folds. The narrative identity of any community, culture or nation is not a rigid structure. Continuous contestation from within renders multiplicity a possibility though it is such a story which transforms itself into many stories (Recoeur 1995). The tale of Reshma and Chuharmal is an instance of a text multiplying itself, each text contains a peculiar social meaning. It is difficult to say which text is earlier one and which is a later one, or which single text is transformed into which multi-texts. What is important is that the narrative identity of these multiple texts should be identified.

In the folk tale of Reshma and Chuharmal, we have tried to search some of the elements of narrative identity of Reshma and Chuharmal. Many versions of this folk tale are popular in

Mokama (the original place of this folk tale) and its neighbouring areas.

Text A

What the story of this folk drama tells us is that Chuharmal, a handsome and healthy youth of Dushadh caste by birth, and Reshma, daughter of a local landlord belonging to the Bhumihar caste get entangled in love. She used to offer him invitation for indulgence.

Chuharmal initially tries to avoid her offers, then narrates to her that she is the daughter of a high-caste landlord, while he belongs to Dushadh caste. Reshma forces him to establish matrimonial relationship with her in which they succeed, and this relationship causes clash between Chuharmal and the landlord father of Reshma resulting in the victory of the virtuous hero, Chuharmal over the landlord and his army. This is the folk version of memory of Chuharmal prevalent in this area. Although this version is more popular among some of the lower castes, many other varied forms of this text are also popular among the people in this area.

Text B

Rani Reshma and Chuharmal, it is said, belonged to Brahmin caste in their previous birth and were couples. They got re-birth at different places near Mokama Ghat in Patna district. Chuharmal got birth in a family of Dusadh living in Anjani village, and his wife got birth in Bhumihar Kshatri Zamindar family. Later on his father sent Chuharmal for schooling. At the same place, Ajab Singh, brother of Reshma also used to study. They became fast friends. Coincidentally, once Ajab Singh fell ill, Chuharmal went to call for Ajab Singh. Reshma saw Chuharmal and was so fascinated by him that she left her meals and started worship of a Goddess for marrying Chuharmal.

Reshma once sent a message for Chuharmal to meet at a lonely place. Chuharmal was a religious, brave, handsome youth. Chuharmal refused Reshma's offer. Reshma was firm to take revenge of this insult. Consequently, there was a fighting between the army of her zamindar father and Chuharmal, but zamindar's army was defeated. Again, with the help of a Tantrik (owning supernatural powers), Reshma tried to defeat Chuharmal. The rest of the tale describes revengeful fighting's of her father's army with Chuharmal. But, due to Chuharmal's bravery, he could not be defeated. This theme is repeated at local dramas and rural theatres.

Analysis

In both the versions (text A and B) supernatural heroism of Chhuramal is projected. In fact, popular Veerakhyan (bravery tales) of Chuharmal is linked with Narashanshi (in the praise of brave persons and kings). Narashanshi is an oral tradition which was compiled in *Rigved Samhita* (Warder 1987). These *gathas*, of which some tales were collected in text and some of them were transmitted from generation to generation orally, are in the praise of human heroes. This set in place a historical tradition. Creative structure of this Narashanshi tradition is being utilised in the folk lore of Reshma and Chuharmal which is in the praise of Chuharmal, a lower caste hero. The Narasanshi tradition of Indian Akhyan later on transformed into Beer Gatha (chivalry) folklore. The Beer Gatha folk poetry developed under the medieval feudal and courtier patronage. These folk poetries contain male-dominated logic and aesthetical sense in their forms. Due to this, in these narratives, the heroes conquer the women and marry with them. In this narrative process the space of eulogisation of hero evolves. In this form of narrative the story of Reshma and Chuharmal has been developed. According to this logic of narrative structure, the abusive and insulting description of Reshma is found here. In the lower castes narrative, the construction of moral character of the hero is based on the character assassination of heroine.[40] The more emphasis has given on the Reshma's episode in which she has been described as sexual and immoral. Another reason may be that the forward have the lower women as kept and seldom rape them.[41] The lower castes are not able to take revenge on upper castes oppressive activities because of their weaker social condition. So they satisfy their desire of revenge to create such narratives in their fantasy and creative imagination. The society accepts these deeds of forward castes but if any lower caste youth relate himself with forward caste women, he is punished by panchayats and society. This types of events are continuously happening in central Bihar and eastern Uttar Pradesh.[42]

Although the narrative of text A and B interacts with each other. But text B is different in its narrative structure from text A that it includes some trades of Brahmnical upper caste morality, e.g., ideas of rebirth, love story of married couple in previous life, meeting by accident, worship of goddess, Chuharmal's religiosity and his devotion for Brahmnical values, victory of the virtuous.[43] In fact, Brahmnical values usually dictates the construction of the form of narrative.[44] Text B is the widely performed version by the local *nautanki* (theatre) group. So in the process of dramatization many narrative element of popular nature be added in this text.[45] In the societies marked by the oral transmissibility the continuum of flow additions and erosions are discernible and this phenomena is constituting of living memory and not memorized texts (Parry 1971).[46]

Text C

Chuharmal was a cowherd. He used to uproot the crop from the fields of people. Being mighty, people could not abstain him. But he was afraid of government employees. Once the landlord's surrogates along with the government employees gheraoed Chuharmal and cut his head. After the murder, again his spirit started to destroy crops of this area; thereupon people of this area fenced the place and started worshipping there.

Analysis

The text C sketches Chuharmal as an evil power who should be killed essentially in public welfare according to the myth. This text is usually fused in memory of forward castes. The main content of marital relation of Reshma and Chuharmal is removed and another tale-theme is added in it. An interesting explanation of Chuharmal was heard during the fieldwork in the area. According to it, the name Chuharmal originated from two words, i.e., 'Chor-Chuhar' which means thief or robber in the folk dialect and 'Chor-Chuhar' (thief-robber) is a compound word popular in the local dialects. The people of forward castes depict him as a dacoit. On rereading the elite name given to subaltern, one may explore different meaning of the word 'dacoit'. A.K. Warder (1987) suggests an interesting inference related to the act of stealing in the history. According to him, Buddhist interpretation holds the view that in primitive society, the concept of individual possession, gave birth to 'theft'. Thus 'individual possession' is synonymous to stealing.[47] Although in a Brahmanical texts like *Manusmriti*, the word '*Daku*' means Saahasi (adventurous). Further *Manusmriti* extends the meaning of 'Saahasi' as kidnapper or plunderer of wealth, and in the law of Manu, killing of 'Saahasi' was supposed to be the duty of the king. On reading the elite name given to subaltern, one may search different meanings of the word 'dacoit' which depict the 'act of dacoiti' in different senses.

According to the law of Manu, the king who forgives a person involved in Sahasik activities, gets ruined shortly, and that king also becomes an object of hatred by people. As observed during the field survey, a 60-year old man Ram Singar Singh uses above justification and mentions the event of murder of Chuharmal by a local feud to be true. The justificatory language itself reveals that mythic discourse and religious discourse parallel closely, atleast in their fundamental principle of the victory of good ever evil. He asks me, "Why Ram killed Ravana?" On the other hand, the Reshma-Chuharmal tale as popular among lower castes puts forward another justification from *Manusmriti* which reflects an opposite image. The justification in

Manusmriti is that if a higher caste girl desires for any lower caste male, then the King should prevent it and may kill the girl, and if Shudra caste male desires for any forward caste girl, then the provision of death penalty is permissible.[48]

The version of this folk tale popular among lower caste mentions the proposal by higher caste girl for lower caste male, while lower caste male is moral. Thus punishing Chuharmal, that even for his morality, instead of punishing Reshma leads us to many inferences. First, this act is regarded as anti-religious act by lower class mentality. Second, it shows that saviour of religion had become violator of religious principles. Third, through this narrative they want to project the degeneration in the feudal culture.[49] On the other hand, forward caste's logic projected Chuharmal as thief and emphasized that Dusadhs worship him because they were traditionally thieves.[50] It is noteworthy that the narrative of sexuality is excluded from the text C. The reason is the sexual narrative about Reshma and Chuharmal embarrassed the forward caste. So, the element of narrative of sexuality is deleted from their versions of Chuharmal's tale.[51]

Text D

Some people remember this tale in other form. According to them, there was a time when thieves and cowherds used to destroy the crops. Then, an incarnation of mighty Chuharmal occurred. He annihilated the destroyers of our crops. Because of this food is offered first to Chuharmal God in Chaitra month.

Analysis

According to the text D Chuharmal was a symbol of good, a saviour of the crops of the people. So people of this area preserve the memory of Chuharmal in divine form. This memory connects them with Chuharmal and his tradition, and is usually preserved among middle castes in the oral narratives and tales.

Memory of Protest and Protest by Memory

The people of Mokama remember this narrative not as myth but as a real event. Myth is simultaneously real as well as unreal (Zimmer 1957). To transform itself into myth, to link with primordial memory, many times a worldly symbol is identified with supernatural powers. In this process traditional societies produce their myths.[52] The myth-making process of subaltern communities provides a different mechanism from myth making process of elites.[53] Those who are established as evil by great tradition,[54] subaltern consciousness adopted some of them as their God and become their worshippers (Guha 1995). Illustrating with the myth of Rahu, he mentions that Rahu, who is demon in 'Samudra Manthan' narrative of *Mahabharata*, and who is assumed as Evil Graha in astrology is worshipped by Dome, Dusadh, Bhangi and Mang castes. This might have been the reason that Varahmihir (Brihad Jatak) excluded shadow planets like Rahu and Ketu in his analysis of astrology.[55]

There are indeed very interesting similarities between the symbolism of Rahu and one of Chuharmal.

Rahu	*Chuharmal*
Cutting the head of Rahu by God Narayan	Cutting the head of Chuharmal by landlord (zamindar)
Role of God Narayan who cut the head of Rahu in the 'Samudra Manthan'	Role of (zamindar) landlord who cut his head in the forward caste version of the myth of Chuharmal
Amrit snatchers worshipped by Dusadh	Snatchers of crops of farmers worshipped by Dusadhs and other similar lower castes

Giving higher religious position to physically and spiritually strong mythological heroes, whose bravery deeds are absolutely anti-social in view of the morality of the great tradition, subaltern culture makes significant the protest against the philosophical and ontological basis of dominant culture.[56] Thus a counter tradition is established, in which dominant symbols are turned upside down----criminals became gods in subaltern myth making. Not only this, lower caste people usually assimilate these symbols in their genealogy. There is a long series of such myths.[57]

Myth	*Worshipper*	*Genealogical Relation*
Chuharmal	Dusadh, Chamar, Dhobi	Dusadh
Sahales	Dom, Dusadh etc.	Dusadh
Gaurayya	Dusadh	Dusadh
Gandak	Maghaiyya, Dom	Dom
Rahu	Dusadh, Dom, Bhungi	Dom
Duryodhan	Scheduled Tribes of Harkiddon Valley	
Shani	Teli in Baghelkhand, Mallah in Gaya District of Bihar	
Bhiyarane	Kachi (Bundelkhand)	Kachi
Doma Dak	Doms, Dusadhs (South Bihar)	Dom
Phul Dak	Doms, Dusadhs (Gaya Bihar)	Dom
Megh Dak	Dusadhs (Patana)	Dusadhs

In Baghelkhand cultural region of Madhya Pradesh in Central India, specially in villages around Satana district, a 'Shanipujak' (worshipper of Shani God) community has constituted itself.[58] They are originally of Teli caste. Shani God is primarily worshipped in their homes. Many villages have even Shani God temples. But what is astonishing is that Shani God is regarded as 'Paapgrah' (bad planet), evil planet in Indian astrological system. Teldan (related to Telis), e.g., iron attached in boats, horse shoes, etc., which are important items of the rituals of Shani worship are usually related to lower castes. Narrative identity of Shani planet although fixed even, keeps on attaching with it narrative identities of many lower castes and is related with their identitics even. Thus, on one hand, 'evil power' like Shani planet assumed to be of lower rank in classical tradition is accepted and worshipped in the communities, while at the same time, the religious identities of the lower and subordinate castes are also defined by it. A 'dissent' from the classical tradition or great is thus integral to their religious identities. In classical Astrological literature, till the time of Varahmihir, that only seven planets exist it was believed, evil planets like Rahu and Ketu, for instance, were not included in the astrological system. Varahmihir had included Shani God in the seven planet system, although he mentioned Shani God as only an evil planet. This shows the influence of memory in the disciplines that are quantifiable.

The warrior lover image of Chuharmal is analogous to many other myths popular in Bhojpur and other cultural regions of Bihar, Uttar Pradesh and Madhya Pradesh and the other neighbouring states, Lorik of Yadavas, Kunwar Vijaymal of middle castes, and the Vaishya caste hero, Shobh Nayak Banjara are all myths of the similar nature.[59]

The narrative identities of subaltern castes interacts with the myths of protest and resistance as tabulated below:

Folk Heroes	*Caste Relation*	*Region of the Influence*
Lorik	Yadav	Bihar, U.P., M.P., Rajasthan, certain parts of Gujarat
Kunwar Vijaymal	Koiri, Yadav, Rajput	U.P., M.P., Rajasthan
Shobh Nayak Banjara	Baishya, Banjara	Rajasthan, Bihar, U.P., M.P., Gujarat, certain parts of Maharashtra

Although different castes link themselves with these myths, these are in true sense folk-heroes. The myth of Chuharmal, however, differs from all other myths that are popular in this region, for it is only this myth that is facing resistance by the hegemonic classes of society. It thus establishes itself as a subaltern myth. It is subaltern myth in a sense that it cannot easily be inserted into master narrative.[60]

Thus, representative symbol of counter-culture in its root contains a consciousness of protest even today. One may call it a symbol of the protest consciousness that refuses to be dormant. The constitution of this myth is very much similar to the myth of Pururva' of the Rigveda that has been recreated in the *Mahabharata*, *Valmiki Ramayana* and *Purana*. In this Akhyan 'Pururava' son of Ila has been killed by the conspiracy of the Devatas. He had fallen in love with Urvashi, a dancer of the Indra Durbur. The qualities of bravery and the struggle for love in Pururva's myth are also evident in the myth of Chuharmal.[61]

All those myths popular among Dusadhs have one commonality. The heroes are all mentioned as very mighty in the narrations although they are generally killed by elite power.[62] Thus these myths are creative expressions of continual tendency of the killing of able and talented potential of the downtrodden sections by the elite and the dominant.

This tradition of narrative in our society exposes the myth of the great eternal tradition of defeat of evil finally.[63] In other words, these myths like Chuharmal expose the falseness of the language of classical morality about the eternal victory of truth and morals. These myths are the record of the social history of the experiences of inequalities and oppression of these castes.

When the technique, by which this memory is communicated and disseminated, is analysed, it is evident that the lower caste in order to retain the memory strengthen its form to make them influential and uses the oral tradition in the representational arena, e.g., through exhibitive performance in ritual, contextual communication, non-verbal relatively archaic form of communication like drums and other aural means, verbal transmissions in a conducive atmosphere, active involvement or a mixture of some or all of the said modes.[64] Consequently, by the mixture of various components of this communication *vak*, *drish*, *krit* and sounds, the lower caste version of the myth of Chuharmal gains ascendancy over other versions of the said myth. The repetitive performance of various rituals related to the worship of Chuharmal gives it an element of mobilizing power.[65] On the other hand, the forward caste in communicating the myth of Chuharmal adopt the single technique of *vak* (oral transmission) and so it is less effective.

Folk Techniques of Communication of Memory

Vak	Oral Tradition and Transmission
Symbol	Non-Verbal Signs, Temple, Festival
Drish	Audience, Statue, Religious Flag
Krit	Ritual, Festival
Dhwani	Aural Sounds
	Large Drums, Flutes[66]

Myth and rituals have close relationship. The performance of rituals gives life to myth and myth maintains the circle of rituals. This ritual re-establishes memories in the consciousness of the people. Memory of Chuharmal recurs through the ritual of his worship, oral and visual media in collective psyche.[67] If this folk tale would have been just a folk tale then probably it could not have become so effective causative factor for struggle and revenge. This is a livened form of memory, some reasons for this can be discovered from the social composition of this place:

(a) Mokama Tal is social structure remains today what it was previously.
(b) Statue of Chuharmal, the hero mentioned in this drama, is erected there and even today, in the Chaitya month of every year there is a fair held. It is a corollary of (a).
(c) Forward and lower castes narrate their respective memories as a struggle for their hegemony even today.

The narration of marital relation between a Dusadh and Bhumihar is enough to make feudal lords fire guns. It hurts the ego of superiority of forward caste prevailed in the Brahmanical social structure.[68] And even when the memory of Chuharmal and Reshma has become not only the oral narrative in the form of folk-tale, but every year 'alive' during the fair, it also arouses the memories of people of this area irritating for the higher ones and satisfying for the lower castes.

Not only in Mokama region, but Patana, Bhojpur of Bihar and Balia, Gazipur, Azamgarh regions of Uttar Pradesh. also this memory has produced similar reactions. Although modern development, mass communication and concomitant changes appear in mentalities of people. Cruelty of reaction might be lessened but form of the reactions will be more or less the same. The experiences of Ramendra Naujawandal Dance Party in Patna district is same as that of Nagesar Nachdal active in Bhojpur district. Ramendra says that villages which are not inhabited by Bhumihar caste they dare to present the play but they do not play the drama where Bhumihar caste people live.

Conclusion

The consciousness of lower castes creates these symbols and myths of protest against the domination of hegemonic power. As they are not able to resist openly against the dominant hegemonic power, the creative energy of consciousness of protest contained within themselves finds expression in these characters, and gets satisfaction of resisting hegemony. Secondly, by identifying oneself with these mythical figures they convert themselves into symbols of protest. Thirdly, when we are not able to strongly oppose anybody, then, mighty myths of resistance are worshipped in the subconscious. Similarly, we perceive a Devatva (virtue of being God) in these protest heroes. Myths channelize and regulate protests through repetition.

In 1995, before parliament elections, Laloo Yadav went to Chuharmal fair and worshipped him. Thus, by political transformation of this myth, firmly residing in consciousness of lower caste, he tried to get support from lower castes linked with the myth. Power has a dual relationship with memory, one it wants to utilize collective memory upto a certain extent; two, it tries to abolish it if the collective memory might become a problem for the power. Thus, social memories have to face basically three kinds of situations. First, political power wants to utilize it for its political interests. Secondly, feudal powers want to abolish those social memories which recur against them repeatedly. And thirdly, people who express their protest through these memories, want to regain and enrich these memories.

Notes

1. Dennis Brutus is very eminent South African poet. This stanza is derived from his poetry "I am the tree" published in Vagarth (1989), a collection of poets from six continents of the world.
2. As conscious recollection of communities (Israel Rosenfield, seminar 1994). Memory provides creative input to the identity formation of the communities and this identity formation determines communities social, cultural, political behaviour at a large extent. Michael Novak also observes the role of memory in the identity construction. He provided the response to his own rhetorical question: What is an ethnic group? "It is a group with historical memory, real or imagined. See Michael Novak, *The Rise of Unmeltable Ethnics*, New York, 1972.
3. The narrative of Chuharmal was initially flowing in pachara song (a tantrik folk song of Dusadhs). See Ram Garib Chaubey, *North Indian Notes and Quarries*, Vol. IV, 1894, pp. 62-63. One may draw inference from this information that dramatization of this narrative has been taken place in the later period. George A. Grierson (1885) in his book on Bihar peasant life, *Being a Discursive Catalogue of the Surroundings of the People of the Province*, Delhi, 1975 (reprinted), mentioned Chuharmal as 'First Thief'.
4. Different from Platonic reminiscence, Hegelian remembrance is an interiorisation and recollection of the spirits movement. It recovers its absolute priority over the sense imagery of perception and imagination. See, G.W.F. Hegel, *Phenomenologie des Giestes* (Frankfurt am main, 1970), p.591. This collective remembrance leads us to the orientation that which burts beyond the confines of personal self. Shifting emphasis of personal experience to a

broader notion of collective remembrance which, in its historical movement, gives sustenance to personal identity. See, Jeffery Andrew Barash, 'The Sources of Memory', *Journal of History of Ideas*, Inc., Vol. 58, No. 4, October 1997). Marc Bloch actually used the concept of collective memory in his work *Feudal Society*, Vol. 1, 'The Growth of Ties of Independence', 1939, (Chicago, 1974).

5. Nietzche while developing his concept of historical memory [Friedrich Nietzche, *Nachgellassene Fragmente*, 1872-74, Werke III, 4 (Berlin, 1978)] forsakes it for the creative activity of imagination but Jeffery Andrew Barash, 'The Sources of Memory' (1997) pointed out the interchangeable function of the historical memory and artistic imagination.
6. Maurice Halbawchs, *On Collective Memory*, edited Lewis A. Coser (Chicago, 1992), pp. 182-89, a French follower of Durkhim who established collective memory as an object of sociological investigation. He emphasised on the selectivity of memory and memory survives through repetiion.
7. Jules Michelet, *Histoire de la revolution francoise*, edited, Gerald Walter, 1847 (Paris, 1939), I, pp. 1-2.
8. The issue of forgetting, and the pushing of awkward thoughts from conscious memory, are central to psychoanalytic theory. Psychoanalytic writers themselves including Freud, often created forgetfullness: as the personal unconscious is remembered, so politics is forgotten. And similarly, as the politics of the personal is remembered. So the politics of social, class and race arc forgotten.
9. While discussing on memory Freud propounded the concept of individual psyche and repressed memory. The critical school especially Herbert Marcuse concentrated on social psyche. Violence protest were seen by Marcuse as distorted release of this specific energy in mankind.
10. Maurice Halbwachs, Les Cadres Sociaux de la memoire (1925), New York, 1975, pp. 83-145.
11. See, Daniel Gordon, A review essay of History as an Art of Memory (P.H. Hutton), *Journal of the History of Ideas. Inc.* Postmodernists, e.g., Furet and Nora deconstructs the idea of vehicle of collective memory, see Maurice Halbawchs, on Collective Memory, edited, Lewis A. Coser (Chicago, 1992).

12. In the view of Arendt (1960), Parsons (1969), Foucault (1980) and Giddens (1981), power represents a phenomenon i.e. primarily creative/productive. But Liberal School and especially Communist Manifesto of Marx and Engels takes power as repression, the prerogative of sovereign. Antonio Gramsci's (1971) concept of elite domination on subaltern and establishment of hegemony is also very near to the liberal notion of power. In post modernist view society is an intricate web of hegemonic structures—from state and critical parties to various social institutions including religion, caste and family—sustains and constantly reproduced by hegemonic structures or roughly parallel to what Marxism calls as dominant ideology. In post modernist theory of power, the power—yes, abstract power—is diffused in all these structures: where distinctions between state power and other forms of power do not count much.
13. In the Machiavellion sense of power, a rural needs power. He must use the force in conjunction with fraud to achieve power. The two taken together constitute 'manipulativeness' (Christie and Geis 1970).
14. Feudal perceives this narrative as an insult because first of all it get down their social prestige. It establish subaltern and lower caste superiority on them. It breaks the hierarchical norms and alter the hierarchical condition of Bhumihar caste in the same feudal society. The whole bunch of upper caste feudal value is based on the Maryada concept described in the Hindu law code *Manusmriti* and other Hindu law texts.
15. It is also indicative that the condition in which the modern project of eliminating caste, ethnic and racial in equalities has not been as successful as envisioned and, in some instances, has failed considerably.
16. In fact the division of human into mutually exclusive group identities of tribe, nation, caste, religion and class thus seems to serve two important psychological functions which prepares the psychological background for conflict and violence. The first is to increase the feeling of well being in the narcissistic realm by locating one's own group at the centre of the Universe, superior to other. The grandiose self maintained by legends, myths and rituals seems to demand a concomitant conviction that other groups are inferior, Sudhir Kakkar, "Some Unconscious Aspects of Ethnic

Violence in India", In *Mirrors of Violence, Communities, Riots and Survivors in South Asia* (edited Vina Das), 1990, Oxford University Press, Delhi. Here memory in the form of myths and rituals plays important role in the construction of Grandiose self of the group which enthrone violence attitude to the groups.

17. In Indian religious epics like Ram Charit Manas, kand denotes the meaning 'chapter' but here it denotes the meaning of specific event.
18. Nath Sect emerged in the U.P. and Bihar near about 13th century A.D. Gorakhpur was the centre of this sect.
19. Bharthari (Bhratrihari in Classical Sanskrit lore) and Sorthi Brijbhar are the popular heroes of the Bhojpuri folk lore.
20. Over the past two decades they lost out in the State's power structure but are not mentally reconciled to the new reality. This led to frustration in their psyche that caused more brutally violence in the Rural Bihar. See Gunshots and Silence: The Killings in Siwan, Bihar, Report of a Fact Finding Mission, May, 1997, Insaf, New Delhi.
21. The corresponding rise in the power and privileges of OBC in Bihar in the recent decades described in detail in the Gunshots and Silence: The Killings of Siwan, Bihar, 1997, New Delhi.
22. 62.1 percent of them own 0-5 acres; 17.9 percent own 5-10 acres and 14.3 percent own more than 10 acres of land.
23. A 1991 publication, the Department of Land Reforms, Government of Bihar cited this data.
24. Michael Kammen (*History and Theory* Vol. 34 No. 3, 1995, p. 261) used the term 'social memory' synonym to 'collective memory'. To detail analysis of concept of collective memory, see Marc Bloch, Feudal Society Vol. I, The Growth of Ties of Dependence (1939), Chicago, 1974.
25. One of the way of expression of dissent of lower castes is that laughter and parody mocking. By these derogatory methods the lower castes tried to frustrate the workings of authority. See Dilip M. Menon, 1993, p. 100. This may be seen as cultural representation of every day forms of resistance of the lower caste people. This description owes its theoretical paradigm by the J. Scot, 'Weapons of the Weak': Every day forms of peasant resistance, Yale University Press, 1985.

26. It may be that these cultural actions were able to propose 'Discourse as Act' (in Sabean's phrase) in their cultural performance. See D.W. Sabean, Power in Blood: Popular Culture and Village Discourse in Early Modern Germany, Cambridge University Press, 1984, p. 84.
27. Safdar Hashmi, a theatre artist of Delhi, very brutally murdered by goons of ruling party (Congress-I) on January 1, 1989, while he and his street theatre group Jan Natya Manch was performing a theatre 'Halla Bol' against the state power. See Sudhanva Desh Pande, Sahmat and Politics of Cultural Intervention, *Economic and Political Weekly*, June 22, 1996. Recently Gaddar, a cultural activist, poet and performer (convenor of Jan Natya Mandali of Andhra Pradesh) was shot at his residence by suspected police agents due to his anti power cultural activities. See Kancha Ilaiah, Gaddar: Embodying many institutions, seminar 456, 1997.
28. Vron Ware, Movements of Danger: Race, Gender and Memories of Empire, History and Theory, Vol. 31, No. 4, 1992.
29. It leads to the reminiscent of ethnic cleansing and hate crimes. See Sowell, 1990.
30. In the 'Invention of Tradition' Hobsbawm and others show that "Some traditions which appear or claim to be old are often quite recent in origin and sometimes Invented. An 'Invented Traditions' is a set of ritual or symbolic practices that inculcate certain values and norms by establishing continuity with a suitable historic past", see Eric Hobsbawm, Introduction: Inventing Tradition in The Invention of Tradition, edited E. Hobsbawm and T. Ranger, Cambridge, England, 1985, pp. 1-2.
31. In fact this shows the trend of mythical construction of the past. Here past is conceived as a set of proposition, often stated in narrative form, i.e., accepted uncritically by a culture or speech community and that serves to affirm its self conception. See Peter Hees, Myth, History and Theory, History and Theory, Vol. 33, No. 1, 1994. About the process of remembering past, John Soronson, 1992, opines that the past is contested terrain, selectively remembered or conveniently forgotten, sometimes invented. Eric Hobsbawm and T. Ranger, 1987, argues that the past can be seen as creation of present and Howard Zinn, 1970, proposed many logic in the defence of the view that there can be no single representative account of any given phenomenon.

32. Mythos (word as authoritative pronouncement) perceived as Logos (word as demonstrable truth). See Peter Hees, Myth History and Theory, History and Theory, Vol. 33, No. 1, 1994. Another work is important in this context is Jacques Le Goff, History and Memory, translated by Rendall and Elizabeth Claman, New York, Columbia University, 1992.
33. This ban is imposed by Bhumihars for the Nautanki artists and other performers.
34. This is the example of typical fear psychosis of the feudal male dominated society. It shows their approach towards women. In fact this ban is imposed by mainly feudal forces and upper castes of the respective society.
35. Mahadeo Prasad Singh village Ayana is folklorist, who has collected the folk drama based on the folk lore of Chuharmal and made extensive field work to trace the geneology of Chuharmal and Reshma.
36. The Chuharmal fair is sacred complex. This is through prescribed propitiatory rites, magic, invocations, incantation designed to please the unseen Chuharmal and to establish communication with him.
37. In many castes, caste heroes imprinted in the historical memory of the group and circulated through oral traditions either real or imagined. They remember narrate and most of the time worshiped them. These historical memories (real or imagined) of the caste contributed much in their identity constructions. While discussing national identity, P. Sahlins defined identity as a socially constructed and continuous process of defining 'friend and enemy'... it depends on subjective experience of difference (P. Sahlins, Boundaries: The Making of France and Spain in the Pyrenes (Berkeley, 1989, pp. 270-71).
38. This ritual shows that lower caste perceived Chuharmal a myth with tone of protest and a saviour of grain and their future dream. Nicholas B. Dirks, rightly suggested that we should evaluate the politics of ritual in terms of a discourse on resistance that seeks out contestatory and confrontational upsurge by the lower castes. See his 'Ritual and Resistance: Subversion as a Social Fact' in 'Contesting Power: Resistance and Every Day Social Relation In South Asia'. Edited Douglas Hynes and Gyan Prakash, 1991. The social and political role of ritual is defined by many scholar. To Geertz

(Geertz, C., 1973, The Interpretation of Culture, New York, Basic Books) rituals provide models of and models for. Asad (T. Asad, 1983, Anthropological conception of religion, reflection on Geertz, Man (NS) 18:237-59) criticises Geertz for neglecting power in his focus and symbols, and following Foucault, wants to study the instrumentalities of rituals, what they do rather than what they mean. To Valeri (V. Valeri, 1985, Kingship and Sacrifice: Ritual and Society in Ancient Hawai, Chicago University: Chicago Press, pp. 341-42) rituals are practices in which the participants do not believe themselves to be the authors of what they do, believing instead that their ritual significations are authorised and prescribed by a superior authority. Bloch (M. Bloch: Book review of Valeri, Kingship and Sacrifice, Man (NS) 22: 218-18, and 1986, From Blessing to Violence: History and Ideology in the circumcision on ritual of the Merina of Medagascar, Cambridge, Cambridge University Press) dismisses Valeri's structuralism and identifies rituals as assertion that brook no arguments, that suggest no alternatives, and cannot be contested. Others then show that ritual is also potent force for change, not merely a conservative power. In Comaroff's view (J Comaroff, 1985, Body of Power, Spirit of Resistance: The Culture and History of South African People, Chicago University, Chicago Press) the ritual is historical practice, a highly encoded resistance to hegemonic order. In Foucauldian or the Boasian view, a history of rituals is a history of reproduction, contestation, transformation and deconstruction of authority. In Gluckman's terms, ritual obviously include a protest against the established order but are intended to preserve and strengthen the established order (Max Gluckman, Custom and Conflict in Africa, Oxford, Blackwell, 1965). But it is rare with the rituals related to Chuharmal is highly politicised in the contemporary time by both-elite forces and forces of resistance. Her ritual acts as a reproduction of protest genere.

39. The Public Festivals described by Jules Michelet, 'Histoire de la Revolution Francoise' edited Gerard Walter, 1847, Paris, 1939 and 'Introductional Histoire Universelle, 1831, in oeuvres completes de Michelet II, pp. 230-255, as resurrections of the living memory. For him the festivals are moment of arrested time.
40. In the lower Caste's text, the Brahmnical values and logics about gender questions are evident here. The cause this may be, what

Kathleen Gough (1987: 26-27) has pointed out that the lower orders as reconciled to a Brahmnical elaboration of the social structure, which instilled a belief in karma, dharma and many other Brahmnical ethical law of life. The demand of morality from a woman is the outcome of the perception emerged from 'masculine view'. Freud expressed the unconscious aspects of the masculine view of his time. Which overtly placed woman on a moral pedestal, when he wrote to his friend Silberstein that 'a woman, let alone a girl, has no inherent ethical standard' (Freud's letter of February 28, 1857, Edward Silberstein).

41. In the March 1994 people of the forward caste of Salaiya, Tejpura and Mahabirpura of Shivpuri district of Madhya Pradesh pressurised Harijan women to celebrate Holi with them in necked form. When Harijan women refused their proposal, they were beaten and their houses were burnt by upper caste people, Janmat, 16-30 September, 1994, Delhi.

42. Three events of this nature is listed below: (a) In August, 1993, in Darbhanga district of Bihar, Jaya, a daughter of Brahman family was given to the Goondas by her own family members because she was in love with Harijan youth. First she was raped by Goondas and then murdered after which her dead body was thrown into river (Janmat, 16-30 September, 1994, Delhi). (b) In February, 1994 in Hendegadha village of Mandu Block of Hazaribagh District, Bihar, Malti a girl of Kurmi caste felt in love of Harijan youth Mahabi Ravidas. Both runs away and married. After some days people of Kurmi caste captured Mahabi Ravidas and presented in front of panchayat. According to decision of panchayat Mahabi was severely beaten and killed (Jansatta, 15 September, 1997, Delhi) Kurmi in Bihar emerged as a powerful feudal caste in the recent decade. (c) 12 September, 1997 in the Murubandra village of Rajrappa police station of Hazaribagh district a tribal youth Chaturgan Karmali was felt in love with a daughter of Manu Mahto (Kurmi). As soon as Kurmi people came to know about this relationship, a panchayat was called a Murubandra. 5000 people of Kurmi community gathered, this panchayat was held under the leadership of Mangal Singh Ohdar of Communist Party of India. According to the decision of panchayat Chaturgan was killed brutally (*Jansatta*, September 15, 1997, Delhi, F.I.R. No. 147/148/149 in Rajrappa Police Station).

43. M. Moffatt (1979, An Untouchable Community in South India: Structure and Consensus, Princeton: Princeton University Press), emphasised a lower castes appropriation of Brahminical morality. That is similar to the trend of Sanskritisation psyche (M.N. Srinivas, *Caste in Modern India and Other Essays*, 1977, Asia Publishing House) of Indian Society. Kathleen Gough (1987) emphasised the lower orders as reconcile to a Brahminical elaboration of social structure. It is interesting to note that a many parts of Bihar Dusadh claims as the descendant's of Arjun and link themselves with Gahlot Kshatriyas. So guided by this memory they tried to prove committed to Brahminical orders. The refusal of Reshma's offer by Chuharmal one may see as to show the commitment to the Brahmnical values.

Rebirth in the narrative structure of a story serves many purposes, e.g., value indicator of specific civilisation and as a style of narrative which expands the time span and canvas of story and gives its epical touch. In the Reshma and Chuharmal's story the rebirth occurs to punish the hero and heroin for the deeds of previous birth but it acts as a narrative style also which joints the two plots in a cohesive whole. Freud studied Rider Haggard's novel 'She'. This is a love story, but what a strange love story. This story described stretches over two thousands years. At the early time we are told, Ayesha (Heroin) kills the man to whom she loves, Kallikrates, out of jealousy, then secures prolonged life and waits the two thousand years for her lover's incarnated form to appear. He appears in the form of Leo, who is the descendant of the original Kallikrates and his Egyptian wife, who had born a child, that child's offspring had continued to perpetuate themselves down unto Leo's father, who passes on his son, in the form of Shard, the assignment to avenge the original murder and to kill Ayesha. Here rebirth plays different role than Chuharmal's love story in both the term-value indication as well as narrative style. In the 'She' rebirth appear to arrange the lover. (Bruce Mazlish, A Triptych: Freud's The Interpretation of Dreams, Rider Haggard's 'She' and Baulwer Lytton's The Coming Race, Comparative studies in society and history, Vol. 39, No. 4, 1993, Cambridge University Press, Cambridge.

44. Ranjit Guha, "The Small Voice of History", Subaltern Study, edited Shahid Amin and Depesh Chakravarty, Vol. IX, Oxford University Press, Delhi.

45. In my observation, this text is popularised by Nautanki groups of the area.
46. Milman Parry, 1971, a Berkeley-trained Anthropologist and Albert Lord in their field work in Yugoslavia observed that the meaning of memory (oral epic) in oral culture transformed in the literacy. They discovered that oral culture has different method to preserve memories than written culture. Written culture usually freezes the living memory. See, Milman Parry, "Cor Huso: A Study of South Slavic Song", in the Making Verse: The Collected Papers of Milman Parry edited Adam Parry, Oxford, 1971, Milman Parry, "The Historical Method in Literary Criticism", in ibid. Milman Parry, "Studies in the Epic Technique of Oral Verse Making". The Homeric Language as the language of an oral poetry, in ibid, 325-61. Albert B. Lord, The Singer of Tales, Cambridge, Mass., 1960, pp. 124-38 and Memory, Fixity and Genre in Oral Tradition Poetries In Oral Traditional Literature: A Festscrift for Albert Bates Lord, edited Miles Foley (Columbus, oh, 1981, pp. 451-61.
47. The Buddhist text Aggiyan Sutt provide the historical narrative about origin of theft, see Rahul Sankrityayan, Pali Sahitya Ka Itihas, 1993, New Delhi.
48. The lower castes logical and cultural reference came from Brahamnical texts because the construction of their cultural memory has been taken shape in the construction of great influence of the Brahamnical power. In the context of South India the same phenomenon analysed by Dilip M. Menon (The Moral Community of Teyyattam, popular culture in late colonial Malabar, studies in history, Vol. 9, No. 2, 1993, New Delhi) that hierarchy was maintained both by the use of power and the inscribing into the every day acts as custom of the lower status of subordinate group. But in a changed political and cultural scenario, they are free to interpret in their own way. One text can be interpreted in multiple way, suggested by Paul Recoeur, 1996, Jacque Derrida, 1978, Howard Zinn, 1970. Pierre Bourdieu, 1991, understand this phenomenon in different way. He suggests that in the symbolic struggle which is going on in the society is based on the struggle for the capturing instruments of symbolic production. Interpretation and the reimagination may also count as instrument of symbolic production. One may take it as a method of subversion

of the Brahamnical dominant logical structure by rereading of the Brahamnical law texts like Manusmriti.

49. The attempted to project the image of local ruling elite as immoral, valueless and religiously corrupt. Because their acts were against moral value and code defined by Manusmriti, Ramayana and other Hindu religious texts.
In this text of narrative Chuharmal depicted as defeated and killed by local landlord but in Text A & B he is described as victorious. This two different construction of same episode shows two different mentalities-mentality of domination and mentality of protest. In the collective remembrance of past the imagination of caste, community and group usually reflects. See Jeffery Andrew Barash, "The Sources of Memory", *Journal of the History of Idea*, Vol. 58, No. 4, October, 1997.

50. Francis Buchanan (an account of the District of Shahabad in 1812-13, Bihar and Orissa Research Society, Patana, p. 198) contradicts this beliefs and informs that in many regions of Bihar like Shahabad Dushads were entirely occupied in agriculture and were not considered thieves.

51. Maurice Halbawchs, 'On Collective Memory', edited Lewis A. Coser, Chicago, 1992, emphasised on the concept of selectivity of Memory and he is of the view that social questions also guides this internal process of selectivity of memory. He repeatedly set out to prove that memory is social phenomena. One may read the narrative of sexuality lies in the Reshma and Chuharmal's folk lore as the representation of in caste desire and transgressive sex but in the society under the study, the sex is the question of prestige especially in the upper caste mentality.

52. See Peter Hees, 'Myth History and Theory', Vol. 33, No. 1, 1994.

53. About subaltern myth making, Kerwin Lee Kelin, 'In Search of Narrative of Mastery, History and Theory', Vol. 34, 1995, pp. 275-298, derived some trends e.g. it is never omniscient, but always aware of its own narrative debts. It cannot easily be inserted into master narrative. It is artistic and imaginative.

54. See, Milton Singer, 1972, 'When A Great Tradition Modernises', New York: Praeger.
The narrative of great tradition proceeds with the description of binary opposites e.g. good and evil, god and demon etc.

55. In the Indian astrological system there are 9 planets Jupiter, Venus, Mercury and Moon are auspicious planets and Rahu, Ketu, Mars and Saturn are evil planets. They are called shadow planets also. Sun is described as lord of planets.
56. Lower castes in their cultural idioms created many way of criticising dominant caste as protest. The lower castes apprehend and attempt to stave off the imposition of authority. See Dilip M. Menon, The Moral Community of Teyyattam, Studies in History, 1993, pp. 187-217.
57. For Schama, myth and memory are closely conjoined. He shows us in his study, how myths were formed by leading us to the places of their origins, then doubling back through the places of their revision and elaboration across the ages. While one of his intention to reaffirm the post modern wisdom that all our myths are human creation. He is also fascinated with myth as the exegesis of primordial memory. (Simon Schama, Landscape and Memory, New York: Alfred Knof, 1995, PP. XI, 652).
58. In the South West Bihar Shanichara (Shani) is worshipped by Turaha (a vegetable seller low caste) community.
59. These are the myths transmitted from generation to generation through oral transmission in the form of folk lore of the region.
60. Myth usually get acceptance across the class and caste boundaries e.g. the myth of Shobh Nayaka Banjara and Lorik do not generate any violent reaction among upper caste but the myth of Chuharmal is contesting myth and upper castes are not even ready to bear this myth.

    For further analysis on the process of interaction between master narrative and subaltern narrative see Kerwin Lee Klein, "In Search of Narrative Mystery: Post Modernism and the People Without History", *History and Theory*, Vol. 34, 1995.
61. One may point out the archetypal function of the myth of Pururava for the imaginative creation of the symbol of Chuharmal. By 'Archetype' Jung means the universal images that have existent since the remotest of the whole ancestral line i.e. the heaped up or pooled experiences of organic existence in general a million times repeated and condensed into types. They are in fact collective unconscious. For further details see Jung's and others discourses on collective unconscious, archetype and memory experience see

S.P. Nagendra, *The Concept of Ritual in Modern Sociological Theory*, 1965, Delhi.

62. The mythical characters of the lower castes who faced the upper caste cruel domination because of those acts which transgressed the space of the upper castes on the sexual issues are evident in the Teyyattam performed only in North Malabar, Dilip M. Menon, 'The Moral Community of Teyyattam', Studies in History, p. 190. But in this case Chuharmal faced the upper caste feudal cruelty because he rejected the offer of sexual indulgence by upper caste girl.
63. In the most of the Akhyan of the Indian tradition evil gets defeat, but here in the text C of Chuharmal narrative, Chuharmal is depicted as defeated and killed by Jamindar (Land Lord). But there is other contesting narrative also. In the text popular among Dusadhs, Chuharmal becomes victorious in the oral narrative. But Chuharmal's long statue erected without head in the fair place near Mokama shows the Chuharmal's killing.
64. Ranjit Guha (Elementary Aspects of Peasant Insurgency in Colonial India, Delhi, 1983) describes the some traditional and relatively archaic forms of communication of local peasants society involve in the protest against Britishers. He suggested that the massage of peasant insurgency transmitted by verbal and non-verbal means of communications. The later were of two kinds-aural and visual. Human communication operates eclectically by a mixture of signs. According to him non-verbal massages were relayed by sight and sound with other means. The means of their communication had the dual function of informing and mobilising at the same time.
65. The memory of Chuharmal contents the potentialities to uniting Dusadhs under the banner of Baba Chuharmal Smarak Samiti a heavy mobilisation of Dusadhs happened recently in Muzaffarpur of Bihar and other places. See Jansatta, Delhi, 28 September, 1997.
66. The drum, the flute and the horn etc. instruments formed a class apart from verbal media in the sense that they helped to realise what Jakobson has called transmutation i.e. an interpretation of verbal signs by means of signs of non verbal sign systems. (Jakobson, Roman questions de poetique, Paris, 1973 quoted in Ranjit Guha, Elementary Aspects of Peasant Insurgency in Colonial

India, Delhi). As such they acted as a surrogate of human speech and were independent enough of the later to permit the decoding of messages directly rather than through linguistic symbolism. In the, Nupe Kingdom of Nigeria drums and wind instruments like trumpets and flutes and among the Tumba community who lived on the east side of the Congo river, the use of drum for communicating messages are the aural means of communications. Through this transmission process the memory of mythic experience can be evoked.

67. See Maurice Halbawchs, 'On Collective Memory', edited Lewis A. Coser, Chicago, 1992, pp. 182, 189.

68. The assertion of caste identity by the political play with caste's memory (historical memory either real or imagined) and the envocation of caste memory by the assertion of identity overlap each other in the complex process of creating violence in rural society which contains both the element of domination as well as protest.

References

Arendt, H., 1960, 'What is freedom?' in *Between Past and Future*, 1960.

Anderson, Benedict, 1983, *Imagined Communities*, London.

Bhatt, Kulluk, *12th Century, Manusmriti* (Tika) Banaras.

Boraclough, Greaffrey, 1979, *Main Trends in History*, New York.

Bourdieu, Peirre, 1991, *Language and Symbolic Power*, Cambridge.

Baxi, Upendra and Mark, Galanter, 1979, Panchayat Justice: An Indian Experience in Legal Access in Access to Justice, Emerging Issue and Perspectives, Vol. 3, Mcappellett and B. Barth, edited, 341-86, Milan: Sijthoff and Noordhoff: Alphenaaderrijn.

Brutus, Dennis, 1989, *Vagarth*, Bhopal.

Christie, R. and F.L. Geis, 1970, *Studies in Machiavellianism*, New York: Academic Press.

Derrida, J., 1978, *Writing and Difference*, Chicago.

Driks, Nocholas B., 1991, *Contesting Power: Resistance and Social Relations in South Asia*, Douglas Hynes and Gyan Prakash, New Delhi.

Foucault, M., 1980, *Power/Knowledge: Selected Interviews and Other Writings*, edited Collin Gordon, Pantheon Books, New York.

---, 1982, 'The Subject/Power' in Hubert L. Dreyfus and Paul Rabinow, *Michel Foucault: Beyond Structuralism and Hermeneutics*, The Harvester Press.

Giddens, Anthony, 1981, *Central Problems in Social Theory*, London and Basingtake.

Guha, Ranjit, 1995, *Nimn Vargiya Prasang*, Vol. 1, New Delhi.

Gramsci, Antonio, 1971, *Selection from the Prison Note Books of Antonio Gramsci* (edited Quintin Hoare and Geoffrey Nowell Smith), New York.

Gough Kathleen, 1981, *Rural Society in South East India*, Cambridge.

Hobsbawm, Eric and Ranger Terence (edited), 1987, *The Invention of Tradition*, Cambridge.

Jung, C.G., 1959, *The Archetypes and the Collective Unconscious: The Collected Works*, Volume 9, Ballingen Series, Panthon Books, New York.

Kosambi, D.D., 1972, *The Culture and Civilisation of Ancient India: An Historical Outline*, Delhi.

Kakar, Sudhir, 1990, 'Some Unconscious Aspects of Ethnic Violence', in *India in Mirrors of Violence, Communities, Riots and Survivors in South Asia* (edited Vina Das), Delhi.

Mishra, M.K., 1987, *Folklore of Kalahandi* (thesis, Sambhalpur University, Orissa).

Menon, M. Dilip, 1993, The Moral Community of Teyyattam: Popular Culture in the late Colonial Malabar, *Studies in History*, Vol. 9, No. 2, 1993.

Narayan, Badri, 1996, *Lok Sanskriti Men Rashtravad*, Delhi.

Nagendra, S.P., 1965, *The Concept of Ritual in Modern Sociological Theory*, Delhi.

Parson, Talcott, 1969, *The Politics and Social Structure*, The Free Press, New York and Collier-Macmillan, London.

Recoeur, Paul, 1996, 'Fragility and Responsibility' in *The Hermeneutics of Action* (edited by Richard Kearney), London.

Rosen, Field Israel, 1994, 'Me and Others', *Seminar*, Delhi.

Singh, Chittaranjan, 1978, 'Tatka', *Ara* (Bhojpuri newspaper)

Sankrityayan, Rahul, 1993, *Pali Sahitya Ka Itihas*, Delhi.

Singh, Mahadev Prasad, 1982, *Reshma-Chuharmal Ka Geet*, Biso Bhag, Calcutta.

Singh, Govind, 1995, *Manusmriti*, Delhi.

Soronson, John, 1992, 'History and Identity in the Horn of Africa', *Dialectical Anthropology*, 17: 227-252.

Sowell, Thomas, 1990, *Preferential Politics: An International Perspective*, New York.

Thyongo, Ngugiwa, 1994, *Bhasha, Sanskriti aur Rashtriya Asmhita*, Delhi.

Zimmer, Heinrich, 1957, *Myths and Symbols on Indian Art and Civilisation*, New York.

Zinn, Howard, 1970, *The Politics of History*, Boston.

Chapter Sixteen

The Exemplar and the Ideologue: The Issue of Friends and Foes

K. Raghavendra Rao

If one examines carefully Gandhiji's attitude towards those whom he regarded as persons worth fighting non-violently, it is clear that he did not consider them as foes in the ordinary sense. In every individual human person, Gandhiji did not see a black-and white blanket picture of a foe or a friend but a mixture of both. Even this is a misleading way of putting things because he viewed every human person as a site where forces of evil and good were locked in a ceaseless internal battle. In short, Gandhiji did not regard any single human person as a simple foe or friend but thought of him or her as a potential friend and a temporary foe in the sense that one could activate the good in them and reduce the evil through the method of non-violent method of love and self-suffering. However, let us assume, for the sake of argument, that those who supported his cause and accepted his principles and programmes as his friends, that is, assume that a Gandhian could be regarded as a friend.

The question then would be: Is there a category that can be legitimately called a Gandhian? We do often indulge in such debates as whether someone, a JP or a Vinobha is a true Gandhian, and, if so, in what sense and to what extent they were Gandhians. Now I suggest that such debates are essentially misconceived. It is because once we penetrate the Gandhian mode of living and thinking, especially focussing on the relationship between living and thinking, the notion of someone being a Gandhian seems irrelevant, if not absurd. While it may make some sense to call someone a liberal or a Marxian, less so in the case of the latter, it seems to make no sense at all to call someone a Gandhian, true or not. At best we can talk about someone trying to practise Gandhian practice, but it would be difficult to talk about someone practising or following a Gandhian theory. The general practice of adding the suffix, 'ist' or 'ian', to underscore commitment to a theory or ideology, does not help in the case of Gandhiji. This is for the very simple reason that nothing can be reasonably construed as Gandhism or a formal and abstract system of thought that can be called Gandhian. We can situate this problematic in terms of two frames of reference. The first may be called the exemplar frame.[1] This frame assumes an important distinction between an exemplar and an ideologue. The second frame assumes a distinction, not between theory and practice, but between either theory and theory-practice or practice and theory-practice. The notion of theory-practice is what Marx called praxis or theory of theory and practice in his early writings, especially in his theses on Feuerbach. From the perspective of the first frame, Gandhiji would be significantly distant from Marx but from the perspective of the second frame he would be significantly close to Marx.

Therefore, the distinctive nature of Gandhian mode can be best articulated in terms of the first frame. What are the implications of this frame? First, it implies that a person is an exemplar insofar as he or she maintains that the thought or theory of an action or practice is structurally so intertwined with that action or practice that any separation of the two would be impossible and untenable. If one were to ask an exemplar to explain his theory or thought, he would hold that his theory and thought are embodied in his life and in his activities, and, therefore his theory and thought are exemplified in his life and practice and they are impossible to grasp in terms of abstract, de-contextualized systems of thought and ideas. The ideologue, in contrast, would be ready to separate his thought and theory from his life and deeds, and give them a considerable degree of abstract autonomy. At this point in our argument, it is very important to note that the exemplar is not a person without thought or theory of his own. It is the case only that the relationship between theory and practice for him is such that a constant reference to his life and action is necessary for any explication of his theory and thought. It would also be equally important to note that the ideologue does not function in a decontextualised, history-free universe of abstract ideas. It is simply the case that he is prepared to constitute in life and action in terms of abstract systems of ideas to a greater extent than an exemplar, but if pressed he would concede ultimately the necessary connection between life and thought, theory and practice. In short, the two modes should not be construed as antithetical or polar but as two moments in a dialectical process. It is because one fails to see this that one is often led to dismiss an exemplar as a theory less man of action. For the same reason, one is led to conclude that an ideologue functions in isolation from the existential pressures and tensions of living and acting.

The question why some become ideologues and others exemplars is not an idle and abstract question. It is a question which can be answered only in historical and sociological terms. To put the matter in simple or even simplistic terms, the exemplar belongs pre-eminently to pre-modern history while the ideologue is a characteristic product of modern history. It is in societies and communities prior to the emergence of modern European social systems that the exemplar flourished while the ideologue made his historical debut in Europe after the onset of modernity brought about by the twin movements of the Renaissance and the Reformation, later reinforced by the Enligtenment. To the question why modernity made it possible for the displacement of the exemplar by the ideologue, the answer can be given in broadly sociological terms. In small-scale societies and collectivities that were prevalent in times prior to the emergence of modern mass societies, created by the industrial capitalist revolution in Europe, conditions were highly conducive to the presence and functioning of the exempler. In the first place, they were very stable and structured systems with little space or scope for any significant degree of moral, political or power conflict based on competing and contending world-views. The autonomy of the individual from the structures of collective life was minimal, and therefore there was very little space for any critical questioning of the status quo or very little room for self-conscious social change. This was a tailor-made situation for the exemplar who tended to embody the existing values and exemplify them authoritatively. Secondly, the fact that the exemplar functioned in a small-scale community where everyone knew everyone else personally and that everyone was exposed directly to the gaze of everyone else, implied that the exempler and his role as an an example were visible to everyone. They could all see him and follow him. In other words, the exemplar is a necessary and functionally relevant category to pre-modern social systems predicated on a high degree of moral and political consensus conjoined with a high degree of inter-personal interaction and mutual visibility. In contrast, the ideologue belongs to a modern history characterized by a conjuncture between a high degree of interpersonal invisibility and a high degree of value dissensus. The emergence of a liberal bourgeois civil society, with its excessive tolerance of ethical and intellectual pluralism in the name of individual freedom, rules out the need for an exemplar excepting for very limited local purposes. In parenthesis, one may note the irony that the modern electronic media which create the possibility of a kind of visibility which is not mutual, may produce what one may call pseudo-exemplars or synthetic exemplars.

In light of the above discussion it is possible to see why in the case of an exemplar, there can be no ideological following or followers, and also why in the case of an ideologue it is not only possible but even necessary. An exemplar functions by projecting his own personal life and example in moral and intellectual terms while an ideologue needs other ideologues to grasp and propagate his ideals and ideas. For leaders in societies in the process of changing from the exemplar to the ideologue systems, the two frames and roles have to be combined in some way or other. Their success depends on their skill and ability to work on two levels, appealing to the vast masses still steeped in an exemplar culture as well as to critical minority groups claiming to have liberated themselves from the shackles of a traditional exemplar society. Gandhiji was precisely in this situation in a colonially and partially modernized India. In his seminal work, *Hind Swaraj*, he argued that, though he was leading an urban educated middle class minority, he pinned his hope and faith on the vast rural masses, still untouched by the disease of modernity. It is this complex historical destiny that drove Gandhiji to become a part-time ideologue, and swing from one mode to another. But there is no doubt that he acted in a predominantly exemplar mode. He was clear in his own mind about his priorities and he decided to invest his energy and time more in the exemplar mode, alienating himself from his immediate followers like the Congress leaders who were under the spell of the ideologue mode. As an exemplar, he constantly exhorted people to follow his personal life and example, but he was also forced to function as an ideologue. His writings and speeches show that he was a subtle and skilful ideologue, though he considered his ideologue role as at best a secondary, rearguard action. That is why he tended to disclaim intellectual originality, and preferred to regard himself as a mere spokesman for ancient truths, as old as the hills, granted to him by intuition, faith or tradition. Because he was reluctant and part-time ideologue, it was problematic for his followers to become Gandhians proclaiming allegiance to a clear-cut system of thought. If one wanted to become a Gandhian, one had no simple system of thought or ideology to latch on to, and one had to engage in the incredible task of perpetually imagining what Gandhiji would have done, not just thought, in any given situation, and then act or thing accordingly! Given such an impossible conditionality, it was not only impossible to become a Gandhian but it was also impossible to know in advance intellectually or theoretically, what it was to be a Gandhian, let alone a genuine or a spurious one.

To establish Gandhiji as an essential exemplar, I offer two citations from a recent anthology of Gandhiana[2] and comment oı them. The first is a forthright one, leaving us in little doubt about his being an exemplar par excellence. He told the Shanti Sena Dal, "... My life is my message..." Instead of explaining or elaborating his ideas or thought or message, Gandhiji told his audience to do their own thinking by applying their mind to the example of his life. Thus, he refused to couch his message in ideological terms. The second citation goes, "...My language is aphoristic, it lacks precision. It is therefore open to several interpretations... " This is an important statement but it can be easily misconstrued. It does not mean that one can interpret Gandhiji in any way one wants to. What it means is that one must interpret Gandhiji in terms of one's own life and experience. In other words, its invitation to polysemanticity refers not to Gandhiji's words strictly but to the result of an interaction between his words and one's life. In a very complicated manner, Gandhiji remains textually intact while its interpretation by us may be several. The severalness derives from the severalness of our life-experience acting on the Gandhian text. This position, too, is essentially an example of an exemplar position. It asks us to read the truth of the Gandhian text not as unilateral but is bilaterally refracted through the truth of the text of our own lives! The essence of the exemplary mode is to create a text out of life and understand a life as a text. I am not trying to push Gandhiji into a bandwagon of post-structuralism or post-modernity here. I am simply interpreting a Gandhian text. Of course, it is possible to maintain that post-structuralism and post-modernity are simply tortuous routes towards the recovery of a lost exemplary mode of life.

Perhaps, the most crucial dimension of the exemplary nature of Gandhian mode is its refusal to postulate the unanchored and de-contextualized individual subject as the author of any text or life. Gandhiji refuses to grant the naked individual the competence to constitute the parametres of his life-context with purely self-generated resources. The individual cannot be the sole author of any text since a text or a life is co-authored by tradition, faith, history and the grace of God. In particular, the individual cannot create a text by employing his rationality only. He needs the back-up of faith in God. Even in this, reason can only be a junior partner and it is faith which will have to be the primary partner. It is this perpetual drive to relate the individual subject to his concrete context and force him to constitute himself and his life in terms of that context which prompts Gandhi to function in the exemplar mode and distance himself from the ideologue mode. In principle, one can re-interpret and re-describe an exemplar in terms of an ideologue but doing so can yield us very limited and questionable payoffs at the cost of disrupting the larger Gandhian canvas. In fact, those who want to become Gandhian or those who thus want to construct an abstract theoretical system called Gandhism would be achieving the precise opposite of their goal----they would end up as anti-Gandhian or at least non-Gandhian. Therefore, it is difficult to resist the conclusion that the quest to become a Gandhian or the search for Gandhism are futile enterprises. They will result in either a dogmatic reduction of Gandhiji to an ideologue or to be a caricature of Gandhian fads and angularities minus the Gandhian strengths. If one cannot become a Gandhian, how then can one relate to

Gandhiji? One can do so only as a person who has tried to internalize Gandhi by trying to live like Gandhi and become some version or edition of the text that is Gandhiji. Gandhi should be re-incarnated, not repeated or limited. In short, you either live like Gandhi or you do not. But you cannot become a Gandhian in the ideologue tradition. If you still persist in using the category of the Gandhian, you will have to identify it not in terms of who follows an abstract theoretical system called Gandhism but in terms who will live a life founded on Gandhi as an exemplar. This fundamental exemplar frame in which the concrete and the abstract, theory and practice, the text and the context, are constantly mediated and related, is one which the post-medieval West and its camp-followers across the globe whether in the name of modernization or globalization, have lost beyond recovery. Does it then mean that our historical trajectory which has brought us to the present crisis of modernity and its confusing rivals, post-modernity or post-structuralism, condemns us to a permanent entrapment in destructive modernity? Apparently we seem to be doomed to such a fate.

But as Gandhiji saw and we can see, the bulk of mankind has escaped the fate of modernity, though they have not escaped the price of modernity. The poor people in the First World and most people in the rest of the world are victims of modernity. Gandhiji speaks for them, and they can only be called his true friends. The few who have benefited from modernity and who have a stake in perpetuating the current historical form of modernity can be called the foes of Gandhiji. If one were to think and act in terms of a fundamentally Gandhian realism, one would have to subvert the present modernity but one would still have the option of arriving at a Gandhian modernity.

Notes

1. I am grateful to Anuradha Shah for drawing my attention to the concept and the problematic of the exemplar.
2. The two citations are from *The Penguin Gandhi Reader* edited by Rudrangshu Mukherji, Penguin Books, India, New Delhi, 1993. The introduction by the editor is as good an illustration as any text of what happens when Gandhiji is coerced into the role of an ideologue.

Index